Accelerating Growth and Job Creation in South Asia

'In this excellent volume, Ejaz Ghani and Sadiq Ahmed have invited the world's leading scholars to apply their talents to understanding the economies of South Asia. They cover a wide range of topics. Scholars interested in South Asia will find the volume most illuminating.'

—ARVIND PANAGARIYA, Columbia University

'The importance of this book cannot be overestimated. It powerfully explores the link between regional integration, economic growth, and job creation. It has several imaginative proposals that can be debated and discussed. It is ambitious but not unmindful of the difficult political economy of the region. But beyond all the rigorous and technical thinking in the volume, it is also a summons to the leadership in South Asia. The destiny of the region is in its own hands. Its people are its greatest asset and should be at the forefront of any policy. And more importantly, however much we may try to deny this fact, the region will swim or sink together. At a time when the region faces two profound challenges, the impact of the global slowdown and regional tensions, this book makes a case for how both these challenges can be addressed simultaneously.'

—PRATAP BHANU MEHTA, Centre for Policy Research

'India and other South Asian countries are not immune to the global downturn. No country is. But South Asia has key assets which are currently underutilized. People and the potential for greater regional trade are among them. The challenge is to reform and integrate so as to mitigate the impact of the global recession in the short run and build a base for continued sustained growth in the longer term … This book … brings insight to the setting of priorities and strategies to accomplish the objective of sustained growth and poverty reduction.'

—MICHAEL SPENCE, Chair of the Commission on Growth and Development, and Nobel Laureate in Economics, 2001

'South Asia is on a path of economic ascendancy, and in spite of India's leading role, economic growth has been widely shared among the countries of the region. Yet, these countries face enormous challenges in reducing poverty, generating employment, and achieving regional economic integration. By addressing these issues with a great deal of analytical rigour and originality, this book provides fresh perspectives on South Asian economic development.'

—WAHIDUDDIN MAHMUD, University of Dhaka

Accelerating Growth and Job Creation in South Asia

edited by

EJAZ GHANI

SADIQ AHMED

OXFORD
UNIVERSITY PRESS

OXFORD
UNIVERSITY PRESS

YMCA Library Building, Jai Singh Road, New Delhi 110001

Oxford University Press is a department of the University of Oxford. It furthers the University's objective of excellence in research, scholarship, and education by publishing worldwide in

Oxford New York
Auckland Cape Town Dar es Salaam Hong Kong Karachi Kuala Lumpur Madrid Melbourne Mexico City Nairobi New Delhi Shanghai Taipei Toronto

With offices in
Argentina Austria Brazil Chile Czech Republic France Greece Guatemala Hungary Italy Japan Poland Portugal Singapore South Korea Switzerland Thailand Turkey Ukraine Vietnam

Published in India by Oxford University Press, New Delhi

First published 2009

ISBN-13: 978-019-806004-8
ISBN-10: 019-806004-1

Typeset in AGaramond 11/13 by Jojy Philip
Printed in India by De Unique, New Delhi 110 018
Published by Oxford University Press
YMCA Library Building, Jai Singh Road, New Delhi 110 001

CONTENTS

TABLES AND FIGURES

TABLE

FIGURES

PREFACE

Even as late as the beginning of the 1980s, South Asia was known as a region suffering from conflict, widespread poverty, and autarkic and slow-growing economies. Some 28 years later, South Asia is drawing international attention for demonstrating rapid growth and substantial poverty reduction. Compared to 3.7 per cent growth per year during 1960–80, South Asia's gross domestic product (GDP) expanded by 5.7 per cent during 1980–2000; growth accelerated further to 6.5 per cent in 2000–7. Growth accounting estimates show that both factor accumulation and total factor productivity contributed to rapid growth. While the growth momentum is led by the largest country, India, other large countries like Bangladesh and Pakistan have also shown signs of growth dynamism. Poverty is declining, falling from around 45 per cent in the early 1980s to about 27 per cent at present. Although substantial inter-country differences remain, poverty has come down in all South Asian countries.

Notwithstanding this impressive progress, South Asia remains home to the world's largest number of poor. There are substantial differences between countries, particularly the differences between the low-income countries of Afghanistan and Nepal and the rest of the region, and the large disparities within countries. Overall, the concentration of poor in the lagging regions of South Asia is generating considerable social and political concern. There is a broad consensus that South Asia must continue to grow rapidly and possibly faster to attack poverty more comprehensively than in the past. There is also an emerging consensus that this growth must be more inclusive to address the dichotomy of the two faces of South Asia resulting from the growing gap between leading and lagging regions. The first face is dynamic, urban, globally integrated, and rapidly growing. These are the leading regions of South Asia. The second face is rural, afflicted with poverty and conflict, and not well integrated with the markets.

These are the lagging regions of South Asia. The concern with the growing gap between these two faces applies to both disparities within countries as well as between countries of the regions. Given long physically open borders, fast growing countries such as India cannot fully ignore the adverse effects of slow growing neighbours. Indeed, unofficial migration resulting from differential income opportunities is already emerging as a major social and political challenge for India and its neighbours. What can be done to sustain and increase growth in South Asia? How can growth become more inclusive? These are leading issues for South Asia's development moving forward.

To provide an input to this debate, the South Asia Region of the World Bank joined hands with the South Asian Association for Regional Cooperation (SAARC) to organize a regional conference, called the Second SAARC Business Conclave, that brought together a number of key players from the private sector, political leadership, policymakers, and academics whose ideas and thoughts could shed new light on the growth challenge. The conference recognized that growth in South Asia is at an early stage. Despite solid progress, the region still suffers from severe policy distortions. If the reform process can be accelerated, South Asia has the potential to achieve and sustain higher growth. The growth practitioners and policymakers identified five key drivers of growth. These are as follows:

- Expanding the industrial base
- Modernizing the service sector
- Strengthening skills
- Strengthening institutions
- Regional cooperation for boosting trade and infrastructure investment

The work and analysis of this book of collected essays are an outcome of high-level dialogue on growth between the private sector, political leadership, policymakers, and academics in South Asia. The growth drivers discussed in this volume are by no means an exhaustive list of growth concerns. Other issues relating to the financial sector, urbanization, agriculture, etc., might be important for growth as well. But these were not discussed at the conference. In each of the five areas identified by experts as growth drivers, the book looks at the types of policies and institutions that could propel South Asia to higher growth, while also promoting growth inclusiveness to address the inequality concerns. The views expressed in the essays are those of the authors. The methodology and approach differ, and the conclusions of some of the works are open to debate. This diversity, however, is also a strength and some of the questions raised will likely spur new research.

Despite the diversity, each chapter intends to address issues affecting growth and employment. Based on the contents of the essays, the book is organized along three themes: an overview of South Asia's growth opportunities and challenges; sources of growth and policies; and the role of regional cooperation in promoting growth.

Part I on growth opportunities and challenges starts with a study by Sadiq Ahmed and Ejaz Ghani that identifies some of the key challenges facing South Asia which, if addressed, would accelerate growth further, especially in the smaller countries. These are in the nature of 'second generation reforms', building on the momentum of reforms in the first phase starting in 1980. These include market integration, both globally and regionally; inclusive growth that would convert the 'demographic dividend' in South Asia into a 'window of opportunity'; improved infrastructure that would behave like second nature geography and propel growth through improved connectivity, allowing its benefits to be shared widely; strengthened institutions that would result in a stronger business environment and less conflict and corruption; and the inclusion of regional public goods into the national development agenda. In the two subsequent brief commentaries, Jeffrey D. Sachs and Paul A. Volcker share their perspectives on South Asian growth opportunities and challenges. Professor Sachs notes the past progress in growth and development in South Asia and recognizes the large potential moving forward. He highlights four priority areas of focus for South Asia: investment in rural areas; regional trade and integration; paying attention to the natural environment, especially water; and the greater role of business leaders to influence political outcomes. Volcker appreciates the progress made by South Asia, in particular in becoming more open and competitive and benefiting from global integration. At the same time he notes the two faces of South Asia. In addition to consolidating the gains from good policies including prudent macroeconomic management and global integration, he emphasizes the critical role of good governance in promoting growth and inclusiveness. Some progress has been made by South Asia in improving governance but there is a long way to go.

Part II looks in-depth at sources of growth for the future and policies and institutions needed to accelerate growth, as well as make growth more inclusive. The key link between growth and inclusiveness is creation of good jobs. South Asia is already undergoing a major structural transformation based on rapid growth of services and manufacturing. The GDP share of agriculture is shrinking fast. This trend is likely to continue in the future, although the growth rates in both manufacturing and agriculture could be accelerated. The employment story is different from the experience of East Asia. South Asia has so far has seen a rapid increase in the contribution of the services sector in employment. However, there is a concern that job creation has been mostly in the informal sector characterized by low skills and low earnings. At the same time, the reduction in the GDP share of agriculture is not matched by a commensurate reduction in the employment share. The manufacturing sector has not shown the dynamism found in the East Asian Tigers. Many experts believe that the ability to convert the manufacturing sector into a dynamic sector with rapid growth in value added will be a key driver for overall economic growth as well as for adequate creation of high-income jobs (called good jobs). What path might the manufacturing sector take to achieve this dynamism? Should South Asia emulate the export-led large scale manufacturing path of the East Asian Tigers? The study by Howard Pack addresses the question of the path of industrialization for South Asia. Pack believes that the path followed by the East Asian Tigers is not a viable option for South Asia because of the difficulties of market penetration in this heavily contested world market. The alternative he suggests is that of a balanced effort at promoting agricultural and rural industry. The small and medium enterprise (SME) strategy, he observes, is not that of a collection of informal sector enterprises whose demonstrated economic benefits are open to question. The type of firms envisioned are factories with 10 to 300 employees, are labour-intensive in nature, and show good total factor productivity. In his view, the balanced path has the advantage of being likely to generate more jobs for the growing labour force, thus limiting the growth of income inequality. It is less exciting, he accepts, but is more politically sustainable. His essay makes an important contribution to the debate on South Asia's industrialization challenge. But this view is likely to be heavily contested.

Kaushik Basu and Annemie Maertens tackle the question of job creation directly in their essay. They observe that a key feature of South Asia is its large labour force and related to this is the expected demographic dividend emerging from a growing labour force. A key challenge facing the region is whether it can create enough good jobs to convert this large population into a productive asset. Drawing on the experience of growth in manufacturing and services sectors in South Asian countries, the study notes the disappointing outcome in terms of creation of good jobs which has limited the poverty reduction impact of rapid growth. Basu and Maertens argue that among the factors that have contributed to this disappointing outcome are restrictive labour laws in the largest country India. These laws have not only reduced employment prospects in organized manufacturing but also constrained its growth by adversely affecting investment and productivity. In all South Asian countries including India, weak infrastructure has also constrained the expansion of the manufacturing sector, thereby adversely affecting both growth and employment creation. The policy conclusions are obvious. South Asia must put much greater emphasis on infrastructure development and addressing the restrictive labour laws in countries where they are binding in order to boost investment and production in the organized manufacturing sector and create more jobs.

In their paper, Ana M. Fernandes and Ariel Pakes focus on the employment challenge facing India's organized manufacturing sector. Using the data from the World Bank's Investment Climate Surveys, the study analyses the labour and capital employment rates of Indian manufacturing firms and their relationships to productivity and various institutional constraints on manufacturing. The essay derives a number of important results from this empirical work that have implications for growth and employment creation in the Indian manufacturing sector. First, there is evidence that labour is underutilized by manufacturing firms in all states, where underutilization is defined as the ratio of optimal labour employment if there were no hiring or firing costs to actual employment. Second, the extent of underutilization of labour differs substantially by states; in particular, states with higher GDP per capita exhibit much less underutilization of labour. Third, the extent of labour underutilization by firms is strongly and positively related with firm productivity. Fourth, the more productive firms tend to overutilize capital more than average, though not to the same extent as they underutilize labour. These results suggest that if labour market restrictions in states with poorly functioning labour markets were liberalized to the level of restrictions in states with better functioning labour markets, labour demand and wages would possibly increase significantly in those states. Also, such liberalization may increase productivity without significant demand for capital.

The growth and employment dividends from the services sector have benefited most South Asian countries. Yet the dynamism experienced in India is yet to be found in other South Asian countries. The study by Aaditya Mattoo looks into the question of how the services sector might be further propelled to provide impetus to higher growth in South Asia. He argues that a number of domestic policy constraints weaken the potential contribution of the services sector as a source of growth. These include regulatory restraints on competition, lack of proper regulations to enforce service standards and quality, weak labour skills due to low investment in education and training, inefficiencies in the financial sector, and restraints on foreign direct investments. In all these areas, progress has been made in most countries with India moving faster than others. Yet a substantial unfinished agenda remains. South Asia can also benefit from stronger regional cooperation in this area to benefit from economies of scale and by reducing the huge transaction costs on trade in regional services.

Raising labour productivity is critical for both growth and job creation in South Asia. While removal of growth constraints, such as weak infrastructure and labour market restrictions, will help increase the demand for labour, this must be matched by a much stronger effort to improve labour skills to sustain more rapid growth and employment. The skills challenge becomes particularly demanding as South Asia opens up to global competition and technology. Michelle Riboud and Hong Tan look at this South Asian challenge and throw light on what needs to be done to gear up. The essay's findings suggest that the educational stock of South Asia is still low compared to other dynamic regions, especially East Asia. Progress on the educational front has been unequal over time across countries, but none of the countries currently upgrade the education of their populations at a speed that would allow them to catch up quickly with East Asia and the rest of the world. The available data also suggest that South Asia invests inadequately in skills development after formal schooling. Similarly, South Asia lags behind other regions in employer provision of in-service training. Clearly, the skills challenge is enormous. A key policy imperative for South Asia moving forward is to put emphasis on higher levels of education without neglecting the unfinished agenda at the primary level. Enhancing the quality of education at all levels is a huge challenge for all South Asian countries. There is also considerable scope for improving the effectiveness of public training institutions in the region, including greater partnership with the private sector to develop and deliver skills training demanded by both employers and the labour market.

The importance of institutions and governance for economic growth and development is now well-established. Ahmed and Ghani and Paul Volcker note the importance of institutions and governance in their essays. There are different dimensions of this long-term challenge. In her contribution Ana M. Fernandes focuses on the differences in institutional quality between South Asia and East Asia. Using measurable proxies for institutional quality, her essay finds that institutions in South Asia on an average are weaker than the rest of the world and in particular in comparison to East Asia. Focusing attention on improving these institutions, especially those that concern improving the rule of law and reduce corruption, can boost the growth momentum in South Asia. Also, greater regional cooperation, as in East Asia, can help the sharing of knowledge and the emulation of good practices, consequently reducing the differences in institutional quality across countries. For all countries, better enforcement of existing laws and regulations can greatly help to strengthen outcomes.

Part III asks the important question of how more and better regional cooperation might help boost growth and equity in South Asia. The region is the least integrated of global regions and barriers to trade and investment among South Asian countries greatly exceed those with the rest of the world. The hostile political environment of the past has caused this, but the environment is changing with much stronger interest in cooperation. There are different dimensions of this cooperation. The initial focus has been on trade, but there is now growing interest in infrastructure and services. The need to broaden cooperation with other regions, especially East and Central Asia, is also recognized. L. Alan Winters in his essay looks into the question of benefits from deepening regional trading arrangements in South Asia. The chapter concludes that the case for increasing integration among South Asian countries is very strong. There are almost certainly major efficiencies to be reaped via increasing trade and competition. The regional agenda clearly should include the removal of additional trade barriers to regional trade and restrictions on transport border crossings. However, the creation of a free trade union is not the best option. Removal of trade restrictions on a global basis to foster international competition for trade and investment is the way to go.

Along with the removal of all trade and non-trade barriers, greater efforts to strengthen regional cooperation on energy and services can provide a substantial boost to growth in South Asia. This is the focus of the next two chapters. Vladislav Vucetic and Venkataraman Krishnaswamy show in their chapter the potential of energy trade in South Asia to be a basis for removing the growing energy constraint to development in the region. Fast-growing India, and to a lesser extent Bangladesh and Pakistan, are energy-thirsty countries. Nepal, Bhutan, and Afghanistan, all relatively poor countries, are endowed with huge water resources that might be fruitfully exploited for generating hydropower for trading with the countries where power is lacking. The outcome is a win–win situation as the income from hydropower can substantially boost GDP growth in these poorer countries. Bhutan to some extent has already demonstrated this through its power trading agreement with India. More generally, South Asia needs to do much more to remove the constraints to energy trade within the region and also from other neighbouring Central Asian, Middle Eastern, and East Asian countries. The essay looks at these constraints and identifies the policy actions needed to spur energy trade in South Asia. Given the long-term nature of these investments, early action is necessary to jump-start the process. In the last chapter of the book, Simon Thomas shows why better regional cooperation in transport is necessary to reduce cost and raise the competitiveness of South Asian production, a point also emphasized by L. Alan Winters. In South Asia, there is a large concentration of poor people along the border areas. Additionally, two of the poorest countries of the region, Afghanistan and Nepal, are landlocked. Enabling these poor people to access markets and benefit from growth centres is critical for poverty reduction. Currently, there are major restrictions on cross-border mobility of goods, services, and people. Most of the transport networks linking the border areas are also in bad shape. Removing these restrictions and improving the transport network to link markets with production centres is essential to raise the income of the poor as well as boost exports. The efforts at improving trade facilitation and the transport networks are being done in a fragmented manner and with little cooperation even where cross-border issues are involved. Establishing corridor-based approaches for improving the transit and transport arrangements for intra-regional trade is an essential step towards resolving the regional transport issues.

In conclusion, South Asia's progress with increasing the rate of factor accumulation and improving factor productivity can be given a further boost by addressing the second generation reforms. This will provide the basis for sustaining growth. The immediate priorities are: expanding the industrial base by removing the infrastructure and labour market constraints; modernizing the services sectors by removing all regulatory barriers; strengthening skills and institutions; and enabling regional cooperation for boosting trade and infrastructure investment. These are by no means a comprehensive set of growth drivers. Other issues such as financial sector reforms, the urbanization challenge, and agriculture sector reforms are also important growth concerns. Finally, South Asia, like other regions, faces substantial downside risks from adverse global developments relating to financial, food, and fuel crisis. Continued prudent macroeconomic management will be critical to keep South Asia on the high growth path.

Can South Asia sustain growth momentum? This has attracted more attention as the downside risks to the global and regional growth outlook have increased. Growth experience has shown that no country can sustain high growth without sound economic management. The global economic downturn makes it even more important that South Asia further strengthens economic management. South Asia also needs to take advantage of its two unique assets: its *people* and its *geography*. The region has a large labour force, which will explode in the future as the share of working age population increases, thanks to demographic dividend. More than 150 million people will enter the prime working age population over the next decade. Demographic dividend can be the future growth catalyst. South Asia's geography can be the second growth catalyst. South Asia is the most densely populated region in the world, and it has the benefit of low distance across countries. Nearly all countries in the region share a common border with India, the largest and the fastest growing economy in South Asia. The potential growth benefits of density and distance have been neutralized by high division, low market integration, poor connectivity, and friction in the region. Increased global and regional market integration will enable South Asia's growth to benefit from proximity, scale, and agglomeration economies that are positively associated with density and distance. The people and geography of the region can help South Asia to transform high growth into inclusive and sustainable growth. Inclusive growth will be the key to poverty reduction in South Asia.

Ejaz Ghani
Sadiq Ahmed

ACKNOWLEDGEMENTS

This book was prepared by a team led by Ejaz Ghani (Task Manager), and it included Aaditya Mattoo, Ana M. Fernandes, Annemie Maertens, Ariel Pakes, Hong Tan, Howard Pack, Kaushik Basu, L. Alan Winters, Michelle Riboud, late Simon Thomas, Venkataraman Krishnaswamy, and Vladislav Vucetic, under the overall guidance of Sadiq Ahmed. Special contributions were made by Jeffrey D. Sachs and Paul A. Volcker.

The book is an outcome of a regional conference organized by the South Asian Association of Regional Cooperation (SAARC) Chamber of Commerce and the World Bank. We are grateful to the SAARC Chamber of Commerce and the participants of the SAARC Business Conclave for making this work possible.

Special thanks are due to a number of people including Barry Bosworth, Carl Dahlman, Mark Dutz, Clive Harris, Isabel Guerrero, Lakshmi Iyer, Homi Kharas, Pravin Krishna, Sandeep Mahajan, Alastair Mckechnie, Ernesto May, Saurabh Mishra, Veronica Minaya, Manish Mohan, Praful Patel, Mark Roberts, Amita Sarkar, Dipak Kumar Singh, John F. Speakman, Graeme Wheeler, and Nobou Yoshida. We are grateful to Lin Chin and Naomi Dass for formatting the document.

ABBREVIATIONS

ADB	Asian Development Bank
ASEAN	Association of South East Asian Nations
ASI	Annual Survey of Industries
ATTA	Afghan Transit Trade Agreement
BASA	Bilateral Air Service Agreements
BIMSTEC	Bay of Bengal Initiative for Multi-Sectoral Tecnhical and Economic Cooperation
BR	Bangladesh Railways
CAPS	Central Asian Power System
CIF	Climate Investment Fund
CGE	Computable General Equilibrium
CPI	Corruption Perception Index
CU	Customs Union
EEC	European Economic Community
FDI	Foreign Direct Investment
FTA	Free Trade Area
GAIL	Gas Authority of India Limited
GATS	General Agreement on Trade in Services
GDP	Gross Domestic Product
GPS	Global Positioning System
ICD	Internal Container Depot
ICS	Investment Climate Surveys
ICT	Information and Communication Technology
IDA	Industrial Disputes Act
IFIs	International Financial Institutions
IR	Indian Railways
ILO	International Labour Organization
IOM	International Organization of Migration
IPCC	Intergovernmental Panel on Climate Change
IWT	Inland Water Transport

KPO	Knowledge Process Outsourcing
LNG	Liquefied Natural Gas
MNC	Multinational Corporation
MFN	Most Favoured Nation
NAVTEC	National Vocation and Technical Education Commission
NGO	Non-governmental Organization
NIC	Newly Industrialized Countries
NTA	Nepal Telecommunications Authority
NTBs	Non-tariff Barriers
NTCIP	National Trade Corridor Improvement Programme
NTPC	National Thermal Power Corporation
NWFP	Northwest Frontier Province
OECD	Organisation for Economic Cooperation and Development
ONGC	Oil and Natural Gas Corporation
OTRI	Overall Trade Restrictiveness Index
PR	Pakistan Railways
PSEB	Pakistan Software Export Board
PICS	Productivity and Investment Climate Survey
SAARC	South Asian Association for Regional Cooperation
SAFTA	South Asia Free Trade Agreement
SAPTA	South Asia Preferential Trade Area
SARIA	South Asian Regional Integration Arrangement
SME	Small and Medium Scale Enterprise
SSA	Sub-Saharan Africa
TERI	The Energy and Resource Institute
TFP	Total Factor Productivity
TVEs	Township and Village Enterprises
UN	United Nations
UNCTAD	United Nations Conference on Trade and Development
UNESCAP	United Nations Economic and Social Commission for Asia and the Pacific
UNSTATS	United Nations Statistics
VAT	Value Added Tax
UI	Unscheduled Interchange
UTL	United Telecommunications Limited
VET	Vocational Education Training

VOIP	Voice Over Internet Protocol
WBES	World Business Environment Survey
WDI	World Development Indicators

I

SOUTH ASIA'S OPPORTUNITIES AND CHALLENGES

1 SUSTAINING RAPID GROWTH IN SOUTH ASIA

Ejaz Ghani and Sadiq Ahmed[*]

Introduction

South Asia continues to grow rapidly and its largest economy, India, is close to becoming a 'Tiger'.[1] This is a remarkable transformation of a region where countries have been infamously dubbed as a 'basket case'. South Asia, which includes eight countries—Afghanistan, Bangladesh, Bhutan, India, Maldives, Nepal, Pakistan, and Sri Lanka—was known for conflict, violence, and widespread and extreme poverty. In the 1950s, when most South Asian countries gained their independence from the colonial masters, the political leadership in the region was motivated by the idealism of balanced growth, commanding heights of the public sector, labour intensive and low technology production, and self-sufficiency. South Asia adopted import substitution growth strategies with heavy trade protection, curbed the growth of private firms, and introduced restrictive labour laws to protect workers. After some 30 years, the outcome of these policies turned out to be very different from what the leadership had in mind. South Asia delivered sluggish growth, continued dependence on low-productivity agriculture, low levels of industrialization, weak export performance, and inadequate creation of good jobs. Much of the labour force was engaged in low-income activities in agriculture and informal services and around 45 per cent

[*] We are grateful for comments to Homi Kharas, Pravin Krishna, Lakshmi Iyer, Carl Dahlman, Dipak Kumar Singh, Rabin Hattari, Nobuo Yoshida, Mark Roberts, Clive Harris, M. Dutz, Isabel Guerrero, and Inder Sud. However, any errors are our responsibility.

[1] See *The Economist*, on 'India Becoming a Tiger', 8 March 2008.

of the population lived below the poverty line. It grew at a feeble growth rate of 3.7 per cent per annum—popularly known as the 'Hindu' rate of growth in India—between 1960 and 1980.

Destiny changed in the 1980s. South Asia adopted pro-growth policies. It opened up markets, replaced the public sector with the private sector as the engine of growth, increased competition, and improved economic management (Ahmed 2006). South Asia averaged an annual gross domestic product (GDP) growth rate of around 5.7 per cent during 1980–2000, which further accelerated to 6.5 per cent during 2000–7. It is now the second fastest growing region in the world, after East Asia. Growth rates in South Asia and East Asia appear to be converging (see Figure 1.1). In 2007, India experienced a GDP growth of 9 per cent, close to that of China. Other South Asian countries like Bangladesh, Pakistan, and Sri Lanka experienced a growth rate of 6.5 per cent. Private investment has boomed, supported by rising national saving rates in South Asia. It now attracts global attention because of rapid growth, global outsourcing, and skill-intensive service exports.

Having achieved high growth, the debate has now shifted to the question: Can South Asia sustain and increase the growth rate further? The experience of East Asia shows that growth that is supported by factor accumulation as well as productivity improvements can lead to higher growth.[2] South Asia stands to benefit from growth hysteresis. Its two key assets, demography and geography, have not yet been fully utilized. It has a young labour force. More workers will join the labour force over the coming decades. Though the small size of the manufacturing sector has prevented the region from converting demographic dividend into a window of opportunity, the large and potentially competitive labour force could be the catalyst that could attract regional and global production centres to be located in South Asia, as firms move in response to wage differences, and globalization benefits low-income countries.[3] South Asia's geography also has the potential to accelerate growth. It has the highest population density in the world, and the second largest proportion of population living in the border areas after Europe. High population density and better access to markets can benefit growth by allowing South Asian firms to take

[2] See Gill and H. Kharas (2007).

[3] See Summers (2006).

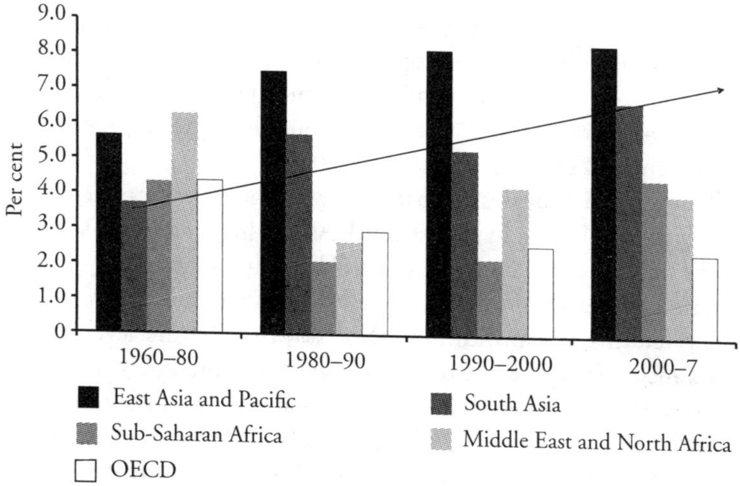

Figure 1.1: Real GDP Growth

Source: World Bank, *World Development Indicators*, various years.
Notes: Data are averages.
South Asia's data include the 2007 growth rate, while the rest of the regions do not.

advantage of agglomeration economies.[4] However, poor connective infrastructure, low mobility, and conflict have prevented the region from taking advantage of its geography and spatial characteristics.

South Asia is also well below the international technology frontier (Dahlman 2007). The scope for productivity gains from improved education, knowledge, and technology is large for all South Asian countries. The continued opening up of the regions' economies to international trade, investment, and finance is an important indicator of improved prospects for acquisition of modern technology. This needs to be complemented with a more rapid pace of investment in education and skill development.

Growth is the best instrument to deal with the formidable challenges that South Asia will face in the years and decades ahead. Rapid growth has already pulled millions of South Asians out of poverty. The average poverty rate has now fallen to around 27 per cent, although there are large inter-country variations. Social indicators have improved. Maldives and Sri Lanka have achieved outstanding success in human development. Despite this progress,

[4] See Ahmed and Ghani (2007: chapter 1).

South Asia still has the largest concentration of poor people in the world. Nearly 400 million people live on less than one US dollar a day. South Asia has the potential to reduce poverty to single digit, if it can accelerate growth to double digit while also improving the inclusiveness of growth (World Bank 2006).

This chapter provides a broad review of the types of policies and institutions which could propel South Asia to higher growth. Growth in the region is at an early stage. There are substantial country variations in terms of size, resource endowment, and progress with policy reforms and institutions. Not surprisingly, the level of per capita income and the rate of growth vary substantially by countries. Yet, sustaining rapid growth remains a challenge for all South Asian countries. Not withstanding past progress with reforms, all countries of the region still suffer from severe policy distortions. If the reform process can be accelerated, South Asia has the potential to achieve and sustain higher growth (Ahmed 2006; Ahmed and Ghani 2007).

Sustaining high growth rates is not easy. Growth is an outcome of complex interactions between policies, institutions, geography, and leadership. These interactions can be uncertain, and the jury is still out on whether initial spurts of growth acceleration, as experienced by South Asia, can be transformed into sustainable growth dynamics. However, growth has some common characteristics: rapid technological adaptation and learning, high rates of savings and human capital accumulation, high rates of public and private investment, rapid diversification, incremental productive employment, and resource mobility across sectors.[5] The South Asian growth experience demonstrates most of these characteristics. For example, South Asia's average savings rate has expanded from around 16 per cent of GDP in the 1970s to 32 per cent in 2006. Investment rate has similarly expanded from the low 20 per cent range in the 1970s to 32 per cent in 2006. While these rates are still lower than in East Asia, the rapidly rising trend is very encouraging.[6] The expansion of savings and investment rates have benefitted from sound macroeconomic management and other market-oriented reforms (Ahmed 2006). At the same time the recent adverse global developments relating to food and fuel show South Asia's vulnerability to external shocks and

[5] See Commission on Growth and Development (2008).

[6] See Ahmed and Ghani (2007, chapter 2 by S. Collins on growth accounting).

suggest that there is no room for complacency. Continued sound macroeconomic management remains essential.

There is no magic bullet for achieving high growth. The growth challenge will vary by country (and within countries by region). Policy and institutional reforms will need to reflect differences in initial economic and social conditions. Several regions in India and parts of Sri Lanka and Pakistan have already reached middle income status. The growth challenge they face will differ from that of Bangladesh, Nepal, Afghanistan, and lagging regions in India and Pakistan, which have per capita incomes of low-income countries. Country-specific strategies that address the main constraints to growth are most likely to be successful. A key challenge for the leadership is to develop a vision and a road map that will help the lagging regions in South Asia to accelerate growth and for the more developed regions to sustain high growth and achieve middle income status.

Leadership plays an important role in growth.[7] Leadership, persistence, and determination matter. A government that acts in the interest of all its citizens rather than for itself or subgroups is important. A lesson emerging from East Asia is that good policies, when spearheaded by a leadership which is pro-growth and pro-private sector, can propel a country towards achieving double digit growth rates. Malaysia and South Korea are examples of countries that have achieved double digit growth. Their leadership, in coordination with the private sector, played a key role in spearheading pro-growth policies.[8] These economies initially relied on a small, dedicated reform team that was connected to the top of the government and in charge of formulating and updating the reform strategy, building consensus, coordinating and mobilizing resources for implementing the strategy, and, crucially, nurturing the reformist political leadership over time.

The rest of the chapter discusses what South Asia can do to achieve and sustain higher growth and achieve middle income status. We believe that for the next stage of South Asia's development, there are at least five key drivers of growth. These are as follows:

[7] Criscuolo and Palmad (2008).

[8] This does not imply that 'government can pick winners' or that this is an invitation to 'corruption and rent seeking'. These arguments are central not only to industrial policy but also to other policies such as education, health, social insurance, and economic stabilization.

- Market integration
- Infrastructure
- Institutions
- Inclusive growth
- Regional public goods

Market Integration

Successful growth experiences are typically associated with greater integration in the world and regional economy—developing countries' domestic markets are much too small to support rapid and sustained expansions of production. Market integration allows economic agents to interact across spatial scales: local, regional, and international. The benefit of this interaction is increased flow of labour, goods, capital, ideas, and technology. Firms benefit from Marshallian externalities (technological spillovers, labour market pooling, access to non-traded intermediate inputs) and non-pecuniary externalities (forward and backward linkages). The extent to which economic agents take advantage of market integration is impacted positively by density, but negatively by distance and division (Fujita, Krugman, and Venables 1999).[9] Divisions, created by conflict, transport costs, and both formal and informal barriers to trade, separate economic agents in one country from the advantages of density in other countries.

The region has significantly more room to benefit from market integration globally, across countries within South Asia, and within country. Globally, South Asia's rapid GDP growth benefited from rapid expansion in trade. It has experienced one of the fastest growth rates in trade (Figure 1.2) averaging 10.8 per cent in 2007, following growth of almost 12 per cent during 2005–6, which was the highest among all regions. Yet, the region has more room to benefit from trade. Despite recent reforms, South Asia continues to have the most restrictive tariff policies compared to other regions (Figure 1.3). Among developing countries, South Asia has the most

[9] Distance here is to be interpreted as an economic and social concept, rather than a purely physical concept. As such, a location that is physically close to a region of high density can, in principle, still be economically distant. This will be the case, for example, if the quality of spatially connective infrastructure linking the two areas is poor or there are economic, social, and institutional barriers to commuting and the free flow of labour between the areas.

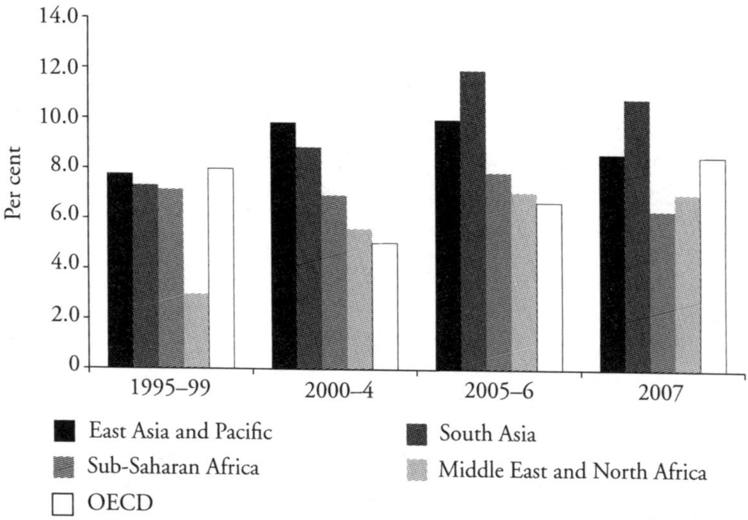

Figure 1.2: Real Growth in Trade of Goods and Services

Source: World Bank (2008b).
Note: Data for 1995–9, 2000–4, and 2005–6 are averages.

protective agricultural trade policies. Its global integration, measured by trade as a ratio of GDP, was 49 per cent in 2007, which although higher than its late 1990s ratio of 20 per cent, is the lowest among developing countries.[10]

Within South Asia, individual countries cannot grow in isolation from each other, and regional cooperation is required. Market integration within South Asia is the lowest in the world as reflected by intra-regional trade between countries being less than 2 per cent of GDP for South Asia compared to 40 per cent for East Asia. Border barriers to trade and services have mostly disappeared in the rest of the world but not in South Asia. Divisions across countries in South Asia have increased dramatically over the last four decades.[11] In 1948, South Asia's share of intra-regional trade as a share of total trade was 18 per cent. In 2000–7, it fell to 5 per cent of the total trade. Cost of trading across borders in South Asia is high. At the Petrapole-

[10] See World Bank (2008a).

[11] Borders and divisions are not the same thing. Borders define a nation state whereas divisions influence the flow of people, goods, services, capital, ideas, and technology across borders.

Benapole, one of the main borders between Bangladesh and India, trucks wait for more than 100 hours to cross the border. It takes 200 signatures in Nepal to trade goods with India, and some 140 signatures in India to trade goods with Nepal. It is estimated that trade between India and Pakistan, currently at US$ 1 billion,[12] could jump to US$ 6–10 billion, if divisions were removed. Divisions in South Asia have been aggravated by conflict.

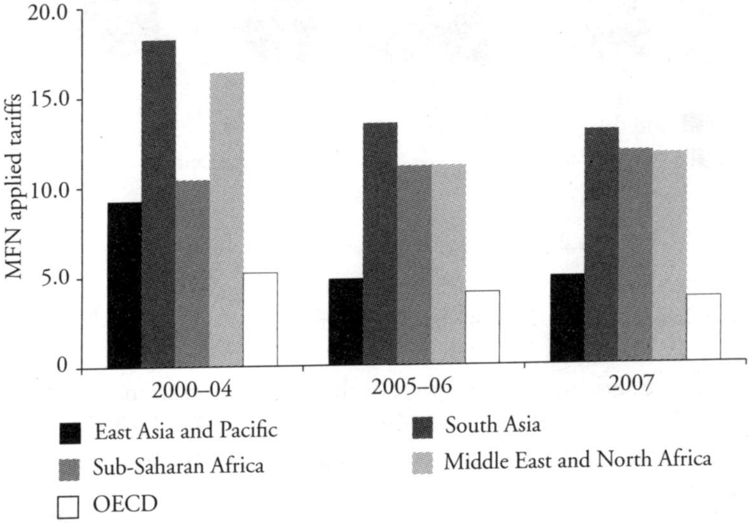

Figure 1.3: Trade Tariff Restrictiveness Index

Source: World Bank (2008b).
Note: Data for 2000–4 and 2005–6 are averages.

Within country, poor market integration is reflected in rising regional disparities. The increase of within country disparities is viewed by many as a potential threat to future growth as tensions between the poorer and richer states are likely to increase if current trends in regional inequality persist or increase in the future. Recent insights from the economic geography literature suggest that increases in regional disparities may be a natural feature of the growth process. However, the best approach to addressing regional disparities is to

[12] Includes both formal and informal trade.

enhance market integration by reducing barriers to trade through improved policies and connectivity.

Growth benefits of market integration are likely to be large but unequal. India, a large country with a big home market, can get by with more restrictive borders, since the size of its economy and population provides the incentive to importers and exporters to overcome these barriers. It is the small, landlocked countries, like Afghanistan, Bhutan, and Nepal, which will benefit most from improved access to the markets of others. Small countries depend more on openness to overcome the disadvantage of size: small population, small markets, and inability to take advantage of agglomeration and scale economies. Even within India, the peculiar geography that isolates the seven north-eastern states (the so-called seven sisters) from mainland India with the location of Bangladesh in-between suggests that market integration requires trade and transit arrangements with neighbours to benefit all regions that are lagging and isolated from the growth centres. Tradable economic activities are inherently scalable in the sense that small economies can expand output without running into diminishing returns (unlike domestic services). Rapid economic growth, associated with modern sector export growth, can be 'lumpy' (Venables 2006). Spatially, it can be uneven, with production being concentrated in some countries, regions or cities. In product space, specialization is likely to increase, with regions specializing in a few tasks rather than production of integrated products. Examples of specialization from South Asia include ICT service export from Bangalore in India; shirts, trousers, and hats exported from Bangladesh; and exports of bed linen and soccer balls from Pakistan. Temporally, rapid growth will happen only once some threshold level of capabilities has been reached. Some countries may experience growth before others, resulting in sequential rather than parallel growth. The benefits of market integration, however, cannot be achieved without improving the infrastructure.

INFRASTRUCTURE

Infrastructure is like second-nature geography, which can reduce the time and monetary costs to reach markets and thus overcome the limitations of physical geography.[13] Improved infrastructure

[13] See Kanbur and Venables (2005a).

that enhances connectivity and contributes to market integration is the best solution to promoting growth as well as addressing rising inequality between regions. The Ganga Bridge in Bihar in India is a good example of second-nature geography. The bridge has reduced the time and monetary costs of farmers in the rural areas in north Bihar to reach markets in Patna, the largest city in Bihar. The Jamuna Bridge in Bangladesh is another good example of spatially connective infrastructure. The bridge has opened market access for producers in the lagging north-west areas around the Rajshahi division. Better market access has helped farmers diversify into high value crops and reduced input prices.

So far, South Asia has achieved impressive growth rates despite poor infrastructure. This may be difficult to sustain in the future. Poor infrastructure and restrictive labour laws (to be discussed later) are among the major factors that have restrained the growth of the manufacturing sector and prevented firms from growing.[14] Table 1.1 shows that the manufacturing share of value added in India is smaller than that share in other large developing economies, though it is similar to that share in smaller countries with GDP per capita similar to that of India (such as Vietnam). However, as Table 1.2 shows, the growth of value added in manufacturing in India is noticeably lower than that in these smaller similar income countries. Indeed the sectoral growth comparisons in Table 1.2 are rather striking. The growth of value added in services in India is comparable to that in China, and about 10 percentage points higher than that in other countries. In rather stark contrast, the growth of value added in manufacturing in India is only about half of that in China and Vietnam.

The service sector in India has done well because it relies less on transportation and is less energy intensive than manufacturing. South Asia has the highest share of services in its exports at 31 per cent, which is higher than OECD (Organisation for Economic Co-operation and Development) high income countries. ICT exports and global outsourcing have benefited from the use of the internet which has reduced information transmission costs dramatically. While other countries can emulate India's successful efforts to boost services export, sustained high growth will require a substantial effort to raise manufacturing growth in all South Asian countries. In general,

[14] See Chapter 6 by Fernandes and Pakes (this volume).

TABLE 1.1: Share of Industry and Manufacturing in Employment and GDP across Countries

	Employment in industry as % of total employment in 2000	*Value added in industry as % of GDP in 2000*	*Value added in manufacturing as % of GDP in 2000*	*2002 GDP per capita (in 2000 US$)*
India	18.2	26.3	15.6	480
Brazil	19.3	28	17.1	3473
China	23	45.9	34.7	1106
Indonesia	17.3	45.9	27.7	844
Pakistan	18	22.6	14.8	532
Vietnam	12.4	36.7	18.6	444
Low-income countries	12.3	26.6	14.1	
Lower-middle-income countries	18.5	38.3	24.2	

Source: World Bank, *World Development Indicators 2005.*
Notes: Industry includes manufacturing, and also mining and quarrying (including oil production), construction, and public utilities (electricity, gas, and water). Lower-income countries and lower-middle-income countries are defined based on the World Bank classification.

TABLE 1.2: Growth in Sectoral Value-Added across Countries

	Growth in value added in manufacturing		*Growth in value added in agriculture*		*Growth in value added in services*	
	1995–2000	*2000–5*	*1995–2000*	*2000–5*	*1995–2000*	*2000–5*
India	28.1%	38.4%	13.7%	14.9%	48.4%	50.3%
Brazil	5.7%	5.6%	17.3%	23.7%	26.5%	31.8%
China	57.6%	67.4%	18.5%	21.2%	57.3%	61.2%
Indonesia	14.6%	27.5%	7.0%	17.3%	-2.4%	35.7%
Pakistan	17.1%	56.6%	26.5%	12.0%	20.9%	29.9%
Vietnam	70.3%	73.8%	24.2%	20.7%	31.9%	40.0%

Source: World Bank, *World Development Indicators 2005.*
Note: The table shows growth rates for each sector in total value added (in constant local currency units) between year t and year t+5.

poor infrastructure has constrained the growth of labour-intensive manufacturing firms in South Asia and prevented the region from making use of its most important asset, its people.

South Asia suffers from three infrastructural deficits. First, there is a *service deficit*, as the region's infrastructure has not been able to keep pace with a growing economy and population. Power outages and water shortages are a regular occurrence in India and Bangladesh. Rural roads are impassable in lagging regions in India (for example, Bihar, Uttar Pradesh) and Sri Lanka. India has 6000 km of four lane highways and China in the last 10 years has built 35,000 km of four to six lane highways. Every month, China adds power capacity equivalent to what exists in Bangladesh. Second, South Asia suffers from a *policy deficit*, given highly distorted pricing, poor sector governance and accountability, and weak cost recovery. It is estimated that eliminating the financial losses from the power and water sectors alone would provide a substantial chunk of the incremental funds for infrastructure investment that India needs. Third, South Asia suffers from a *cooperation deficit*. India, one of the energy thirsty nations, sits next to an immensely energy-rich neighbour, Nepal. Yet there is very little exploitation of Nepal's hydropower potential because of inadequate cooperation with India. Similarly, India, which has attracted global attention in ICT, contrasts with other South Asian countries that are lagging in ICT. In South Asia, only 7 per cent of the international calls are regional compared to 71 per cent in East Asia.

South Asia needs to overcome a huge gap in infrastructure. The region has invested only 3.5 to 4 per cent of GDP per year in infrastructure over the period 2000–5. This is lower than what the East Asian countries have invested: Vietnam and China had investment rates of around 8 per cent to 10 per cent of GDP. In 1980, India actually had higher infrastructure stocks—in power, roads, and telecommunications—but China invested massively in infrastructure, overtaking India by 1990 and the gap is currently ever widening. It is estimated that for the South Asian region to sustain a growth target of 8 per cent, it will require an investment in infrastructure amounting to 7.6 per cent of GDP (Harris 2008). Higher growth rate in the 10 per cent range will require an even more rapid pace of investment to modernize the infrastructure.

Much of the infrastructure investment gap has to be financed at the national level along with necessary improvements in sector policies and institutions. Yet, regional cooperation can be of great help to meet a significant part of this need. The three priority areas for regional cooperation include telecom and internet, energy, and transport. A regional telecom network and a high-bandwidth, high-speed internet-based network could help improve education, innovation, and health. A regional network would facilitate better flow of ideas, technology, investments, goods, and services. It would facilitate greater interactions between knowledge workers in areas such as high-energy physics, nanotechnology, and medical research. There are untapped positive synergies at the regional level that would come from information sharing and competition in ideas among universities, non-university research and teaching entities, libraries, hospitals, and other knowledge institutions. It also could help in the building and sharing of regional databases, and in addressing regional problems, including multi-country initiatives such as flood control, disaster management, climate change, and infectious disease control. Importantly, such an effort could help spark higher and more sustainable regional growth.

Regional cooperation in the telecom sector and the internet could strengthen the competitiveness of South Asia in the services-export sector. India has established itself as a global player in ICT and outsourcing. Other countries in South Asia could potentially benefit from neighbourhood and spillover effects. The expansion of services exports would contribute to growth, create jobs, and other sectors would benefit from improved technology and management (Hamid 2007). The service-export sector, although less infrastructure intensive than manufacturing, needs different types of infrastructure than the traditional export sectors. For these exports, there would be a need to invest in fibre optic highways, broadband connectivity, and international gateways and uplink facilities. Investments in tertiary education, and in technical and English proficiency would need to be increased. South Asia would need to remove barriers to trade in ICT services, eliminate restrictions on the flow of intra-regional foreign direct investment (FDI), and remove visa restrictions on the flow of people.

The potential gains from regional trade in energy are substantial. After decades of insignificant cross-country electricity trade and the absence of any trade in natural gas through pipelines, regional political leaders and businessmen have recently evinced a great deal of interest and enthusiasm in cross-border electricity and gas trade, not only within South Asia but also with its neighbours in the west (Central Asia and Iran) and in the east (Myanmar). There are two regional energy clusters in South Asia. The Eastern market includes India, Bangladesh, Bhutan, Nepal, and Sri Lanka, extending to Myanmar, and the Western market includes Pakistan, Afghanistan, and India, extending to Central Asia and Iran. India bridges the two clusters. While all countries would benefit from energy trade, in relative terms the gains would be especially large for Nepal, which could double its GDP if it could trade its hydropower with India and Bangladesh.

What can governments do to promote energy trade? They need to continue reducing political and security tensions; consider energy trade as enhancement of energy security and political and economic cooperation; continue energy sector reforms; improve commercial performance of the utilities; improve the credibility, competence, and accountability of regulation; adopt sustainable (cost-reflective) tariffs and a social protection framework; promote commercial approach to energy trade; encourage private sector participation in the form of public–private partnership (PPP) structures in cross-border investments; help the transit countries—especially Afghanistan—integrate; engage in reaching water-sharing agreements; seek accession to international agreements (such as Energy Charter Treaty); strengthen regional institutions at both political and technical levels; and identify priority trade-oriented investment projects and pursue their implementation. The success of India–Bhutan electricity trade should offer useful lessons to other countries.

Restrictions in transport border crossings are a major constraint to global and intra-regional trade in South Asia. Removing these restrictions would boost trade within the region as well as lower the cost for international trade in general as many landlocked countries and regions will benefit from access to the closest ports. Currently, the efforts at improving trade facilitation and transport networks are being done in a fragmented manner and with little cooperation even where cross-border issues are involved. Establishing corridor-based approaches for improving the trade–transport arrangement for intra-regional trade would be essential for improving the efficiency of regional transport and for reducing trade costs.

INSTITUTIONS

Many good policies can be implemented immediately while institutions are built over time. Economic governance[15] in South Asia has improved over time with the implementation of the first-generation policy reforms. First, market-creating institutions have improved since the 1980s, as the policymakers replaced resource allocation based on centralized planning with market-based allocation. Global integration, by fostering competition and transferring knowledge, has further helped to strengthen market-creating institutions. Second, market-stabilizing institutions have strengthened as the policymakers have improved economic management.[16] The good aspects of the market-stabilizing institutions have allowed South Asia to achieve one of the lowest inflation rates in the world during the last three decades. Output variability in South Asia over the period 1960–2000 has also been low compared to other regions. Third, some progress with institutions on conflict management has helped to avoid extreme outcomes in South Asia, such as famines, or the disintegration of states (such as seen in the Soviet Union, former Yugoslavia, and Sudan). Fourth, South Asia is credited with achieving large growth responses with small policy changes. It is the underlying institutions, which encourage consensus and policy stability, that have helped magnify the effect of policy changes on growth. Governance institutions have improved, although slowly, as a result of the increased role of the civil society, right to information, and education. Are these institutions strong enough to support and sustain high growth?

South Asia's institutions are particularly weak in three areas: business environment, labour laws, and conflict management.

[15] Economic governance is defined as the legal and institutional framework to support economic activity and economic transactions by protecting property rights, enforcing contracts, and taking collective action to provide physical and social infrastructure. Security of property rights provides incentives to save, invest, achieve efficient allocation of assets, and enable productive use of labour. Enforcement of contracts removes the fear of counterparty cheating which constrains mutually gainful transactions.

[16] See Rodrik (2002) for a detailed discussion of market-creating and market-stabilizing institutions.

Business Environment

South Asia has the second worst business environment in the world. Figure 1.4 shows a comparison of the business environment in South Asia with other regions. South Asia performs poorly on most indicators of business environment and also fares poorly in terms of corruption (Figure 1.5), although it is is home to some of the most dynamic entrepreneurs in the world. These entrepreneurs have managed to overcome regulatory barriers, and grow like the banyan tree which spreads around concrete barriers. Restrictive regulatory policies and corruption are associated with the loss of productivity and investment. South Asia could check corruption by mainstreaming 'one stop' licensing agencies (which combine central, state, and local authorities); introducing competing authorities (but one license) so that bribes can be competed down to zero; improving access to land titles; and making the right to information more effective. Law and order could be improved to strengthen the protection of property rights. Business institutions, chambers of commerce, and media can guard against government's predation.

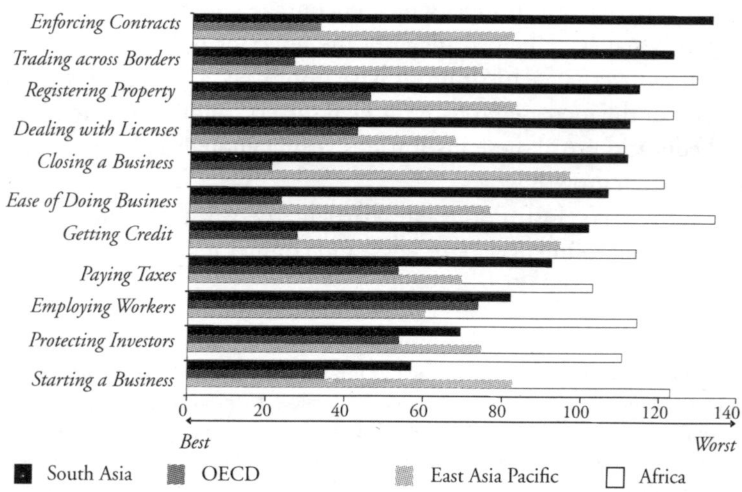

Figure 1.4: Ranks of Doing Business Indicators

Source: Doing Business Reports.
Note: Data are average of 2003 to 2007.

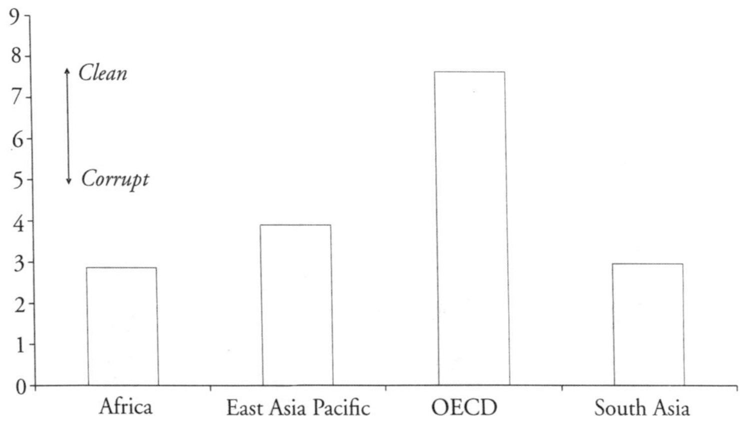

Figure 1.5: Corruption Perception Index in 2007

Source: Transparency International.
Notes: The CPI should be interpreted as a ranking of countries with scores ranging from 0 (highly corrupt) to 10 (highly clean).
Data are averages of sample countries in each region.

Labour Laws

A key regulatory weakness of South Asia is rigid labour laws that protect workers rather than jobs. South Asia has one of the most restrictive sets of labour regulations in the world. Figure 1.6 shows global perspectives on the restrictiveness of hiring and firing workers. India and Sri Lanka are rated very restrictive on hiring and firing. Average severance pay is 75 weeks in South Asia compared to 33 and 63 weeks in other parts of the world. However, not all South Asian countries suffer from rigid labour laws. Pakistan and Bangladesh have market-friendly labour laws. The World Bank has developed an index, ranging from 0 to 100, of how hard it is to let go workers, where 0 denotes the easiest and 100 the hardest. India scores 90 on this scale while Bangladesh and Pakistan score 20 and 30, respectively, and Bhutan scores 0.

The adverse implications of rigid labour laws for the manufacturing sector are illustrated by the experience of India. The Indian manufacturing sector includes a much larger share of relatively small firms than the manufacturing sectors in other economies. This is shown in Figure 1.7 which compares the size distribution of firms in India to that in China, Brazil, and Indonesia.

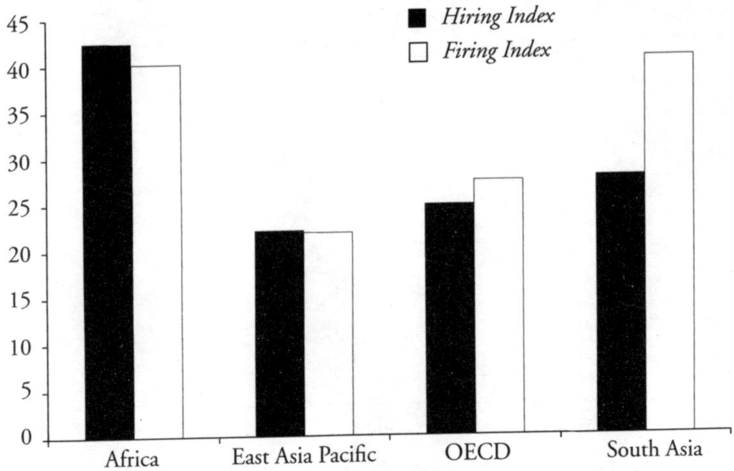

Figure 1.6: Hiring and Firing Indices

Source: Doing Business Reports.
Note: Data are averages of 2003 to 2007.

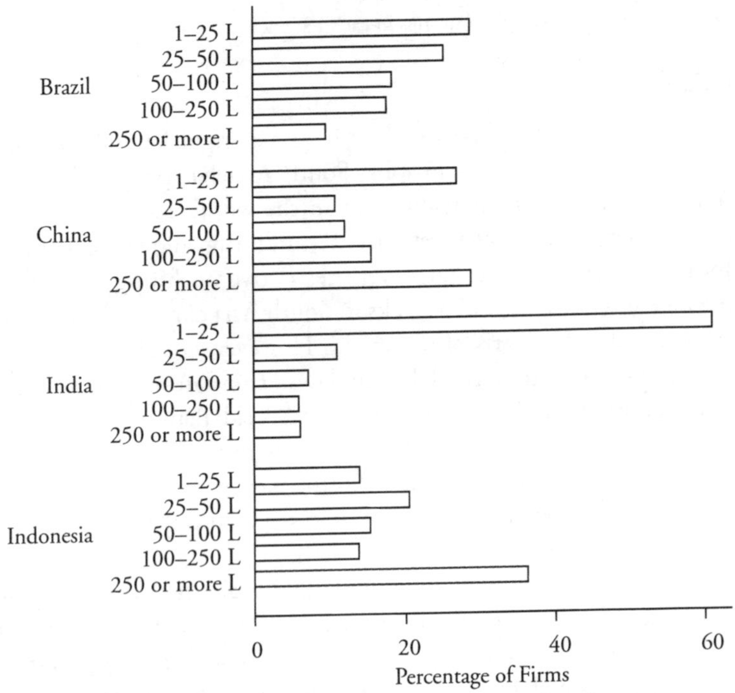

Figure 1.7: Percentage of Firms by Size Group across Countries

Source: Investment Climate Surveys for Brazil, China, India, and Indonesia.

In a recent study, Fernandes and Pakes (2008) examine the issue of factor utilization in the Indian manufacturing sector. They find that labour is underutilized in manufacturing firms in the formal sector in India. That is, given the amount of capital used by firms, their productivity, and the cost of labour, firms are employing less labour than they would employ if they faced no hiring and firing costs. In contrast, there is overutilization of capital in Indian firms. One important implication of this finding is that the reduction of labour restrictions will create more employment in the manufacturing sector. More generally, several studies (Beesley and Burges 2004; Aghion and Burges 2003; Kochar et al. 2006) have shown that labour restrictions tend to hurt investment and productivity in India's organized manufacturing sector.

Conflict Management

The South Asian region suffers from a high degree of conflict, both within and across countries. Nepal witnessed a long-running civil war from 1996 to 2006, in which more than 12,000 people were killed. Afghanistan and Sri Lanka have also been the scenes of long-running conflicts. The provinces of Balochistan and North West Frontier Province (NWFP) in Pakistan are widely regarded as conflict-ridden places. In India, 749 people were killed in incidents of Naxalite violence in 2006; such incidents have been reported from 13 different states, and 70 per cent of these deaths occurred in the lagging regions of Chhattisgarh, Jharkhand, and Bihar.[17] More than 70 million people have been displaced by conflict in South Asia and incidents of terrorism are also on the rise across these countries.

There are several potential causes for a higher degree of conflict in the lagging regions, many of which have been found to be significantly associated with the incidence of conflict in cross-country studies. These include geography, economic factors such as poverty and unemployment, social diversity, and institutional factors such as poor property rights, landlessness, inequality of access to public infrastructure, and weak state capacity in the delivery of services. Within South Asia, areas with historically poor property rights have been found to display higher levels of violent crime.[18]

[17] Asian Centre for Human Rights (2007).

[18] Banerjee and Iyer (2005).

District-level research in Nepal finds that geography and poverty are very significantly associated with the intensity of conflict, while measures of social diversity based on caste or language play a much smaller role.[19]

In addition to dealing with conflict within countries, the region also suffers from significant conflict across countries. Two well-known examples are the long-drawn conflict between Pakistan and India over Kashmir, and the Afghan-Pakistan conflict over the Taliban issue. Less open yet unfortunate is the low-level conflict between Bangladesh and India over the perceived rise of terrorism in the region. The development costs of these conflicts have been tremendous in terms of loss of life, restrictions on people to people contact across countries within the region, high financial cost of military and other security-related operations, and the loss of benefits from lack of economic, social, and political cooperation. Cross-country conflict is the most important reason why South Asia is the least integrated region of the world.

What can South Asia do to transform conflict into cooperation? South Asian countries have implemented different measures to control internal conflict. In most countries, the official government policy has been to combine implementation of development schemes with the deployment of additional security forces. By and large, efforts to curb ethnic conflict with force appear to have exacerbated the intensity of conflict. In Nepal, after several years of trying a military response, the government signed a peace deal with the Maoist rebels in 2006.

The challenge for South Asia is how conflict can be converted into cooperation and the resources channeled towards achieving growth and sharing the benefits of growth with minority and disadvantaged groups. Nepal's success in reaching a peace accord with the Maoists and bringing them into the democratic process sets a good example for other countries regarding how to address long-term conflict at its source. Ensuring good governance that allows participation and voice of all citizens in the development effort can play a key role in reducing in-country conflicts. Better economic cooperation and stronger trade relations can be helpful in reducing cross-country conflicts.

[19] Quy-Toan Do and Iyer (2007).

INCLUSIVE GROWTH

Can South Asia achieve both high and inclusive growth? Good examples of factors that can contribute to high and inclusive growth are labour mobility, better job creation, skills and education, and resolution of internal conflict. Inclusive growth is not about balanced growth but shared opportunities. Spatial disparities in growth are inevitable when growth accelerates and countries make the transition from being an agricultural to an industrialized economy. Regional policies to support balanced growth do not work, as shown by India's experience. In the 1960s, India promoted uniformity in economic production, which turned out to be

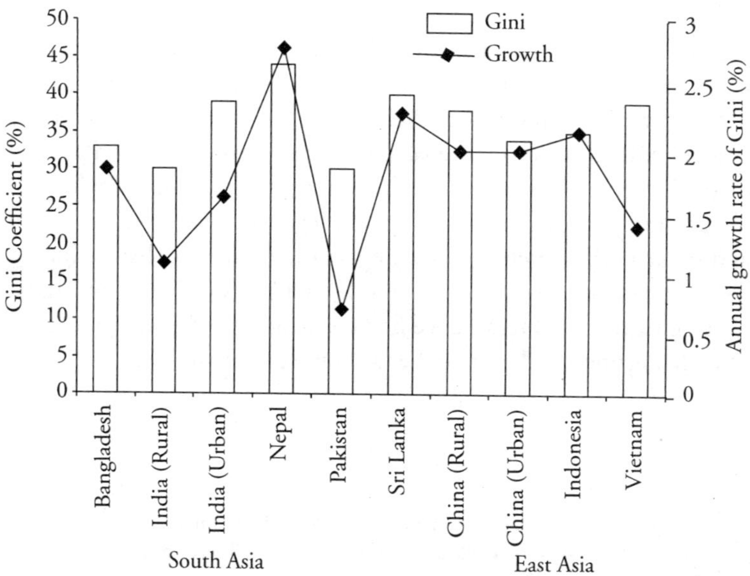

Figure 1.8: Gini Coefficient (the latest available) and the Annual Growth Rate of Gini (%)

Source: World Bank staff estimation using household income and expenditure surveys of each country.
Note: Source data for Bangladesh—HIES 1991–2 and 2005; Pakistan—PIHS 1998–9 and PSLM 2005–6; India—NSSO 50th and 55th rounds; Sri Lanka—HIES 1990–1 and 2002; Nepal—NLLS 1996–7 and 2003–4. Data for all East Asian countries are in the World Bank's data department; and survey years are 1993–2004 for China; 1999–2004 for Indonesia; 1992–2004 for Vietnam.

expensive.[20] Since the liberalization of these policies in the 1980s, the dynamics of growth have changed from 'race to the bottom' to 'race to the top'. Is South Asia's growth inclusive? Is growth creating jobs? Do people have skills to support and sustain high growth?

Figure 1.8 shows economic inequality as measured by the Gini coefficient.[21] Inequality in South Asia is rising but less than in East Asia.[22] This is apparent when comparing the growing inequality between the rich and the poor in India compared to China. Nepal and Sri Lanka have the highest levels of inequality in South Asia. They also have the highest growth in inequality. Pakistan and rural India have the lowest levels of inequality. Is inequality between regions, that is, spatial inequality, also rising?

For most countries, growth in inequality across leading and lagging regions is rising faster than growth in inequality across individuals. Figure 1.9 reports regional inequality at the sub-national level using the Theil inequality measure.[23] The figure shows that *regional* inequality is rising at a much faster pace than *pure between-individual* inequality in all countries except for Nepal and, to some extent, India. Regional inequality generally increases as an economy shifts from agriculture to manufacturing. There are some signs of regional convergence in Nepal and India, as the extremely poor areas in these countries have achieved faster growth rates in consumption. Poorer parts of Nepal and India have benefited from remittance flows as workers have moved to areas of higher economic density either at home or abroad.

[20] Economic imperatives cause economic activity to concentrate in some regions and not in other regions. Government efforts, based on tax breaks and subsidies to capital and labour, to alter the location of economic activity are likely to be ineffective or very expensive. Instead, government policy should focus on addressing problems of distance and divisions, and allow the market to respond accordingly.

[21] We are grateful to Nobuo for this work.

[22] Based on their survey of evidence of over 50 developing nations, Kanbur and Venables (2005a, 2005b) argue that the uneven spatial impact of trade and globalization played a major role in the increase in regional and urban spatial inequalities in developing countries in recent years. Moreover, they argue that, in addition to geographic remoteness, the backward regions and rural areas suffered from an inequitable distribution of infrastructure, public services, and policies that constrained the free migration of people from backward places.

[23] The Theil inequality measure has a convenient property: it can be decomposed into inequality across areas, or '*regional* inequality', and inequality between individuals, after controlling for the former, or '*pure between-individual* inequality'.

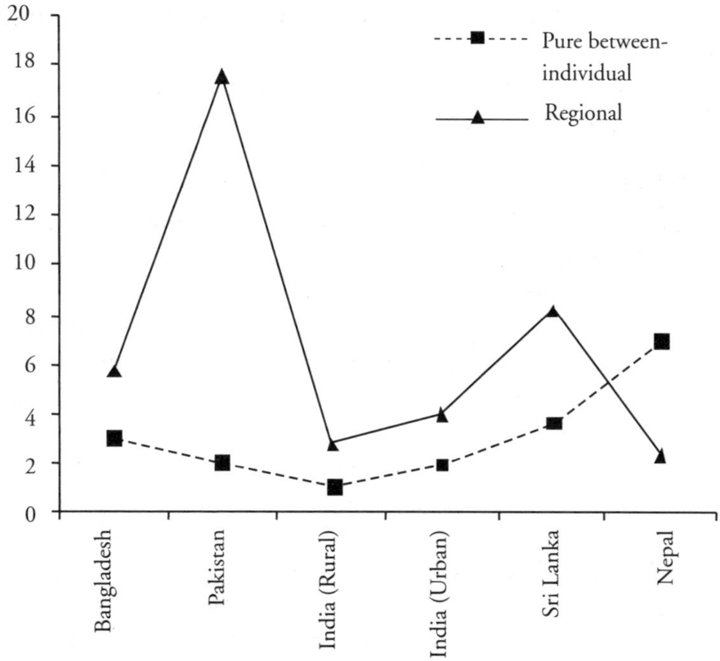

Figure 1.9: Annual Growth Rate of Regional Inequality and the Pure Individual Effect for Selected South Asian Countries

Source: World Bank staff estimation using household income and expenditure surveys of each country. Data sets are the same as Figure 1.1.
Notes: The sub-national level indicates division for Bangladesh; province for Pakistan and Sri Lanka; state for India; and region for Nepal.
For all countries but Pakistan, per-capita household expenditures are used for computing Theil inequality measures. For Pakistan, household expenditure per adult equivalent is used.

The strongest indicator of inclusive growth is poverty reduction. As mentioned earlier, all South Asian countries have reduced poverty. Going forward, however, poverty reduction is likely to be complicated by the fact that income is increasingly concentrated in the leading regions, while poverty is concentrated in the lagging regions. Most lagging regions in income terms are also lagging in terms of having higher than average incidence of poverty. Based on national sample surveys and national poverty lines, there are more than 330 million people in South Asia who are considered poor. An estimated 200 million poor people live in the lagging regions. The evidence also suggests that lagging regions are growing slower than leading regions. What can South Asia do to achieve high growth and reduce poverty given this spatial asymmetry between income per capita and poverty incidence?

Migration

Labour mobility is the natural mechanism for promoting faster and inclusive growth regionally and globally. In the case of South Asia, remittances are almost twice as large as private debt and portfolio equity, three times as large as foreign direct investment, and seven times as large as official development assistance. It is estimated that over 22 million people, or 1.5 per cent of the South Asian population, live outside their country of birth. Intra-regional migration is the largest share of international migration movement in South Asia (mostly illegal), while high-income non-OECD and high-income OECD countries are the second and third largest destinations. In 2007, the top recipient countries of recorded remittances in South Asia were India (US$27.0 billion), Bangladesh (US$6.4 billion), and Pakistan (US$6.1 billion), collectively making the South Asian region the third largest regional recipient of remittances. As a percentage of GDP, remittances are most important for Nepal and Bangladesh. Migration contributes to the movement of surplus labour from rural to urban areas, from lagging to leading sectors, and from lagging to leading regions. This promotes higher productivity, wages, and inclusive growth.

The flow of resources and products to areas where demand and prices are higher allows more efficient use and higher incomes. In India, inequality is emerging between the populous northern and interior states where there are few jobs, and the coastal states that are creating more jobs but face labour shortage, due to low labour mobility. Labour mobility in South Asia is low within countries. For example, over 96 per cent of the Indian population lives in the state in which they were born. The parallel number is dramatically lower for China, Turkey, Mexico, and other large developing countries. Among the factors that inhibit labour mobility are internal distances, poor infrastructure (such as roads), cultural factors (such as language), poor education, and *location*-specific safety net programmes such as rural employment guarantee schemes in India, which prevent migrant workers from using safety nets in states where they were not born.

Given the positive role of migration and remittances in reducing inequality and poverty, policy efforts should focus on removing restrictions on migration and to lower the cost of sending remittance by facilitating money transfer through official channels. South Asia can learn from the positive experience of countries such as Brazil in helping reduce the cost of sending remittances.

Job Creation

Job creation is good for both growth and equity. South Asia has a young population (Figure 1.10) and the lowest female participation rate in the labour force (Figure 1.11). The demographic dividend will result in more workers entering the labour force in the future. More than 150 million people will enter the prime working age population over the next decade. Labour supply growth is 2.3 per cent per annum in South Asia, above the global average of 1.8 per cent. The increased bulge within the labour force can contribute to additional growth; so will the increased female participation in the labour force. This will also contribute to equity as, in the absence of unemployment and pension benefits, employment of a family member is the biggest safety net for families in South Asia. Labour markets are the main channels through which economic growth is distributed across people. How has South Asia done in job creation?

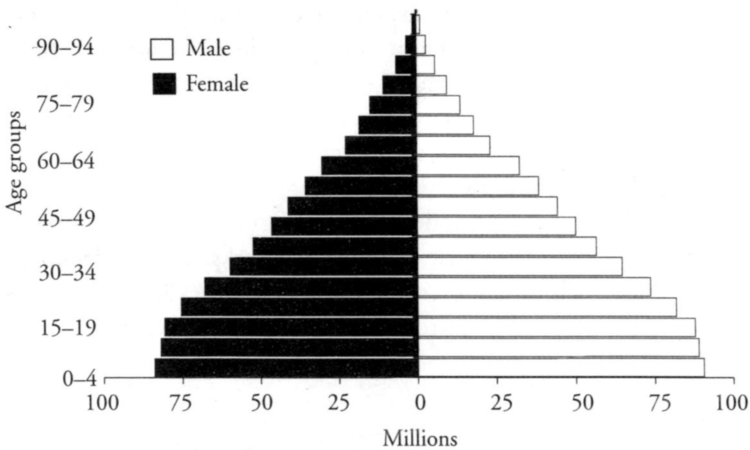

Figure 1.10: South Asian Population Structure in 2005

Source: UN Population Database.

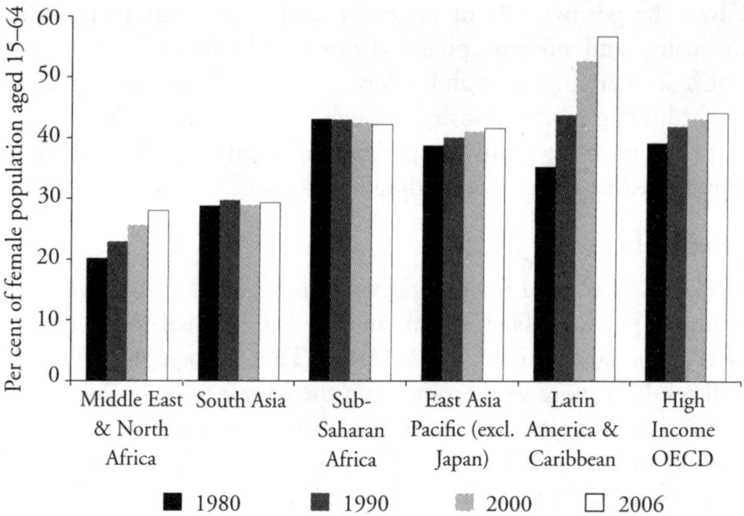

Figure 1.11: Labor Force Participation Rate, Female

Source: World Bank, *World Development Indicator*, various years.

In terms of numbers, South Asia is one of the fastest job creators in the world. Figure 1.12 presents data on total job creation (formal and informal sectors). South Asia is the second fastest job creator in the world, after East Asia. Job creation has increased over time. Over the period 2000–5, India generated 11.3 million net new jobs per year, on average. The figure was 7 million in China. In India the employment growth in 2000–5 was 2.8 per cent while in China it was 1 per cent.[24] The largest job creation in South Asia is in the services sector, but the manufacturing sector is also showing progress. Jobs in the agriculture sector are shrinking in South Asia. As the agriculture sector modernizes, and farmers move up the value chain, and make better use of retail networks, storage facilities, refrigeration facilities, and transportation facilities from the fields to the markets, more jobs are likely to migrate from agriculture to other sectors.

[24] Nearly 90 per cent of job creation in India is in the informal sector compared to only 50 per cent in China. In addition, the growth in formal employment in urban China is much higher than the growth in formal employment in urban India (3.1 per cent versus 1.7 per cent in the last five years).

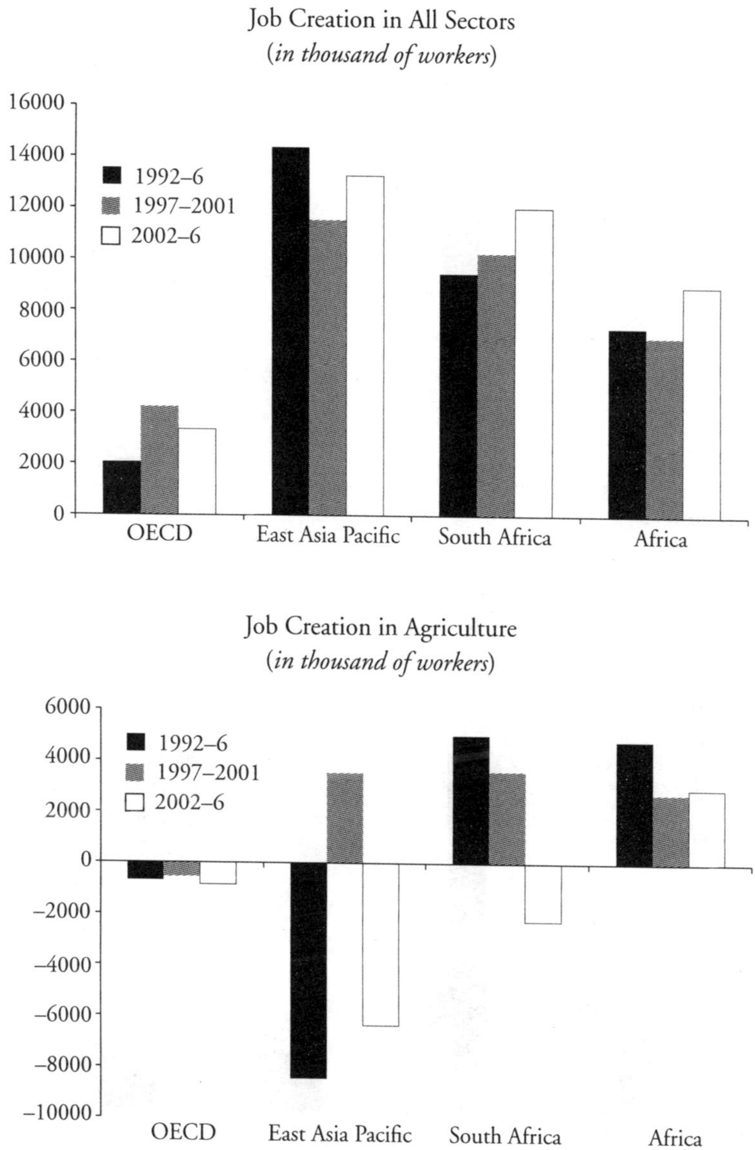

Figure 1.12: Job Creation

(contd ...)

Figure 1.12 (contd ...)

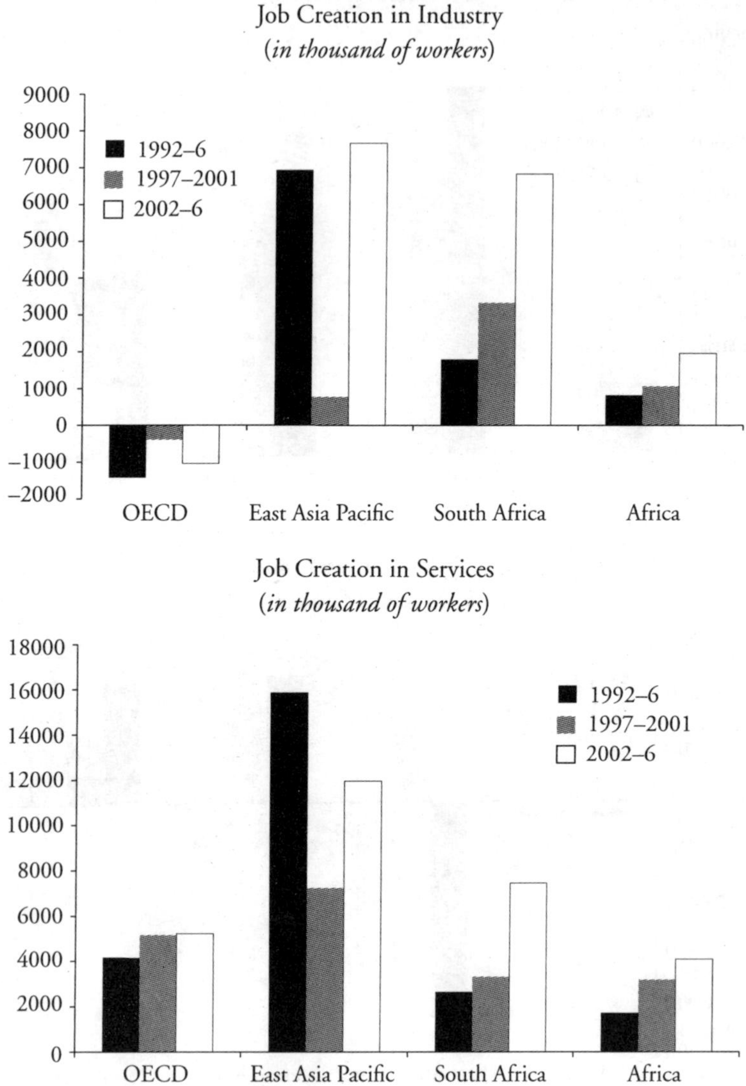

Figure 1.12: Job Creation

Source: International Labour Organization (2008).
Notes: All data are averages of respective times.
Job creation is defined as difference of total employment in t and t-1.
Includes formal and informal sectors.

From the numbers it will appear that South Asian economies are modernizing and the transfer of labour from agriculture to services and manufacturing is a sign of this transformation. Yet this is misleading. In addition to country differences, even for the most dynamic economy, India, the employment story is not a happy story. Overall, the deceleration of real wage growth—and even decline of urban casual wage—in India suggests that it is the supply of workers and self-employment that is driving job growth. The employment challenge facing South Asia is how to create 'good' jobs in sufficient quantity so as to productively absorb the increasing number of people entering the labour market.[25] A large number of jobs being created in South Asia are 'bad' jobs. Nearly 90 per cent of jobs created are in the informal sector of the economy, with difficult working conditions and low wages. The absence of unemployment insurance and limited safety nets mean that open unemployment in South Asia is limited. Most people accept any job that allows them to survive. These people are employed but they have a 'bad' job.

What will create 'good' jobs? First, rapid growth is essential to create more and better jobs. Second, restrictive labour laws need to be reformed to remove barriers to creating jobs in the formal sector. Labour market reforms should be accompanied by improved social protection. Third, for South Asia to accelerate growth and create good jobs, it will require much better training and education to produce more skilled labour.

Technology, Education, and Skills

South Asia has a large technology gap. In developing countries, innovation should be interpreted as knowledge that is new to the country, although not necessarily new to the world. This means that an important element of innovation is not only the investments in domestic research and development (R&D) and its output such as technical and scientific papers and patents, but also the extent to which an economy taps into global knowledge through trade, direct foreign investment, technology transfer, foreign education and training, etc. South Asian economies have been weak in both the domestic innovation effort (except India) and in the extent to which they have tapped into global knowledge. Figure 1.13 shows how

[25] See Bourguignon (2005) for definition of good and bad jobs.

South Asia compares to the other five developing country regions (Africa, Europe and Central Asia, East Asia, Latin America, Middle East, and North Africa), and the developed country triad (Europe, Japan, and the United States) on an index of innovation that includes both components. Within South Asia, India does better than the other countries because it does have critical mass in R&D, although it is not very integrated into global markets.

On a broader measure of the knowledge economy[26] that includes not only innovation but also the basic economic and institutional regime, education, and R&D, South Asia does not do any better. Figure 1.14 shows the results, where the bars indicate the relative score on each of the four components. In this broader measure, Sri Lanka is the South Asian country that has improved its performance compared to its position in 1995. It does better than India, particularly because of much higher scores on education, and on the basic economic and institutional regime. For South Asia as a whole, the knowledge gap is substantial.

There is a large policy agenda for addressing South Asia's technology gap. The main priorities include: tapping into global knowledge; creating new knowledge through investments in R&D; disseminating existing knowledge; and networking and collaboration among South Asian countries (Dahlman 2007).

Adoption of new technology suggests the need for continuous learning over the work-life. How educational and training systems respond to these challenges will have far reaching implications for economic growth and competitiveness of South Asian countries, and for income growth, employment, job creation, and poverty reduction.

The educational stock of the workforce in South Asia is still low compared to other parts of the world, in particular East Asia (see Figures 1.15 and 1.16 on secondary and tertiary education). There is both a 'quantity' and a 'quality' challenge at all levels of education. Progress on the educational front has been unequal over time across countries. The countries in the region are making efforts to upgrade the education levels of the population. Yet this progress is rather slow and the focus has been mostly on increasing access. The demand for quality education is growing. The returns to higher secondary and tertiary education have remained high and even increased relative to lower schooling levels, especially in business services as compared to

[26] See Dahlman (2007) for more details on this concept and its measurement.

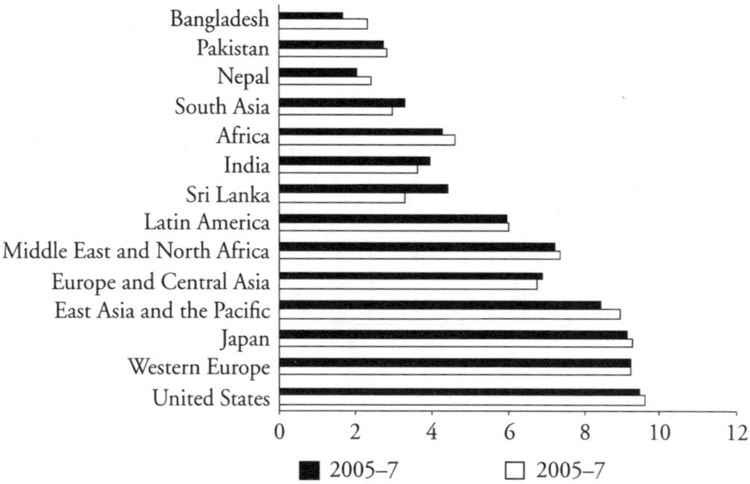

Figure 1.13: Innovation Index

Source: World Bank (2008a).

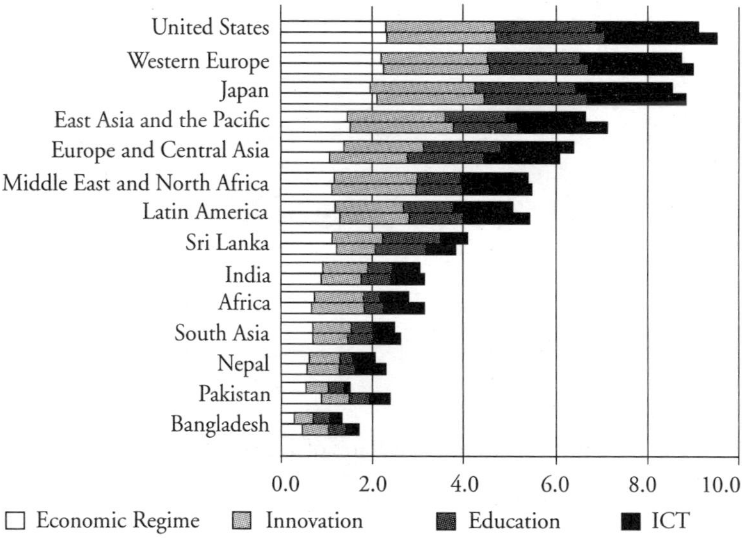

Figure 1.14: Knowledge Economy Index

Source: World Bank (2008a).
Note: For each country grouping, the first bar is the score for the most recent period (based on indicators for 2005–7), while the lower bar is the score for 1995.

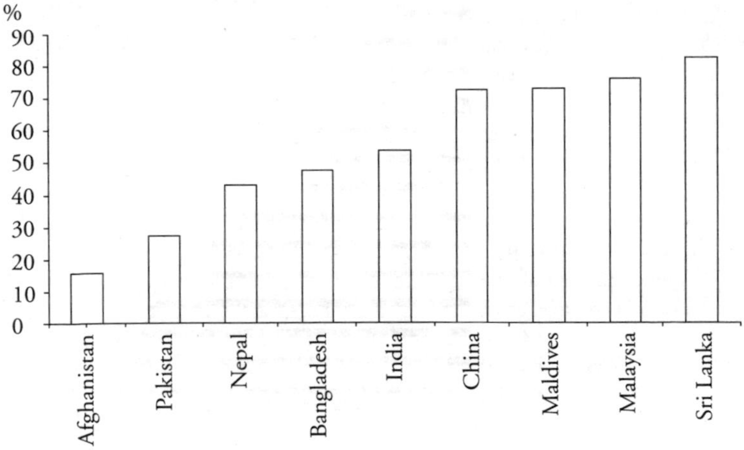

Figure 1.15: Gross Enrolment Rates of Secondary Education, 2004

Source: Riboud and Tan (2008).

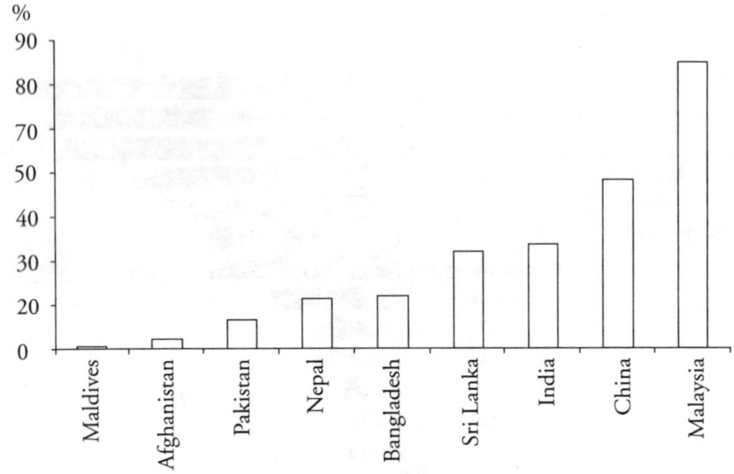

Figure 1.16: Gross Enrolment Rates of Tertiary Education, 2004

Source: Riboud and Tan (2008).

industry. The inability to meet the fast growing demand for skills is an indication that education policies have not yet responded adequately.

Evidence also suggests that South Asia invests inadequately in skills development. The estimated returns to post-school training are high and comparable to returns to formal schooling. Despite high returns, the efforts to provide post-school training is low, being lowest in Pakistan and highest in Sri Lanka, with other countries falling somewhere in between.

Regarding employer provision of in-service training, the story is similarly disturbing; South Asia lags behind other regions. Evidence suggests that in-service training in manufacturing firms in South Asia is among the lowest in the world, which is less than half of the average for Europe and Central Asia, East Asia, and Latin America and the Carribean (Figure 1.17). The deficit is particularly large when South Asian countries are compared to their competitor countries in East Asia, such as Malaysia (where the incidence is twice as high) and China (where the incidence is three times higher). A low incidence of training has negative implications for the industrial competitiveness of countries in the region.

Policymakers are increasingly aware that an educated and trained workforce is critical for technological change and creating a knowledge economy. But countries are yet to put education and training at the top of their priorities. For most countries, education and training policies and programmes are still not responsive to the needs and signals from the labour market. In the low-income regions, the immediate challenge for South Asia is to promote basic education, which would enable its labour force to find employment outside of agriculture and

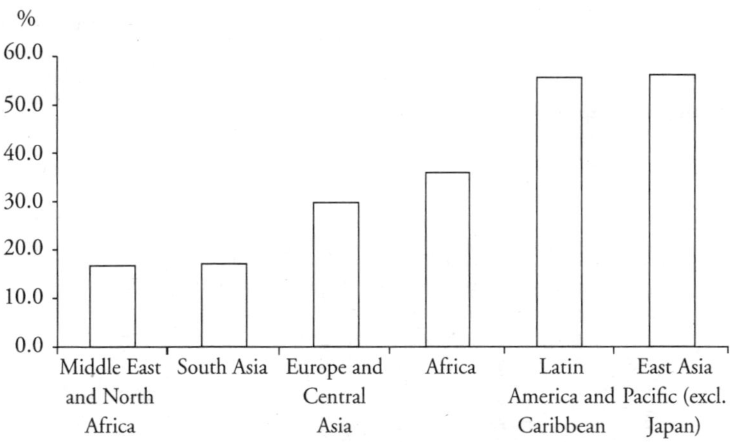

Figure 1.17: Regional Comparisons of In-Service Training in Manufacturing

Source: Riboud and Tan (2008).

especially in industry. In the high-income regions, the challenge is to shift emphasis to higher levels of education without neglecting the unfinished education agenda at the primary level. There is also considerable scope for improving the effectiveness of public vocational training institutions in the region, including greater partnership with the private sector to develop and deliver skills training demanded by employers and by the labour market. Promoting inclusive growth would call for increased emphasis to improve workers' skills, by taking steps to improve the training institutions and enhancing incentives for both firms and workers to invest in life-long learning. This needs to be complemented with well-targeted support to improve learning opportunities for the low-skilled workers, who have less access to on-the-job training than skilled workers.

Regional Public Goods

High growth in South Asia cannot be sustained without better management of natural disasters and regional public goods. Figure 1.18 shows the impact of natural disasters in terms of the share of

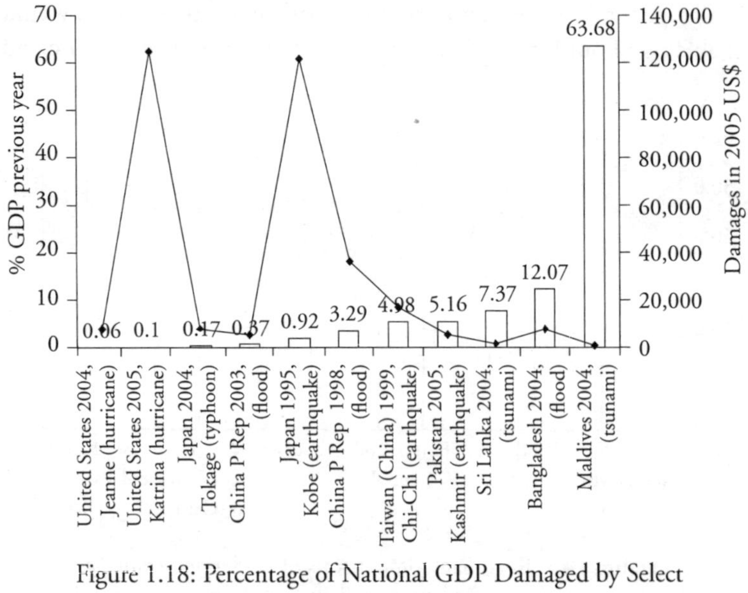

Figure 1.18: Percentage of National GDP Damaged by Select Natural Disasters

Source: http://www.unisdr.org/disaster-statistics/top50.htm

GDP lost. South Asia has lost a significant amount of its GDP because of natural disasters. This loss has been significant for Maldives, Bangladesh, Sri Lanka, and Pakistan. The impact of natural disaster is particularly strong in South Asia because of its high population density. The losses are typically not insured in the financial market. It is the poor who are adversely affected by disasters.

Benefits of regional cooperation in water and climate change would be immense in South Asia. From the Himalayas, where glacier melt is already changing water flows in ways that remain to be understood, to the coastal floodplains of Bangladesh and Pakistan, South Asian countries need to adapt to climate change. The melting of Himalayan glaciers leading to the disastrous prospect of reduced water availability in the South Asian rivers, the frequency of floods and cyclones, and the evidence of rising sea level have given South Asia a wake up call for collective action for managing climate change to reduce vulnerability and poverty over the longer term. This can provide the much-needed trigger for opening a dialogue on regional water cooperation. Cross-border cooperation on water between India, Bangladesh, and Nepal offers the only long-term solution to flood mitigation, and would benefit over 400 million people. The benefits of cooperation are clear. For example, watershed management and storage on Ganges' tributaries in Nepal could generate hydropower and irrigation benefits there and flood mitigation benefits in Nepal, India (Uttar Pradesh, Bihar), and Bangladesh; water storage in northeast India could provide hydropower and flood benefits in India and Bangladesh; and both would also provide increased and reliable dry season flows. There is an emerging and promising opportunity on the specific cooperation between India, Nepal, and Bangladesh on the Ganges.

More generally, regional cooperation can be instrumental in facilitating the design and implementation of effective country-level strategies for addressing a range of global public goods, improving water management, disaster management, climate and environmental management, combating HIV/AIDS, narcotics and drug trafficking, and security and arms trade. Geographic proximity and common borders mean there are areas where common action by neighbours will eliminate negative externalities, reduce transaction costs of monitoring and implementation, and allow learning from sharing of best practices. South Asia's track record on regional cooperation is not without any success. The Indus Valley Water Treaty between India and Pakistan is an example of successful regional cooperation that helped to bring about the green revolution in agriculture in the two Punjabs. The challenge is to build on this success.

South Asia needs to strengthen regional governance institutions. This is vital for managing the provision of regional public goods and management of common pool resources. South Asia suffers from numerous prisoners' dilemmas such as free riding and overuse of resources, because of a lack of effective institutions. This problem can be overcome by engaging the government, the private sector, NGOs, and communities in formal and informal social institutions (networks, norms, and sanctions) based on collective action. Regional cooperation initiatives could unlock the growth benefit of South Asia's geography and people, consistent with improved management of regional public goods. Better regional cooperation can also contribute to reducing regional conflicts, which will remove an important long-term constraint to growth.

Conclusion

The challenge of South Asia to further accelerate growth and strive for middle income status is a 'stretch target' but not an impossible target to attain. South Asia's transition from low income to middle income status is not only an enormous economic challenge; it is also a major social and political challenge. There is no magic formula that will propel the region towards higher growth rates. This is not a reason to give up trying. As South Asia's experience since 1980 shows, reforms of policies and institutions can yield large supply responses. There is ample room to achieve and sustain higher growth rates if South Asia can take advantage of its geography and demography and accelerate the implementation of second generation reforms. These include market integration, both globally and regionally; inclusive growth that will convert the 'demographic dividend' in South Asia into a 'window of opportunity'; improved infrastructure that will behave like second nature geography and propel higher and inclusive growth through improved connectivity, allowing its benefits to be shared widely; strengthened institutions that will result in a stronger business environment and less conflict and corruption; and mainstreamed management of regional public goods into the national development agenda.

REFERENCES

Ahmed, Sadiq. 2006. *Explaining South Asia's Development Success: The Role of Good Policies*. Washington, D.C.: World Bank.

Ahmed, Sadiq and Ejaz Ghani. 2007. *South Asia: Growth and Regional Integration*. New Delhi: Macmillan.

Asian Centre for Human Rights. 2007. *Naxal Conflict in 2006*. New Delhi: Asian Centre for Human Rights.

Banerjee, Abhijit and Lakshmi Iyer. 2005. 'History, Institutions and Economic Performance: The Legacy of Colonial Land Tenure Systems in India', *American Economic Review*, 95(4): 1190–213.

Bourguignon, F. 2005. 'Development Strategies for More and Better Jobs'. Mimeo, Washington, D.C.: World Bank.

Commission on Growth and Development. 2008. *The Growth Report: Strategies for Sustained Growth and Inclusive Development*. Washington, D.C.: World Bank.

Criscuolo, A. and Vincent Palmad. 2008. 'How the Most Successful Reformers Organized Themselves', Finance and Private Sector Development, Note number 318, February, Washington, D.C: World Bank.

Dahlman, Carl. 2007. 'Improving Technology, Skills and Innovation in South Asia', in Sadiq Ahmed and Ejaz Ghani (eds), *South Asia: Growth and Regional Integration*. New Delhi: Macmillan.

Dixit, A. 2008. 'Governance Institutions and Development', Poverty Reduction and Economic Management (PREM) Seminar Paper. Washington, D.C.: World Bank.

Do, Quy-Toan and Lakshmi Iyer. 2007. 'Poverty, Social Divisions and Conflict in Nepal', World Bank Policy Research Working Paper, No. 4228. Washington, D.C.: World Bank.

European Union. 2007. *Growing Regions, Growing Europe*, Fourth Report on Economic and Social Cohesion. Brussels.

Fernandes, Ana M. 2008. 'Comparing Property Rights Institutions and Growth in South Asia and East Asia', Draft Paper, South Asia Region. Washington, D.C.: World Bank.

Fujita, M., P. Krugman, and A.J. Venables. 1999. *The Spatial Economy: Cities, Regions, and International Trade*. Cambridge, Mass.: MIT Press.

Gill, I. and H. Kharas. 2007. 'East Asian Miracle'. Washington, D.C.: World Bank.

Hamid, Naved. 2007. 'South Asia: A Development Strategy for the Information Age', in Report on the South Asia Department Economists' Annual Conference 2006. Manila: Asian Development Bank.

Harris, Clive. 2008. 'Is South Asia Closing the Deficit in its Infrastructure?'. Mimeo, Washington, D.C.: World Bank.

Haussmann, R., L. Pritchett, and D. Rodrik. 2005. 'Growth Accelerations', *Journal of Economic Growth*, 10: 303–29.

Hausmann, R. and D. Rodrik. 2003. 'Economic Development as Self-discovery', *Journal of Economic Growth*, 72.

International Labour Organization. 2008. *Global Employment Trends, 2008.*

Kanbur, Ravi and Anthony J. Venables. 2005a. 'Spatial Inequality and Development', in R. Kanbur and A. J. Venables (eds), *Spatial Inequality and Development.* Oxford: Oxford University Press.

———. 2005b. 'Spatial Inequality and Development: Overview of UNU-WIDER Project'. Available at http://www.arts.cornell.edu/poverty/kanbur/WIDERProjectOverview.pdf

Kanbur, Ravi, Anthony J. Venables, and Guanghua Wan. 2006. *Spatial Disparities in Human Development: Perspectives from Asia.* New York: United Nations Press.

Kanbur, Ravi and Xiaobo Zhang. 2005. 'Fifty Years of Regional Inequality in China: A Journey Through Central Planning, Reform and Openness', *Review of Development Economics*, 9(1): 87–106.

Kochar, K., U. Kumar, R. Rajan, A. Subramaniam, and I. Tokatlidis. 2006. 'India's Pattern of Development: What Happened, What Follows', Working Paper No. 12023, National Bureau of Economic Research, Cambridge, MA.

OECD. 2005. *Building Competitive Regions: Strategies and Governance.* Paris: OECD.

———. 2007. *Employment Outlook*. Paris: OECD.

Rajan, R. G. 2006. 'India: The Past and its Future', Asian Development Bank, Vol. 23, No. 2.

Riboud, M. and Hong Tan, 2008. 'Improving Skills for Competitiveness', Draft paper, South Asia Region. Washington, D.C.: World Bank.

Rodrick, D. 2002. 'Trade Policy Reform as Institutional Reformer', in B. Hoekman, A. Mattoo, and P. English (eds), *Development, Trade, and the WTO.* Washington, D.C.: World Bank.

Stewart, F. and E. Ghani. 1991. 'How Significant are Externalities for Development?' *World Development*, Vol. 19, No. 6.

Summers, Lawrence. 2006. 'The Global Middle Cries Reassurance', *Financial Times*, 29 October.

Venables, A.J. 2006. 'Shifts in Economic Geography and their Causes'. Federal Reserve Bank of Kansas City, Economic Review, Fourth Quarter.

World Bank. 2006. 'Can South Asia End Poverty in a Generation?' Mimeo, Washington, D.C.: World Bank.

———. 2008a. Knowledge for Development Program, Knowledge

Assessment Methodology 2008. Available at www.worldbank.org/KAM.

———. 2008b. 'World Trade Indicators: Benchmarking Trade Policies and Outcomes', Mimeo. Washington, D.C.: World Bank.

———. 2008c. *Doing Business*. Washington, D.C.: World Bank.

———. 2008d. 'South Asia: Ending Poverty in a Region of Growing Contrasts', Mimeo. Washington, D.C.: World Bank.

———. 2008e. *World Development Report 2009: Reshaping Economic Geography*. Washington, D.C.: World Bank.

Yoshida, Nobou. 2008. 'A Note on the Trend of Regional Inequality Across Areas in the South Asia Region', Mimeo. Washington, D.C.: World Bank.

2 SOUTH ASIA STORY OF DEVELOPMENT

OPPORTUNITIES AND RISKS*

Jeffrey D. Sachs

The real challenge is to make our political processes work at something that even remotely resembles the efficacy of our technological know-how right now, in getting us connected from miles apart. Bringing together the business community of the South Asian region is one of the most promising ways forward. We have a remarkable mix of positive progress and trust, while at the same time, certain areas are experiencing stagnation. The region presents great opportunity, but also enormous risk. On the one side, we have fast economic growth, as is absolutely the case in India—one of the fastest-growing economies in the world, an economy that has now grabbed the attention and captured the imagination of the world in a way that China had before. At the same time, several other countries in the South Asian region are also experiencing brisk economic growth. Yet what we also still see is a considerable amount of turmoil, a failure to complete peace processes in several parts of the region, and a failure to achieve the cooperation in economic enterprise within the region, with skills being divided along ethnic, or sectarian, or political lines. I am a big believer in business communities everywhere being in the lead in solving such problems. I believe that this will be true for South Asia as well.

I spend most of my time on the Millennium Development Goals (MDGs) project in Africa, which has the highest poverty rates in the world, and where economic growth has not come in the way that

* This is an abridged version of the speech delivered by Professor Jeffrey D. Sachs, Director, the Earth Institute, Columbia, through video conferencing to Mumbai on 18 February 2007.

it has to South Asia. But it is no secret that South Asia remains the region with the largest absolute number of people living in extreme poverty. While the count is debated, it is still over 300 million people in South Asia, and there may be as many as 400 million people living in what we would call extreme poverty, meaning poverty that is so severe that life is a struggle for survival.

The good news, of course, is that South Asia has made a tremendous amount of progress over the last 25 years, unlike sub-Saharan Africa. In South Asia, the rate of extreme poverty has come down from around 50 per cent back in the 1970s, to perhaps 25 to 30 per cent today. But in a region of 1.5 billion people, it represents a considerable number of people who are in extreme poverty. While there has been marked improvement in the important indicators—life expectancy, child mortality rates, literacy rates, etc., it is also true that the levels of those critical indicators, which really signal the poverty of life, show that South Asia is still between where it once was and where it aspires to be. Life expectancy in South Asia remains between 60 and 65 years, while in high-income countries, life expectancy is pushing beyond 80 years. Under-5 mortality rates in the high-income countries are well under 10 for 1,000 live births, whereas in South Asia they remain at 80 to 100. Of course, these statistics are averaging over very diverse regions, as well as disparities across countries, to give an overall picture.

We see many of the social problems still continuing. So, from my point of view as one who focuses on meeting basic needs and achieving the MDGs, South Asia again presents a mixed picture: some significant progress, still vast numbers of extreme poor, and some really notable shortcomings. Very high undernutrition rates remain a problem throughout the region. Children who do not get proper nutrition during the infancy stage and early years of life, constitute about one-fourth of the children of the region. This is shocking because the more we learn, the more we know that early nutrition for children is critical for a healthy and safe life, for cardinal and physical development, and that undernutrition not only affects children's ability to learn and develop, but also increases the risk of diseases—cardiovascular disease, diabetes (which is now an epidemic in South Asia), and many other serious problems.

However, the region's potential for growth cannot be denied, given the level of progress made so far. I would like to discuss some of the challenges, as well as their likely solutions, and what the role of the business community can be. The rate of poverty still signals intense pressures, particularly in the countryside. There is much urban poverty, too, but the concentration of poverty in South Asia remains in the countryside, partly because that is where most people live, and partly because the rates of poverty are higher in rural areas than in urban ones. The starting point in looking for the causes is the incredible population densities in South Asia. This has been true for two millennia now, but it has become much more extreme in the past 50 to 100 years. South Asia's land-to-person ratio is about the lowest in the world, and it continues to decline. So there is rapid population growth, particularly in rural areas, in the face of what are already extraordinary rural densities and extraordinarily small land sizes. Not surprisingly, the poverty head count is strongly correlated either with landlessness in rural areas or very small farm sizes—sometimes 0.1 hectares or 0.2 hectares.

We also find that the population growth continues to be high because the fertility rates of women remain very high. Even though there has been much demographic transition in several key indicators, the total fertility rates in rural South Asia remain, perhaps, four children per woman. It implies that each woman is raising, among surviving children, on an average, perhaps 1.5 daughters per mother, and that means continued rapid population growth. If today the population is 1.5 billion in South Asia, the United Nations' medium forecast projection for the region is about 2.5 billion people by mid-century, which will make it the most crowded place in the world, and where the farm sizes will decline.

A third aspect is the still low levels of social investment in critical areas, particularly education and health, to which I will come back. Though it is true that the overall literacy rates have gone up, the number of young girls who do not finish primary school, who do not become functionally literate, still remains very high, and that is part of the syndrome of their poverty, and is part of the syndrome of the high fertility rates that continue as well.

The fourth point that I would mention is especially relevant not only in the light of crowding, but also in the light of global changes. South Asia is extraordinarily vulnerable to environmental risk, and I would put water risk right at the top. In fact, the water challenge in South Asia is so significant that nobody can yet find an answer. It is not only a grave problem, but also highly complex and multifaceted. Many parts of South Asia are inherently water-stressed regions. Many parts of South Asia depend on rain-fed agriculture, which is highly vulnerable, and life may become more vulnerable with global climate change. Also, hundreds of millions of people depend on groundwater. One of the great revolutions of the last 25 years is the pumping from bore holes in the Ganges Valley, the Brahmaputra, and the other great river systems in South Asia. However, it is now leading to a collapse of water tables. In Punjab and some other places, the water table is now down to 500 feet below the surface, and increasing numbers of dry bore holes are leading farmers to utter desperation. But let me add one more major consideration on the environmental side, and that is global climate change, which is so well appreciated now. It was the subject of the major UN study by the Intergovernmental Panel on Climate Change (IPCC) led by Dr R.K. Pachauri of The Energy Research Institute (TERI) in New Delhi. The IPCC has confirmed that human-made climate change is accelerating, and it threatens the water situation throughout South Asia in a number of ways. But truly the one that is most important is deforestation, which would change the monsoon patterns in ways that are difficult to know with certainty, but probably would result in more intense monsoons over shorter periods of time, while dry areas will be getting still drier because of higher temperatures. Perhaps most predictably, climate change is having a serious impact by melting the glaciers of the Himalayas, and is also changing the pattern of snow melt in the Himalayas so that the water flow is becoming lower and lower every spring in the whole region of the Indus, Ganges, Jamuna, and Brahmaputra rivers. As a result the great river systems of South Asia are changing their water flows significantly, which threatens the viability of summertime buoyancies in much of the region.

Hence there are very serious environmental challenges, which would be tough enough even if the population was not expected to increase by another 50 per cent. But to load these environmental challenges together with another, maybe 1 billion people in South Asia, is really a quite extraordinary challenge to face over the next 45 or so years.

At the same time, I see South Asia as a region with tremendous dynamism, and a tremendous potential for breakthrough. I see India as perhaps the fastest-growing major economy in the world right now, certainly catching up with China's economic development. A tremendous surge in the number of qualified graduates and engineers and scientists is thrilling. But at the same time, some very major risks exist—first, the continuing population pressure, undernourishment, water stress, high fertility rates, and lack of investment in social and human capital. Second, the conflict situations prevailing in the region—domestic strife in Sri Lanka and Nepal, and the ongoing conflicts between Pakistan and India—pose a major challenge. The risks are exacerbated due to the region being extraordinary in social, ethnic, linguistic, and religious divisions.

While outlining the risks and opportunities, I believe that there are practical solutions to all these problems. I believe that the South Asian Association for Regional Cooperation (SAARC) and the business community have to be in the lead. SAARC is critical because regional integration is going to be the only way to find solutions to these problems. Regional integration is the only solution for the conflicts, for the environmental challenges, and for economic development through increased trade, just as it was in Europe. At the same time, as the engines of growth, the business community needs to continuously be in the lead to tell politicians to get serious, make peace, build infrastructure, and invest in people, so that business can get on with providing practical solutions.

First, I would put great stress on real integrated development of rural areas. This is where hundreds of millions of extremely poor people live, and where their isolation and lack of services is profound. The evidence is overwhelming. If roads and power, schools, and clinics are available in rural areas, life can be transformed. Not only the agricultural productivity will rise sharply, but non-agricultural manufacturing and services can develop sharply in rural areas as well. One of the stunning facts of most of South Asia is the systemic underinvestment in rural areas for decades, and this has occurred in health care; to some extent in schooling, though that is improving; and in other basic services. The situation has improved gradually over the last decade. But when I look at the situation in rural India which I know best, the underinvestment, for example, in health care remains remarkable. India and the rest of South Asia still spend less than 2 per cent of GNP on public health. Sometimes it is just 1 per cent of GNP. This is a completely inadequate level, and it then contributes to continuing high undernourishment, high child mortality rates, and high fertility rates.

Hence, increasing investments in rural areas, ensuring connectivity of all rural villages with roads, power, telecommunications, and the Internet, ensuring a network of public health facilities, ensuring that children are in proper public schools and are completing not just primary education but secondary education, are other important things. The rural areas tend to get underserved. But voices are being raised, and it is vital that the politicians respond. We know businesses can make money in rural areas as well. But that depends on a basic structure of public investment to build out the infrastructure, roads, power, telecom, Internet, public health, and education. All of this is essential, and I think it is a great challenge ahead.

The second big challenge is regional integration in trade. SAARC has been around for many years now, but its ability to make change has always been impeded by the poverty of the region. Regional integration could be the most crucial engine of growth for a true boost in South Asia. The market is vast. The ability to integrate from a feasible point of view is very large. Yet the amount of actual infrastructure for transport, communications, and port services within the region still lack significantly, and the trade data shows that the GNP for most of the SAARC countries remains between 10 per cent and 15 per cent, whereas it should be, perhaps, 25 per cent. The amount of trade that India or Pakistan or Bangladesh engaged in within the SAARC region is a tiny share of their total trade.

The lessons of Western Europe are profoundly important. We are now in the fiftieth year of the European Community, now the European Union (EU). This is the fiftieth anniversary of the Treaty of Rome. The worst wars in human history took place in Europe, and just in the shadow of those wars came a durable peace and the deepest economic integration among countries of any part of the world. If Germany and France can make peace, Pakistan and India can also make peace and have the same kind of dramatic progress of economic development because these are countries in Europe that had exhausted each other in mass murder and in mass war, and then decided enough is enough. SAARC should be able to put forward a development agenda that is truly dynamic and brings countries together at this point in the twenty-first century. I believe that regional integration would lead to a dynamism of trade of huge proportions and the export-to-GNP ratios would double within the SAARC region if proper infrastructure, air travel, fibre optic connections, regular overland—rail, road, and bus—services are integrated, and roads are expanded and built between the regions. I think it would have a phenomenal effect, and I think it would be of huge benefit for the well-being of the people.

The third area, already mentioned, is regional environmental management. It may be true that there is no region that has greater environmental stress than South Asia by virtue of the mass deforestation, which is a centuries-old story. There is also the extraordinary population growth. The whole region is the most highly densely populated part of the world. I think it needs major thinking about how to handle the existing water stress and the coming water crisis.

Since all water supplies of the region are from river systems that cut across national boundaries, all being part of the Himalayan river systems, there is no way to solve the water problems except through peaceful development and peaceful integration. Even the safety of the water that is being used right now is not adequate because of arsenic poisoning and fluoride poisoning in some places. Those people in Bangladesh and elsewhere who are drinking water that is contaminated with arsenic through natural processes, leading to arsenic houses and to serious long-term diseases, need to be assisted urgently. This is an urgent problem, which the whole world should be helping with, not just forcing Bangladesh to solve it on its own.

The fourth point is related to the business community. My experience in many parts of the world has told me that business leadership plays a crucial role in political development, democratization, and peace. Business people are practical and only want expanded markets for doing their businesses. They do not really care too much who their customers are. I think that this is the right way to solve problems, to get down to business, create employment, and improve the economic prospects of people. The business community is also, to an important extent, the eyes and ears of their countries vis-à-vis the world community. They are out in the international markets ahead of the general public. They have to emphasize that this is a competitive world, that SAARC does not have time to lose, that the jobs that do not come to South Asia, go to East Asia, or that the opportunities for getting ahead are not going to wait on South Asia.

Let me finally conclude by saying it is not only South Asia, it is all of Asia where, I think, the world looks right now. Asia will be the centre of gravity of the world's economy in the twenty-first century. It is where most of the people are. I find it thrilling to watch the Indian Ocean trade come back to life as it was during the great history of centuries past. Now Africa, where I work a lot, and South Asia and East Asia are all becoming integrated in regional trade again. This is a marvellous thing for a very large part of the world. It is a success on which the whole world depends. The initiatives being taken by the business community today can play an important role in furthering the integration of the trade between Africa, South Asia, and East Asia.

3 IMPROVING GOVERNANCE IN SUSTAINING EQUITABLE GROWTH

Paul A. Volcker

When I recently set foot in India after 30 years, I came face-to face-with two facets of development. In Bengaluru, I saw companies at the leading edge, exploiting sophisticated technology to serve the needs of the most demanding clients, not primarily in India, or even South Asia, but all around the world. Notably, that includes large firms in the financial markets of my hometown of New York. Indian companies are working 24 hours a day, seven days a week, for businesses that simply cannot tolerate errors or breakdowns in service. On the other hand, I could also see the gap between the high-tech wonders of Bengaluru and life in Indian villages. Those villages may have a computer or two, but they lack even basic sanitary facilities or a reliable supply of potable water. Of course, the same contrast exists even in Mumbai—luxury hotels alongside urban squalor.

Hence the challenge is obvious: how to build upon and extend the unprecedented economic progress in the region, and to bring more of the potential benefits to the hundreds of millions still trapped in poverty, without the resources and education required.

A big part of what is required is hard, slogging work on the ground, in villages one by one. That is the kind of thing I see in government projects (supported by the World Bank) that are beginning to have a real impact in Maharashtra. Step by step, organizing the men and women to plan and participate, a more reliable water supply, and basic sanitary facilities are being developed. I am well aware of the success elsewhere in this region in encouraging sources of local 'micro' finance, an approach that seems beyond the capacity of established financial institutions.

That work is local by its nature. The particulars may vary nation by nation, state by state, and city by city. But there is important common ground, and the impulse here in South Asia to learn from one another and to work together is natural. It parallels efforts in other parts of the world to work towards regional integration. There are potential political, as well as economic, benefits. However, I want to emphasize that we cannot lose sight of a larger reality.

The recent success of India and South Asia, of China and Asia generally, of Eastern Europe, and now hopefully beginning in Africa as well, is not so much a matter of unique national or regional accomplishment, but of effective response to the opportunities provided by the globalization of business and finance. The fact is that almost all countries are growing—by one tabulation, every country grew in 2006, something that had not been true for almost half a century.

In part, that common success has been inherent in today's technology—the speed and economy of communication and transport. But it is also a result of deliberate policy. Barriers to trade and investment have been reduced and even removed, and international trade and finance have provided enormous impetus to growth. Initially, the benefits were largely seen in the opportunities to expand exports and build manufacturing, offered to low-wage countries in Asia and elsewhere. Today the main thrust has been on services, partly mundane but increasingly high-tech. These services are built on technology that was literally unknown two or three decades back; today, these high-tech services are the quintessential characteristic of the global economy.

Another characteristic of that economy is the immense growth and complexity of international finance. India and other South Asian nations for a while chose to wall off the international money markets. Then, as those markets opened, it was only a decade ago that some Asian economies were thrown into turmoil by financial crisis. It was a dramatic demonstration of the potential volatility of capital flows and exchange rates. There were lessons to be learned.

South Asia escaped the full force of that crisis, in part because its economies and markets were then not so financially exposed. Closing markets is no longer a real option. But I also believe emerging economies now have generally learned how better to protect themselves against the potential risks and volatility. That is a matter of recognizing the importance of sound fiscal and monetary policies, of maintaining a cushion of reserves, and, most importantly, of avoiding inflationary excesses.

All of that is now common ground in economic thinking and public policy around the world. And the result is that South Asia is much better positioned to benefit from the flows of international capital.

Surely, the needs are obvious. Basic infrastructure needs to be improved to support growth, more electricity is basic both to industry and living standards, and a growing manufacturing industry requires access to large amounts of capital. Internal savings cannot meet all those needs. Even more clearly, the investments by internal savings do not bring with them the technology transfer, managerial strengths, and long-time perspective that, at its best, are characteristics of direct foreign investments.

There is not any real doubt that India and South Asia are now seen as providing potentially profitable opportunities for international business and finance. Steps have been taken here in India and elsewhere to facilitate flows of capital, and loans and direct investment from abroad have increased significantly—although still far below their potential. And there have been dramatic illustrations of the willingness and ability of Indian businesses themselves to participate in the rationalization of manufacturing and services on an international scale.

What needs particular emphasis is another aspect of participation in global markets. It is of key importance precisely because it is necessary to unlock the full benefit that international flows of funds can provide in meeting the obvious needs for resources and technology.

Economists have struggled for decades to develop consistent approaches and policies towards enhancing economic development. Intellectual fashions change, but at this time there is indeed a broad consensus. Disciplined fiscal and monetary policies, the importance of price stability, the need for efficient domestic financial institutions, and the benefits of open markets are all recognized as fundamental. For South Asia, there is still a lot to be done in those areas.

But there is something further, something less tangible but in a real sense even more important if growth is to be encouraged and sustained. What I am referring to is something that can be broadly labelled as 'good governance'. By good governance I am not thinking of specific public policies or practices, but the basic framework within which both governments and businesses work.

- Is there a strong sense of the 'rule of law'—that is, are there defined rules that are fairly and consistently understood and applied?
- Is the system of justice independent, characterized by integrity, and are court decisions respected as reasonably speedy and fair?
- Are management processes in both government and businesses reasonably transparent and open to debate?
- Are contracts enforced, and the system of taxation bearable and equitable?
- Is there a willingness to accept and conform to international standards in accounting, auditing, financial regulation, and other areas essential to a well-functioning international system?
- Then, there is the truly important, sensitive, and difficult issue: is corruption—bribery, collusion, and cheating—tolerated?

An effective international system rests on a negative answer to the last question and on affirmative answers to the rest. I am also aware that perfection in these respects is beyond reach. Even the United States, having prided itself to the point of a certain arrogance about its own approaches, has had to face the embarrassment of a succession of accounting, auditing, and compensation scandals. The legislative and administrative procedures are also not free of corruption. However, in the United States, it can be claimed fairly that substantial reforms are in place. There are prominent men and women shamed and in jail. Ordinary citizens have made their views known in the recent electoral process.

In fact, while circumstances differ widely even within countries, my sense is that progress is being made in India and elsewhere in South Asia. There is greater recognition of the importance of the rule of law and means for enforcing it. There is pressure for greater transparency. Financial practices and accounting standards are slowly being brought into line with international standards. Particularly, there is a growing sensitivity to corruption. It has become a pressing political issue.

Nonetheless, the hard fact remains that South Asia ranks low on the international scale of governance, according to surveys of business attitudes as well as the judgement of independent agencies and non-governmental organizations (NGOs). Its relative position has not improved much, if at all, in recent years. It hurts in the competition for capital, in the efficiency of industry, and in perceptions of fairness of who wins and who loses.

A lot is heard these days about the competition between the two population giants, China and India, for growth and for reducing poverty. But there are two areas in which India is plainly lagging, areas that are limiting its potential. I am referring to manufacturing and infrastructure. They are 'big-ticket' items. They take capital. They should attract employment at wages that may be low by international standards but are very attractive to those in poverty-stricken rural areas or the unemployed. Those sectors of the economy won't prosper without substantial international participation, most particularly foreign capital and foreign markets. And those are precisely the areas where China—and before China, Taiwan, South Korea, and Hong Kong—are way ahead. Still others are catching up.

There is one aspect of governance with which I have had direct contact in recent years, and that is corruption—corruption not just in the United States, but also in the United Nations. Corruption in the Oil-for-Food Program has left deep wounds in the UN organization, impairing its effectiveness. The woes of the UN may not be at the top of the agenda. However, the problem strikes home when the work of development economists and surveys of business firms coincide in ranking corruption as a leading threat—perhaps the leading threat—to investment and development. It is often correctly cited as a tax on the poor.

Corruption is not only pervasive, it also takes many forms. In some societies it cannot be effectively controlled and eliminated without public understanding and a strong political commitment, without insistence on transparency in contracting, and without simplifications and effective administration of regulations. These cannot be achieved overnight, but cannot be avoided, either. That is why the approach of the World Bank, and of other international institutions, to focus more attention and effort in this area is to be welcomed. Both the OECD and the United Nations have adopted strong conventions about foreign corrupt practices. If and as those conventions are made effective through domestic legislation and determined law enforcement, corrupt practices could and will become even more self-defeating for countries needing investment.

It needs to be realized that this is a sensitive issue in this part of the world, and I have wondered a bit as to whether to brush over the subject lightly. I have raised that question among businessmen and other friends here in India. They have been virtually unanimous in encouraging me to speak out here. More importantly than a speech here in Mumbai, they support the efforts of the World Bank and other providers of investment to strengthen their surveillance and to enforce strong standards. I believe that in another eight or ten years, South Asian economies could double in size. Hundreds of millions can be lifted out of poverty. Asia, with more than half the world's population, should become the driving force for the world economy. However, sustaining this growth would require open markets, strong competition and, not least, effective governance.

There is a lot upon which to build, more than I could have imagined 30 years ago. That is a great tribute to the businessmen in this room, and to your governments. I trust the sense of competitive vitality in this visit will be translated into good governance as well as good business.

II

POLICIES AND SOURCES OF GROWTH

4 SHOULD SOUTH ASIA EMULATE EAST ASIAN TIGERS?

Howard Pack

INTRODUCTION

It is often suggested that the South Asian nations require a greater emphasis on manufacturing in order to provide more job opportunities for their growing labour forces. Some of the economies of East Asia, particularly China, the Republic of Korea, and Taiwan (China), are often used as models for such growth. This chapter will argue that the East Asian export-led model is misapplied. But to fix ideas, it is helpful to examine some very simple patterns Figure 4.1 shows the share of manufacturing in GDP for the major regions of the world, as defined by the World Bank. The data are derived from the standard international source, the World Bank's *World Development Indicators*, and for some years data are missing. The exceptionalism of East Asia is starkly clear. While Latin America was above other developing regions in 1970, and close to East Asia and Pacific (EAP), reflecting a quarter century of fairly inefficient import substitution, over the next three decades all regions converged on a VAM/GDP (value added in manufacturing as a ratio of GDP) figure of about 15, whereas East Asia was almost double this ratio. South Asia looked like all the other regions. East Asia is not the norm.

A similar pattern appears when looking at a range of individual countries. For example, in 2004, VAM/GDP was 11 per cent for Brazil, 14 per cent for Colombia, 16 per cent for Bangladesh and India, and 18 per cent for Pakistan, with the Latin American countries having considerably greater per capita income. Only in comparison with China (32 per cent) and Korea (29 per cent), do the South Asian countries appear to be distinctly different.

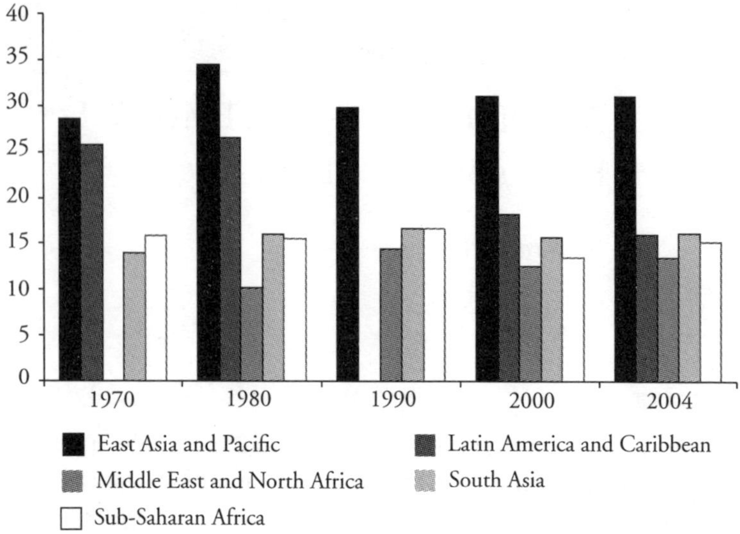

Figure 4.1: Manufacturing Value Added as a Percentage of GDP

Source: World Bank, *World Development Indicators*, various years.

Part of the difference with respect to East Asian countries is simply due to the rapid accumulation of capital in East Asia, which led to a growing capital–labour ratio that favoured manufacturing. Figure 4.2 shows the regional value for fixed capital formation as a percentage of GDP, I/GDP. Again, the East Asian countries far exceed other regions, and by 2004 were investing roughly twice as much as the others. The rapid accumulation of capital, and the resulting drop in the real cost of capital, was conducive to entering manufacturing. Even more stark are the differences in the rate of growth of the capital–labour ratio $(K/L)^*$ shown in Table 4.1. In the decades 1980–2000, $(K/L)^*$ for the South Asian grouping was considerably less than half that of the East Asian countries in their period of rapid industrialization, 1960–80.[1] Even comparing the same decades, 1980–2000, the East Asian nations had roughly twice the value of $(K/L)^*$. It is not surprising that the South Asia region has not experienced a comparable transformation. And I will show

[1] Clearly the 'East' Asian countries are basically those exhibiting rapid growth—several would normally be viewed as being in Southeast Asia.

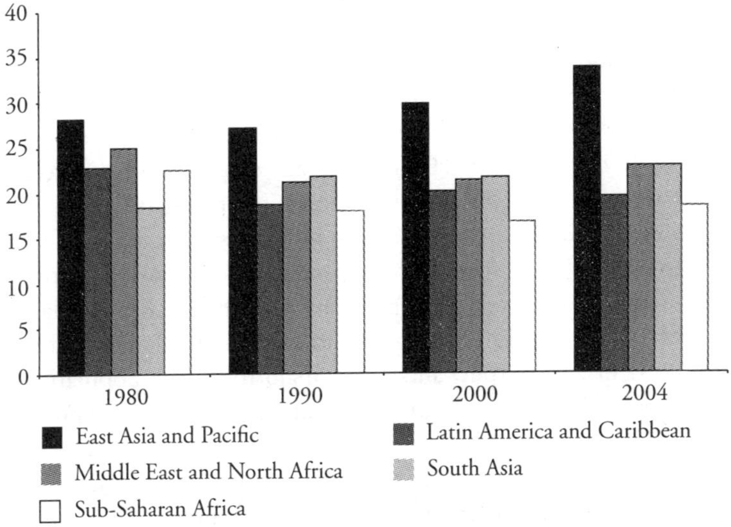

Figure 4.2: Gross Domestic Capital Investment as a Percentage of GDP

Source: World Bank, *World Development Indicators*, various years.

TABLE 4.1: Growth Rate of Fixed Capital–Labour Ratio

	1960–70	*1970–80*	*1980–90*	*1990–2000*
East Asia				
Malaysia	5.6	6.8	5.7	7.0
Singapore	12.8	10.1	5.7	5.6
Taiwan (China)	10.4	10.5	6.3	7.6
China	0.1	4.6	6.0	9.3
South Korea	5.5	10.7	8.1	7.1
South Asia				
Bangladesh	3.3	–0.3	1.5	1.7
India	2.5	1.7	3.0	3.8
Sri Lanka	0.5	4.3	5.6	3.0
Pakistan	10.8	1.6	2.7	1.4

Source: Data from unpublished tables, Bosworth and Collins, 2003.

that simple capital accumulation, even if it were accelerated, is no longer sufficient to ensure a shift to a more manufacturing-intensive development process.

The Evolution of Thought about Industrialization

The evolution of economic thought about industrialization has been striking. In the early post–World War II period, it was assumed that growth in the manufacturing sector was a *sine qua non* of sustained economic development. There was an emphasis on protecting domestic manufacturing production from international competition in order to provide time for infant industries to learn sufficiently well to be able to compete without protection. The assumed context was usually that of relatively populous nations, such as India and Pakistan, which exhibited a small urban sector, limited manufacturing employment and output, and a vast majority of the population in rural areas engaged in both agricultural and non-agricultural pursuits. The envisioned growth scenario was that of continuing investment in the manufacturing sector, which generated a rise in the demand for labour by that sector, and a gradual transition of the centre of economic activity from rural to urban areas. That had been the model of at least one late-developing nation, namely, Japan.

Several subsidiary features were part of the context of the analysis. The food supply would increase to feed the new industrial labour force, while the additional output of urban goods would find a market because of the growing income of rural areas. Most of the industrial goods would be relatively simple and not imported, that is, the economy envisioned was largely a closed one. Balanced growth between the sectors could prevent a decline in the price of industrial goods relative to food.

Two developments in the world changed this view of how poor economies were likely to develop. First, numerous countries, including many in South Asia, embarked on efforts to stimulate the local production of heretofore imported manufactured goods, under the process of import substituting industrialization (ISI). Local industries were protected from international competition by a variety of measures, including import quotas and tariffs. The results in most countries were disappointing. Output grew, but it was inefficient. Protected firms, secure behind tariffs or quotas, had little incentive to learn. Not only did production take place at high cost, but there was little evidence that learning occurred, despite the promise of the proponents of ISI. The higher prices of domestic production were borne by local consumers. Employment growth in these sectors was disappointing, explained largely by the unintended side effects of ISI, which artificially raised wages to employers and lowered the cost of utilizing machinery. For residents of rural areas, there was a double squeeze—higher prices for the industrial products they purchased, and few job opportunities in the urban areas. Whatever skills were accumulated by firms under ISI were insufficient to propel nations pursuing such policies to accelerated growth. Industrial exports did not grow particularly rapidly, which was understandable given the low productivity of firms, the high cost of imported inputs used in the production of exports, and the appreciated real exchange rate that was a concomitant of ISI.

A number of much smaller Asian economies—Korea, Taiwan, Hong Kong , and Singapore—pursued different strategies beginning in the mid-1960s, emphasizing manufactured exports largely targeted at the OECD nations. At the beginning of this process, even the largest of these nations, Korea, was small in population, with less than 40 million, and Singapore, the smallest, had a population of roughly 3 million. The total population of these four nations was less than 60 million. These countries had growth that was propelled by high investment rates, in excess of 30 per cent per year; high initial education which then grew rapidly, an emphasis on science and engineering education, and by and large good macroeconomic policies. Korea and Taiwan gradually abandoned their previous ISI regimes, but nevertheless protected industries until well into the 1980s. Hong Kong was largely a free-trading country, and Singapore relied heavily on inflows of investment and technology from multinational corporations (MNCs).

The Asian 'gang of four' overturned many of the views that had been held about both the desirability of the 'balanced' growth and the ISI paths. The rapidly growing manufactured exports in these nations to some extent reduced the need for growth in domestic demand. The international market, rather than rural consumers, served as the market for rapidly growing industrial output. Manufacturing that depended on exporting could not be inefficient, though protected domestic markets still afforded inefficient industries some time for achieving efficiency gains. Exporting was conducive to growth as firms had to compete on both price and quality (including delivery times and style), and could not afford the luxury offered to domestically oriented producers to continue with low productivity. To many observers, manufacturing exporting (though initially relatively protected domestic markets) became the model for growth.

The successful early industrializers all exhibited rapid employment growth in manufacturing. Appropriate factor use is a key in considering the implications of any efforts to stimulate the growth of manufacturing exports. The South Asian nations may be characterized as ones of high labour force numbers relative to both land and physical capital. To absorb the large numbers of currently unemployed, underemployed, and future labour force entrants requires the expansion of labour-intensive sectors. The need for labour-intensive sectors follows from the fundamental facts of macroeconomic life. For the region as a whole for 2003–4, the ratio of annual gross domestic capital formation in current dollars to the annual change in the labour force was roughly $21,000 (WDI 2006). But this total investment figure is gross, not net of depreciation; and some fraction, perhaps 50 per cent based on data for countries in which investment by sector is available, is devoted to social overhead capital such as roads, dams, schools, and hospitals. Thus, the region-wide 'productive' investment per new labour force entrant is less than $10,000. It is roughly US$ 8,500 in Bangladesh, US$ 14,000 in India, US$ 3,500 in Nepal, and US$ 4,000 in Pakistan. Such low investment per new worker is hardly characteristic of manufacturing sectors that might offer unexplored opportunities for high capital and technology exports.

Labour-intensive sectors, such as clothing, sports equipment, wigs, and athletic shoes, were precisely the ones that exemplified Korean and Taiwanese growth in the 1960s and 1970s. The manufacturing sectors that now spring to mind in portraits of the gang of four—LCD television sets, semiconductors, automobiles, steel, and laptop computers—were hardly the original sectors of growth. Autos and others grew only in the 1980s and 1990s, after decades of huge amounts of capital accumulation that allowed the financing of US$ 2 billion semiconductor or LCD plants. An important correlate of manufacturing export growth in the first newly industrialized countries (NICs) was a rapid increase in the number of workers employed in the sector. The growth in Korea and Taiwan, which was initially labour intensive, was able to absorb many workers from the agricultural and informal urban sectors. Employment growth was rapid as the product mix of new exports conformed to the countries' initial supplies of large quantities of unskilled and semi-skilled labour, though there was also growth in the quality of labour. Not only were these labour-intensive sectors, but the machinery employed was on the labour-intensive side of the technology spectrum. For example, semi-automatic looms, rather than high-speed air-jet looms, were employed in Korean weaving.

What lessons can be gleaned for contemporary South Asian nations trying to accelerate both the growth of output and manufacturing employment? Are the paths that were open four decades ago still available? The answer is surely no. When the initial industrial acceleration began in the gang of four, there were few competitive exporting nations. Not only did they face a level playing field, they had the field largely to themselves. Importers from the OECD nations, such as clothing chains, quickly realized that a potential source of large additional profits could be garnered by outsourcing their requirements to these nations. But the initial path pioneered by the gang of four is now well understood by all developing nations, from Latin America to Eastern Europe. While there are laggard regions in this respect—the Middle East and North Africa, and Sub-Saharan Africa—the explosion of manufactured exports from the initial

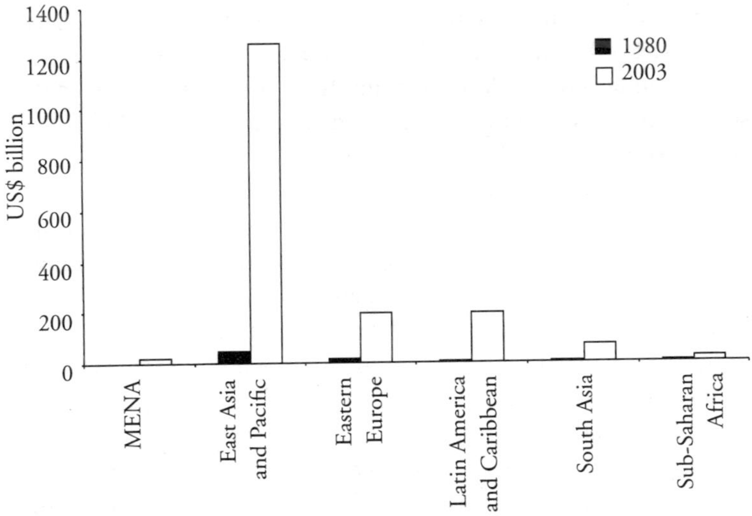

Figure 4.3: Manufacturing Exports

Source: COMTRADE Database, August 2005.

Asian tigers, the follower Asian nations of Indonesia, Malaysia, and Thailand, Eastern Europe, and most importantly China, has greatly increased the supply and competitiveness in international markets.

Figure 4.3 vividly demonstrates the fact that the South Asian nations are entering world markets very late. One implication of the enormous growth of manufacturing capacity throughout the world is that it is difficult to break into export markets, and even if one succeeds, the private (and social) profitability of doing so is likely to be limited. Firms in nations that already export are likely to have gone through a learning curve that has reduced their factory gate prices, generated extensive marketing contacts, and been able to build adequate infrastructure, such as a dependable electricity supply and reasonably good internal transport and port facilities so that they already enjoy considerable cost advantages.

Lessons from the Indian Service Sector

Changing perspective from manufacturing to services can illuminate the problems that are faced by new manufacturing firms in all countries. Briefly reviewing the spectacular development of the Indian software sector, the obstacles that face new software firms in other countries can be readily seen and underlines the problems that will be faced by nascent manufacturers attempting to enter export markets.

In the 1980s, there were a large number of graduates with serious programming skills at levels ranging from post-secondary technical schools to those trained at the Indian Institutes of Technology (IITs). Almost all had been educated in English. Many were familiar with major computer hardware systems, computer-aided software engineering tools, object-oriented programming, graphical user interface, and client networking. Nevertheless, there was limited demand for these graduates, and many emigrated. A major impetus to demand came from abroad from of a set of 'accidents'. In the 1990s, the ratio of world prices for programming services relative to those in India increased due to a global shortage of programmers and the demands for solutions to the anticipated Y2K problem. Enterprising businesses in India capitalized on this opportunity by setting up firms that were essentially employment agencies. Indian software programmers were hired by local firms on behalf of clients in the United States on short-term contracts (either for a fixed period of time or on a project basis) to provide onsite services. 'Bodyshopping', as this practice was called, became the predominant mode of Indian software exports because the development work was performed on the client's premises, saving software firms the high costs of acquiring computer hardware. NASSCOM, the Indian software trade association, reported that the software sector earned US$ 2.5 billion from Y2K billing from 1996 to 1999, a critical period in the growth of the industry. As late as 1988, software exports had been less than US$ 200 million, but rose to US$ 3.6 billion by 1998, accounting for over 10 per cent of total Indian exports.

Indian software firms also benefited from another serendipitous event, the European Union's move to the euro. Many Indian software professionals were actively involved in adapting existing computer systems and databases to accommodate the euro. Between 2000 and 2002, it is estimated that India earned approximately US$ 3 billion in revenues from these euro-related IT projects. Clearly a contributing factor was the low relative level of programming costs in India that conferred a Ricardian comparative advantage in some software sub-sectors. As late as 1995, after substantial wage increases because of a rising demand for Indian software, the annual wages of Indian software professionals were only 14 per cent to 59 per cent that of their counterparts in Switzerland, the United States, Canada, and the United Kingdom. Given the skills of Indian programmers, these cost savings led firms in some of the industrial countries to outsource their software development requirements to India.

Once the sector had demonstrated its success entirely without government help, a number of government efforts to reinforce this success were undertaken, including software parks and greater attention to infrastructure such as roads. On the other hand, the software sector did not require much other facilitation, and given the nature of its inputs, downloaded from satellite, and its output, uploaded to satellites, the sector was not exposed to the vagaries of the investment or business climate. For example, speedier or lower cost access to imported inputs that had to be cleared through customs was not an issue, nor was the quality of roads and ports. Obviously, a critical input was the quality of the IITs, but these had begun decades before the information technology sector came into being.

Having established its success, the Indian IT sector immediately entered onto the radar screen of foreign firms seeking to reduce their programming costs. The reputation and demonstrated success of firms such as Wipro and Infosys generated a virtuous circle that encouraged still more contracts emanating from OECD firms. The sector now has a huge amount of accumulated experience in dealing with a wide range of software issues, marketing know-how, and visibility, and is the employer of choice for many local graduates, and increasingly for foreign graduates. Firms in other nations, even quite advanced ones, are now at a huge disadvantage relative to Indian firms in obtaining contracts. But this is precisely the type of disadvantage facing South Asian firms that attempt to enter manufacturing markets in industries in which 'first movers' have accumulated advantages that the Indian software sector now enjoys. Other countries with a large English-speaking labour force, such as Pakistan, suffer from a huge disadvantage in reputation, in accumulated experience and hence costs, and in the difficulty of even demonstrating their potential to firms in other countries.

Prospects for Export Manufacturing

It is not that India planned the software sector's growth and fostered it. Fundamentals (education) and fortune (Y2K and the euro) were the keys, but once the growth began, the sector realized a huge windfall. Consider now the scenario facing manufacturing firms in South Asia contemplating exports. For most mass production commodities, there are established firms that have benefited from 25 years (China) to 30 years (Thailand) to 40 years (Korea) of manufacturing products of high quality, delivered by a specified date, at an internationally competitive price. Many of these firms are already part of international production networks (Dell) or international purchasing networks (Wal-Mart, Carrefour), and have worked over many years to rectify the inevitable problems that arise in international sourcing. Moreover, in all of the major manufacturing exporting countries, many of the problems of infrastructure, permits, and other potential hindrances to exporting have been addressed. Locally owned firms have already established local supply networks of subcontractors that have also been the beneficiaries of experiencing their own learning curves, often with the help of the parent Chinese, Korean, or Japanese firm.

Are Niche Markets Feasible?

New manufacturing exporters must thus be able to offer a combination of price and quality that match existing producers, but the latter have benefited from the learning noted in the previous paragraph. Thus, entering existing mass product markets in manufacturing may be very difficult. The first movers currently have a huge advantage, similar to the one accruing to the Indian software sector. While it is always possible to perhaps gain a foothold in clothing or footwear, the private and social profitability is likely to be very small in mature markets due to previous entrants. This leaves one possibility for new manufacturing exporters, namely, identifying a niche market that is not populated by many existing suppliers. But even if this unlikely configuration can occur in a few markets, it is unlikely to hold in the large numbers that are required to make a dent in the looming problem of absorbing huge numbers of still poor individuals. Even after 15 years of spectacular growth, the Indian IT industry today employs little over 700,000 workers and another 2.3 million in indirect industries (NASSCOM-McKinsey Report, p. 15), which is a small fraction of the labour force, estimated at over 400 million workers.[2]

The issue of whether firms can enter niche markets is a controversial one. There is considerable debate among academic economists and within international financial institutions about the ability of governments to identify such opportunities and facilitate entry of national 'champions' into such markets. However, the niche markets that do not face considerable competition lie at the capital-, education-, and technology-intensive end of the spectrum of manufacturing goods. Consider one example, American production of agricultural machinery—such machinery being typical of the entire machinery sector in its technical requirements. At a factory in Waterloo, Iowa,

> ...thousands of workers are building high-tech John Deere tractors that are equipped with satellite-tracking technology and are intended for export to China, India, Central Europe, and the former Soviet republics in Central Asia, among other destinations. Foreign sales of these tractors have doubled in the last five years. 'There are more lines of computer code in these tractors than there is in the space shuttle,' says Dave Everitt, president of the North America, Australian, and Asian regions of the agricultural division of Deere & Company.

[2] Even with optimistic estimates, the IT industry is expected to employ 2.3 million workers by 2010. Clearly, the IT industry is not labour intensive and will not be able to absorb the 70 million additional workers who are expected to enter the workforce over the next five years (*The Economist 2006*).

Although the cheaper dollar has helped, particularly in sales to Western Europe, the tractors are selling because they can be guided precisely by satellite and because of an 'intelligent power' system that can provide extra horsepower when needed, while still meeting emission requirements. 'We are not competing on cost. We are not competing on volume,' Mr. Everitt says. 'We are competing on providing value to the customer.' (Holstein 2007)

This quotation exemplifies the problems South Asian nations face in entering higher technology niche markets, of which this would be an example. Many of the products are exceptionally complex—obviously beyond the capability of countries such as Bhutan, Nepal, Pakistan, Sri Lanka, and Bangladesh. For 2004, the last year for which data are available, according to the *World Development Indicators*, high technology exports from Pakistan were US$ 150 million, compared to US$ 2.8 billion from India.[3] Some Indian manufacturers may have some of the required skills. But sectors such as machinery production require exceptionally complicated manufacturing abilities, very skilled designers and production staff, complicated and expensive machine tools, and in this case, involve integrating GPS systems into the final product. In this and many other niche products in manufacturing, there is a high capital–labour ratio, and few jobs for unskilled workers. Moreover, these are products in which cumulative learning in OECD nations is enormous, extending over a century, and in which the production process itself is very complicated, requiring the coordination of many suppliers whose quality and price must themselves be internationally competitive.

The depth of the problem facing South Asian nations in seeking a niche between mass production in China and a few other established low-cost LDC manufacturers and the technologically advanced OECD countries and higher technology exports is also illustrated by a recent description of the rebound in the German economy:

The crucial factor in Germany's (recent) success…is that it churns out… global niche products: sophisticated high-technology tools that have worldwide but narrow markets. Fast-growing developing economies, like China's, are keener to buy such rarefied products than to make them. Only Japan currently competes in many of these areas. 'We are protected because

[3] High technology exports 'are products with high R&D intensity, such as in aerospace, computers, pharmaceuticals, scientific instruments, and electrical machinery'. Data are in current US dollars.

the big Asian gorillas are not interested,' Mr. von Witzleben said. 'If I were in the business of flat-panel television screens, it would be a different story.' Jenoptik, which was built on the ruins of an East German state enterprise, concentrates on making lasers used in medical devices and chip factories. It also builds sensors that steer satellites. Of its US$645 million in sales, 57 percent comes from exports. Its order book is running well ahead of last year. (Landler2007)

Note the implications that even a relatively high-tech niche product of five years ago—flat-panel TV sets (both LCD and plasma)—has become a commodity, with prices falling at roughly 30 per cent per year, and almost surely all rents have long disappeared. While a few individual South Asian manufacturers might be able to identify a market in which they possess a comparative advantage, most are likely to be caught between the high technological capacity in the OECD nations—building on a century or more of high-quality research in universities and business, sustained university and vocational education, and worker experience—and the mass production capabilities and agglomeration economies that have developed over the last four decades in China, the gang of four, and more recently in some parts of Eastern Europe. Extant mass production, and the close links already established between international production and purchasing networks, is particularly important. To add to the difficulties, China is increasingly entering high-technology sectors.

China is demonstrating a surprising ability to parlay its dominance in low-end manufacturing into a new strength in producing sophisticated high-tech goods. Already the place where many of the world's computers and mobile phones are put together, it is expected to become home to a multibillion-dollar integrated-circuit plant run by Intel Corp., the world's biggest maker of computer chips. The speed at which China is moving into more complex manufacturing is a sign that its transition from a low-wage economy making cheap goods to a high-wage economy producing valuable ones may not be as difficult as once thought. (Batson, 2007)

Is It Easy to Enter the Commodity Market?

This does not mean that China will vacate its labour-intensive sectors to newcomers. There are still hundreds of millions who have not benefited significantly from its growth, and the focus on encouraging still more exports of labour-intensive products is one reason underlying its unwillingness to allow an appreciation of the yuan.

Moreover, technical production competence, even if achieved, is not sufficient. Firms attempting to enter export markets cannot assume that producing goods at a low cost is enough to achieve foreign sales. There is no guarantee that lead firms in international networks will have a small number of firms in new potential exporting nations on their radar screen. The existence of supply networks imposes a significant challenge for South Asian firms that are not already embedded in such networks.

Consider recent developments in the clothing supply chain. Huge retailers such as Wal-Mart and Target buy in quantities of millions. This typically exceeds the production capacity of small nations, or even large ones that only have a small number of efficient producers. The special economic zones in China have become a series of clusters that produce enormous quantities of socks, ties, and other clothing. Retailers and wholesalers place very large orders that are well beyond the total production capacities of smaller firms, even if these have learned sufficiently rapidly to become cost competitive. 'These days, buyers from New York to Tokyo want to be able to buy 500,000 pairs of socks all at once, or 300,000 neckties, 100,000 children's jackets…' (Barboza 2004). European firms buy smaller, more varied products, but impose even greater demands on local suppliers expecting 'in-house design and sample making capabilities that would allow them to translate and adapt the design from Europe' (Sturgeon and Lester 2002, p. 49).

In textiles, clothing, electronics, auto parts, and other sectors, being a part of an international network is critical to exporting and upgrading of quality. Firms that are not part of such networks may not succeed, even if they are initially as efficient as members. Some of the requirements of the leading firms in such networks are not good news for firms with lower capabilities in the South Asian nations, as they must 'label track, respond to product orders in real time on the basis of style, color, fabric, and size; exchange information on an...electronic basis, provide goods to a retailer's distribution centre that can be efficiently moved to stores…including containers with bar codes concerning contents' (Yusuf et al. 2003, p. 283). These requirements, now fairly standard in many product areas, suggest that successful penetration of OECD markets will become increasingly difficult for nations that have only begun sustained industrialization and are not yet exporting.

In electronics, an important efficient, labour-intensive growth sector in the past for countries such as Korea and Taiwan, and which might offer some possibilities for growth, much of the production is now carried out by contract manufacturers whose size has grown enormously in the last decade. Firms such as Solectron and Flextronics now undertake activity that was formerly under the aegis of major firms in developed countries, but that now have outsourced the activity. Examining the location of several activities, such as headquarters, manufacturing, materials, purchasing and management, new production introduction centres, and after-sales repair centres, Sturgeon and Lester (2002) show that most of these activities of Solectron, the largest of the contract manufacturers, take place in developed countries or the more advanced semi-industrialized economies contiguous to them, such as Mexico, Puerto Rico, Romania, and Turkey. Ernst (2002) confirms these results and points out that specialized clusters in countries such as the Nordic nations, the United States, France, and Germany are major sources as are Singapore, Hungary, Israel, Korea, and Taiwan (China). Poorer countries, even if they achieve a potential cost advantage after a long learning period, will have trouble breaking into these existing circuits.

Are FDI or Export Processing Zones a Solution?

None of this is to say that the South Asian countries are eternally locked into their current product areas and exporting status. Greater competitiveness and scale will eventually occur, building initially on sales in domestic markets. But it is unlikely that manufacturing exports can be the major short-term source of growth in aggregate demand as they were for Korea and Taiwan in the 1960s. Greater investment by MNCs could provide some possibility to circumvent the existing constraints—the effect of Daewoo's initial investment in Bangladesh's clothing industry is well known. But in general, foreign direct investment (FDI) is unlikely to be sufficiently important quantitatively to alter the picture unless MNCs decide to substantially diversify who they purchase from away from China and towards nearby nations.

FDI was attracted to China partly by its special economics zones and the possibility of utilizing a low-wage cost platform for exports. There are many lessons to be learned from China, which in turn modelled itself on the early export processing zones (EPZs) in Korea and Taiwan. But EPZs are not always successful, though certain policies increase the probability of success.[4] But even if all of the prerequisites are implemented, so that EPZs would rank highly on the World Bank's investment and business climate indicators, large inflows of FDI are not likely to be commensurate as a percentage of GDP (except in India), with those that flowed into China. China had the advantage of a huge potential domestic market that foreign firms wanted some familiarity with, in the hope that local sales would eventually become possible.

Moreover, it is important to note that most MNC investment is relatively capital and skill intensive. While there might be some growth in output and employment, it will not generate large demand for unskilled labour. That avenue has already been blocked by China. Take an example from a recent study by the consulting firm McKinsey & Co. of the potential for FDI in India (Luthra et al. 2005). The sectors McKinsey identified as potential areas of investment were automotive components, specialty chemicals, and electronics and electronic components. A typical reason offered for the potential competitiveness of these sectors is one given for automotive parts, 'the industry has the advantage of skills in process, product, and capital engineering ...its process engineering skills which can be applied to such tasks as the redesign of manufacturing processes to make them more labour and less capital intensive enable multinationals to reduce their overall costs substantially.' The skills may well exist and the industry could be successful, but even with some changes in the production process, the firms locating in India would be education intensive and generate very few jobs for unskilled labour. By extension, FDI is unlikely to provide productive employment in nations such as Nepal and Pakistan, which are less well-endowed with highly educated workers.

But another path may well exist, which has been overlooked in the recent emphasis on China's success in manufacturing exports. In both Taiwan and China, and to a lesser extent in Korea, the expansion of small and medium enterprises (SMEs) had been an important source of growth of output and employment early in the industrialization process and I now turn to this issue.

[4] Calanog (2005) provides a thorough survey of the literature on export processing zones.

The Role of Small and Medium Enterprises

If nations seek a solution to low rural incomes and the generation of new, more remunerative jobs both on and off the farm, one path was followed a half century ago, but has recently been ignored given the visibility of the export-led super-performers in Asia. Rather than simply achieving some arbitrary normative notion of the desirable level of the share of manufacturing in GDP and exports, growth in rural incomes and employment can be propelled by an expansion in agricultural productivity that gives rise to increased demand by rural families for many household products and agricultural inputs that can be efficiently produced in rural areas. Despite the most obvious characteristic of China, Korea, and Taiwan—namely the enormous growth and move up the value chain in manufacturing—all three underwent a dramatic increase in agricultural productivity and growth in the small- and medium-enterprise sector that sold consumer and production goods to farms. The SME emphasis is also the only one that is consistent with the actual investment available per new worker, cited above, that characterizes these economies.

The Chinese Experience with TVEs

In none of these countries was there a one-time jump into modern manufacturing. Rather, there was an evolution into it while simultaneously, in the background, a rapid increase in agricultural productivity occurred, along with a growth in small enterprises servicing this demand. In light of the intense focus often directed at the spectacular growth of Chinese manufacturing, a more balanced picture can be obtained by examining the growth of the rural enterprises that are referred to as TVEs (township and village enterprises). There are many accounts of this transformation that began soon after the liberalization in the late 1970s. A very recent synthesis of the material by Naughton (2007) carefully documents many of the relevant points and the following liberally uses his summary of the existing literature.

While the entire Chinese industrial sector grew after the liberalization beginning in the late 1970s, the relatively small-scale TVEs grew at an astonishing rate. Employment increased from 28 million in 1978 to 135 million in 1996, an annual growth rate of 9 per cent. The share of value added in GDP in the TVE sector grew from 6 per cent to 26 per cent in the same years.[5] The TVEs also performed a valuable function of providing discipline for large firms through their competition. 'TVEs drove price relationships into line with underlying costs... In the foreign trade area, TVEs provided opportunities for Chinese exporters to move into new labour-intensive manufactures.'[6] An important element of the success of the TVEs was that 'they faced factor prices that reflected China's true factor endowment'. (This, as noted earlier, was one of the foundations of the success in manufacturing in Korea and Taiwan). They 'rarely had access to subsidized capital...most was provided at near-market interest rates or came from internally generated funds with a high opportunity cost'.[7] They were 'specialized in those sectors with low capital–labour ratios where the competitive advantage of their low wages was biggest'.[8] The transforming effect of the TVEs was significant. 'A whole series of new markets were created by the sudden growth of rural incomes...rural housing construction took off and new rural industries developed to supply building materials.'[9]

Could South Asia replicate the TVE success in manufacturing? First, it is important to note that a considerable part of sales of the rural manufacturers was destined for rural markets, implying that growing income in these areas occurred simultaneously with growth in industry. Second, there was continuing investment, financed out of profits of the TVEs. Third, some fraction of was what produced was sold to urban firms that subcontracted to the rural firms. It is likely that the continuing investment stemmed from successful rural sales so that increases in rural income may, paradoxically, be a prerequisite to a more rapidly growing manufacturing sector in South Asia. Many of the requirements for improved agricultural productivity for simple implements, irrigation pipes and wells, can be produced without large-scale economies, as can a large variety of simpler consumer goods.

To bring out the potential of agricultural expansion-induced industrialization, a simple arithmetic example is helpful using figures typical of some South Asian nations. If agricultural income (which

[5] Ibid.: 274.
[6] Ibid.: 275.
[7] Ibid.
[8] Ibid.: 276.
[9] Ibid.: 277.

is less than rural income) accounts for 25 per cent of GDP, and manufacturing 15 per cent, an increase of 40 per cent in agricultural income, half of which is spent on manufacturing, would generate a 33 per cent growth in demand for the latter. The posited increase in agricultural income is well within technical bounds given the current low level of agricultural productivity of the nations in the region. And even such an increase in farm productivity would still leave farmers with very low productivity relative to other sectors. For example, in 2000, the last date for which the requisite data are available, labour productivity in agriculture was 40 per cent of the national average in Bangladesh, and 45 per cent in Pakistan. In both countries 'industry', which is more inclusive than manufacturing, had more than twice the national labour productivity, implying either greater capital intensity or greater total factor productivity (TFP), or probably both.

Conclusions

The major thrust of this chapter is the need to take a realistic account of the current conditions in South Asia—large rural populations, many of whom are involved in agriculture, who are often poor and exhibiting low productivity, and the limited possibility of ameliorating these conditions by rapid industrialization through labour-intensive manufacturing exports. While the export route provided a path for earlier industrializers such as Korea, it is largely precluded because of the rapid development of Chinese, East European, and Latin American exporters, along with the earlier Asian entrants such as Indonesia, Malaysia, and Thailand. The alternative suggested is a balanced effort for agricultural and rural industries. This alternative is by no means meant to imply a replication of earlier misguided efforts to limit the growth of the large-scale industrial sector by industrial licensing or other such artificial means. These measures in India and other nations were clearly counterproductive by limiting the ability of efficient firms to increase their share of output.

There are no secrets about the requirements for improved agricultural productivity, and indeed in the 1960s, India and Pakistan benefited enormously from adoption of the Green Revolution package. Much more is now understood about the requirements for rural development, and the main issue is one of whether political will exists. Rapid growth in specialty chemicals or auto components is always easier to boast about than improved rural roads and more agricultural research stations and extension agents. And the beneficiaries of these rural-oriented policies are likely to be more quiescent politically. While not underestimating the problems, both technical and political, of greater rural development, the generation of more SMEs outside of major cities may be more difficult.

The SME strategy is not geared towards the informal sector, or where demonstrated economic benefits are open to question. The types of firms envisioned are factories with 10 to perhaps 300 employees. But unlike other regions in the world, there are large numbers of small firms, noted two decades ago in a World Bank study of India (Little, Mazumdar, and Page 1987) and studies in Bangladesh and Pakistan. Moreover, the evidence in that volume and other analyses suggests that such firms suffer no systematic disadvantage in total factor productivity as compared with larger firms, but do exhibit the desirable property of being more labour intensive even in the same industry as they face a set of factor prices more in line with the nations' endowments. Recall the aforementioned Chinese TVE description. Without entering into specific policies to allow the growth of the sector, it is worth noting that a growth in rural demand would militate in its favour, as would, importantly, an improved business and investment climate. While large firms can often undertake private measures such as owning generators to fill gaps in the reliability of electricity supply, or to overcome bureaucratic delays, small firms cannot afford to do so. On the other hand, if the SME sector is the desirable social alternative to large manufacturing, it should not be artificially stimulated. Preferential policies such as low-interest loans would undercut the need for firms to make decisions based on socially appropriate factor prices.

None of this is to suggest that there is no role for the large-scale factories that can generate efficient production. They can probably best be stimulated by improved business and investment climate policies including, importantly, liberalized labour markets. Growing exports are important as a source of foreign exchange to finance imports, which themselves may help, through a greater variety of intermediate inputs and improved machinery, to augment productivity. But to argue for special promotion using fiscal incentives for large manufacturing firms is not the first order of business. In Bangladesh, special fiscal incentives were not the source of the spectacular growth in clothing production and exports (Rhee 1990). In India, government measures ratified rather than initiated software growth. In the latter case, high-quality specialized education was important as a precondition for taking advantage of the fortuitous circumstances that arose in the 1990s, but financing the Indian Institutes of Technology was hardly initiated as an effort to anticipate future IT development.

The manufacturing sector in South Asia is unlikely to duplicate the trajectory in Korea and Taiwan, nor the more recent Chinese experience. Partly because of the very success of these economies, the conditions facing the South Asian nations are less propitious for such a heavy reliance on export-propelled growth. This does not in any way condemn these nations to a largely agricultural development path. Given the natural economic interactions between the rural and smaller-scale manufacturing sectors, both can grow simultaneously. Given the higher income elasticity for manufactured than agricultural goods, there will inevitably be a slow shift in the centre of economic gravity towards the industrial sector. The more balanced path also has the advantage of being likely to generate more jobs for the growing labour force, thus limiting the growth of income inequality. It is less exciting but more politically sustainable.

References

Barboza, David. 2004. 'In Roaring China, Sweaters are West of Socks City', *The New York Times*, 24 December.

Batson, Andrew. 2007. 'Soon Made in China: High-Tech Products—Intel Investment Shows How Nation's Economy is Climbing Value Chain', *The Wall Street Journal*, 23 March.

Bosworth, Barry F. and Susan M. Collins. 2003. 'The Empirics of Growth: An Update', *Brookings Papers on Economic Activity*, 2: 113–79.

Calanog, Victor. 2006. 'Essays on the Economics of Development Strategies', Ph.D. dissertation, The Wharton School, University of Pennsylvania, Philadelphia.

Economist.com. 2006. 'Survey: Business in India—Now for the Hard Part', 1 June.

Ernst, Dieter. 2002. 'Global Production Networks in East Asia's Electronics Industry', Economics Study Area Working Papers, East–West Centre, Economics Study Area. Honolulu, Hawaii.

Holstein, William J. 2007. 'Catching a Wave of High-Tech Exports', *The New York Times*, 11 March.

Landler, Mark. 2007. 'A Tradition of Quality and Strong Brands Leads Export Growth', *The New York Times*, 13 April.

Little, Ian M.D., Dipak Mazumdar, and John M. Page, Jr. 1987. *Small Manufacturing Enterprises—A Comparative Study of India and Other Economies*. New York: Oxford University Press.

Luthra Shashank, Ramesh Mangaleswaran, and Asutosh Padhi. 2005. *When to Make India a Manufacturing Base*. McKinsey & Co.

NASSCOM–McKinsey & Co. 2005. *Extending India's Leadership of the Global IT and BPO Industries,* Report.

Naughton, Barry. 2007. *The Chinese Economy—Transitions and Growth*. Cambridge, Mass.: MIT Press.

Rhee, Yung W. 1990. 'The Catalyst Model of Development: Lessons from Bangladesh's Success with Garment Exports', *World Development*, 18(2): 333–46.

Sturgeon, Timothy and Richard Lester. 2002. 'Upgrading East Asian Industries: New Challenges for Local Suppliers'. Cambridge, Mass.: Industrial Performance Centre, MIT.

Yusuf, Shahid (with Altaf, Eichengreen, Gooptu, Nabeshima, Kenny, Perkins, and Shotten). 2003. *Innovative East Asia: The Future of Growth*. Washington, D.C. and New York: World Bank and Oxford University Press.

World Bank. *World Development Indicators*, various years.

5 THE GROWTH OF INDUSTRY AND SERVICES IN SOUTH ASIA AND ITS IMPACT ON EMPLOYMENT

ANALYSIS AND POLICY

Kaushik Basu and Annemie Maertens

INTRODUCTION

The recent boom in all major South Asian economies has been the subject of huge global interest and analysis. Yet the patterns of development differ across countries, with Bangladesh making strides in living standards' indicators, Sri Lanka showing buoyancy in manufacturing, Pakistan recording reasonable overall growth, and the Indian economy showing an outstanding resurgence of growth. But if we agree that growth is valuable only to the extent that it raises the general standard of living across the population, and especially among the most disadvantaged, then some troubling questions arise about the South Asian experience. South Asia's defining characteristic is its large labour force, along with the anticipated 'demographic dividend'—an increase in the share of working-age people in the population. This raises important questions about the ability of these countries to absorb this labour and turn this 'population glut' into a window of opportunity. We know from past experience that this opportunity cannot be seized simply by having the government plan and commandeer the use of labour-intensive technology through licensing and by decree (Mohan 1992). If this opportunity is to be seized, policies will have to be crafted that do not disregard the laws of the economy, and that take into account the incentive structure of markets. The aim of this chapter is to analyse the patterns of growth of the manufacturing and services sectors in the South Asian countries and study, in particular, their impact on employment and job creation. It then goes on to discuss the policy options open to the governments of the various South Asian nations.

One message that emerges forcefully from this multi-country study is this. Analysts and policymakers engaged in economics have a predilection to look for a single sufficient cause. But if we are to understand what causes growth that is inclusive (in the sense of engaging and benefiting the labouring classes), then we have to recognize the multiplicity of causes. A nation needs an educated and healthy labour force, basic infrastructure, appropriate labour market and trade policies, and the right kind of social norms and institutions. Even if we leave out the latter as belonging largely to disciplines beyond economics, the list for the economist is long and likely to cause impatience in the policymaker looking for a quick, focused remedy. This complementarity of policies is worth keeping in mind when studying the nations of South Asia because, as we shall presently see, despite the shared history of much of this region, the factors that have held back good performance, and in particular inclusive growth, in various nations are different. We will argue that different bottlenecks are of salience in different nations—labour market regulations in some but not in others, inadequate education in some but not in others, and so on. The one common deficiency that plagues the entire region is inadequate infrastructure investment, but even here the way this problem has to be approached may have to vary for different nations, depending on a country's fiscal situation. What is also common to this entire region is the prospect of good times. After decades of stagnation, it suddenly appears that South Asia can follow in the footsteps of East Asia. Moreover, we argue that the region can not only ask for rapid growth, but also for the fruits of this aggregate growth to be better distributed. This chapter is a small contribution for formulating policies towards this grand objective.

A Preview

Most South Asian countries came into their own in the middle of the last century, inheriting a structure of labour laws and regulations from the British. Starting from this common heritage, the nations have veered off in different directions, amending some of the laws, repealing some, and enacting new ones. These changes have no doubt had huge impacts on labour market outcomes, along with sectoral patterns of growth. Hence, the chapter focuses on the growth in services and industry, and the linkages of these with labour market policies and outcomes.

One feature of the Indian growth experience that has some interesting similarities and contrasts with other South Asian economies and has attracted much attention is the phenomenal expansion of the services sector, coupled with, at best, lukewarm growth of industry and agriculture. Important questions have arisen about this unusual and unprecedented pattern of growth on the part of India and the commonalities and contrasts with other South Asian economies, and a part of this chapter will be concerned with this phenomenon.

As a preview, let us begin by noting that the structural shift in India is indeed striking.[1] In 1950, 57 per cent of India's GDP came from agriculture, 14 per cent from industry, and 29 per cent from services. As a country grows, it is only natural to expect the share of agriculture to shrink and industry to grow. But what happened in India and most South Asian nations is striking. In today's India, around 20 per cent of the GDP comes from agriculture, approximately 25 per cent from industry, and well over 50 per cent from services. This kind of sharp rise in the services sector, which essentially took place after 1991, has little parallel elsewhere in the contemporary world or in history. Interestingly, the little parallel that exists can be found in South Asia. Bangladesh, surprisingly, has a similar structure: 20 per cent of GDP from agriculture, 21 per cent from industry, and 59 per cent from services. Pakistan also has similarities. The shares of agriculture, industry, and services in Pakistan's GDP are, respectively, 22 per cent, 24 per cent, and 54 per cent. To see how sharply this contrasts with other Asian countries, note that 12 per cent of China's GDP comes from agriculture and 48 per cent comes from industry; and 3 per cent of Korea's GDP comes from agriculture and 45 per cent from industry.

The chapter will study these structural differences in the SAARC countries but, instead of doing this as an end in itself, the aim is to understand labour market outcomes, especially those relating to employment, and to make policy recommendations. It is arguable that growth in all these countries is not filtering down enough to the

[1] The numbers cited in this preview are from various sources—scholarly and popular—and may not match exactly the more detailed statistical texts that occur in the body of the chapter with the formal source always cited.

workers and the poor. In the case of India, it has been argued that unless the manufacturing sector picks up more—since that is usually a more labour-intensive sector than services—growth in employment will not be robust. It is indeed interesting to see that in India, while 21 per cent of the GDP comes from the agricultural sector, over 60 per cent of the labour force works in that sector. Industry produces 26 per cent of the GDP and employs 12 per cent of the labour force, and the services sector produces 53 per cent of the GDP and employs only 28 per cent of the labour force. It would therefore appear that an increased emphasis on manufacturing could boost employment.[2] Also, if we look at other Asian countries, we find that much more labour has already moved out of agriculture. For example, in Korea, less than 7 per cent of the labour force is in agriculture. There is clearly room in South Asian countries for drawing labour away from agriculture and into manufacturing. Behind the inadequate performance of employment and the relatively weak growth of manufacturing, there may be some common, more fundamental causes, which are institutional and founded in government policy and the law.

When comparing the employment situation in South Asia with other regions in the world, one is tempted to conclude that South Asia has not done so badly after all (see Table A1.12 in the Appendix). For 2006, the International Labour Organization (ILO) reports employment growth in South Asia of 2.36 per cent, versus 2.66 per cent in Sub-Saharan Africa, and 0.94 per cent in East Asia. In absolute numbers, this implies that South Asia has 'created' an additional 13 million 'jobs', and sub-Saharan Africa and East Asia have both created 7 million. To conclude from these numbers that South Asia is doing better on the employment front than East Asia, however, is incorrect. Underlying these figures are two very different economies. Take the cases of India and China, for instance. The population of China is 1.3 billion; the population of India is 1.1 billion. The total labour force in China is 782 million; India's labour force is only 443 million. China's population growth rate is 0.56 per cent; India's population

[2] It may appear that an emphasis on agriculture would create even more jobs. This is true, but if this is done at the expense of industry and services, it may hold up the country's overall growth rate, since agricultural growth seldom measures up to the maximum feasible in these other sectors.

growth rate is 1.38 per cent. China's labour force growth rate is 0.83 per cent; the figure for India is 1.85 per cent.[3] In China, 53 per cent of employment is classified as informal sector employment; the corresponding figure for India is 94 per cent.[4] As the unemployment rate in India is only around 4 per cent, the high employment growth is just a reflection of the underlying higher population growth and population structure (32 per cent of the population is under age 15 in India, compared to 21 per cent in China).[5] The majority of these entrants are absorbed by the informal economy.

While the causality between jobs and the pattern of growth is something that we explore in this chapter, a striking fact worth noting is the sharp decline in the number of workers in Indian firms employing more that 100 workers, which occurred after 1984, when India amended its Industrial Disputes Act of 1947, so as to make the dismissal of workers much harder for firms that employ over 100 workers. In 1983 there were 898,000 workers in firms employing over 100 workers; the number fell to 569,000 in 1990. This suggests that the decline in employment was the market's response to the policy change, and leads to the policy implication that India can benefit by amending its Industrial Disputes Act and enabling the use of a wider range of contractual agreements between workers and firms.

But complications arise when we look at the experience of other nations in the region. Suppose we maintain that India's performance in the labour market was weakened by its rigid labour laws. Given that India was the best performer in this region, one may, at first blush, expect the labour laws to be even more rigid in the other nations. But that is not the case. Through a series of changes since independence, Pakistan and Bangladesh have liberalized their labour laws greatly (in fact there are open questions as to whether they have not overdone it and whether they have done it in the right way). The World Bank has developed an index, ranging from 0 to 100, of how hard it is to fire workers, where zero denotes the easiest and 100 the hardest. India scores 90 on this scale. In comparison, Bangladesh and Pakistan score 20 and 30, respectively, while Bhutan scores zero. So clearly, the flexibility of labour laws is not all there is to it.

[3] *World Development Indicators 2007*, Data from 2006.

[4] *OECD Employment Outlook 2007*, Tables 1–6.

[5] *World Development Indicators 2007*, Data from 2006.

In the case of India the top-heavy Indian education system, which through the 1970s and 1980s produced a glut of engineers and a body of unemployed technically-trained personnel, helped the country position itself strategically to gain from the meteoric rise of the Silicon Valley, the demand from which and its secondary effects implied that the glut in skilled labour quickly vanished. Also, the colonial legacy of the English language has helped most South Asian economies and shaped their destinies to a certain extent, giving South Asia a relative edge in the services sector, in which language skills are of greater importance. This has created a handicap for nations without this history, such as Nepal, Bhutan, and Afghanistan, and this may be one reason why they have been less able to capitalize on globalization.

By the same token, it may have led to the relative neglect of the employment-generating manufacturing sector. The structure of South Asian education has also contributed to the poor growth in employment and the rise of the services sector. India's basic literacy rate trails behind that of most Sub-Saharan African countries, even ones that are poorer than India. Yet India has been very successful in promoting higher education and science. There is need now in India and all of South Asia (except Sri Lanka and the Maldives, which have already done well in this regard) to promote basic literacy, which would enable its labour force to find employment outside of agriculture, and especially in industry.

It should also be mentioned that industrial growth hinges critically on infrastructure—ports, airports, roads, and electricity—and so there is the need to build up infrastructure rapidly. This is likely to lead to some fiscal strain but, if it can be managed while keeping a lid on the revenue deficit, it should not give rise to inflationary pressures. This is a policy that the entire region of South Asia can benefit from, but particularly the large economies of India, Pakistan, and Bangladesh.

While India's primary policy focus has to be on labour markets, literacy, and infrastructure, for other South Asian nations, to have more successful labour market outcomes, more attention needs to be paid to policies that lie beyond the labour market. These include general macroeconomic and fiscal policies, and also to raising more capital and foreign investment in the domestic markets. The aim of this essay is to, first, systematically collate the available data on intersectoral growth in South Asian countries, and then to study the employment-generating capacity of different sectors in different nations of the region, and to directly address policy questions on how to generate greater gainful employment.

We shall not be going into matters of globalization in any great detail, since our focus will be on national and regional policy options. But it should be pointed out that how much a government can do is, in today's globalized world, bounded by what happens in other nations. If, seeing the level of inequality and poverty in a certain nation, the government decides to raise the corporate tax in order to divert some of the money to the poor, it is entirely possible that some corporations will move to another nation, resulting in the government collecting less revenue than before, and being unable to help its poor. This shrinkage in national policy space is not specific to developing nations. There is evidence from the OECD countries that there has been some competitive lowering of corporate taxation going on over the last 20 years (Weise 2007). This suggests an increasing need for the coordination of anti-poverty and inequality-related policies across nations, and international organizations can play a useful role (see Basu 2006b). But our focus here is on what the governments of the South Asian nations can do—and there is a lot that they can—so we stay away from the larger question of *global* policy coordination in this chapter.

Introducing the Eight Countries

The eight South Asian countries considered in this essay are Afghanistan, Bangladesh, Bhutan, India, Maldives, Nepal, Pakistan, and Sri Lanka. These countries constitute the member nations of SAARC, established in 1985 with all these nations except Afghanistan, which joined the group earlier this year.

Table 5.1 presents some basic statistics of these countries in 2005. India is the largest, both in terms of population and GDP, followed by Pakistan and Bangladesh. Bhutan and the Maldives are population-wise, the smallest countries in SAARC. The current average population growth in the region, not including Afghanistan, is 1.60 per cent, the average GDP growth is 8.65 per cent, and the average GDP per capita growth in the region, not including Afghanistan, is 6.94 per cent.[6] The age dependency ratio, that is,

[6] *World Development Indicators 2007*, data from 2005.

TABLE 5.1: Basic Economic Statistics, South Asia in 2005

	GDP (current US$ millions)	*GDP/Capita (current US$)*	*Total population*	*GDP growth (annual, %)*[1]	*Population growth (annual, %)*	*Population dependency ratio*
Afghanistan	7,308	315	23,200,000[2]	14.00	2.03[2]	0.97[3]
Bangladesh	60,034	423	141,822,276	5.96	1.86	0.64
Bhutan	844	1,326	636,638[5]	6.06	3.35	0.75
India	805,714	736	1,094,583,000	9.23	1.37	0.60
Maldives	766	2,327	329,198	–5.19[4]	2.46	0.79
Nepal	7,391	272	27,132,629	2.71	2.02	0.74
Pakistan	110,732	711	155,772,000	7.78	2.41	0.73
Sri Lanka	23,479	1,196	19,625,384	5.30	0.84	0.46

Source: World Bank, *World Development Indicators 2007*.

Notes: [1] Annual percentage growth rate of GDP at market prices based on constant local currency.

[2] Data from 2004. *Afghanistan Statistical Yearbook* (2005).

[3] Calculated from Table 2.1 in the *Afghanistan Statistical Yearbook* (2005) using the definition of the World Bank for dependency ratio.

[4] The negative GDP growth rate in the Maldives in 2005 is due to the tsunami in 2004.

[5] The population figures for Bhutan are debatable. The government of Bhutan only counts the official residents of the country. There are other estimates that suggest that the population is closer to 2 million residents.

the ratio of the non-working population (people under 15 or over 65) to the working population (people 15 to 64), is 62 per cent for the South Asian countries, excluding Afghanistan. For the OECD countries it is 49 per cent.[7] This high dependency ratio implies that relatively few workers are responsible for a large number of children and elderly. However, the structure of the population (33 per cent of the population is under the age of 15 years in South Asia, versus 18 per cent in the OECD countries[8]), combined with a decreasing fertility rate, implies that in the future, this dependency ratio might fall considerably. Especially for India, the 'demographic dividend' is expected to be substantial over the next 25 or 30 years, comparable to Ireland in 1979, when it legalized contraception, faced a rapid decline in the dependency ratio, and prospered economically in the decades that followed, earning it the nickname the Celtic tiger. The dynamics of the population structure are an important element to be taken into account when discussing the current and future labour force of a country.

Table 5.2 presents a selection of the most recent available social indicators. The adult literacy rate in South Asia was estimated by the World Bank to be 58 per cent in 2005. This is 3 percentage points lower than the rate for Sub-Saharan Africa. The gap between the female and male literacy rates in South Asia is the greatest in the world, with an estimated 45 per cent female literacy rate, and a 70 per cent male literacy rate in 2005.[9] The life expectancy at birth is 63 years for males and 64 years for females. An estimated 21 per cent of the population is undernourished, versus 30 per cent in sub-Saharan Africa.

It is immediately evident that though the entire region is still poor and has poor standard of living indicators, it is also characterized by a vast diversity, ranging from the Maldives and Sri Lanka with high literacy rates, high life expectancy, and low poverty rates, to Afghanistan, destroyed by two decades of war, with an adult female literacy rate of only 13 per cent and almost 70 per cent of the

[7] Data from 2005, excluding Afghanistan, from the *World Development Indicators 2007*.

[8] Data from 2005, excluding Afghanistan, from the *World Development Indicators 2007*.

[9] *World Development Indicators 2007*.

TABLE 5.2: Basic Social Statistics, South Asia, 2004–6

	Literacy rate adult female (15 years & above) (2006)	*Literacy rate adult male (15 years & above) (2006)*	*Life expectancy at birth (female) (2005)*	*Life expectancy at birth (male) (2005)*	*Poverty rate head-count PPP at $1 a day*	*Prevalence of under-nourish-ment (%) (2004)*
Afghanistan	13	43	45[1]	47[1]	[2]	67[1]
Bangladesh	41[3]	50[3]	65	63	41 (in 2000)	30
Bhutan	49 (in 2005)	69	65	63	[4]	[4]
India	48	73	64	63	34 (in 2004)	20
Maldives	96	96	67	68	less than 1[5]	10
Nepal	35	63	63	62	24 (in 2004)	17
Pakistan	36	63	65	64	17 (in 2004)	24
Sri Lanka	89	92	77	72	6 (in 2004)	22

Source: World Bank, *World Development Indicators 2007*.

Notes: [1] Data from 2004; *Afghanistan Statistical Yearbook* (2005).

[2] No estimates are provided by the *Afghanistan Statistical Yearbook* (2005).

[3] Data from 2001; *2002 Statistical Yearbook of Bangladesh* (2005).

[4] No estimates are provided by WDI, ADB, or the *Bhutan Statistical Yearbook* (2005).

[5] Data from 2005, *Millenium Development Goals Maldives Country Report* (2005).

TABLE 5.3: GDP Annual Growth Rates, South Asia (1971–2005)

	Afghanistan	*Bangladesh*	*Bhutan*	*India*	*Maldives*	*Nepal*	*Pakistan*	*Sri Lanka*
1971	–4.8	–5.5	2.7	1.8	5.2	–1.2	1.5	0.5
1972	–1.8	–14	1.2	–0.6	2.4	3.1	6.6	3.2
1973	11.4	9.6	1.5	3	1.6	–0.5	5.3	3.5
1974	5.5	–4.1	5.2	1.2	5.7	6.3	3.2	4
1975	6.2	5.7	–3.3	9.2	–8	1.5	4.6	3.4
1976	5.5	2.7	9	1.8	0.6	4.4	3.8	3.8
1977	–5	7.1	7.9	7.2	11.3	3	8	4.1
1978	7.4	4.8	7.1	5.5	14.7	4.4	4.8	8.7
1979	–2.6	0.8	4.8	–5	10.7	2.4	8.7	6.1
1980	–3.7	3.4	5	6.6	18.6	–2.3	6.9	6.2
1981	2.2	1.2	10	6.5	11.8	8.3	6.5	5.5
1982	2	4.9	5.3	3.8	–3	3.8	6.8	5.2
1983	4.9	5.4	8	7.4	16.3	–3	5.1	4.8
1984	1.8	3	7	3.7	27	9.7	7.6	5.1
1985	0.3	4.3	3.7	5.5	13	6.1	5.5	5
1986	3	4.2	10.2	4.9	9.4	4.6	6.5	4.3
1987	–10.3	2.9	17.8	4.8	8.9	1.7	7.6	1.6
1988	–8.3	2.5	1.1	9.9	8.7	7.7	5	2.8

(contd ...)

Table 5.3 (contd ...)

	Afghanistan	*Bangladesh*	*Bhutan*	*India*	*Maldives*	*Nepal*	*Pakistan*	*Sri Lanka*
1989	–7.1	6.6	4.7	6.6	9.3	4.3	4.5	2
1990	–3.1	3.4	6.6	5.7	16.3	4.6	5.5	6.2
1991	6.5	4.2	3.5	0.4	7.7	6.4	7.8	4.8
1992	1.6	4.6	4.5	5.4	6.3	4.1	1.3	4.4
1993	–20.3	4.1	6.1	5	6.2	3.8	3.7	6.9
1994	–7.8	4.9	2.9	7.5	6.6	8.2	5	5.6
1995	5	4.6	7.3	7.6	7.1	3.5	4.8	5.5
1996	9	5.4	5.8	7.4	8.8	5.3	1	3.8
1997	10.1	5.2	4.2	4.5	11.5	5.3	2.6	6.4
1998	11.9	4.9	5.8	6	9.3	2.9	3.7	4.7
1999	–5.9	5.9	7.8	7.1	7.8	4.5	4.3	4.3
2000	–33.6	5.3	9.5	3.9	4.4	6.1	2.7	6
2001	–9.4	4.4	8.6	5.1	3.3	5.6	1.9	–1.4
2002	29.7	5.3	7.1	4.1	6.1	–0.6	3.2	4
2003	18.6	6.3	6.8	8.6	9.2	3.4	5	5.9
2004	8	5.4	8.7	7.1	9.6	3.4	6.4	5.4
2005	13.8	5.5	8.8	8.7	-0.2	2.5	7.8	6.2

Source: GDP annual growth rate, 1990 prices, US$ (UN estimates).

population undernourished. In growth, the entire region seems to be showing buoyancy, with the exception of Afghanistan, even though the latter had a large bounce-back effect in 2005, as shown in Table 5.1. The Maldives shows up poorly in this table, but only because of the tsunami, which hit this small nation severely. To move away from these one-year blips, we need to look at growth over the years, and that is what we do next.

Table 5.3 and Figure 5.1 present the growth figures of the SAARC nations from 1971 to the present times. In Figure 5.1, we have graphed the natural log of the GDP, rather than the actual GDP, so that one can read the growth rate directly from the slope of the graph. A straight line represents a constant rate of growth. Table 5.3 presents annual averages of growth rates from 1971 until 2005.

From Figure 5.1 and Table 5.3, one can see that the series for Afghanistan has shown large movements, fluctuating between –33 per cent at one extreme, to 18 per cent at the other. Bangladesh's growth rate since the early 1980s has fluctuated around 4 to 5 per cent per year, rising to above 5 per cent by the end of the 1980s and

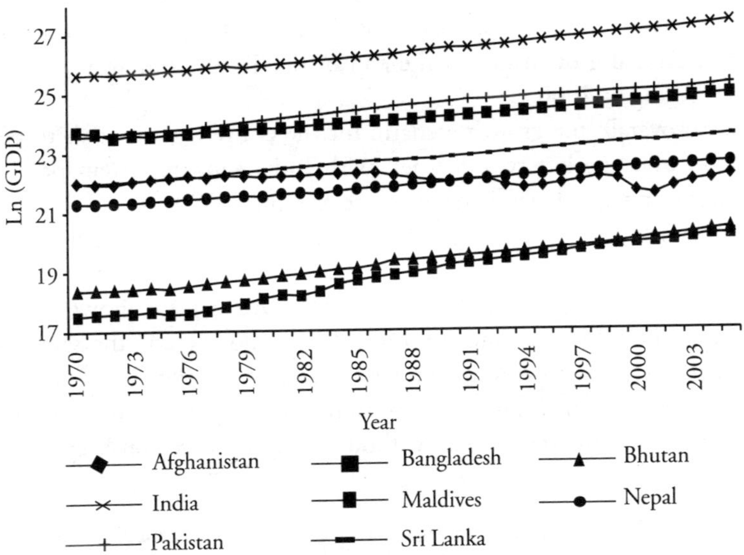

Figure 5.1: GDP Growth in South Asia

Source: UN—GDP at market prices, 1990 prices, US$ (series code 19470).

start of the 1990s (Salimullah, Huq, and McNicol 2000). Bhutan's annual growth rate has been fluctuating around an average of 6 to 7 per cent since the early 1980s. In India, the rate of growth in the 1970s had been fluctuating around 3.5 per cent per year, which had been India's consistent average since the early 1950s. In 1975–6, India had an upward spike in growth, breaking through the 9 per cent mark for the first time, and in fact, from the mid-1970s, the Indian rate of growth exhibits an upward trend, averaging around 6 per cent for the period 1975–2005, despite the fact that 1979–80 was the worst year for India in terms of overall economic growth. Over the last three years, India has had over 8 per cent growth per annum.[10] Apart from three years with negative growth, the Maldives experienced consistent high growth rates. Nepal had shown a considerably higher average growth rate in the period 1980–2000, compared to the pre-1980s and post-2000 period, averaging around 5 to 6 per cent annual growth in the former. In Pakistan, economic growth slowed down from the early to mid-1990s; but since 2003, the economy seems to have picked up its 5 to 6 per cent per year growth rate once again. But by that point, the region's average growth was much higher, so in relative terms it does not appear to be as good. Sri Lanka had seen a dip in its 5 per cent to 6 per cent annual growth rate at the end of the 1980s, and again at the beginning of 2000.

So overall, the growth scenario for the entire region seems to be good over the last two decades, with India showing a remarkably steady and good performance since the mid-1990s. Over the last three or four years in particular, India has begun to look like the East Asian economies in the 1970s.

The discerning reader would have observed that the growth rates shown in Tables 5.1 and 5.3 for 2005 are not exactly the same—especially for Maldives, the growth rates seem markedly different.[11] We have chosen to present these somewhat disparate numbers that originate in different places, without trying to force consistency on

[10] For analyses of India's growth experience, see Ahluwalia (2000, 2002); Basu (2004); Forbes (2002); Kelkar (2004); Panagariya (2004); Rodrik and Subramanian (2004); Virmani (2004); and Srinivasan (2005).

[11] *The Statistical Yearbook of the Maldives* of 2006 mentions –5.6 per cent as the annual growth rate in 2005 (at basic prices, using 1995 constant price series).

them. This is harmless, since averaged out over the years, the differing sources make little difference.[12]

THE SECTORAL BREAK-UP OF GROWTH

We are now in a position to go beyond this overall picture to the underlying structure and, in particular, to study the sectoral components of national economic growth. Figures A1.1 to A1.8 in the appendix show the evolution of the structure of the economy in the eight South Asian countries. Table 5.4 gives the structure of the economies at selected years. In 1980, the shares of agriculture, industry, and services in South Asia were, respectively, 37 per cent, 24 per cent, and 39 per cent. In 2005, these shares were, respectively, 19 per cent, 27 per cent, and 54 per cent.[13]

Afghanistan's sectoral structure and growth look different from the rest of South Asia. In 1965, the shares of agriculture, industry and services were, respectively, 53 per cent, 11 per cent, and 31 per cent. In 2005, these were 36 per cent, 24 per cent, and 39 per cent. It must be noted that data for Afghanistan are not easy to get, and the GDP estimates from various sources tend to vary widely. In fact, the 2005 *Statistical Yearbook* was the first one in English in its series.

In Bangladesh, the share of agriculture has declined from 32 per cent in 1980 to 21 per cent in 2006. The share of services has increased slightly, from 48 per cent in 1980 to 51 per cent in 2006. The share of industry has increased from 21 per cent in 1960 to 28 per cent in 2006.

For Bhutan, we have data only from 1980. According to the *World Development Indicators*, in 2003, the share of agriculture was 33 per cent of the GDP, that of services was 27 per cent, and industry accounted for 39 per cent. According to the statistics of the government of Bhutan however, the primary, secondary, and tertiary sector account for, respectively, 26 per cent, 35 per cent, and 40 per cent of GDP in 2004.

[12] Note that this difference in growth rate, in theory, cannot be due to a different base year used in the two calculations. For Table 5.3, we have opted to use the UN estimates because while the World Development Indicators are available from 1961 onwards, the series for Afghanistan, Bhutan, and the Maldives are incomplete.

[13] *World Development Indicators 2007*. These figures exclude the Maldives for both years and Afghanistan for 1980.

TABLE 5.4: Structure of the Economy, South Asia (1960–2006)

% of GDP	*1960*	*1965*	*1970*	*1975*	*1980*	*1985*	*1990*	*1995*	*2000*	*2005*
					Afghanistan					
Agriculture	–	53	–	62	62	58	48	64	57	36
Industry	–	11	–	24	26	29	38	20	21	24
Services	–	31	–	14	12	12	14	16	22	39
					Bangladesh					
Agriculture	–	–	–	–	32	33	30	26	26	21
Manufacturing	–	–	–	–	14	14	13	15	15	17
Industry	–	–	–	–	21	21	21	25	25	28
Services	–	–	–	–	48	46	48	49	49	51
					Bhutan					
Agriculture	–	–	–	–	57	53	43	41	36	26
Manufacturing	–	–	–	–	3	5	8	11	8	7
Industry	–	–	–	–	12	19	25	34	35	35
Services	–	–	–	–	31	28	32	25	29	40
					India					
Agriculture	47	45	46	41	39	34	31	28	23	21
Manufacturing	14	14	14	15	16	16	17	18	16	15
Industry	19	21	21	22	24	26	28	28	26	26
Services	34	34	33	36	37	40	41	44	50	53

(contd ....)

Table 5.4 (contd ...)

% of GDP	*1960*	*1965*	*1970*	*1975*	*1980*	*1985*	*1990*	*1995*	*2000*	*2005*
					The Maldives					
Agriculture	–	–	–	–	34	19	16	12	9	11
Manufacturing	–	–	–	–	3	9	9	8	8	8
Industry	–	–	–	–	15	12	12	13	14	17
Services	–	–	–	–	50	73	76	79	80	76
					Nepal					
Agriculture	–	65	67	72	62	52	51	41	40	40
Manufacturing	–	3	4	4	4	6	6	9	9	9
Industry	–	11	12	8	12	15	16	22	21	23
Services	–	23	21	20	26	33	33	37	39	38
					Pakistan					
Agriculture	46	40	37	32	30	29	26	26	26	22
Manufacturing	12	14	16	17	16	16	17	16	15	17
Industry	16	20	22	23	25	22	25	24	23	24
Services	38	40	41	45	46	49	49	50	51	54
					Sri Lanka					
Agriculture	32	28	28	30	28	28	26	23	20	16
Manufacturing	15	17	17	20	18	15	15	16	17	15
Industry	20	21	24	26	30	26	26	27	27	25
Services	48	51	48	43	43	46	48	50	53	59

Sources: Same as for Figures A1.1–A1.8; Bhutan figures for 2004 come from Table 14.7 in the *Bhutan Statistical Yearbook 2005*.
Notes: The figures for Maldives add up to 100 per cent when adjusted using Financial Services Indirectly Measured (FISIM), which is negative for most years. The figures for Afghanistan for 1965 do not add up to 100 per cent as 5 per cent depreciation is not included. The figures for Bhutan in 2004 include a –1.3 per cent imputed bank service.

In India, the share of agriculture had declined from 47 per cent in 1960 to 21 per cent in 2006. The majority of this decline has been absorbed by an increase in the share of services, from 34 per cent in 1960 to 53 per cent in 2006. The share of manufacturing has remained stable over the last 40 years, fluctuating around 15 per cent.

In the Maldives, the tertiary sector had grown from 50 per cent of GDP in 1980 to 76 per cent in 2005. The manufacturing sector had grown from 3 per cent in 1980 to 8 per cent in 2005. In 2005, the secondary sector represented 17 per cent of GDP, and the primary sector 11 per cent.

In Nepal, agriculture and services had an approximately equal share of the economy, at around 40 per cent in 2006. The manufacturing sector, despite its increase in share in the last 40 years, was still very small, representing 9 per cent of the economy in 2006.

Pakistan's transition has been similar to that of India. The share of agriculture declined from 46 per cent in 1960 to 22 per cent in 2006. The share of services increased from 38 per cent in 1960 to 54 per cent in 2006. The share of manufacturing grew from 12 per cent in 1960 to 17 per cent in 2006.

In Sri Lanka, the share of agriculture had declined from 32 per cent in 1960 to 16 per cent in 2006. The share of the service sector increased up until the early 1970s, then dropped suddenly, and showed a steady increase again from the mid-1990s. Today, the service sector represents 59 per cent of the economy. Manufacturing today has an equal share of the economy as it had 45 years ago, at 15 per cent.

Let us now look at the disaggregate figures of the annual growth rate in Tables A1.1 and A1.2 and Figures A1.9 to A1.16 in the Appendix.

As data on Afghanistan is limited, little can be said with any degree of authority. Economic growth in Afghanistan has historically been characterized by large volatility. It is a region that has been plagued by war and insurgency. Much of this is local—small tribal chiefs fighting for turf and citizen control; but it has also been the theatre of global politics, with the United States and Russia fighting proxy wars on its soil. We know that agriculture recorded small negative growth, and industry and services have grown slowly. Unfortunately, no serial data is available (in English at least) on manufacturing separately. Despite the war in the area, according to the data of the United Nations Economic and Social Commission for Asia and the

Pacific (UNESCAP) in Table A1.3, since 1996, trade, transport, and finance have shown a sharp growth spike, with annual growth rates of well over 5 per cent. The high average growth in each of these three sectors is, however, associated with great volatility and year-to-year fluctuations.

One has to be careful in interpreting the Bangladesh data (Table A1.1). The World Bank often gives data from 1960, but Bangladesh was only created in 1971. So the data for 1960 to 1971 pertains to East Pakistan. This means that there is a huge break in the middle of the series—the formation of the country itself, with all its political implications. With this in mind, agriculture has grown in Bangladesh at an (arithmetic) average of 2 per cent since 1960. The standard deviation of this series is 4 per cent. Manufacturing has grown at an (arithmetic) average of nearly 6 per cent. This series displays large volatility, with a standard deviation of almost 14 per cent. The service sector has grown at an (arithmetic) average of 4 per cent; the standard deviation of this series is 3 per cent. Thus, overall since 1960, agriculture and services have fared poorly compared to the industry sector. Looking at the last decade, however (since 1995), the service sector seems to have done consistently better, with an (arithmetic) average of over 5 per cent and a standard deviation of under 1 per cent.

Within the manufacturing sector, from 1995 to 2001, large-scale manufacturing has grown at an arithmetic average of 5 per cent, and small-scale manufacturing has grown at an arithmetic average of 6 per cent. The fast-growing industry sectors of the last decade are apparel, pharmaceuticals, and iron and steel, growing at an (arithmetic) average, respectively, of 14 per cent, 8 per cent, and 12 per cent between 1994 and 2001.[14] Several scholars have analysed this growth in the manufacturing sector in the last 20 years, looking for its sources. Salim (2003) uses firm-level data of the food manufacturing sector and concludes that it was the input growth that accounted for the output growth in most sectors, and not an increase in total factor productivity. The results of Hossain and Karunaratne (2004), using manufacturing data of Bangladesh from 1978 to 1994, show that the overall technical efficiency of the manufacturing sector and the

[14] Authors' calculations from the *Statistical Yearbook of Bangladesh* (2002) from series GDP of Bangladesh by broad activity categories at constant 1995/96 prices.

technical efficiencies of the majority of the individual industries have increased over time. Within the service sector, transport, storage, communication, and trade have done relatively well since 1995. The data of the last few years in Table A1.4 show that the other service sectors, such as hotels and restaurants, financial intermediation, public administration, education, health, community services, and personal services, have been booming.

In Bhutan, manufacturing represents 7.4 per cent of GDP. The Bhutan manufacturing industry is dominated by cement production, food processing, and wood and paper products, and consists of a small number of major operators. Besides these, there are a number of other small manufacturing plants in the food processing sector and cottage industry.[15] The growth rate series of manufacturing (Table A1.2) of the last 20 years has been very volatile. In recent times, average growth has been just short of 5 per cent in the manufacturing sector. The tertiary or services sector represents 40.3 per cent of GDP. The main growth within this sector has been in hotel and restaurants, wholesale trade and transport, storage, and communication, and to a certain extent in finance.[16]

Continuing with India, the largest country in South Asia, it is clear from Table A1.1 that the growth rate of the agricultural sector has been extremely volatile. Despite the fact that the figures of the last few years do not seem structurally different than the growth figures of the previous decades, there is talk of an agrarian crisis in India. This is caused by declining public investments in agriculture (a trend that started in the early 1980s); the decline in agriculture as a share of the GDP, associated with relatively little reallocation of employment; the fact that poverty in India is a predominantly rural phenomenon; and the rise in farmer suicides, mainly in the states of Karnataka, Andhra Pradesh, and Maharashtra (Vaidyanathan 2006). As we have discussed elsewhere (Basu and Maertens 2007), the industry series for India seems at first sight to be quite volatile. According to Balakrishnan and Parameswaran (2006), the manufacturing series exhibits three structural breaks. The first negative structural break occurred in the mid-1960s. The second structural break, which was positive, took place in 1982–3, and the third structural break, which was negative,

[15] *Bhutan Statistical Yearbook 2005*; figures from 2004.

[16] *Bhutan Statistical Yearbook 2005*; figures from 2004.

happened in 1994–5. They interpret these figures as evidence against the hypothesis that manufacturing had led the acceleration in the GDP growth rate at the beginning of the 1980s. Virmani (2004), however, reaches the opposite conclusion: 'This (analysis) shows that the growth rate of manufacturing accelerated after 1980–81. This contributed to the acceleration of the rate of growth of GDP from 1981.' From Table A1.7 in the appendix, one can see that the fastest-growing sectors within the manufacturing industry over the last 10 years in India are beverages, tobacco and related products, machinery and equipment other than transport, and rubber, plastic, petroleum, and coal products.

The source of the recent (post-reform) growth (or lack of growth) in the manufacturing and industry sector in general has been the subject of debate in India. According to Kalirajan and Shashanka (2004), growth in the manufacturing sector in the late 1990s is input-driven rather than efficiency driven, with significant levels of technical inefficiency. Bosworth et al. (2007) come to a similar conclusion. According to them, the total factor productivity growth of industry is slowing down, not accelerating, during the post-reform period. They conclude that 'these results are disappointing in light of the attention that has been devoted to the on-going liberalization of the trade and regulatory regimes for goods production'. Their conclusions related to manufacturing are very similar to the ones for industry as a whole. They, among others, thereby seem to provide counter-evidence to the studies of Ahluwalia (1995) and Unel (2003), who claim that manufacturing experienced a surge of productivity in the 1990s. Goldar and Mitra (2002) take the more skeptical line that these differences in findings can be attributed to a variety of measurement issues. Recent work of, for instance, Falk (2005), using firm-level data instead of national data, indicates that the labour and capital productivity estimates of recent years vary by industry and by the financial health of the individual firms.

Finally, let us look at the service sector figures for India.[17] Table A1.1 shows that since the 1980s, services have shown a more consistent higher annual growth rate than the industrial and the agricultural sectors of the economy. Bosworth et al. (2007) show that

[17] For surveys of the recent performance of the services sector in India, see Singh (2006) and Chanda (2007).

according to their growth accounting analysis, this increase in the growth rate is mainly due to an increase in total factor productivity. This is rather puzzling as services are normally considered an area of limited productivity growth. They suggest a number of explanations for this phenomenon, such as an incorrect measurement of the prices in the service industry. Srinivasan (2005) similarly suggests that the higher wages in the public sector might be driving spurious increasing total factor productivity.

In a recent essay, Playforth and Schundeln (2007) put forth the interesting hypothesis that, thanks to the attractiveness of the government sector, many educated Indians have chosen to enter this sector, and because the government is not a very productive sector, education in India has not yielded the level of benefit that it could potentially have done. While this sounds eminently plausible, and they back it up with substantial statistical evidence, it is possible to argue that this 'reservoir of education' that the state sector provided was a blessing in disguise. It was the presence of the state sector—productive or not—that made it attractive for middle- and lower-middle-class Indians to acquire education (since that was the only way to get those jobs). When the Indian economy took off in the early 1990s, and then the demand for educated labour in the corporate sector surged, especially over the last three or four years, the surge was not stymied by a lack of educated labour force, precisely because the state sector turned out to be the grand reservoir where the educated people were effectively 'human capital in waiting'. The new corporate entrepreneurs could simply draw on this.[18]

According to Table A1.6, the best performers in the service sector in India during the last 10 years are banking, insurance, and

[18] There is also plenty of anecdotal evidence of this. From the 1960s up to the mid-1990s, the Delhi School of Economics (DSE) produced a steady stream of around 120 graduates with a master's degree in economics. And throughout this period, around 350 students took the admissions test to get into the DSE. For graduating students, the targets were roughly the same. The best five to ten wanted to complete a PhD and become an academic, and the rest strove to get government jobs or teaching jobs in colleges (which are also to a certain degree government jobs). The change over the last 10 years is nothing short of dramatic. Roughly the same number (120) graduate each year, but virtually all seek and get corporate jobs, which pay a much higher salary than the government, and some 1,500 students now take the admissions test. There are complaints that the government and teaching institutions are suddenly understaffed.

communication. One of the industries in the service sector that is doing particularly well is software. Indeed, in the popular press, India's booming economy is often associated with the software sector. While this sector has seen an impressive growth in production and exports throughout the 1990s, it still only accounted for 3.7 per cent of the GDP in India in 2005–6 (see Table 5.5). Even though the software sector has never been subject to the many regulations and licenses that other sectors were (Forbes 2002), the recent growth should still be partially attributed to the policy changes of the 1990s (see Murthy 2004). Today, FDI of up to 100 per cent is permitted in all information technology units set up exclusively for exports, and automatic approval is available for foreign equity in software and almost all areas of electronics (Panagariya 2004). In addition, the dependence of software production on the abundant pool of qualified engineers, and the dependence of trade in software on telecommunications infrastructure, rather than on standard infrastructure such as roads and railway transportation, has provided the necessary conditions for the current growth of the industry. Given that success in the software industry depends crucially on reputation (Banerjee and Duflo 2000), one might expect that the Indian software industry, having built a strong reputation, will continue to grow at

TABLE 5.5: Software Production and Exports, 1996–2006

	Software exports (million US$)	*Software production (million US$)*	*Software production as a percentage of GDP*
1996–7	1099	1775	0.46
1997–8	982	2683	0.65
1998–9	2600	3777	0.91
1999–2000	3958	5619	1.24
2000–1	6206	8263	1.79
2001–2	7653	9933	2.08
2002–3	9526	12294	2.43
2003–4	12674	16210	2.70
2004–5	17845	22683	3.27
2005–6	23310	29286	3.67

Sources: Ministry of Information Technology, Annual Report 2005–2006 and previous editions. Exchange rate and GDP (current prices) used for conversions and calculations of column 3 from the Reserve Bank of India.

impressive rates in the future. But to have a major impact on the whole economy, this growth would have to be quite large (Rodrik and Subramanian 2004).

Let us continue our discussion with one of the smallest countries, the Maldives. From Table A1.2 we can see that agricultural growth in the Maldives has been volatile, with a high of 14.7 per cent in 1985, and low of –50 per cent in 1984, and a low overall (arithmetic) average of around 2 per cent per annum. The manufacturing and service sectors each have an (arithmetic) average of 10 per cent. Growth in both sectors has declined in the last few years; both series since 1995 have an (arithmetic) average of 6 per cent. From Table A1.8, we observe that government administration and transport and communications are booming, and that financial services are also doing relatively well. In the case of Maldives, special attention should be given to the tourism sector. In 2003, it comprised 31.2 per cent of GDP (Yahya et al. 2005). Tourism has shown positive growth in all years except 2005, presumably a result of the 2004 tsunami.

In Nepal, the manufacturing and service sector growth rates have been lower in the last 10 years compared to the average of the entire series from the 1970s (see Table A1.2). Since 1995, manufacturing output has grown at an (arithmetic) average of 3 per cent per year, while services have grown at a slightly higher rate. Within the service sector, transport, communication, and storage have grown very rapidly since 1995 (see Table A1.9). According to the analysis of Kishor, Sisara, and Okzkowski (2002), productivity growth in the manufacturing sector was negative before and after the reforms of the 1980s, but there was some improvement in the latter period. Higher productivity growth took place in industries with relatively large-scale production and foreign investment.

In Pakistan, growth of the agricultural sector has been equally volatile. The series shown in Table A1.1 has an (arithmetic) average of 3.8 per cent and a standard deviation of 3.8 per cent. The manufacturing series has an (arithmetic) average of almost 7 per cent, and a standard deviation of 3.5 per cent. The service sector series has an (arithmetic) average of 6 per cent and a standard deviation of 3 per cent. Within the service sector, the finance and insurance sector, and the community, social, and personal sector, have shown the highest (arithmetic) average growth (around 6 per cent each). Within the industrial sector, vegetable ghee, cooking oil, liquids, cement, trucks, billets, shuttles, motor tires, electric household appliances, and paints are all among the fast-growing industries (see Table A1.10).

In Sri Lanka, manufacturing and services both have shown an (arithmetic) average growth of 5 per cent since the 1960s (Table A1.1). In the last 10 years (since 1995), the growth has been a consistent 5–6 per cent. From Table A1.11, it appears that it is mainly the factory industry and small industry that is responsible for the manufacturing growth of the last decade. Within the service sector, post and telecommunications are booming, and financial services are also doing relatively well. In Embuldeniva's (2000) analysis of the effects of the reforms initiated in 1977 on large-scale industry in Sri Lanka,[19] he observes that in Sri Lanka, large-scale companies began a process of diversification starting in the late 1970s.

Population and Employment

While we have discussed growth—overall and sectoral—at length, we are acutely aware that growth is important only instrumentally, for what it can confer on the people and in particular on the poor and the most disadvantaged in society. In this essay we are particularly concerned with the labouring classes, who are typically at the bottom end of the economy. This is not to deny that there are the aged poor, the disabled, the homeless widows, and others who may be even poorer than those who are lucky enough to be labourers. Nevertheless, in most societies the workers constitute the lower end of the income scale, and their well-being is a reasonable indicator of what is happening to the poor.

Before we can study the policy options open to the South Asian governments for creating more productive employment and, more generally, enhancing worker welfare, it is important to take stock of the facts of the employment situation in the South Asian economies. Let us begin by taking a cursory look at the statistics of the economically active population in Tables 5.6 and 5.7. According to the ILO, the 'economically active population', which includes the 'usually active'

[19] The reforms of 1977 went far beyond sectoral and macroeconomic policies, and heralded a shift away from the social welfare system that Sri Lanka had used for a long time with large positive benefits for its standard of living indicators. The newly elected government cited fiscal strain as the reason to dismantle this system (see Sen 1988; Basu 1990).

and 'currently active' (the 'currently active' is also known as 'the labour force'), comprises all persons who furnish the supply of labour for the production of economic goods. The 'economic activity rate' is, therefore, the economically active population as a percentage of the total population. Due to issues with comparability among the different countries, we decided to refrain from stating the averages for South Asia as a whole. From Table 5.6, one can see that the economic activity rate in South Asia fluctuates around 40 per cent. In fact, the rate has not changed much in the last 20 years.[20] The economic activity rate in 2000 varied from a low of 37 per cent in Pakistan to a high of 52 per cent in Bangladesh. In the United States and China, this rate is, respectively, 51 per cent and 60 per cent.

TABLE 5.6: Economic Activity Rate in South Asia (1980–2000)

	1980	*1990*	*1995*	*2000*
Afghanistan	42.76	40.54	42.6	42.01
Bangladesh	47.13	46.15	49.5	52.83
Bhutan	51.5	49.97	48.95	47.98
India	43.58	42.45	43.28	44.37
Maldives	47.06	41.15	40.62	40.50
Nepal	48.47	46.47	46.13	46.42
Pakistan	35.42	35.64	36.33	37.46
Sri Lanka	36.82	40.16	41.84	43.88

Source: International Labour Organization estimates from UNSTATS Series 4270. Economic activity rate by sex, 13 age groups, 1950–2010.

Table 5.7 shows the economic activity rate by gender. South Asia appears to be a region with a large gender differential. While in the United States the gap between males and females is only 11 per cent, in the South Asian countries, this gap is over 20 per cent for all countries except the Maldives, where the gap is only 9 per cent.

[20] Assuming that labour force equals employed population (and therefore ignoring the unemployment rate), one could algebraically decompose the growth in GDP/capita in two terms: labour productivity growth and a (weighted) term of growth in the ratio of working population over population. Seeing that the latter ratio has not changed much, one could conclude that the observed GDP/capita growth of the last 20 years in South Asia must be mainly due to labour productivity growth.

In China, the economic activity rate for is 56 per cent for women and 64 per cent for men. The relatively low economic activity rate of women in South Asia versus East Asia is due to a different population structure and low female labour market participation. Recall that the age dependency ratio for South Asia is 62 per cent. In comparison, the figure for China is 40 per cent.[21] In addition, in China more than 90 per cent of the women in the age group 20 to 50 years participate in the labour market. For India, this figure fluctuates around 40 to 45 per cent.[22]

Table 5.8 presents the employment shares by sector in the three broad categories—agriculture, industry, and services. This data comes from three main sources, the *World Development Indicators*, the *Key*

TABLE 5.7: Economic Activity Rate in South Asia by Gender (1980–2000)

		1980	*1990*	*1995*	*2000*
Afghanistan	Men	54.37	51.84	54.12	52.93
Afghanistan	Women	30.53	28.5	30.46	30.57
Bangladesh	Men	52.74	52.51	55.84	59.27
Bangladesh	Women	41.15	39.41	42.8	46.04
Bhutan	Men	61.93	60.21	58.77	57.37
Bhutan	Women	40.93	39.61	39.02	38.48
India	Men	55.77	56.52	57.22	58.22
India	Women	30.5	27.4	28.39	29.59
Maldives	Men	55.49	46.78	45.66	44.96
Maldives	Women	37.72	35.22	35.3	35.77
Nepal	Men	57.94	55.03	54.35	54.51
Nepal	Women	38.53	37.79	37.73	38.11
Pakistan	Men	52.16	52.15	51.77	51.85
Pakistan	Women	16.91	17.8	19.78	22.13
Sri Lanka	Men	52.83	52.77	54.23	56.20
Sri Lanka	Women	20.18	27.53	29.6	31.81

Source: ILO estimates from UNSTATS series 4270, Economic activity rate by sex, 13 age groups, 1950–2010.

[21] *World Development Indicators 2007*. Data from 2006.

[22] ILO estimates from UNSTATS series 4270. Economic activity rate by sex, 13 age groups, 1950–2010.

Table 5.8: Employment Shares by Sector in South Asia (1960–2006)

Afghanistan

% of employment	*1960*	*1965*	*1970*	*1975*	*1980*	*1985*	*1990*	*1995*	*2000*	*2002*
Agriculture	–	–	–	–	73	–	70	–	–	82
Industry	–	–	–	–	10	–	11	–	–	6
Services	–	–	–	–	18	–	19	–	–	–

Sources: For 1980 and 1990: ILO, *KILM*, 2003; for 2002: *Afghanistan Statistical Yearbook*, 2005.

Bangladesh

% of employment	*1960*	*1965*	*1970*	*1975*	*1980*	*1985*	*1990*	*1996*	*2000*	*2003*
Agriculture	–	–	–	–	48	58	66	63	62	52
Industry	–	–	–	–	33	12	13	10	10	14
Services	–	–	–	–	19	26	16	25	24	35

Sources: For 1985–2003: *WDI 2008*; for 1980: *Census at a Glance Bangladesh*, 2007.

Bhutan

% of employment	*1960*	*1965*	*1970*	*1975*	*1980*	*1985*	*1990*	*1995*	*2000*	*2004*
Agriculture	–	–	–	–	95	–	94	–	–	63
Industry	–	–	–	–	1	–	7	–	–	10
Services	–	–	–	–	4	–	5	–	–	27

Sources: For 1980 and 1990: ILO, *KILM*, 2003; for 2004: *Bhutan Statistical Yearbook*, 2005.

(contd ...)

Table 5.8 (contd ...)

India

% of employment	1960	1965	1970	1975	1980	1985	1990	1995	2000	2006
Agriculture	–	–	–	–	–	–	69	67	–	–
Industry	–	–	–	–	–	–	14	13	–	–
Services	–	–	–	–	–	–	17	20	–	–

Source: *WDI 2008*.

The Maldives

% of employment	1960	1965	1970	1975	1980	1985	1990	1995	2000	2006
Agriculture	–	–	–	–	–	–	25	22	14	11
Industry	–	–	–	–	–	–	22	24	19	24
Services	–	–	–	–	–	–	48	50	50	59

Sources: For 1990: *The 25 Years of Statistics, the Maldives*; for 1995, 2000: *WDI 2008*; for 2006: *Statistical Yearbook of the Maldives*, 2007.
Note: The figures of the Ministry of Planning and National Development do not add up to 100% due to a set of 'not stated' workers.

Nepal

% of employment	1960	1965	1970	1975	1981	1985	1990	1995	2001	2005
Agriculture	–	–	–	–	91	–	83	78	66	–
Industry	–	–	–	–	1	–	2	6	13	–
Services	–	–	–	–	8	–	14	21	20	–

Sources: For 1981: ILO, *KILM*, 2007. For 1990–5: *WDI 2008*; for 2001: *Statistical Yearbook of Nepal*, 2005.

(contd ...)

Table 5.8 (contd ...)

Pakistan

% of employment	1963	1965	1970	1974	1980	1985	1990	1995	2000	2005
Agriculture	60	59	58	55	53	51	51	47	48	43
Industry	15	18	19	18	20	20	20	18	18	20
Services	24	24	23	27	27	29	29	35	34	36

Sources: For 1980–2000: *WDI 2008*; other years: *Handbook of Statistics of the Pakistan Economy*, 2005.

Sri Lanka

% of employment	1960	1965	1970	1975	1981	1985	1990	1995	1998	2003
Agriculture	–	–	–	–	46	49	48	37	42	34
Industry	–	–	–	–	19	19	21	23	22	23
Services	–	–	–	–	29	28	30	34	33	39

Source: *WDI 2008*.

Indicators of the Labour Market of the ILO, and the yearbooks of the respective countries. The original sources of all data are the labour force surveys and censuses of the respective countries.

From Table 5.8, we can see that, from the point of view of employment and location of the labour force, all the South Asian countries except Sri Lanka and the Maldives, are still largely agrarian societies. In Sri Lanka, 34 per cent of the population was located in the agricultural sector in 2003. In the Maldives, this percentage was 14 in 2000. Services clearly is the major employer in the Maldives, with 59 per cent of the workforce employed in that sector in 2006.

The most agricultural society in South Asia is Afghanistan, where 82 per cent of the economically active population is in the agricultural sector. The industry sector represents only 6 per cent of the economically active population.

Bangladesh in 2000 and Bhutan in 2004 had similar structures. The employment shares of agriculture, industry, and services were approximately 60 per cent, 10 per cent, and 25 per cent, respectively. The structure of employment is changing rapidly in both countries though, and in 2003 the employment shares of agriculture, industry, and services in Bangladesh were, respectively, 52 per cent, 14 per cent and 35 per cent.

In India, the shares of agriculture, industry, and services in employment in 1995 (the most recent years for which figures were available) were, respectively, 67 per cent, 13 per cent, and 20 per cent.

It must be noted, however, that the sectoral employment shares can be calculated directly from the National Sample Survey (NSS) data.[23] Table 5.9 presents the employment shares of the 55th round of the NSS in India. In rural India, around 70 per cent of the usually employed people worked in the agricultural sector. In urban India, the majority of usually employed people, or around 60 per cent, worked in the tertiary sector.

In Nepal, the employment shares of industry and services were, respectively, 13 per cent and 18 per cent (in 2001). Compared to the situation in 1980, the employment share of agriculture had declined drastically, from 91 per cent to 66 per cent.

[23] As such, a time series of almost yearly data since the mid-1950s of employment shares could be calculated.

TABLE 5.9: Employment Shares in India (2004–5)
(in %)

	Urban		*Rural*	
	Male	*Female*	*Male*	*Female*
Primary	6.6	17.7	71.4	85.4
Secondary	32.8	29.3	12.6	8.9
Tertiary	60.6	53.0	16.1	5.7

Source: Authors' calculation based on the *Handbook of Statistics on the Indian Economy 2006*, Table 173.

In Pakistan in 2005, 43 per cent of the population worked in the agricultural sector, 20 per cent in the industrial sector (almost all in industry), and 36 per cent worked in services. From an employment perspective, Pakistan, and even Bangladesh, are less agricultural societies than their larger neighbour, India.

Table 5.10 shows the labour productivity growth rates of several selected countries. One has to be careful when interpreting these figures. First, international comparability is difficult: the PPP correction differs according to country, the labour unit in the denominator is sometimes labour force, sometimes the employed (and the self-employed are often not correctly integrated). Similarly, the number of working hours is not consistently defined over the different countries. In addition, different countries use various output GDP measures (at different prices).

Second, many processes can lead to increased labour productivity: increased efficiency of the workers themselves, increased use of other inputs, or a shift from less productive sectors to more productive sectors. Because there are so many caveats, we present these figures only because they are available and are often discussed. The aforementioned limitations have to be kept in mind when looking at some of the figures.

India's overall labour productivity growth stands at 3.4 per cent. The manufacturing labour productivity growth rate is 5.1 per cent, and the agricultural labour productivity growth rate is 1.7 per cent. The figures for China are, respectively, 5.3 per cent, 7.3 per cent, and 3.5 per cent. This seems to contradict a popular view that China's growth rate comes from its high savings and investment whereas for India, in relative terms, it is higher productivity that contributes to growth. One reason for the discrepancy is that Table 5.10

TABLE 5.10: Labour Productivity Growth Rates (1980–2003) in Selected Countries

Country	*Total Economy*		*Manufacturing*		*Agriculture, forestry, and fisheries*	*Transport and communications*	*Wholesale and retail trade, including hotels and restaurants*
	Value added per person employed	*Value added per hour worked*	*Value added per person employed*	*Value added per hour worked*	*Value added per person employed*	*Value added per person employed*	
Belgium	1.5	1.9	4.4	4.8	3.9	2.0	
United States	1.6	1.7	4.0	3.9	4.0	2.4	3.2
United Kingdom	1.9	2.3	4.7	5.0	3.0	3.8	2.3
Bangladesh	1.9				–0.7		
India[a]	3.4		5.1a		1.7	4.6	
Nepal					1.6		
Pakistan	2.6				1.9		
Sri Lanka	2.3				1.2		
China[b]	5.3		7.3b		3.5		
Kenya	–0.5				–0.8		
Ghana	0.6				–0.6		
Tanzania	0.1				1.7		

Source: International Labour Organization, *Key Indicators of the Labour Market,* 2006, Figure 18A.
Note: [a] 1990–2002; [b] 1980–99.

considers a time period in the middle of which India's big growth surge takes place, whereas China's growth surge coincides fully with the table's time period. We must consider the jury to be out on this.

A conceptual instrument that is widely used by economists for linking aggregate production to employment is 'employment elasticity'. Essentially, 'employment elasticity' is a number (in particular, a ratio) that describes how employment growth varies with growth in economic output. An elasticity of 1 implies that every 1 percentage point of GDP growth is associated with a 1 percentage point increase in employment. The usefulness of employment elasticities for understanding the labour market and even providing policy recommendations is not beyond criticism. The main critique concerns causality and the use of this instrument to predict how many jobs will be created with growth. Any employment elasticity that we calculate simply tells us what happened in the past. It does not tell us that there is a fundamental and unchanging relation between output increases and new jobs. The relation between jobs and output is mediated by a variety of variables, and shifts in these can cause the nature of the relation to change. The decision of producers to use more or less labour, and what kind of labour to use, depends on many aspects of the economy, such as prevailing prices, laws, and regulations. As such, using employment elasticities to predict future employment generation is a risky enterprise.

Also, linking elasticities to the welfare of the people at the bottom end also poses risks. Assuming that the population equals the employed labour force, there exists an algebraic relationship between elasticity and labour productivity growth, but one needs to be careful in interpreting this link. Low elasticity and high labour productivity growth does not necessarily imply high average labour productivity, high wages, or welfare.

The fault lies not in the concept of elasticity, but in the user who tries to get more out of it than can be theoretically justified. Clearly, employment elasticities have to be used with handsome doses of common sense and economic intuition.

With these caveats in mind, let us turn to definitions. Employment elasticities can be calculated in two ways. One could calculate the arc-elasticity between two points in time using the following definition:

$$\varepsilon = \frac{\frac{\Delta L}{L}}{\frac{\Delta Y}{Y}},$$

where L refers to the amount of labour used, Y to the level of output produced and the variable in front of a variable refers to a change in the value of that variable. Alternatively, one could run a regression with the natural logarithm of labour as the left-hand variable and the natural logarithm of output as the right hand variable. The coefficient associated with the logarithm of the output is the so-called 'point elasticity of employment'.

Both methods have problems. The first one, since it entails averaging over discrete changes, often results in wide variations in employment elasticities for the same countries for different periods

TABLE 5.11: Employment Elasticities and Average Annual GDP Growth

	Employment elasticities			*Average annual GDP growth*		
	1991–5	*1995–9*	*1999–2003*	*1991–5*	*1995–9*	*1999–2003*
World	0.34	0.38	0.30	2.9	3.6	3.5
Developed Economies and EU	0.25	0.34	0.21	2.2	3.1	2.1
Central and Eastern Europe (non-EU)	0.28	0.21	0.10	–7.8	0.5	6.2
East Asia	0.14	0.14	0.18	11.6	7.4	7.7
Southeast Asia and the Pacific	0.39	0.20	0.42	7.4	1.6	4.8
South Asia	0.40	0.49	0.36	6.0	5.8	5.1
Latin America and the Caribbean	0.64	0.68	0.41	3.4	2.8	1.4
Middle East and North Africa	0.66	1.01	0.70	3.1	3.7	4.3
SSA	0.73	0.82	0.53	1.1	3.2	3.2

Source: International Labour Organization, *Key Indicators of the Labour Market*, 2006, Box 19a.

of time as *Y* fluctuates. The second method requires a times series and assumes no structural change in the economy during the period for which the regression is run, and as such provides an average point-elasticity. Despite these limitations, employment elasticities can give useful information about the structure of the economy, as long as we are careful not to take the numbers too literally and are prepared to moderate the analysis with common sense.

Table 5.11 gives the employment elasticities of different regions of the world together with the average GDP growth.[24] The current average employment elasticity in the world is 0.30. For the developed economies and the EU, this number is 0.21, and for South Asia this is 0.42. The employment elasticity of the developed economies and the EU falls between the employment elasticity of SSA, one of the poorest regions in the world, and East Asia.

Table 5.12 shows the sectoral employment elasticities in the world for the period 1991–2003. From this table, one can see that economic growth in agriculture in South Asia has been relatively more employment intensive than in the world as a whole, and the elasticities are, respectively, 0.71 and 0.41. This is consistent with the figures in Table 5.10 that indicate that agriculture in India has indeed been a low (labour) productivity growth sector. In industry, economic growth has been less employment intensive compared to South Asia, Latin America, and SSA, but more intensive than East Asia. In the case of services, economic growth has been associated with less growth in employment than in East Asia, the developed economies, SSA, and South Asia. In fact, only Central and Eastern Europe and the CIS have an employment elasticity that is lower than that of South Asia, 0.25 versus 0.36. According to SAARC (2005) this low elasticity is associated with a low elasticity in the transport, storage, and communication sector, and the finance, insurance, and real estate sectors. It is through this last figure that one can see the growth–employment debate currently going on in South Asia. The concern is this: if service becomes the dominant sector of the economy, and this sector, judging by its employment elasticity, absorbs relatively little labour, would economic growth of this kind not result in jobless

[24] ILO calculates the employment elasticities using a multi-country regression with country dummy variables (see *Key Indicators of the Labour Market*, 2006: chapter 1A).

Table 5.12: Sectoral Employment Elasticities and Growth (1991–2003)

	Agriculture		*Industry*		*Services*	
	Elasticity	*VA growth*	*Elasticity*	*VA growth*	*Elasticity*	*VA growth*
World	0.41	2.0	0.28	2.1	0.57	3.0
Developed Economies and EU	–0.43	1.2	0.28	1.3	0.56	2.9
Central and Eastern Europe (non-EU) and CIS	–0.24	–0.1	0.29	–0.4	0.25	1.5
East Asia	0.23	3.7	0.06	12.5	0.50	8.8
Southeast Asia and the Pacific	0.20	2.1	0.68	5.4	0.99	4.6
South Asia	0.71	2.9	0.37	5.9	0.36	6.9
Latin American and the Caribbean	–0.32	2.5	0.51	2.2	1.04	2.7
Middle East and North Africa	1.06	3.3	0.35	2.0	0.73	4.4
SSA	0.82	2.3	0.90	2.0	0.79	2.8

Source: International Labour Organization, *Key Indicators of the Labour Market*, 2006, Box 19a.

growth? This is a genuine concern and, as we argue below, there is need for South Asian economies, and especially India, to level the playing field so as to enable manufacturing and industry to grow. Interestingly, the manufacturing sector in India, as it stands, does not have high employment elasticity either.[25] But it is arguable that the same policies (discussed below) that have thwarted the growth of the manufacturing sector impeded the growth of the labour-intensive parts of the manufacturing sector. Hence, correcting these policies should not only give rise to further industrial development, but lead to the more labour-intensive parts of the industrial and manufacturing sectors to grow.

Let us continue and look at the disaggregate figures of Table 5.13. Note that the figures for Afghanistan and the Maldives were not available through ILO. From Table 5.13, one can see that there is a lot of underlying diversity in South Asia. It seems that India and Pakistan, given their size, are driving the average figures of South Asia. In Sri Lanka, the service sector elasticity is negative. This, together with positive economic growth, implies that Sri Lanka faces negative employment growth in the service sector. The elasticities for the industrial sector in South Asia are all positive. In Nepal, however, this elasticity is larger than 1, implying employment growth but negative labour productivity growth.[26]

We conclude this section with comments on the unemployment situation in South Asia. In most developing countries, the unemployment rate, that is, the ratio of the unemployed to the total labour force, does not correctly reflect the actual situation in the labour markets. Underemployment also needs to be considered. Workers might be working fewer hours than they ideally would want to work.

Table 5.14 provides the latest summary statistics. From this table, one can see that the unemployment rate in India, Bangladesh, the

[25] The manufacturing employment elasticiticy of South Asia in the 1990s is estimated at 0.29. The manufacturing employment elasticity for India for the period is estimated at 0.33 for the period 1993/94–2000. Interestingly, East Asia had an employment elasticity of 0.48 in the 1980s and 0.01 in the 1990s, according to SAARC (2005, Regional Poverty Profile 2005, Poverty Reduction in South Asia through Productive Employment). It must be noted that SAARC elasticity estimates are quite different from the ILO estimates, again illustrating the difficulty of computing elasticities and cautioning us against over-interpretation.

[26] Again, assuming that the population equals the employed population.

Table 5.13: Sectoral Employment Elasticities and Growth in South Asia (1991–2003)

Country	*Agriculture employment to value added elasticity*	*Industry employment to value added elasticity*	*Services employment to value added elasticity*	*Agriculture value added growth*	*Industry value-added growth*	*Services value-added growth*	*Total GDP growth*
Bangladesh	0.35	0.51	0.03	3	7.2	4.9	4.9
Bhutan	0.59	0.47	0.40	3.4	9.9	7	6.8
India	0.78	0.27	0.41	2.8	6	7.7	6
Nepal	-0.64	3.05	1.60	2.6	5.5	5.3	4.3
Pakistan	0.69	0.65	0.37	3.4	4.2	4.5	3.8
Sri Lanka	2.67	0.04	-0.16	1.7	5.6	5.2	4.6

Source: International Labour Organization, *Key Indicators of the Labour Market*, 2006.

TABLE 5.14: Unemployment in South Asia (2000)

Country	*Year*	*Gender*	*Labour force (thousands)*	*Unemployed (thousands)*	*Unemployment rate*
Bangladesh	2000	MF	53512.0	1749.0	3.3
Bangladesh	2000	M	33452.0	1083.0	3.2
Bangladesh	2000	F	20060.0	666.0	3.3
India	2000	MF	346241.4	14858.7	4.3
India	2000	M	246992.9	10803.6	4.4
India	2000	F	99248.5	4055.1	4.1
Maldives	2000	MF	87.1	1.7	2.0
Maldives	2000	M	57.7	0.9	1.6
Maldives	2000	F	29.4	0.8	2.7
Nepal	1999	MF	9455.0	104.0	1.1
Nepal	1999	M	4800.0	72.0	1.5
Nepal	1999	F	4571.0	32.0	0.7
Pakistan	2002	MF	40207.0	3147.0	7.8
Pakistan	2002	M	33925.0	2117.0	6.2
Pakistan	2002	F	6282.0	1030.0	16.4
Sri Lanka	2003	MF	7805.3	701.1	9.0
Sri Lanka	2003	M	5245.0	324.2	6.2
Sri Lanka	2003	F	2560.4	376.6	14.7

Source: International Labour Organization, *Key Indicators of the Labour Market*, 2006, Table 8a.

Maldives, and Nepal is below 5 per cent. In Pakistan and Sri Lanka, the unemployment rates for men are around 6 per cent, and for women around 15 per cent.

Table 5.15 provides some more recent details on the unemployed population in the four most populous South Asian countries. In India, 27 per cent of the unemployed received education up to the primary level, 41 per cent up to the secondary level, and 32 per cent up to the tertiary level. In Bangladesh and Sri Lanka, about half of the unemployed received education up to the primary level. In Pakistan, the majority of the unemployed whose education status is known have received education up to the tertiary level.

It is evident that the overall employment situation in South Asia is much less optimistic than the growth statistics. Though there

TABLE 5.15: Details of the Unemployment Situation in South Asia

Country	*Year*	*Sex*	*Total unemployed ('000)*	*Less than one year of education (%)*	*Pre-primary (%)*	*Primary (%)*	*Secondary (%)*	*Tertiary (%)*	*Not defined (%)*
Bangladesh	2000	MF	1750	14.5		54.3	22.7	8.4	
Bangladesh	2000	M	1083	11.6		55.3	22.9	10.2	
Bangladesh	2000	F	666	19.1		52.9	22.4	5.7	
India	2003	MF	41389			27	41.1	31.9	
India	2003	M	30636			27.6	41.5	30.9	
India	2003	F	10752			25.3	40	34.7	
Pakistan	2002	MF	3506	44.9	3.5	14.7	12.3	24.1	0.5
Pakistan	2002	M	2381	35.7	4.5	17.1	15.4	26.8	0.5
Pakistan	2002	F	1125	64.4	1.4	9.7	5.6	18.5	0.4
Sri Lanka	2000	MF	497	0.2		49.7		49.9	
Sri Lanka	2000	M	241	0.4		61.4		38.2	
Sri Lanka	2000	F	256	0.0		39.1		60.9	

Source: International Labour Organization, *Key Indicators of the Labour Market*, 2006, Table 11.

have been some desirable changes, such as the 'feminization' of the labour force in Bangladesh (Mahmud 2003), or the decline in the dependency ratio in most nations, and especially India, the growth in jobs has not been commensurate with the growth of the economy. Indeed, critics have described the Indian economy as one of jobless growth. Even if this is a matter of debate, what is beyond dispute is that the employment in the organized manufacturing sector of the economy has been virtually stagnant since the early 1990s, hovering between 6 million and 6.4 million (Srinivasan 2007; see also Nagaraj 2004, Gokarn 2006). The stagnation is worrying, but equally worrying is that it is such a small number for a country of India's size. All this leads us to the inevitable question: What should be done?

Infrastructure and Institutions

Evidently, manufacturing needs a boost in all South Asian countries. But we know from past experience that this cannot be done through centralized planning, licenses, and decrees. Such interventions have, at best, no effect, and can lead to a proliferation of bureaucracy that can thwart productivity and take years to dismantle. The right way to approach this problem is to see if there are hurdles to the expansion of the manufacturing sector, remove the hurdles identified, and then let the economy take its course. The chances are, once the hurdles are removed, the industrial and manufacturing sectors will take off. And if they do not, then we simply have to brace for an unusual path to development. It has been much debated if the Indian economy could leapfrog the manufacturing phase that all developed nations go through before achieving prominence in services (Rakshit 2006). To us, this is a somewhat idle debate. We do not need to solve it. We simply have to analyse whether the playing field is level, put policies in place to level the humps and flatten out the slopes, and then sit back.

As it happens, the playing field is not level, and we can easily discern special hurdles with which the industrial and manufacturing sectors in the South Asian region have to contend. First and foremost is the problem of underdeveloped infrastructure and overdeveloped bureaucracy. This is something that is shared by all South Asian nations. The inadequacy of infrastructure—poor ports and roads, and undependable electricity supply—is easily visible and has been written about at length. A simple revealing piece of datum is that to move a garment from a factory in India to a store in New York

Table 5.16: Infrastructure in South Asia (Selected Indicators), 2005

	Roads, paved (% of total roads)	*Air transport-freight (million tons per km)*	*Rail lines (total route-km)*	*Broadband subscribers (per 1,000 people)*	*Population covered by mobile telephony (%)*	*Telephone subscribers*	*Personal computers (per 1,000 people)*
Bangladesh	9.5 (2003)	183.5	2855	–	80	10070000	11.86 (2004)
Bhutan	62 (2003)	0.25	–	–	–	70551	20.42
India	–	773.2	63465	1.187667	–	140000000	15.53
Maldives	–	0.01	–	6.3518	81 (2004)	185689	112.08 (2004)
Nepal	30.3 (2004)	7	59	–	–	697459	4.37 (2004)
Pakistan	64.7 (2004)	408	7791	0.286316	–	18048750	–
Afghanistan	23.6 (2004)	–	–	0.007367	–	1300000	–
Sri Lanka	81 (2003)	310.4	–	0.717031	85	4605768	27.21 (2004)

Source: *World Development Indicators 2007*.

takes on an average 30 days, whereas from East Asia it takes half that time.[27] This is caused in part by the bureaucracy involved in sending ship cargo but, more importantly, by the fact that because the ports are of poor quality and outdated, large liners cannot come to South Asia, and feeder vessels have to carry the goods to a mother vessel elsewhere, which then sets sail to the United States.

Table 5.16 presents some of the key indicators on the infrastructure facilities in the South Asian countries (see also Siddiqui 2007). In India, Pakistan, and Bangladesh, the railway systems are relatively well-developed. In Bhutan, the Maldives, and Afghanistan, no functional railway system has been developed. Transportation of goods happens almost entirely via roads, which, particularly in Afghanistan, are of poor quality.

Inadequate infrastructure and overzealous bureaucracy adversely affect all sectors, but especially manufacturing and large-scale agriculture. Many of the service industries can leapfrog over the bureaucratic and infrastructural hurdles. New software does not have to wait at ports to be shipped abroad, it can be sent electronically. Many of the financial services likewise can prosper even if the infrastructure is inadequate and bureaucracy malicious. This could well be a reason why India, and to a certain extent Bangladesh, have done well in services but not in manufacturing and large-scale agriculture.[28]

The burden of bureaucracy is well-documented by the World Bank in its 'Doing Business' data (see Table A1.14 in the appendix). This indicator ranks economies in terms of their 'ease of business', from 1 to 175, with 1 referring to the best. This index averages the country's per centile rankings on 10 categories, giving equal weight to each category. Each category averages the country's per centile rankings on different subcategories. We reproduce some of this here, in Table 5.17, and it is immediately evident that the South Asian countries, except for the Maldives, do not do well. The average rank for high-income countries is 27. India and Bhutan score worst on the 'starting

[27] These numbers were obtained by one of us (Basu) from a conversation with Sudhir Dhingra, CEO of one of India's largest textile and apparel companies, Orient Craft, in Gurgaon, outside of New Delhi, and were reported in http://news.bbc.co.uk/2/hi/south_asia/4294679.stm.

[28] For accounts from the horse's mouth of India's software services sector and manufacturing, and the successes and failures of these sectors, see Murthy (2004), Bharat-Ram (2007), and Tata (2007).

a business' rank. South Asia (except for the Maldives) overall does not do well in dealing with licenses, with India and Bhutan being the worst performers.

From the time taken to start a business, through the difficulties of enforcing a contract, to the time taken to close an insolvent business, the burdens are huge. At one level, cutting bureaucracy, unlike building a new port or power plant, is costless. At the same time, this is very hard politically. It entails stepping on vested interests and taking away what people may have come to view as entitlements. In some ways, it is easier to deal with what may be expensive, but does not entail political hurdles. It is not the aim of this essay to detail how to de-bureaucratize a system and improve governance, but to emphasize the importance of this. Given that India has been growing so rapidly despite the impediments of its bureaucratic system is reason for hope. It can get a lot of further mileage, virtually without cost, simply by dismantling some of these bureaucratic hurdles. This is true for all of South Asia—poor governance and bureaucracy continue to be a major growth hurdle (see Haque 2006, in the context of Pakistan).

Building up infrastructure is a different kind of problem. Here the main stumbling block is money. The need for better infrastructure is self-evident in all South Asian nations. But how rapidly a country should strive to improve infrastructure will vary from one nation to another. Much will depend on the nation's fiscal position and the ability of its finance ministry to shoulder the financial burden. The other important determinant involves forecasting the future of the economy. Any infrastructural investment entails sinking money into the projects without immediate returns.

Take the case of a new or upgraded airport. This is a hugely expensive investment. Whether in retrospect this will be called a good investment will depend on how actively the airport is used once it has been built or revamped, and how much money it generates. And from this it is immediately obvious that much depends on the future demand for that particular investment. In that respect, there is always an element of gambling involved in making an infrastructural investment.

History is replete with examples of investments that, in retrospect, were wrong. In the early part of the last century, the world's largest airport was Gander in Newfoundland, Canada, on the Atlantic. Gander International Airport was opened in 1938 and rapidly

TABLE 5.17: Selected Doing Business Indicators, South Asia

	Afghanistan	*Bangladesh*	*Bhutan*	*India*	*Maldives*	*Nepal*	*Pakistan*	*Sri Lanka*
Total Rank	162	88	138	134	53	100	74	89
Starting a Business Rank	17	68	79	88	31	49	54	44
Procedures (number)	3	8	10	11	5	7	11	8
Time (days)	8	37	62	35	13	31	24	50
Dealing with Licenses Rank	–	67	145	155	9	127	89	71
Procedures (number)	–	13	26	20	10	15	12	17
Time (days)	–	185	204	270	118	424	218	167
Employing Workers Rank	74	75	116	112	5	150	126	98
Difficulty of Hiring Index	67	11	78	33	0	67	78	0
Rigidity of Hours Index	40	40	40	20	0	20	20	20
Difficulty of Firing Index	30	40	0	70	0	70	30	60
Rigidity of Employment Index	46	30	39	41	0	52	43	27
Non-wage Labour Cost (% of salary)	0.0	0.0	1.0	16.8	0.0	10.0	12.0	15.0
Firing Costs (weeks of wages)	4.3	51.0	94.7	55.9	8.7	90.0	90.0	177.7
Getting Credit Rank	174	48	159	65	143	101	65	101
Enforcing Contracts Rank	165	174	56	173	83	105	163	90
Procedures (number)	–	50	34	56	28	28	55	20
Time (days)	1.642	1.442	275	1.42	665	590	880	837
Closing a Business Rank	151	93	151	133	114	95	46	59
Time (years)	No practice	4.0	No practice	10.0	6.7	5.0	2.8	2.2
Cost (% of estate)	No practice	8.0	No practice	9.0	4.0	9.0	4.0	18.0

Source: Doing Business 2006—online World Bank.

expanded in the belief that, since trans-Atlantic flights were bound to increase, and since of course no aircraft could cross the Atlantic between the United States and Europe without having to do a refuelling stop, the demand for this airport would be large and growing. The success of the Gander investment seemed certain. The fly in the ointment was the unanticipated development of jet aircrafts with long-range flight capacity in the 1960s. And the demand for Gander International Airport rapidly waned. In retrospect, it was not a good investment.

One has to be careful in what one makes of this 'Gander dilemma'. Most South Asian economies have erred on the side of caution, so it is easy for these governments to point to the Gander experience and shy away from investment. That would of course be wrong. One has to make a measured judegment, using the best available information about whether an investment is worthwhile. Of course, some will go sour, but that fear must not freeze into permanent inaction.

Based on the economic situation in the South Asian nations that we have described above, we feel it is certainly time for India to make aggressive infrastructural investments, and perhaps also for Pakistan and Bangladesh.[29] From the growth spurt that has occurred over the last 15 years or so, and the particularly sharp growth over the last four years, along with the good press coverage that India is receiving internationally, there is reason to expect that the international demand for goods and services from India will continue to grow, at least for some years. So it seems worthwhile for India to borrow money to invest in infrastructure that will make it easier for the country to respond to this heightened demand. It is true that the new fiscal responsibility law prevents the Indian government from running up large deficits, but that is only on the revenue account. It is feasible for the government to run up a large capital account deficit, and we believe that at this stage of buoyancy, it is worthwhile for India to do so. Major investments in ports, rail freight carrying capacity, roads, and power should yield large dividends within the next five to 10 years. This may cause some interim inflationary pressures, but monetary instruments can be used to hold these down. Also, the great

[29] A recent study from Pakistan (Ghani and Din 2006) shows that investment has a positive impact on growth; but, while this is clear and significant for private investment, that is not the case with public investment.

revenue boom that the Finance Ministry has had over the last three years means that there is money to spare, and this should be directed disproportionately to investment (see Chidambaram 2007).

Pakistan and Bangladesh should also step up infrastructural investment, but they need to be more cautious. Their growth has been high, but not as high as India's, and their fiscal buoyancy has not been as great. So they face a bigger risk that, after the investment is undertaken, there will not be enough demand for the new facilities. So the risk of being unable to earn back the investment seems to be higher. Nevertheless, the prognosis for both these economies is very good, and using greater investment to leverage this is a good idea.

Alongside these changes, there must be ongoing efforts to hone the institutions of governance and law in these nations. If government can play one role, that of enforcer of contracts, efficiently and at a low cost, much of the problems of development would be taken care of by ordinary people and businesses. The mortgage market is a good example. To have it flourish, we do not need government to provide mortgages, but to provide the institutions and rule of law that enable such a market. This means enabling the courts to enforce mortgage contracts and recover money without large costs. As the boom in India's mortgage market shows, once these institutions are in place, the private sector can provide the actual money. But once again, like curtailing bureaucracy, installing good institutions is easier said than done. Our aim here is merely to flag the importance of this.

Labour Market Policies

In matters of labour market reform, South Asia is a varied place, with needs that differ substantially across the nations. As already mentioned, most of the nations started from a shared history, but have tended to go their own ways, changing or choosing to stay with the laws inherited from a colonial or feudal past. While laws can be altered, customs and culture are often more bound by inertia. So the 'culture' of labour is arguably more similar across all the South Asian nations than the laws, which are remarkably distinct. Culture is important and needs to be researched more. Hence, our focus here is primarily on the laws and the regulatory frameworks of labour.

The big changes that are needed on this score are in India, since the other nations have made many of the necessary alterations already. The most controversial piece of labour legislation is the Industrial

Disputes Act, 1947. This was the last labour legislation enacted by the British in India. It became an Act in April 1947, months before India and Pakistan became independent. Hence, this was a law that was inherited by both nations.[30] This law appears to be very protective of labour since it places heavy restrictions on laying off or retrenching workers. It is arguable, however well-meaning though the law may be, that it has been an impediment to job creation and, to that extent, has hurt rather than helped labour. It is possible to show theoretically that this becomes especially so once a nation's wages rise above a certain level (Basu, Fields, and Debgupta 2007); so this law is now an even greater burden (see also Basu 2006a). Given India's democracy and powerful labour unions, this law has been a bulwark in the firmament of the nation's labour regulation—and, in fact, there have been several amendments strengthening it in seemingly pro-labour fashion (see Besley and Burgess 2006).

Pakistan, on the other hand, which slid into martial law and military dictatorship in 1957, showed much greater impatience with this law. It amended the law in important ways, weakening the bargaining power of workers, in 1948 and 1956. In the mid- to late 1950s, there were a series of strikes in East Pakistan, the most famous being the strikes of the Adamjee Jute Mill workers and the workers of the Chanderguna Paper Mills. There were riots, and 300 people were killed (Amjad 2001). Ayub Khan's military government would have none of this, and in 1959 effectively repealed the Industrial Disputes Act and replaced it with the Industrial Disputes Ordinance, 1959, which was later modified into the Industrial Disputes Act, 1968. This, in turn, was later annulled and ultimately replaced with the Industrial Disputes Ordinance, 1969. The power of trade unions and the rights of workers were severely limited. While this was an act of oppression, the fact of the matter is that it abolished the Industrial Disputes Act of 1947 out of the way and cleared the way for possibly better laws.

Bangladesh, which was culled out of Pakistan in 1971, was born without this legislative encumbrance, even though this is a part of its cultural and political history. Soon after its founding, Bangladesh went on to set up a fairly modern system of labour regulation and management, much of which was founded on a progressive, liberal

[30] And since Bangladesh was part of Pakistan till 1971, this legal setting is also, indirectly, an inheritance of Bangladesh.

constitution. The balance of labour rights, especially women worker's rights, and the flexibility for different kinds of employment contracts, creates hope, particularly in the garment industry of Bangladesh (Mahmud and Kabeer 2003; Beena 2006). At the same time, this has been achieved without being unmindful of basic labour rights. What really separates Bangladesh from the other nations of the region is its remarkable non-governmental organization (NGO) activity. There are some 22,000 NGOs active in the country, with 35 per cent of the nation's population directly benefiting from their activities, and 85 per cent of the villages touched by some NGO presence (Kabeer 2003). Moreover, some of these NGOs are there not to deliver money or service, but to help the poor articulate and demand their rights. The NGO Nijera Kori, which has been active since 1980, is founded on the principle that poverty is not merely a matter of resource shortages, but of a lack of voice and rights.

The Grameen Bank, though organized for a very different purpose—to extend credit to the small farmer and the poor—has had a salutary affect on the organization of labour that is often not recognized. While lending money, Grameen insists on the contractual nature of this transaction—the borrower has to pay back the money with no excuses. As Kabeer (2003, p.10) quotes some rural women, who state that the officials of Grameen say, 'Even if you have a dead body in the house, you have to pay the instalment. On that basis if you are willing to take the loan, then take it.' Given the feudal past of most of South Asia, this is a quite radical way of thinking. In a feudal setting, the contract is not very important. An individual can always plead some crisis and expect the feudal lord to be forgiving. Modern industries cannot run in such a way. The contract is crucial. Not letting kindness obstruct contracts is kinder in the long run because it makes the poor businessworthy. Building the sanctity of the contract into labour market agreements is the crucial reform that we talk about below.

India's labour history turned out to be very different from that of all other South Asian nations, given its democracy and the socialist predilections of its early leaders.[31] Laws to monitor the labour

[31] India's democratic system has had an intricate relationship with the economy, and understanding this is germane to understanding the economic performance of India (Sen 2004).

market proliferated and, despite the best of intentions, have now become a stumbling block for industrial and manufacturing sector growth. In India, there are 45 laws at the national level and close to four times that many at the state government level that monitor labour market functioning. This complexity is reflected in the World Bank's Ease of Business Indicators, where in 2006, India ranked 112 out of 175 countries in the category 'employing workers', (with 1 indicating the best). Even though recent changes in the regulations of several Indian states have resulted in lower 'difficulty of hiring index', 'rigidity of hours index', 'rigidity of employment index', and 'firing costs', India still scores high on the 'difficulty of firing index' (70/100), which is considerably higher than the average of the low-income countries (44/100).

Some of these labour laws date back to the nineteenth century. They were meant to control conflict and keep the labour market efficient. Unfortunately, the experience has been the contrary. According to recent World Bank estimates, in 2004 there were 482 cases of major work stoppages, resulting in 15 million human days of work loss (Ahsan 2006). Between 1995 and 2001, around 9 per cent of factory workers were involved in these stoppages. The figure for China is close to zero. On the other hand, the wages of Chinese workers are rising much faster than those of India's. These facts, we would argue, are not unrelated.

Most of India's labour laws were crafted with scant respect for 'market response'. If a particular situation seemed bad, the presumption was that the government had to simply enact a law banning that particular situation. But the fact that each law leads entrepreneurs and labourers to respond strategically, often in complicated ways, was paid no heed. In a poor country, no one with any sensitivity wants workers to lose their jobs. So what does one do? The instinct is to make it difficult for firms to lay off workers. That is exactly what India's Industrial Disputes Act, 1947, did, especially through the amendments of 1976 and 1982, for firms in the formal sector and employing more than 100 workers.

But in today's globalized world, with volatile and shifting demand, firms have responded to this by keeping their labour forces as small as possible. It is little wonder that in a country as large as India, less than 10 million workers are employed in the formal private sector. Some commentators have argued that India's labour laws could not have had much of a consequence, since most apply only to the formal sector. What they fail to realize is that one reason the formal sector has remained miniscule is because of these laws, and also because of the culture that these laws have spawned (Basu 2006a).

Several recent studies have analysed the impacts of labour regulations on firm productivity, patterns of specialization, and technological progress. According to Besley and Burgess (2004), increasing pro-worker regulation has a negative impact on investment and productivity in the registered manufacturing sectors. What is also interesting about their findings is the lack of evidence that such policies improve labour interests. Aghion and Burgess (2003) confirm these results, and show that the negative impact of having stricter labour regulations on productivity has increased in the period post-liberalization. Kochar et al. (2006), based on their analysis of the patterns of specialization of Indian firms, suggest that not only is the level of productivity of existing firms affected by stringent regulations, but new firms are kept from entering the industry as a result.

What is needed in India is not a law that allows employers to fire workers at will, but one that allows for different kinds of contracts. Some workers may sign a contract for a high wage, but requires them to quit on short notice; others may seek the opposite. This would allow firms to employ different kinds of labour, depending on the volatility of the market in which they operate.

Much of the debate on labour laws has been misconstrued. What is needed is not change in labour laws and policy to elicit sacrifice from organized labour, as some economists have suggested. Indian workers, whether they be in the organized sector or not, are too poor for that. The need is for changes in order to create greater private-sector demand for labour, which would boost wages and employment.

We believe that India's poorly construed labour laws have been so persistent because of an intellectual failure, to wit, the inability to grasp that it may be in the worker's own interest (in some contexts) to have the right to waive some rights that have been granted. Complicated models and empirical analysis can be developed to illustrate this, but the basic conceptual idea underlying it is well known in the context of game theory. To see this, consider a simple game in which a firm or an investor has to decide whether to make a small or a large investment in India (such as to start a new firm). The worker (which stands for the collectivity of all workers in this firm) can (in the future) call a strike or never call one (the 'no strike' option). The pay-off for the investor is the first number in each cell, and the pay-off for the worker is the second number. If the worker calls a strike (or at least has the ability to do so), he/she earns a higher income no matter what the size of the investment of the investor happens to be. This is what leads to the popular opinion that if we want workers to be better off, we should give them the right to strike. This deduction, however, is not true, as we are about to illustrate. Assume further that the investor, after he has chosen his investment size, is always worse off if the worker calls (or can call strikes). However, if a strike takes place and his investment is large, his loss is disproportionately large, since his capital is held up. All these features can be summed up in the game described below in which the investor chooses between rows and the worker chooses between columns.

THE WORKER–INVESTOR GAME

	Strike	*No strike*
Large	2, 5	10, 4
Small	4, 2	5, 1

It is now easy to see that in this game the worker will always choose the 'strike' option and, that being so, the investor will choose to make a 'small' investment. So the investor and the worker will have earnings of, respectively, 4 and 2.

While the worker will always choose the strike option in the above game, if before the game began, she was asked if she would like to waive the right to strike, clearly it would be in her interest to say yes. Once she gives up this right, she is confined to the right column, and if that is the case, the investor will make the 'large' investment. Hence, the worker earns 4 instead of 2 by having the added ability to give up a right. Also, the choice of larger investment by firms in general could mean a higher investment rate for the nation as a whole, which could translate into not just higher short-run benefits, but long-run gains through higher growth.

By way of caution, it should be clarified that we are not making the case to give all workers the right to give up their right to call strikes, but simply illustrating that there are *contexts* where it is worthwhile giving them such meta rights. One has to weigh lots of pros and cons before making a general recommendation. We feel that the right to strike has other advantages so that, barring some very special cases, workers should always have this right. On the other hand, it is arguable that at the current stage of South Asian development, where the manufacturing sector is poised to take off, workers should be given the right to sign contracts with different kinds of firing or retrenchment rules and doing so is likely to cause such a rise in aggregate demand for labour that all workers would be better off. While much of the current debate in South Asia on labour laws is conducted as though worker interests are pitted against business interests, in reality, it is between thinking clearly and not thinking clearly.

It should be added that flexibility in hiring and firing is not the only problem. India's complex web of legislation leads to a system of dispute resolution that is incredibly slow. Data from the Ministry of Labour reveal that in 2000, there were 533,038 disputes pending in India's labour courts. Of these, 28,864 had been pending for over 10 years. If India is to be a vibrant global economy, this has to change.

In brief, the need is to move to a system that (*a*) makes room for more flexible contracts in the labour market, (*b*) has a minimal welfare net for workers who are out of work, and (*c*) resolves labour market disputes more quickly.

Some of this applies to other South Asian nations as well. The aim has to be to strike a balance between basic rights and rights that ex post hurt the very same people they are meant to protect. Given the vast power of capital, workers need to have the right to strike collectively. At the same time, firms need to have the freedom to sign different kinds of contracts with workers with different rules of disengagement. This freedom can unleash a demand for labour and therefore jobs, which the government cannot provide, no matter how well-meaning it happens to be. Minimally, these are matters that ought to be brought into the public space for debate. In most countries, these are treated as such sensitive matters that the urge is to push them under the carpet. But that is not in the best interest of the economies of South Asia in the long run.

Conclusion

The economy is an enormously complex organism that we understand only partially. It is foolish to pretend that we have definitive knowledge of what causes growth and what leads to greater employment. Yet years of painstaking research in economics, theoretical and empirical, have begun to give us an outline of how a nation ought to proceed and what kinds of policies it should try to put into place. Some of these are unsettled matters and so a new policy will be a bit like testing the waters, with all its associated risks. At the same time, it is possible to argue that the waters must be tested for it is too costly, especially for the poor and the labouring classes, to sit back with the smugness that the policy regime that currently is in place is the best.

We have argued in this essay that the recent history of South Asia raises hope for the region. Growth has been rapid, and some parts of the region are beginning to resemble the economies of East Asia of the 1970s, or China of the late 1980s. Yet this growth has not had a matching impact on employment, so the incidence of poverty remains large and, despite some small downward movement in recent times, at record levels by global standards. This also means that the concomitants of poverty, such as low literacy rates, malnutrition, and poor working conditions, persist. It is therefore important for us to turn our attention to spreading the benefits of growth to larger segments of the population. Some of this can be done through government programmes and subsidies, but in the end we have to rely on job creation and private initiative.

This essay tries to (*a*) collect and organize the scattered economic data of this region, and (*b*) draw on our knowledge of the best practices for creating more demand for labour and, as a consequence, greater employment. The prescriptions that we have outlined for the nations of South Asia have a common core, but also nation-specific idiosyncrasies. We view the essay more than an academic exercise, as an advocacy for action and discussion in the public space for policy changes that can make the region's new growth more inclusive.

REFERENCES

Aghion, Philippe and Robin Burgess. 2003. 'Liberalization and Industrial Performance: Evidence from India and the UK', Paper presented at the conference, The Future of Globalization at Yale University.

Ahluwalia, Isher J. 1995. 'India: Industrial Development Review', The Economist Intelligence Unit and UNIDO.

Ahluwalia, Montek S. 2000. 'Economic Performance of States in Post-reform Period', *Economic and Political Weekly*, 35 (6 May): 1637–48.

Ahluwalia, Montek S. 2002. 'Economic Reforms in India since 1991: Has Gradualism Worked?' *Journal of Economic Perspectives*, 16 (3): 67–88.

Ahsan, Ahmad. 2006. 'India's Employment Challenge: Creating Jobs, Helping Workers', Report 35772 (draft), Poverty Reduction Management, South Asia Region, World Bank, Washington, D.C.

Amjad, Ali. 2001. *Labour Legislation and Trade Unions in India and Pakistan*. New Delhi: Oxford University Press.

Asian Development Bank. 2005. *Key Indicators 2005. Labour Markets in Asia: Promoting Full, Productive, and Decent Employment*. Asian Development Bank.

———. *Key Indicators of Developing Asian Countries*, various issues since 1973. Asian Development Bank.

Balakrishnan, P. and M. Parameswaran. 2006. 'Identifying Growth Regimes in India', Paper presented at the South and South East Asian Econometric Society, Chennai, India, 19 December.

Banerjee, Abhijit V. and Esther Duflo. 2000. 'Reputation Effects and the Limits of Contracting: A Study of the Indian Software Industry', *Quarterly Journal of Economics*, 115(3): 989–1017.

Bangladesh Bureau of Statistics. *Statistical Yearbook of Bangladesh*, various issues. Dhaka: Government of Bangladesh..

Basu, Kaushik. 1990. 'The Elimination of Endemic Poverty in South Asia', in Jean Drèze and Amartya Sen (eds), *The Political Economy of Hunger*, Vol. 3. Oxford: Clarendon Press.

——— (ed.). 2004. *India's Emerging Economy: Performance and Prospects in the 1990s and Beyond.* Cambridge, MA: MIT Press.

———. 2006a. 'Labour Laws and Labour Welfare in the Context of the Indian Experience', in Alain de Janvry and Ravi Kanbur (eds), *Poverty, Inequality and Development*. New York: Springer Verlag.

———. 2006b. 'Globalization, Poverty, and Inequality: What is the Relationship? What is to be Done?" *World Development*, 34(8): 1361–73.

——— (ed.). 2007. *Oxford Companion to Economics in India.* New Delhi: Oxford University Press.

Basu, Kaushik, Gary S. Fields, and Shub Debgupta. 2007. 'Labour Retrenchment Laws and Their Effect on Wages and Employment: A Theoretical Investigation', Mimeo, Cornell University.

Basu, Kaushik and Maertens, Annemie. 2007. 'The Patterns and Causes of Growth in India', *Oxford Review of Economic Policy*, 23(2): 143–67.

Beena, P. L. 2006. 'Limits to Universal Trade Liberalisation: The Contemporary Scenario for Textiles and Clothing Sector in South Asia', Working Paper No. 279, Centre for Development Studies, Thiruvananthapuram.

Besley, Tim and Robin Burgess. 2004. 'Can Labour Regulation Hinder

Economic Performance? Evidence from India', *Quarterly Journal of Economics*, 119(1): 91–134.

Bharat-Ram, Vinay. 2007. 'Manufacturing Hub', in Kaushik Basu (ed.), *Oxford Companion to Economics in India.* New Delhi: Oxford University Press. .

Bosworth, Barry P., Susan M. Collins, and Arvind Virmani. 2007. 'Sources of Growth in the Indian Economy', Forthcoming in *India Policy Forum.*

Central Bank of Sri Lanka. *Economic and Social Statistics of Sri Lanka*, various issues.

Central Bureau of Statistics Nepal. *Statistical Yearbook of Nepal*, various issues. Central Bureau of Statistics.

Central Statistics Office, Afghanistan. 2005. *Afghanistan Statistical Yearbook.* Central Statistics Office.

Chanda, Rupa. 2007. 'Services', in Kaushik Basu (ed.), *Oxford Companion to Economics in India.* New Delhi: Oxford University Press..

Chidambaram, P. 2007. 'Fiscal Policy Reforms since 1991', in Kaushik Basu (ed.), *Oxford Companion to Economics in India.* New Delhi: Oxford University Press..

Department of Census and Statistics Sri Lanka. *Statistical Abstract*, various issues. Department of Census and Statistics.

Dyson, Tim, Robert Cassen, and Leela Visaria. 2004. *Twenty-First Century India, Population, Economy, Human Development and the Environment.* Oxford University Press.

Embuldeniya, Don. 2000. 'Economic Reforms and the Corporate Sector in Sri Lanka', *Contemporary South Asia*, 9(2): 165–79.

Economic and Social Commissions for Asia and the Pacific, United Nations. *Statistical Yearbook for Asia and the Pacific*, various issues from 1968. United Nations.

Falk, Rahel. 2005. 'Industrial Sickness in Indian Manufacturing', PhD dissertation. Department of Economics, Ruprecht-Karls Universität, Heidelberg, Germany.

Federal Bureau of Statistics of Pakistan. *Pakistan Statistical Handbook*, various issues. Federal Bureau of Statistics.

——. 2007. *Labour Force Survey*, 2005–2006.

Forbes, Naushad. 2002. 'Doing Business in India: What has Liberalization Changed?' in *Economic Policy Reforms and the Indian Economy*, pp. 129–67. Chicago and London: University of Chicago Press.

Ghani, Ejaz and Musleh-ud Din. 2006. 'The Impact of Public Investment on Economic Growth in Pakistan', *Pakistan Development Review*, 45.

Gokarn, Subir. 2006. 'Industrial Growth and New Business', Mimeo, CRISIL.

Goldar, Bishwanath and Arup Mitra. 2002. 'Total Factor Productivity

Growth in Indian Industry: A Review of Studies', in B.S. Minhas (ed.), *National Income Accounts and Data Systems* pp. 218–37. New Delhi: Oxford University Press.

Haque, Nadeem ul. 2006. 'Beyond Planning and Mercantilism: An Evaluation of Pakistan's Growth Strategy', *Pakistan Development Review*, 45.

Hossain, M.A. and N.D. Karunaratne. 2004. 'Trade Liberalisation and Technical Inefficiency: Evidence from Bangladesh Manufacturing Industries', *The Journal of Development Studies*, 40(3): 87–114.

International Labour Organization. 2003. *Key Indicators of the Labour Market*, 3rd edn. International Labour Organization.

———. 2006. *Key Indicators of the Labour Market*, 4th edn. International Labour Organization.

Kabeer, Naila. 2003. 'Growing Citizenship from the Grassroots: Nijera Kori and Social Mobilization in Bangladesh', *Bangladesh Development Studies*, 29: 1–20.

Kalirajan, Kaliappa and Shashanka Bhide. 2004. 'The Post-reform Performance of the Manufacturing Sector in India', *Asian Economic Papers*, 3(2): 126–57.

Kelkar, Vijay. 2004. 'India: On the Growth Turnpike', Special lecture, ANU, Canberra, Australia.

Kezang and Jason Whalley. 2004. 'Telecommunications in the Land of the Thunder Dragon: Recent Developments in Bhutan', *Telecommunications Policy*, 28(11): 785–800.

Kishor, Sharma, Jayasuriya Sisara, and Edward Oczkowski. 2002. 'Liberalization and Productivity Growth: The Case of Manufacturing Industry in Nepal', *Oxford Development Studies*, 28(2): 205–22.

Kochar, Kalpana, Utsav Kumar, Raghuram Rajan, Arvind Subramanian, and Ioannis Tokatlidis. 2006. 'India's Pattern of Development: What Happened? What Follows', Working Papers WP No. 06/22, International Monetary Fund.

Mahmud, Simeen. 2003. 'Is Bangladesh Experiencing a Feminization of the Labour Force?' *Bangladesh Development Studies*, 29.

Mahmud, Simeen and Naila Kabeer. 2003. 'Compliance versus Accountability: Struggles for Dignity and Daily Bread in the Bangladesh Garment Industry', *Bangladesh Development Studies*, 29.

Ministry of Finance. *Economic Survey*, various issues. Ministry of Finance, India.

Ministry of Labour and Human Resources. 2006. *Labour Force Survey Report.* Bhutan: Ministry of Labour and Human Resources.

———. 2007. *Labour Act 2007.* Bhutan: Ministry of Labour and Human Resources.

———. 2007. *Labour Market Information Bulletin*. Bhutan: Ministry of Labour and Human Resources.

Ministry of Planning and National Development. 2005. *Millennium Development Goals Maldives Country Report*. Maldives: Ministry of Planning and National Development.

———. 2005. *The 25 Years of Statistics: Maldives*. Maldives: Ministry of Planning and National Development.

———. 2005. *Statistical Yearbook*, various issues. Maldives: Ministry of Planning and National Development.

Mohan, Rakesh. 1992. 'Industrial Policy and Controls', in Bimal Jalan (ed.), *The Indian Economy: Problems and Prospects*. New Delhi: Penguin.

Munro, Lauchlan, T. 1989. 'Technology Choice in Bhutan: Labour Shortage, Aid Dependence, and a Mountain Environment', *Mountain Research and Development*, 9(1): 15–23.

Murthy, N.R. Narayana. 2004. 'The Impact of Economic Reforms on Industry in India: A Case Study of the Software Industry', in Kaushik Basu (ed.), *India's Emerging Economy: Performance and Prospects in the 1990s and Beyond*. Cambridge MA: MIT Press and New Delhi: Oxford University Press.

Nagaraj, R. 2004. 'Fall in the Organized Manufacturing Employment: A Brief Note', *Economic and Political Weekly*, 39 (July 24).

National Statistics Bureau of Bhutan. 2003. *Statistical Yearbook of Bhutan*. National Statistics Bureau.

——. 2005. *Statistical Yearbook of Bhutan*. National Statistics Bureau.

Nepal Rastra Bank. *Economic Report*, various issues. Nepal Rastra Bank.

Panagariya, Arvind. 2004. 'Growth and Reforms during 1980s and 1990s', *Economic and Political Weekly* (19 June): 2581–94.

OECD. 2007. *OECD Employment Outlook 2007*. Organisation for Economic Co-operation and Development.

Playforth, John and Mathias Schundeln. 2007. 'Private versus Social Returns to Human Capital: Education and Economic Growth in India', Mimeo, Harvard University, Cambridge, MA.

Rakshit, Mihir. 2006. 'Services-led Growth: The Indian Experience', Mimeo, ICRA, Kolkata.

Reserve Bank of India. 2006. *Handbook of Statistics on Indian Economy*. Reserve Bank of India.

Rodrik, Dani and Arvind Subramanian. 2004. 'Why India Can Grow at 7 Per cent a Year and More: Projections and Reflections', *Economic and Political Weekly* (17 April): 1591–6.

SAARC. 2005. *Regional Poverty Profile 2005, Poverty Reduction in South Asia through Productive Employment*. South Asian Association for Regional Cooperation.

Salim, Ruhul Amin. 2003. 'Economic Liberalization and Productivity

Growth: Further Evidence from Bangaldesh', *Oxford Development Studies*, 31(1): 85–98.

Salimullah, Mohammed, Mozammel Huq, and Iain McNicol. 2000. 'Structural Change and Performance of the Bangladesh Economy, 1986–87 and 1992–93: An Application of the Growth Decomposition Model', *Bangladesh Development Studies*, 26.

Siddiqui, Anjum. 2007. *India and South Asia: Economic Development in the Age of Globalisation.* New York and London: M.E. Sharpe.

Sen, Amartya. 1988. 'Sri Lanka's Achievements: How and When?' in T.N. Srinivasan and Pranab Bardhan (eds), *Rural Poverty in South Asia*. New York: Columbia University Press.

———. 2004. 'Democracy and Secularism in India', in Kaushik Basu (ed.), *India's Emerging Economy: Performance and Prospects in the 1990s and Beyond.* Cambridge, MA: MIT Press and New Delhi: Oxford University Press.

Singh, Nirvikar. 2006. 'Services-Led Industrialization in India: Assessment and Lessons', Mimeo, University of California, Santa Cruz.

Srinivasan, T.N. 2005. 'Comments on "From 'Hindu Growth" to Productivity Surge: The Mystery of the Indian Growth Transition', *IMF Staff Papers*, 52(2).

———. 2007. 'Employment and India's Development Reforms', Mimeo, Yale University, New Haven, CT.

State Bank of Pakistan. *Handbook of Statistics on the Pakistan Economy*, various issues. State Bank of Pakistan.

———. *Annual Report 2005–2006.* State Bank of Pakistan.

Tata, Ratan. 2007. 'Tata, the House of', in Kaushik Basu (ed.), *Oxford Companion to Economics in India.* New Delhi: Oxford University Press.

Unel, B. 2003. 'Productivity Trends in India's Manufacturing Sectors in the Last Two Decades', Working Paper, WP/03/22, International Monetary Fund, Washington, D.C.

Vaidyanathan, A. 2006. 'Farmers' Suicides and the Agrarian Crisis', *Economic and Political Weekly,* 23 September, pp. 4009–13.

Virmani, Arvind. 2004. 'India's Economic Growth: From Socialist Rate of Growth to Bharatiya Rate of Growth', Working Paper No. 122, Indian Council for Research on International Economic Relations, New Delhi.

Weise, Kristian. 2007. 'Corporate Tax Warning', *OECD Observer*, 261 (May): 22–3.

World Bank. 2007. *World Development Indicators 2007.* Washington, D.C.: World Bank.

Yahya, Faizal, Ashvin Parameswaran, and Rodney Sebastian. 2005. 'Tourism and the South Asia Littoral: Voices from the Maldives, South Asia', *Journal of South Asian Studies*, 28(3): 457–80.

6 EVIDENCE OF UNDEREMPLOYMENT OF LABOUR AND CAPITAL IN INDIA MANUFACTURING

Ana M. Fernandes and Ariel Pakes

Introduction

There has been some concern with the lack of growth, particularly of employment growth, in Indian manufacturing, and its relationship to various institutional constraints. Partly this is a result of the fact that the Indian manufacturing sector is much smaller than that sector in other economies of similar size. Table 6.1 illustrates this fact. It indicates that the manufacturing share of value added in India is smaller than that share in other large developing economies, though it is similar to that share in smaller countries with GDP per capita similar to that of India (Pakistan and Vietnam). However, as Table 6.2 shows, the growth rate of value added in manufacturing in India is noticeably lower than that in these smaller, similar-income countries. Indeed, the sectoral growth rate comparisons in Table 6.2 are rather striking. The growth rate of value added in *services* in India is comparable to that in China, and about 10 percentage points higher than that in any other country on our list. In rather stark contrast, the growth rate of value added in manufacturing in India is only about *half* of that in China and Vietnam, and quite a bit lower than that in Pakistan.

Why is the relative performance of the Indian manufacturing sector, relative both to the service sector and to the manufacturing sectors in other comparable countries, so poor and what are its implications for employment and income distribution in India? This chapter uses the World Bank Investment Climate Surveys to examine a component of this question. In particular we analyse the labour and capital employment rates of Indian manufacturing firms and their relationship to productivity and various institutional constraints.

TABLE 6.1: Industry and Manufacturing Share of Employment and GDP across Countries

	Employment in industry as % of total employment in 2000	*Value added in industry as % of GDP in 2000*	*Value added in manufacturing as % of GDP in 2000*	*2002 GDP per capita (in 2000 USD)*
India	18.2	26.3	15.6	480
Brazil	19.3	28.0	17.1	3473
China	23.0	45.9	34.7	1106
Indonesia	17.3	45.9	27.7	844
Pakistan	18.0	22.6	14.8	532
Vietnam	12.4	36.7	18.6	444
Low-income countries	12.3	26.6	14.1	
Lower-middle-income countries	18.5	38.3	24.2	

Source: *World Development Indicators 2005*.
Notes: Industry includes manufacturing, along with mining and quarrying (including oil production), construction, and public utilities (electricity, gas, and water). Lower-income countries and lower-middle-income countries are defined based on the World Bank classification.

Several researchers have argued that the restrictiveness of labour market regulations in India is one of the most important constraints on the performance of its manufacturing sector. Our analysis focuses exclusively on the formal (organized) manufacturing sector in India for which data is available and to which labour market regulations are applicable.[1]

[1] Indeed, recent data from the ILO and OECD (2007) suggest that overall employment growth in India between 2000 and 2005 was a quite rapid 2.8 per cent per annum (compared to only 1 per cent in China). However, the OECD (2007) also reports that close to 90 per cent of the population employed in India work in the informal sector (versus only 50 per cent in China), and there is some indication that the recent strong job creation in India has been mostly 'bad' jobs, that is, those in the informal sector. For example, the OECD (2007) report estimates that growth in formal employment in urban China is much higher than growth in formal employment in urban India in the same period (3.1 per cent versus 1.7 per cent).

TABLE 6.2: Growth in Sectoral Value-Added across Countries

	Growth in value added in manufacturing		*Growth in value added in agriculture*		*Growth in value added in services*	
	1995–2000	*2000–5*	*1995–2000*	*2000–5*	*1995–2000*	*2000–5*
India	28.1	38.4	13.7	14.9	48.4	50.3
Brazil	5.7	5.6	17.3	23.7	26.5	31.8
China	57.6	67.4	18.5	21.2	57.3	61.2
Indonesia	14.6	27.5	7	17.3	-2.4	35.7
Pakistan	17.1	56.6	26.5	12	20.9	29.9
Vietnam	70.3	73.8	24.2	20.7	31.9	40

Source: *World Development Indicators 2005*.
Note: The table shows growth rates in total value added for each sector (in constant local currency units).

Labour market regulations are described in detail in Ahsan and Pages (2005) and in World Bank (2006). Here we only point out the most controversial of those regulations: the 1982 amendment to the Industrial Disputes Act (IDA) of 1947, which made the firing of workers illegal for firms employing more than 100 workers, except with previous permission from the appropriate state government.

The evidence indicates that the permission to fire workers is rarely granted (see Ahsan and Pages 2005). Early work by Fallon and Lucas (1991) found that the introduction of employment laws restricting the firing of workers in India led to a substantial decline in the demand for labour by manufacturing industries. Hence, the objective of the regulations—to protect jobs—resulted in fewer jobs being created. More recently, Besley and Burgess (2004) found that Indian states that amended labour market regulations to make them more restrictive (that is, to give greater protection to workers) experienced lower output, lower employment, lower investment, and lower productivity in the manufacturing sector. Ahsan and Pages also found important employment losses in Indian manufacturing as a result of restrictive regulations on the firing of workers, particularly in labour-intensive industries such as textiles.

In this chapter, we ask whether factor employment in manufacturing firms in India is 'abnormally' low or 'abnormally' high, conditional on: (*a*) firm productivity, (*b*) the amount of other factors employed by firms, and (*c*) the factor costs faced by firms. With respect to labour, our measure of 'abnormal' is constructed as the ratio of (*a*) the labour employment that would be optimal for the firm if there were no hiring and firing costs (or constraints), and (*b*) the firm's actual employment of labour. That is, if our measure, which we will call 'underutilization of labour' for a firm equals *x,* then a firm without hiring and firing costs that had the same productivity, capital, and factor costs as the given firm would increase its demand for labour relative to the given firm by a factor of *x*. To get a different perspective on the implications of the empirical magnitudes obtained, we also compute the percentage difference between the actual cost of labour and the cost of labour that would make a firm without hiring and firing costs just satisfied with its current labour employment.

We then look at differences in our underutilization of labour measures across Indian states, and at the relationship between our underutilization of labour measures and measures of productivity, underutilization of capital (described below), and data on institutional constraints to doing business collected by the World Bank Investment Climate Surveys. We find very large differences in the extent of underutilization of labour across Indian states. Although it is probably impossible to eliminate all the employment constraints faced by Indian manufacturing firms, we think it is possible that the states with 'poorly functioning' labour markets—that is, states with large underutilization of labour—could, with institutional improvements, approach the figures for underutilization of labour in those states with better functioning markets. We delve deeper into the meaning of the expression 'poorly functioning' in the last part of the chapter, where we summarize the relationship between our underutilization figures and other characteristics of the firm and the state in which it operates.

We want to be clear at the outset that our underutilization figures should not be taken as literal predictions of what would happen to the manufacturing demand for labour were policymakers to eliminate all hiring and firing costs in a given state. This is because if policymakers eliminated these costs and constraints for all firms in a state, and the firms began to respond by employing more labour, the cost of labour would likely rise, and the output price would likely fall below what our current estimates predict. The current estimates do not take into account the impact on a firm's sales if a competitor increases the quantities it produces. These two processes would decrease the firm's marginal revenue product for labour and hence their incentive to hire more workers. For precise predictions of what would happen to employment patterns in a state where labour market institutions were improved, we would need to analyse a general equilibrium model that endogenized both the wage rates and the output prices of firms in the manufacturing sector. Developing such a model is left for future research.

This chapter also considers an analogous measure of 'underutilization' of capital. This measure is constructed as the ratio of: (*a*) the optimal capital for the firm if there were perfect rental markets for capital goods, and (*b*) the firm's actual capital stock. The perfect rental markets concept is quite abstract; it assumes that firms could rent each different kind of capital good at an annual rental cost equal to the sum of the current rate of interest on loans to manufacturing firms, plus the depreciation rate on those capital goods. Still, our results on capital are both comforting in that they correspond to our intuitions on the capital market, and surprising in how different they are from our labour underutilization patterns.

In particular, there is evidence that capital markets are much better at arbitraging differences across states than labour markets. First, the differences in both the cost of capital and the underutilization of capital across states are noticeably smaller than the differences in both labour costs and the underutilization of labour across states, and the magnitudes are striking. The interstate variance in the percentage of underutilization of labour is about three-and-a-half times the interstate variance in the percentage of underutilization of capital. Second, though we obtain large positive numbers for the underutilization of labour—that is, labour is 'underutilized' compared to what would happen if there were no hiring and firing costs or constraints—the numbers for the underutilization of capital are negative. That is, given the amount of labour employed by firms, firm productivity, and cost of capital, firms are employing *more* capital than they would employ if they were facing perfect rental markets for capital goods.

Of course, the overutilization of capital may just be a response to the fact that firms are underutilizing labour. That is, firms that face many constraints in the hiring and firing of workers may respond by increasing their use of capital relative to labour. Indeed, as we show below, firms that underutilize labour disproportionately tend to overutilize capital disproportionately. Moreover, it is clear that if labour employment were to rise, say in response to an improvement in labour market institutions, the marginal revenue product of the capital in place would rise, and our measure of the overutilization of capital would fall. Moreover, the overutilization of capital figures that we obtain is much smaller in magnitude than the underutilization of labour figures. Consequently, improvements in labour market regulations that may be feasible may also eliminate the overutilization of capital. Unfortunately, to answer whether this is likely to be true would require a more detailed general equilibrium model alluded to above.

The last section of this chapter investigates the reduced form relationships: (*a*) among our measures of underutilization of labour, underutilization of capital, and productivity, and (*b*) between these three measures and answers to questions posed on the investment climate survey. Perhaps the most striking finding of this analysis is that the extent of underutilization of labour by a firm is strongly and positively related to the firm's productivity. The more productive firms also tend to overutilize capital somewhat more than the average, though not to the same extent that they underutilize labour. The results in prior sections indicated that liberalizing the labour market in states where there is high underutilization of labour is likely to result in significant increases in both labour demand and wages in those states. The results in the last section give us reason to believe that a lowering of labour market constraints would also increase productivity, and it would do so without significant increases in the demand for capital. We should expect an increase in productivity, both because the more productive firms are likely to increase their output disproportionately, and because each firm's productivity should increase as labour and capital employment move towards their efficient levels.

Other relevant reduced form findings include the following: (*a*) firms that suffer more production losses due to electricity outages are less productive than the average firm in their states, and firms in states in which the average production losses due to outages are high underutilize labour and capital more than firms in states with less frequent outages; (*b*) firms reporting more problems with corruption are the more productive firms in the state, and they have relatively high underutilization of both factors of production; (*c*) within states, it is the relatively more productive firms that are more likely to receive loans, suggesting that the loan-granting institutions are able to select the more productive firms; and (*d*) states in which a disproportionate number of firms received loans are the states with less underutilization of both factors of production, particularly of capital.

DATA ANALYSIS

Our analysis requires the use of data on factors of production and sales for manufacturing firms in India. Our data is taken from the Investment Climate Surveys conducted in India jointly by the World Bank and the Confederation of Indian Industry (CII) in two rounds: 2002 and 2005. The surveys cover formal manufacturing firms across 12 Indian states and seven industries based on a random sample designed to be representative of the population of firms according to their industry and location. The surveys provide information on firm characteristics, investment climate variables, and accounting variables. Accounting variables were collected for the two years immediately preceding the administration of the two survey rounds (2001 and 2004), as well as for prior years through retrospective questions. To avoid measurement problems associated with retrospective data, we use only the accounting variables for 2001 and 2004. The 2005 survey round covered all firms from the 2002 survey round that were still in business and willing to respond to the questionnaire, as well as additional firms not covered in the 2002 survey. Appendix A6.1 at the end of the chapter provides more details on the data and shows some descriptive statistics for the sample.

INGREDIENTS FOR THE UNDERUTILIZATION MEASURES

Production Functions and Factor Costs

In order to obtain our measures of the underutilization of labour and capital, we need to know what labour and capital employment would be for a firm facing no hiring and firing costs or constraints (perfect rental markets for capital goods). For this purpose we use

- estimates of a production function, or more precisely of a 'sales generating' function; and
- estimates of the cost of employing labour and capital.

The availability of a sales generating function enables the calculation of the increment in sales for a unit increase of employment at different employment levels for each firm. The labour that the firm would employ if there were no hiring and firing costs or constraints is equivalent to the labour employment level that would set the firm's increment in sales due to a new worker exactly equal to the cost of employing that worker. An increase in employment above this 'statically optimal' level would generate more labour costs than sales, and an employment level below this static optimum would mean that the firm would raise sales more than costs if it increased its employment. Our estimates of underutilization of capital are obtained analogously based on the cost of capital.

Sales Generating Functions

Our sales generating function is obtained by multiplying an inverse demand function, which gives us prices as a function of output, by a production function for output. It is assumed that the demand function has a constant elasticity form, and that the production function is Cobb-Douglas. The location of the demand curve and the efficiency of production are allowed to vary across firms. Also, as is explained below, we had to modify the Cobb-Douglas assumption somewhat to account for the institutional detail of the Indian manufacturing sector. The sales generating function coefficients allow us to aggregate inputs into one index, and differences in sales per unit of this input index will be called 'productivity' in what follows.

The literature on estimating sales generating functions is quite extensive. We follow the general approach initiated by Olley and Pakes (1996), but a reader with a deeper interest in how we obtained our estimates should refer to the longer version of our background paper (Fernandes and Pakes 2008), and the literature cited there. We do, however, want to emphasize the two aspects of the estimation that differ somewhat from the standard literature. Both are designed to accommodate some special features of the Indian manufacturing sector.

First, the Indian manufacturing sector includes a much larger share of relatively small firms than the manufacturing sectors in other economies. This is illustrated in Figure 6.1, which compares the size distribution of firms in India to that in China, Brazil, and

Indonesia, based on data from Investment Climate Surveys. As a result, we shall pay special attention to small firms in the analysis. In this context, our concern was that the smaller firms might be systematically different from large firms in the production processes used. To address this, we examined whether there were differences in sales generating function coefficients by firm size, and found that the largest differences occurred when we split the sample at employment levels of 50 workers. Accordingly, we estimate a sales generating function that allows for different production function parameters for firms employing more than 50 workers and those employing less than 50 workers.

Second, the earlier production function estimation literature assumed that labour can be optimized out in the short run, that is, that hiring and firing costs for labour are negligible. This assumption

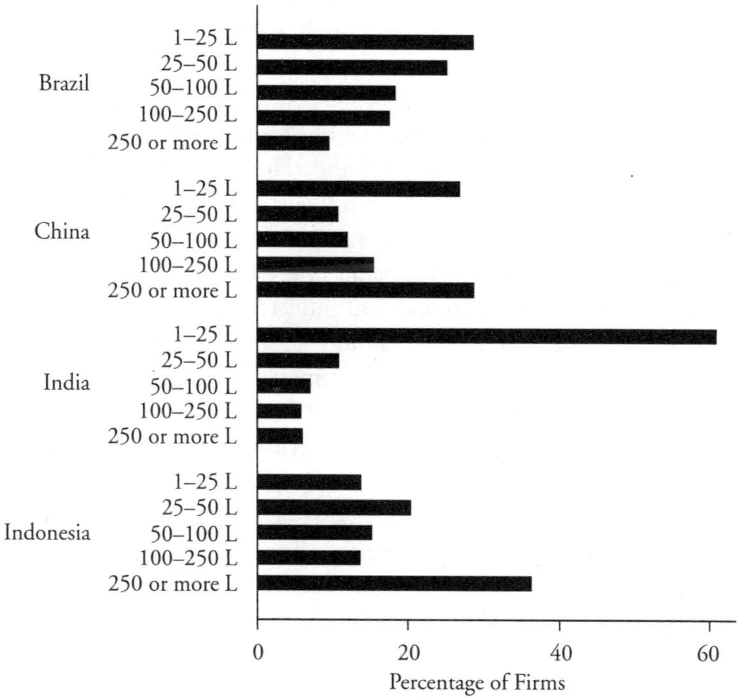

Figure 6.1: Percentage of Firms by Size Group across Countries

Source: Investment Climate Surveys for Brazil, China, India, and Indonesia.

stands in stark contrast with India's labour market regulations. Our survey classifies workers as either permanent or temporary. Specifically, the questionnaire defines temporary labour as all (paid) short-term (that is, for less than a year) workers with no guarantee of renewal of their employment contract, while permanent labour is defined as all paid workers who are not classified as temporary. Our estimation results indicated that we should use separate production function coefficients for the two types of labour, and that we should allow for hiring and firing costs for permanent labour. Therefore, we do not assume that permanent labour is freely adjustable in the short run, as does most prior research.

Factor Costs: Labour

We begin by discussing labour costs. The immobility of labour across states could enable interstate differences in labour costs to develop. Also, our analysis treats permanent labour as a homogenous product. Unfortunately, information on schooling that would allow us to differentiate workers in our analysis was not consistently available. As a result, our underutilization of labour estimates should probably be interpreted as underutilization of labour for the same mix of workers as the firms are currently employing. However, if some types of workers contribute more to the firm's output than others, and there are systematically different fractions of different types of workers in different industries, then this would imply that we should allow for different costs of labour in different industries.

To determine whether we should allow the costs of labour to vary by industry or by state, we estimated a regression of average wages from our survey on industry and state dummies. The industry dummies were neither jointly nor individually significant, whereas many of the state dummies were significant. Consequently, we allowed for differences in labour costs across states but not across industries. Table 6.3 provides the state-level average wages from the Indian Annual Survey of Industries (ASI), using the most inclusive definition of wage in that survey, and compares them to the average wages in our survey. We use the ASI wages in what follows since the ASI sample is more representative than our sample, and because for the vast majority of states, ASI wages are higher than the average wages from our survey. Hence, by using the ASI wages we will, if anything, *underestimate* the extent of labour underutilization.

TABLE 6.3: Average Cost of Labour
(in thousand of Rs)

	Year	*Average wages and benefits per worker*	
		From annual survey of industries	*From investment climate surveys*
Andhra Pradesh	2001	47.6	60.2
	2004	55.8	59.4
Delhi	2001	90.7	45.6
	2004	109.0	91.7
Gujarat	2001	87.6	53.5
	2004	108.1	48.0
Haryana	2001	99.3	56.1
	2004	122.9	106.1
Karnataka	2001	87.1	70.8
	2004	104.4	29.7
Kerala	2001	55.9	35.7
	2004	57.9	33.8
Madhya Pradesh	2001	89.8	51.0
	2004	95.9	16.9
Maharashtra	2001	129.9	80.9
	2004	151.9	29.8
Punjab	2001	59.9	47.6
	2004	71.2	64.2
Tamil Nadu	2001	63.0	62.0
	2004	70.8	57.4
Uttar Pradesh	2001	77.8	49.3
	2004	85.3	65.4
West Bengal	2001	84.6	50.1
	2004	92.6	80.1

Sources: Annual Survey of Industries and Investment Climate Surveys for India.

Factor Costs: Capital

Table 6.4 shows the state-level averages of our measures of the components of the cost of capital. The Indian ASI contains measures of average interest rates on loans and average depreciation rates of capital. Our cost of capital measure is the sum of these two averages.

TABLE 6.4: Average Cost of Capital

		Average cost of capital			
		From annual survey of industries		*From investment climate survey*	
	Year	*Average interest rate*	*Average depreciation rate*	*Average interest rate*	*Median interest rate*
Andhra Pradesh	2001	15.4	8.3	13.4	14.0
	2004	14.0	9.4	9.0	9.3
Delhi	2001	17.1	13.3	11.1	10.0
	2004	11.5	15.0	17.9	14.0
Gujarat	2001	16.4	8.5	13.8	14.0
	2004	10.7	9.4	16.8	10.0
Haryana	2001	19.2	11.0	13.0	14.0
	2004	16.5	13.5	12.2	12.3
Karnataka	2001	12.3	7.3	12.9	12.5
	2004	11.0	9.0	12.2	11.8
Kerala	2001	15.3	9.2	17.0	13.5
	2004	13.8	9.9	11.1	10.5
Madhya Pradesh	2001	14.9	8.6	13.4	12.5
	2004	13.3	9.5	10.1	10.0
Maharashtra	2001	18.4	9.5	13.6	14.0
	2004	13.0	9.1	10.2	10.0
Punjab	2001	21.8	11.3	13.3	14.0
	2004	13.7	11.8	22.1	14.0
Tamil Nadu	2001	19.9	10.0	11.8	12.0
	2004	12.2	10.2	10.9	11.0
Uttar Pradesh	2001	16.0	8.1	13.0	14.0
	2004	12.0	10.0	18.4	12.0
West Bengal	2001	15.6	8.2	13.3	14.0
	2004	8.9	8.6	9.9	10.0

Sources: Annual Survey of Industries and Investment Climate Surveys for India.

Our surveys provide a measure of the interest rate on loans. The mean and median of this measure for each state are shown in the last two columns of the table, and they are quite similar to the interest rates from the Indian ASI.

Note that there is much less variance in the cost of capital across states than there is in the cost of labour. The coefficient of variation of the cost of capital across states is only half that of wages (respectively, 15 per cent and 14 per cent in 2001, and 28 per cent and 30 per cent in 2004). We also regressed the average interest rate of loans from our survey on industry and state dummies. Neither the industry nor the state dummies were jointly or individually significant. Recall that the state dummies were significant in the wage regression. This difference suggests that capital markets in India are able to arbitrage interstate differences in the returns to capital reasonably effectively, while labour markets and labour flows are much less able to arbitrage interstate differences in the returns to labour. For consistency with the labour results, we use the cost of capital from the ASI and allow it to vary across states in the calculations that follow.

Underutilization of Labour

The most striking result that we obtain is the extent of underutilization of labour across manufacturing firms in India. Overall, we estimate

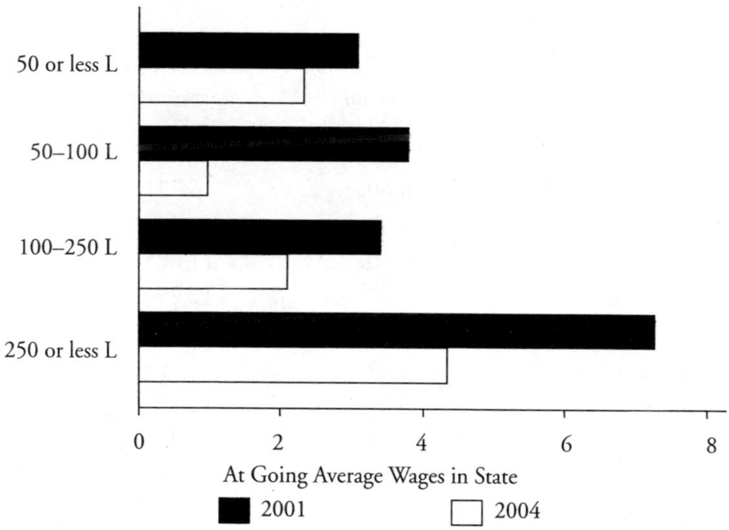

Figure 6.2: Underutilization of Labour by Size Group in India

Source: Authors' calculations based on the Investment Climate Surveys for India.
Notes: In the Y-axis L stands for employees. The figure shows for each year the weighted sum of the measured underutilization of labour across firms, where weights are given by each firm's share in total employment for its size group.

underutilization of 5.8 times current manufacturing employment in 2001, and 3.4 times in 2004. Further, underutilization is estimated to be large and positive for every size group of firms (see Figure 6.2) and every state (see Table 6.5).

The extent of underutilization of labour varies *dramatically* across states. Higher GDP-per-capita states have less underutilization. A similar correlation is evident in the time series dimension. Table 6.6 and Figure 6.3 compare the changes in underutilization of labour by state to the changes in GDP per capita by state between 2001 and 2004. Again, there is a striking negative correlation. Indeed, if we omit one outlier, West Bengal (which exhibits a very large decline in the underutilization of labour), the data look like they were generated by a simple linear model. That is, high GDP-per-capita states exhibit less underutilization of labour, and states where underutilization is falling are states where per-capita GDP is rising. Uttar Pradesh has the lowest GDP per capita and the second-lowest growth rate in

TABLE 6.5: Underutilization of Labour and GDP per Capita by State

	Underutilization of labour	*Level of GDP per capita*
	Average over 2001 and 2004	
Uttar Pradesh	8.60	6,721
Madhya Pradesh	0.37	8,694
West Bengal	8.10	11,825
Andhra Pradesh	6.47	12,290
Kerala	1.77	13,157
Karnataka	1.47	13,793
Tamil Nadu	3.35	14,798
Gujarat	1.58	17,211
Haryana	0.51	17,063
Maharashtra	1.30	17,698
Punjab	0.45	17,697
Delhi	0.22	27,864

Sources: Authors' calculations based on the Investment Climate Surveys for India and indiastat.com.

Note: Per capita GDP is expressed in billion of constant 1993–4 rupees.

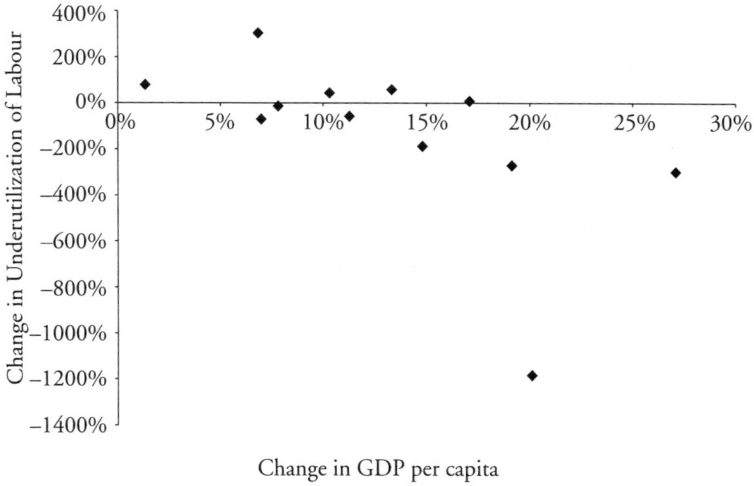

Figure 6.3: Change in Underutilization of Labour and in GDP per Capita across States

Source: Authors' calculations based on the Investment Climate Surveys for India.
Note: Each dot in the figure represents one Indian state and shows the change between 2001 and 2004 in GDP per capita and in the underutilization of labour.

GDP per capita, and hence is considered a 'lagging region'. It has both the highest percentage of underutilization of labour, and the highest growth in that percentage (indeed it is one of the few states where underutilization is growing).

To put these figures in a different light, we calculated what the wage would have had to be for the firm's current employment to be 'statically optimal' (that is, the wage equal to the firm's marginal revenue product of labour at its current employment level). Across manufacturing firms, this wage averaged 6.8 times the current wage rates in 2001 and 4.6 times the current wage rates in 2004. Moreover, in the three states with highest underutilization of labour—Uttar Pradesh, Madhya Pradesh, and West Bengal—this wage averaged about nine times the actual wage in the respective state, a number that is probably larger than the average tenure of a manufacturing worker. In contrast in Delhi, which was the state with the lowest underutilization of labour, the wage averaged about 20 per cent of a worker's year's wages. If nothing more, the large divergence in these numbers across states suggests there is impact from the different labour market regulations across states.

TABLE 6.6: Change in Underutilization of Labour and in GDP per Capita by State

	Change in underutilization of labour between 2001 and 2004	*Change in level of GDP per capita between 2001 and 2004*
Uttar Pradesh	304.2	6.8
Madhya Pradesh	–57.5	11.3
West Bengal	–1182.7	20.1
Andhra Pradesh	–187.2	14.8
Kerala	–270.3	19.1
Karnataka	–69.9	7.0
Tamil Nadu	80.1	1.3
Gujarat	–298.0	27.1
Haryana	58.2	13.3
Maharashtra	8.3	17.1
Punjab	–13.6	7.8
Delhi	43.8	10.3

Sources: Authors' calculations based on the Investment Climate Surveys for India and indiastat.com.

The extent of underutilization of labour decreased significantly between 2001 and 2004. The decrease occurred in all size groups of firms, but was most pronounced among firms with 50 to 100 workers (see Figure 6.2). The size cut-off at which firms must start abiding with restrictive employment regulations in most Indian states is 100 workers, so there is some indication that institutional changes have moderated the impact of those regulations during this period. We note that this occurred at the same time as the fraction of the manufacturing labour force employed by firms in the 50- to 100-worker group increased, so the fall in underutilization of labour in this group was not a result of this size group discarding a disproportionate number of workers. A related fact is that there was a distinct tendency over this period for manufacturing employment to shift from large firms (with more than 250 workers) to moderately sized firms (with 50 to 250 workers).[2]

[2] See Appendix Tables A6.2.1 and A6.2.2.

Underutilization of Capital

The differences between our estimates of the underutilization of capital and that of labour are striking. In particular, there is overutilization of capital; that is, the marginal revenue product of the capital employed at firms tends to be *less* than the cost of capital. As Table 6.7 and Figure 6.4 show, this is true for all size classes of firms and all states in 2001 and in 2004. Indeed, the overutilization of capital is, on average, equal to about three-quarters of the capital stock.

This magnitude is much smaller than the corresponding magnitudes for the underutilization of labour. To see this in a more intuitive way, we calculated what the cost of capital would have had to be for the firm's current capital to be 'statically optimal' (that is, the cost of capital equal to the firm's marginal revenue product of capital at its current capital level). On average, this 'statically optimal' cost of capital was 58 per cent of the current cost of capital in 2001, and 64 per cent in 2004. These numbers are different from one, but only by

Table 6.7: Overutilization of Capital and GDP per Capita by State

	Overutilization of capital	*Level of GDP per capita*
	Average over 2001 and 2004	
Uttar Pradesh	–0.40	6,721
Madhya Pradesh	–0.80	8,694
West Bengal	–0.72	11,825
Andhra Pradesh	–0.88	12,290
Kerala	–0.63	13,157
Karnataka	–0.92	13,793
Tamil Nadu	–0.66	14,798
Gujarat	–0.86	17,211
Haryana	–0.67	17,063
Maharashtra	–0.66	17,698
Punjab	–0.69	17,697
Delhi	–0.59	27,864

Sources: Authors' calculations based on the Investment Climate Surveys for India and indiastat.com.

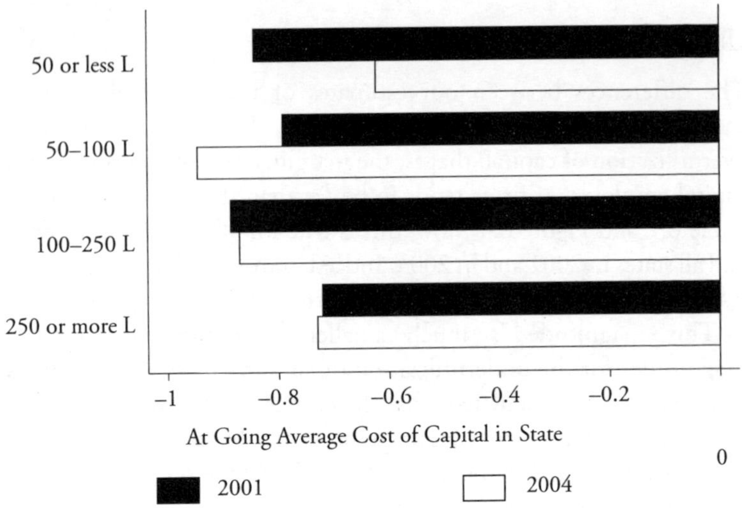

Figure 6.4: Overutilization of Capital by Size Group in India

Source: Authors' calculations based on the Investment Climate Surveys for India. *Notes*: In the Y-axis L stands for employees. The figure shows for each year the weighted sum of the measured overutilization of capital across firms, where weights are given by each firm's share in total capital for its size group.

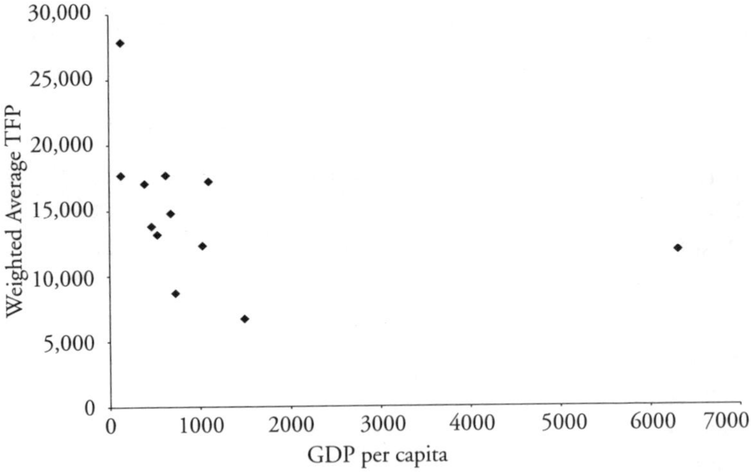

Figure 6.5: Weighted Average TFP and GDP per Capita across States

Source: Authors' calculations based on the Investment Climate Surveys for India. *Note*: Each dot in the figure represents one Indian state and shows the average across 2001 and 2004 of GDP per capita and of weighted average TFP, where weights are given by each firm's share in total sales for its state.

about 40 per cent (recall that the underutilization of labour resulted in ratios of wage rates to marginal productivity of labour of about 600 per cent). Moreover, unlike the figures on underutilization of labour, the extent of overutilization of capital did not change much between 2001 and 2004, it does not vary much across states or size groups, and it is not correlated with differences in GDP per capita across states.[3]

Manufacturing Productivity

While the focus of this chapter is not on the determinants of total factor productivity in the Indian manufacturing sector, we are interested in the relationship between our underutilization measures and productivity. Therefore, we now discuss one

Table 6.8: Average TFP and GDP per Capita by State

	Weighted average TFP	*Unweighted average TFP*	*Level of GDP per capita*
	Average over 2001 and 2004		
Uttar Pradesh	139.41	47.98	6,721
Madhya Pradesh	207.37	63.06	8,694
West Bengal	518.40	81.68	11,825
Andhra Pradesh	66.75	45.72	12,290
Kerala	74.83	36.35	13,157
Karnakata	41.30	33.08	13,793
Tamil Nadu	81.45	61.26	14,798
Gujarat	127.08	40.71	17,211
Haryana	68.98	63.62	17,063
Maharashtra	78.88	40.39	17,698
Punjab	32.23	32.11	17,697
Delhi	33.41	29.41	27,864

Sources: Authors' calculations based on the Investment Climate Surveys for India and indiastat.com.

Note: In calculating weighted average TFP, the weights are given by each firm's share in total sales for its state.

[3] Interestingly, we also find evidence of important underutilization of labour and overutilization of capital in another South Asian country with restrictive labour regulations: Sri Lanka. See Appendix A6.2 for a discussion of those results.

finding on manufacturing productivity that is of interest for the subsequent results. It is presented in Table 6.8 and the accompanying Figure 6.6.

The table and figures show that interstate differences in average manufacturing productivity are not positively correlated with interstate differences in GDP per capita. The precise nature of the relationship between manufacturing productivity and GDP per capita differs depending on whether we consider a sales share weighted average of firm productivity, or an unweighted average of firm productivity. However, it is clear that among all states except those with a very high GDP per capita, there is a negative relationship between manufacturing productivity and GDP per capita, although the relationship flattens out and may turn positive among the highest GDP-per-capita states. If states with higher GDP per capita are those in which overall productivity is higher, the higher productivity levels are coming from sectors other than manufacturing (for example, services).

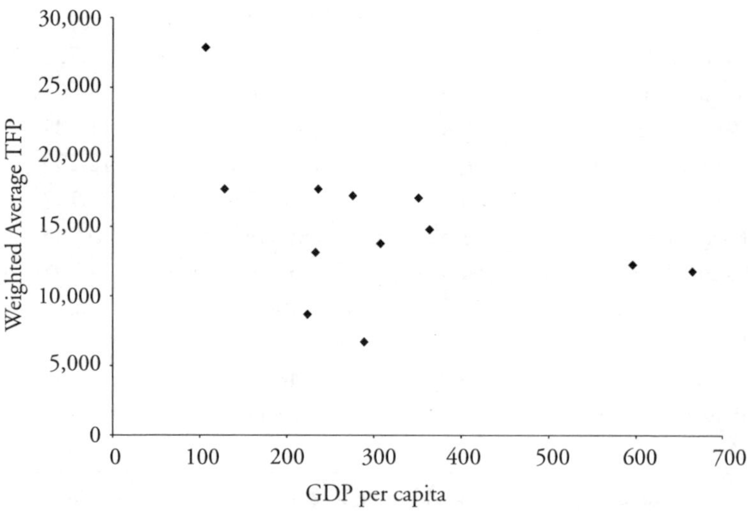

Figure 6.6: Unweighted Average TFP and GDP Per Capita across States

Source: Authors' calculations based on the Investment Climate Surveys for India.
Note: Each dot in the figure represents one Indian state and shows the average across 2001 and 2004 of GDP per capita and of unweighted average TFP.

Relationships between Underutilization Measures, Productivity Measures, and Responses to the Investment Climate Survey

In this section we discuss the findings from a reduced form analysis of the relationships between our firm-level underutilization measures and firm-level productivity, and the relationships between these three variables and the responses to questions in the Investment Climate Surveys. To facilitate the analysis, we estimated a three-equation system using our measures of the underutilization of labour, the underutilization of capital, and productivity, as dependent variables. The 'explanatory' variables are the same in all equations, and are based on information from the Investment Climate Surveys. We put the word explanatory in quotation marks because we want to emphasize that we make no attempt to infer cause and effect from the estimates. We present them only as correlations that a causal model would have to rationalize. The estimates were obtained using seemingly unrelated regression techniques and are shown in Table 6.9.

The variables included from the Investment Climate Surveys were the fraction of the firm's workforce that is unionized, whether the firm had a loan, production losses at the firm due to electricity outages, an indicator of corruption in inspections, the state-year level averages of these variables among the firms in our data set, and the average share of temporary labour in total employment in the state-year (as an indicator of flexibility of local labour markets). Since for each firm-level variable we also include the state-year level averages of these variables, the effects of the firm-level variables should be interpreted as within coefficients; that is, they provide the impact on the dependent variable of the difference between the right-hand side variable and the average of that right-hand side variable in the given state-year.[4]

We begin with the coefficients from the equation that has productivity as the left-hand-side variable, that is, column 3 in Table 6.9. All four of the firm-level variables have significant coefficients in this equation. The estimated positive coefficient on the firm-level

[4] The 'explanatory' variables are described in detail in Appendix Table A6.2.5. For the within interpretation, see Mundlack (1978), who shows that one can allow for group-specific fixed effects in linear equations by including, as additional right-hand-side variables, the group-specific averages of all included right-hand-side variables.

unionization variable indicates that firms with a larger fraction of unionized labour force are more productive than the average firm in their state. This finding could either be a result of it being easier to unionize in more productive firms, or of unionization increasing productivity. All the coefficients on the state-year level variables are more difficult to interpret as the link between a change in the value of the covariate they are attached to and the firm-level outcomes of interest is indirect. Still, if there are regional economies to organizing union activities, the fact that the average level of unionization in the state-year is positively related to productivity would reinforce the possibility that unions find it easier to unionize where manufacturing productivity is higher. Note that the results in Table 6.9 also indicate that states with a higher degree of unionization tend to be states with relatively high underutilization of both capital and labour. Of course, this need not be causal; it may be that there are omitted variables that cause underutilization and are correlated with state-level unionization.

The relationships between productivity and the other firm-specific variables are somewhat easier to interpret. Since our productivity estimates take direct account of the impact of capital on sales, the most obvious interpretation of the positive interaction between productivity and the firm-level loan variable is that loan-granting institutions are able to select out the higher productivity firms in a region. In contrast, the corresponding state-year level variable indicates that the states in which a disproportionately high number of firms received loans were states with lower manufacturing productivity. About three-quarters of loans granted in India are granted by governmental institutions, so the regional pattern of loans might reflect the goals of those institutions. The states in which a disproportionate share of firms has loans are states in which firms have significantly less underutilization of both labour and capital. We note that this finding is not because states that have a higher fraction of firms with loans are the more developed states—at least if we measure development by GDP per capita. We tried adding GDP per capita as a right-hand-side variable to all equations. None of the results presented in Table 6.9 changed notably, and the GDP-per-capita coefficients were all insignificant.

Provided not all production losses due to electricity outages were planned for we would expect the firms within a region that lose a

TABLE 6.9: Underutilization of Labour, Capital, and Productivity

	Dependent Variable is:		
	Under-utilization of labour	*Under-utilization of capital*	*TFP*
	(1)	(2)	(3)
Share of temporary labour in total labour—avg. state-year	6.649 [17.428]	15.814 [30.086]	0.109 [0.129]
Share of workforce unionized	23.276 [21.952]	–23.746 [37.897]	1.275 [0.162]***
Share of workforce unionized—avg. state-year	280.012 [129.199]**	688.058 [223.043]***	4.249 [0.956]***
Dummy for firm with loan	15.236 [8.883]*	–7.157 [15.335]	0.292 [0.066]***
Share of firms with loan—avg. state-year	–77.554 [34.608]**	–181.481 [59.746]***	–1.353 [0.256]***
Production losses due to outages	–14.469 [45.466]	12.919 [78.490]	-0.600 [0.336]*
Production losses due to outages—avg. state-year	343.424 [200.498]*	961.361 [346.130]***	3.680 [1.483]**
Corruption among inspections	18.387 [11.099]*	35.186 [19.160]*	0.231 [0.082]***
Corruption among inspections—avg. state-year	–57.940 [34.661]*	–125.275 [59.837]**	0.492 [0.256]*
Number of observations	1,500	1,500	1,500
'R-squared'	0.014	0.018	0.097

	Variance of:		
	Under-utilization of labour	*Under-utilization of capital*	*TFP*
Total	25,351.1	75,899.4	1.51
Within	24,953.7	75,261.5	1.47
Between	635.4	604.8	0.05

(contd ...)

Table 6.9 (contd ...)

	Variance of Residuals of Equation for:		
	Under-utilization of labour	*Under-utilization of capital*	*TFP*
Total	25,005.8	74,524.4	1.37
Within	24,862.6	74,321.1	1.36
Between	283.4	214.2	0.01

	Under-utilization of capital	*TFP*
Covariance between Residuals of Equation for:		
Underutilization of Labour		
Total	–846,037.0	69,432.7
Within	–802,618.6	70,143.1
Between	–43,418.4	–710.5
Underutilization of Capital		
Total		–24,250.0
Within		–24,311.2
Between		61.1

	Under-utilization of capital	*TFP*
Correlation between Residuals of Equation for:		
Underutilization of Labour		
Total	–0.0131	0.250***
Within	–0.0124	0.253***
Between	–0.0007	–0.0025607
Underutilization of Capital		
Total		–0.051*
Within		–0.051*
Between		0.0001

Source: Authors' calculations based on the Investment Climate Surveys for India.
Notes: Seemingly unrelated regressions estimation used. Standard errors in parentheses. ***, **, and * indicate statistical significance at a 1 per cent, 5 per cent, and 10 per cent confidence levels, respectively. The regressions include year fixed effects.

higher fraction of their output due to electrical outages would have lower productivity, and this is what the results in Table 6.9 show. Also, provided that average production losses across a state influence a firm's perceptions about its own likely future production losses, we should expect a relationship between the state-year level measure of electricity outages and the employment of inputs that have a sunk component to their costs. And we have found that both labour and capital should be treated as inputs with sunk costs in India. As a result, the strong positive relationship between the state-year level measure of production losses due to outages and both our underutilization measures should not be a surprise. Interestingly, there is a positive relationship between productivity and the average production losses due to outages across state-years. This finding suggests that states where manufacturing is productive are the states that are pushing the boundaries of current electricity generating capacity.

The firm-level corruption variable has a positive coefficient in the productivity equation, a finding that might reflect the possibility that it is the more productive firms that are most averse to corruption, and therefore most likely to complain about it. The firm- and state-level coefficients on corruption in the utilization equations are opposite in sign. Firms that complain about corruption tend to employ less labour and capital, *ceteris paribus*, than other firms in the region. On the other hand, the average number of complaints about corruption is higher in states with less underutilization of labour and capital.

None of the other firm-level variables exhibit a significant relationship to either underutilization variable. Indeed, the most striking information on the underutilization variables is contained in the residuals. Note first that the residual variance in both the underutilization regressions is about 98 per cent of the total variance, and about 97 per cent of that variance is within-state variance. Given this, the residual covariances imply that the variable most closely related to underutilization of labour in our data is firm-level productivity. That is, the more productive firms in a region are more likely to be holding back on hiring than less productive firms in the same region. Consequently, if we were able to institute changes in labour regulations that resulted in all firms hiring labour up to the point where the marginal revenue product of labour equalled the wage, we would not only increase employment, but also most likely redistribute output in a way that would increase overall productivity.

Interestingly, the residuals also indicate that the more productive firms do not hold back on investment more than less productive firms. If anything, they utilize relatively more capital. This finding, taken together with the negative correlation between the underutilization of labour and capital residuals, suggests that one effect of the labour regulations in India might be to induce firms, especially more productive firms, to substitute capital for labour.

CONCLUSION

This chapter uses the World Bank Investment Climate Surveys to examine the labour and capital employment rates of Indian formal manufacturing firms, and their relationship to productivity and investment climate variables. We are motivated by our desire to understand the factors underlying the relatively weak performance of the Indian formal manufacturing sector relative to the Indian services sector or the manufacturing sectors in similar countries (for example, China). We define measures of underutilization of labour for Indian firms as the ratio of (*a*) the labour employment that firms would optimally choose if there were no hiring and firing costs at current wage costs, and (*b*) firms' actual employment of labour. Analogously, we construct measures of underutilization of capital for Indian firms.

We find that labour is underutilized in manufacturing firms operating in all states. That is, given the amount of capital used by firms, their productivity, and the cost of labour, firms are employing less labour than they would if they faced no hiring and firing costs. The extent of underutilization of labour differs substantially across Indian states. In particular, states with higher GDP per capita exhibit much less underutilization of labour. In contrast, our results show overutilization of capital in Indian firms, though the extent of this overutilization is much smaller than the extent of underutilization of labour, and does not vary a great deal across states. The overutilization of capital may be a response to the underutilization of labour as firms and states that underutilize labour disproportionately also overutilize capital disproportionately.

The most striking finding from our analysis of the relationships between the underutilization of labour, the underutilization of capital, and productivity, and between these three variables and investment climate variables, is that the extent of underutilization of labour by firms is strongly and positively related to firm productivity. Also, the more productive firms tend to overutilize capital more than the average, though not to the same extent that they underutilize labour.

Overall, our findings suggest that if labour market restrictions in states with 'poorly functioning' labour markets were liberalized to the level of restrictions in states with better functioning labour markets, labour demand and wages would likely increase significantly. Also, such liberalization would likely increase productivity, without significant increases in the demand for capital. Our results suggest that this would occur both because an improvement in the functioning of labour markets would cause the more productive firms to increase their output disproportionately, and because firm productivity should increase as labour and capital employment move towards their efficient levels.

We also obtained a number of other more detailed findings. Firms that suffer more production losses due to electricity outages are less productive within their states and underutilize both labour and capital more than firms in states with less production losses due to electricity outages. Firms reporting more problems with corruption are shown to be the more productive firms in their state, and they also exhibit relatively high underutilization of both factors of production. The relatively more productive firms within states are more likely to receive loans, suggesting that loan-granting institutions are able to target the more productive firms. Finally, we find that states in which a disproportionate number of firms received loans are the states with less underutilization of both factors of production, particularly of capital.

Appendix A6.1: Investment Climate Surveys Data and ASI Data

The sample used for the Investment Climate Survey (also known as Firm Analysis and Competitiveness Survey) of India in the 2002 round was designed to cover firms in the top 40 industrial cities in India (located in 12 states) that account for more than 90 per cent of India's industrial GDP. In the 2005 round, the survey covered additional states, but we exclude them from our analysis that requires information from both 2001 and 2004. See World Bank (2004) and Mengistae, Xu, and Yeung (2006) for more details on the survey and the data.

The measure of output used in our production function estimation is firm value added, defined as total sales minus purchases of raw materials minus consumption of energy minus other costs (for example, overhead expenses, selling and general administration expenses, design department). The measure of capital for 2001 is the sum of the firm reported value of (*a*) replacing all machinery and equipment at the end of 2001, and (*b*) replacing all business premises or leasehold at the end of 2001. Since data on replacement cost for capital was not collected in the 2005 survey round, we constructed the measure of capital for 2004 based on replacement value in 2001, and on the change in book value of fixed assets (machinery and equipment plus land, buildings, and leasehold improvement) between 2001 and 2004. As mentioned in the main text, our measure of labour is the number of permanent workers (all paid workers that are not temporary), and we also consider a measure of temporary labour to equal all (paid) short-term (that is, for less than a year) workers with no guarantee of renewal of their employment contracts.

Appendix Tables A6.2.1, A6.2.3, and A6.2.4 show the distribution of sample firms considered for our analysis of the underutilization of factors across size groups, states, and industries.

In Table A6.2.3 we show a measure of compensation to workers from the Investment Climate Surveys, calculated as the average of firms' total compensation paid to workers (including wages, salaries, and benefits) in each state, divided by the firms' number of permanent workers. In order to compute underutilization of labour across firms, we use the average wage and benefits across Indian states shown in Table A6.2.3, taken from the Annual Survey of Industries. This survey is conducted annually and covers all manufacturing factories employing 10 or more workers using power and those employing 20 or more workers without using power across all Indian states (more information can be found at www.mospi.nic.in). Our measure of average wages and benefits is total emoluments obtained as the sum of the three items below, divided by the total number of manufacturing workers in each state and year.

1. *Wages and salaries*: They are defined to include all remuneration in monetary terms and also payable more or less regularly in each pay period to workers as compensation for work done during the accounting year. This includes: (*a*) direct wages and salary (that is, basic wages/salaries, payment of overtime, dearness, compensatory allowance, house rent and other allowances), (*b*) remuneration for the period not worked (that is, basic wages, salaries and allowances payable for leave periods, paid holidays, payments due to layoffs, and compensation for unemployment, if not paid from sources other than

employers), (*c*) bonuses and ex gratia payments paid both at regular and less frequent intervals (that is, incentive bonuses, good attendance bonuses, productive bonuses, profit-sharing bonuses, festival or year-end bonuses, etc.). The wages are expressed in terms of gross value, that is, before deductions for fines, damages, taxes, provident funds, and employee's state insurance contributions.

2. *Employers' contributions to provident funds and other funds*: including old age benefits, pensions, gratuities, etc., and employers' contributions towards other social security charges, such as employees' state insurance, compensation for work injuries and occupational diseases, provident fund-linked insurance, retrenchment and layoff benefits.
3. *Staff welfare expenses*: including group benefits like direct expenditures on maternity, day care, canteen facilities, educational, cultural and recreational facilities, and grants to trade unions, and cooperative stores for employees.

In Table A6.2.4 we show a measure of cost of capital from the Investment Climate Surveys, calculated as the average in each state of the interest rate on loans taken by firms since 1992. In order to compute underutilization of capital across firms, we use the average cost of capital across Indian states shown in Table A6.2.4, taken from the Annual Survey of Industries.

Our measure of the average cost of capital is obtained as the sum of the average interest rate, calculated as the ratio of items (i) and (ii) below, and the average depreciation rate obtained as the ratio of items (iii) and (iv) given below.

1. Interest paid
2. *Outstanding loans*: represent all loans (short term or long term, interest bearing or not) outstanding according to the books of the factory on the closing day of the accounting year.
3. *Depreciation*: is consumption of fixed capital due to wear and tear and obsolescence during the accounting year, and is taken as provided by the factory owner or is estimated on the basis of cost of installation and working life of the fixed assets.
4. *Fixed capital*: represents the depreciated value of fixed assets owned by the factory on the closing day of the accounting year. Fixed assets are those that have a normal productive life of more than one year. Fixed capital includes land, including leasehold land, buildings, plant and machinery, furniture and fixtures, transport equipment, water systems and roadways, and other fixed assets such as hospitals, schools, etc., used for the benefit of the factory personnel.

Appendix A6.2: Underutilization of Labour and Capital in Sri Lanka

This appendix briefly examines the underutilization of labour and capital in Sri Lanka, another country characterized by restrictive labour market regulations, as discussed by the World Bank (2007). Note an important difference in the restrictiveness of labour market regulations in India versus Sri Lanka. In India, the restrictiveness lies in the difficulty of firing workers. However, Indian workers who are fired are entitled to low severance payments by international standards (see Ahsan and Pages 2005). In Sri Lanka, the restrictiveness lies in the very high severance payments to which fired workers are entitled.

Our approach is similar to that used for India: that is, we construct underutilization of labour at current wage rates and underutilization of capital at current capital costs. However, we modify the approach, given Sri Lanka's much smaller size and different regulatory environment. Sri Lanka is a unitary state and its provinces do not have legislative power on labour market regulations as the Indian states do. Thus, we consider Sri Lanka as a single labour market and a single capital market, not examining differences across provinces. Our analysis uses data from the World Bank Investment Climate Survey conducted in Sri Lanka in 2004. This dataset suffers from some caveats relative to India's dataset. First, the Sri Lanka data is from a single survey round rather than two survey rounds. Thus, we are forced to use retrospective data for the accounting variables, which as we mentioned in the second part of the chapter, can suffer from measurement problems. Second, the measure of capital used for firms in Sri Lanka is book value of capital, since replacement value information was not collected. Third, since we do not have data from a Sri Lanka census source similar to the Indian ASI, we use measures of average compensation per worker from the Investment Climate Survey, which may under- or over-estimate the true labour costs faced by firms in the manufacturing sector. Fourth, some numerical problems constrain us to estimate the production function using the standard Olley and Pakes (1996) technique; that is, allowing labour to be adjustable in the short run, in contrast to India, where labour was assumed to be fixed in the short run. However, our production function estimation allows for different coefficients for firms employing more than 50 workers and for firms employing less than 50 workers, as in the case of India. These caveats imply that the numbers below need to be taken with a lot of caution, as they are only broadly indicative of the patterns of underutilization of factors. In particular, one should not compare the magnitudes of underutilization of factors between India and Sri Lanka since they are based on different data and on production function coefficients estimated using different techniques.

Our main finding is strong evidence of underutilization of labour across manufacturing firms in Sri Lanka. Overall, we estimate underutilization of 1.1 times current manufacturing employment in 2003. Underutilization of labour is estimated to be positive for every size group of firms. We also calculated what the wage would have to be for firms' current employment to be 'statically optimal' (that is, the wage equal to a firm's marginal revenue product of labour at its current employment level). This wage averaged 2.1 times the current wage rates in 2003. As mentioned in the third section of this chapter, one has to be careful with the interpretation of these magnitudes. These figures do not imply that if there were no hiring and firing costs and constraints in Sri Lanka, and firms were maximizing profits, they would increase their employment by 110 per cent. If firms started increasing their employment, wages would rise, output would rise, and the prices of the firms' outputs would fall (beyond what we are allowing for here). These two factors would moderate the actual equilibrium employment implications of reducing hiring and firing costs and constraints.

For manufacturing firms in Sri Lanka we also find evidence of overutilization of capital. Specifically, the overutilization of capital is on average equal to about a third of the capital stock in 2003. As in the case of India, this magnitude is much smaller than the corresponding magnitudes for the underutilization of labour. We also calculated what the cost of capital would have to be for the firm's current capital to be 'statically optimal' (that is, the cost of capital equal to the firm's marginal revenue product of capital at its current capital level). On average across manufacturing firms this 'statically optimal' cost of capital was 58 per cent of the current cost of capital in 2003. While this number is not too far from 100 per cent, recall that the underutilization of labour resulted in a ratio of current wage rates to marginal productivity of labour of about 210 per cent.

TABLE A6.2.1: Distribution of Sample Firms across Size Groups

	2001	*2004*
50 or less employees	81.4	78.4
50–100 employees	7.2	9.4
100–250 employees	5.6	6.7
250 or more employees	5.8	5.6
Number of observations	1,296	721

Source: Authors' calculations based on the Investment Climate Surveys for India.

Table A6.2.2: Share of Total Employment across Size Groups

	Distribution of total employment across firm size groups	
	2001	*2004*
50 or less employees	16.9	16.6
50–100 employees	7.3	8.8
100–250 employees	12.3	15.4
250 or more employees	63.5	59.1

Source: Authors' calculations based on the Investment Climate Surveys for India.

Table A6.2.3: Distribution of Sample Firms across States

	Distribution of sample firms states	
	2001	*2004*
Gujarat	9.7	15.0
Karnataka	11.1	3.5
West Bengal	9.2	4.3
Punjab	9.0	10.8
Tamil Nadu	9.0	9.2
Kerala	3.6	2.1
Delhi	5.9	6.4
Andhra Pradesh	7.6	6.7
Uttar Pradesh	10.0	11.4
Maharashtra	10.8	12.3
Haryana	6.3	6.9
Madhya Pradesh	7.7	11.5
Number of observations	1,296	721

Source: Authors' calculations based on the Investment Climate Surveys for India.

Table A6.2.4: Distribution of Sample Firms across Industries

	2001	*2004*
Textiles	12.2	8.5
Garments and leather	18.7	11.9
Metals and machinery	8.8	9.2

(contd ...)

Table A6.2.4 (contd ...)

	2001	*2004*
Electronics	16.4	16.6
Chemicals and pharmaceuticals	18.6	21.2
Transport equipment	15.7	21.5
Food	9.7	11.1
Number of observations	1296	721

Source: Authors' calculations based on the Investment Climate Surveys for India.

TABLE A6.2.5: Definition of Variables Used in System of Equations

Variable	*Definition*
Share of workforce unionized	Dummy variable equal to 1 if the firm has a bank loan or overdraft from a financial institution.
Production losses due to outages	Percentage of sales lost due to electricity interruptions, including lost production time from the outage, time needed to reset the machines, and production and sales lost due to processes being interrupted.
Corruption in inspections	Dummy variable equal to 1 if the firms reports that a gift or an informal payment was expected or requested during inspections from the tax inspectorate, labour, fire and building safety, sanitation/epidiemology, police, and environmental agencies.

REFERENCES

Ahsan, A. and C. Pages. 2005. 'Helping or Hurting Workers? Assessing the Effects of De Jure and De Facto Labour Regulation in India', Mimeo, World Bank.

Besley, T. and R. Burgess. 2004. 'Can Labour Regulation Hinder Economic Performance? Evidence from India', *Quarterly Journal of Economics*, 119: 91–134.

Fallon, P. and R. Lucas. 1991. 'The Impact of Changes in Job Security Regulations in India and Zimbabwe', *World Bank Economic Review*, 5: 395–413.

Fernandes, A. and A. Pakes. 2008. 'Factor Utilization in Indian

Manufacturing: A Look at the World Bank Investment Climate Surveys Data', NBER Working Paper 14178.

Mengistae, T., C. Xu, and B. Yeung. 2006. 'China vs. India: A Microeconomic Look at Comparative Macroeconomic Performance', Mimeo, World Bank, Washington, D.C.

Mundlak, Y. 1978. 'On The Pooling of Time Series and Cross Section Data', *Econometrica*, 46: 69–85.

OECD. 2007. *OECD Employment Outlook*.

Olley, G. and A. Pakes. 1996. 'The Dynamics of Productivity in the Telecommunications Equipment Industry', *Econometrica*, 64: 1263–97.

World Bank. 2004. *Improving the Investment Climate in India*. World Bank.

———. 2006. *India's Employment Challenge: Creating Jobs, Helping Workers*. World Bank.

———. 2007. *Doing Business in South Asia*. World Bank.

7 IS SERVICE SECTOR A SOURCE OF GROWTH?

Aaditya Mattoo

INTRODUCTION

The performance of the services sector is vital for development in South Asia. First of all, services—which include finance, communications, transport, distribution, health and education—are already the largest and often the fastest-growing part of the economy in South Asian countries (see Basu and Mertens, this volume). Value added generated in services accounts for over 50 per cent of GDP in all South Asian countries except Nepal. Apart from their direct contribution to GDP, services affect the performance of other sectors of the economy and the productive potential of the people. Despite recent improvements, access to services remains inadequate in the region. These inadequacies hurt South Asians not just in their role as consumers, but also perpetuate poverty by undermining the productivity of firms and farms, as well as their ability to engage in trade. Sustaining high economic growth and achieving poverty reduction therefore critically depends on the improved performance of the services sector in South Asian countries.

International integration of services markets—encompassing cross-border trade in business and transport services, consumption by foreigners of tourism, health and education services, foreign direct investment in banking, communication, and distribution, and temporary migration of doctors, teachers, and construction workers—has a powerful influence on the performance of services sectors. Much of this integration has been driven by changes in technology, but policy reform has also played a role. Greater regional and global integration alleviates, in principle, the constraints on the development of the services sector due to the limited endowments of South Asian countries in terms of capital and skills, as well as the smallness of some markets.

Despite the striking growth in services exports from some Indian states and the remarkable dynamism of the liberalized telecommunications sector in South Asia, the gains for this region from international integration are small so far compared to the unexploited opportunities. But there are also significant challenges. Exposing previously 'non-tradable' sectors to international competition could imply changes in income distribution and adjustment costs, fears that could lead to the persistence of protection at home and abroad. Also, some of the smaller and poorer countries and regions within countries may be no better equipped to engage in services trade than they were in merchandise trade, and hence there is a danger of further marginalization. This creates a vital question for policymakers and the development community: How can South Asian countries secure the benefits from the internationalization of services without painful disruption and widening inequalities?

This chapter presents the results of some preliminary research on four questions:

- What prevents the success of some Indian states in services trade from being replicated in other regions of South Asia?
- Why do policies affecting international integration matter?
- How can further domestic reforms in services, including liberalization, improve overall economic performance as well as the attainment of social goals?
- How can international cooperation help?

The Determinants of Services Output and Exports

Basu and Maertens (this volume) provide a detailed discussion on sectoral growth experience in each country of the region, so only a few observations would be made here. If we look at the cross-country relationship between the share of services in GDP and GDP per capita, India is a marginal outlier (Figure 7.1, upper panel). But in the cross-country relationship between the share of services exports in total cross-border exports and GDP per capita, India is a significant outlier (Figure 7.1, lower panel). Since the mid-1990s, the business services exports of India grew by over 10 per cent per annum, and included not just call centre services, but an ever-

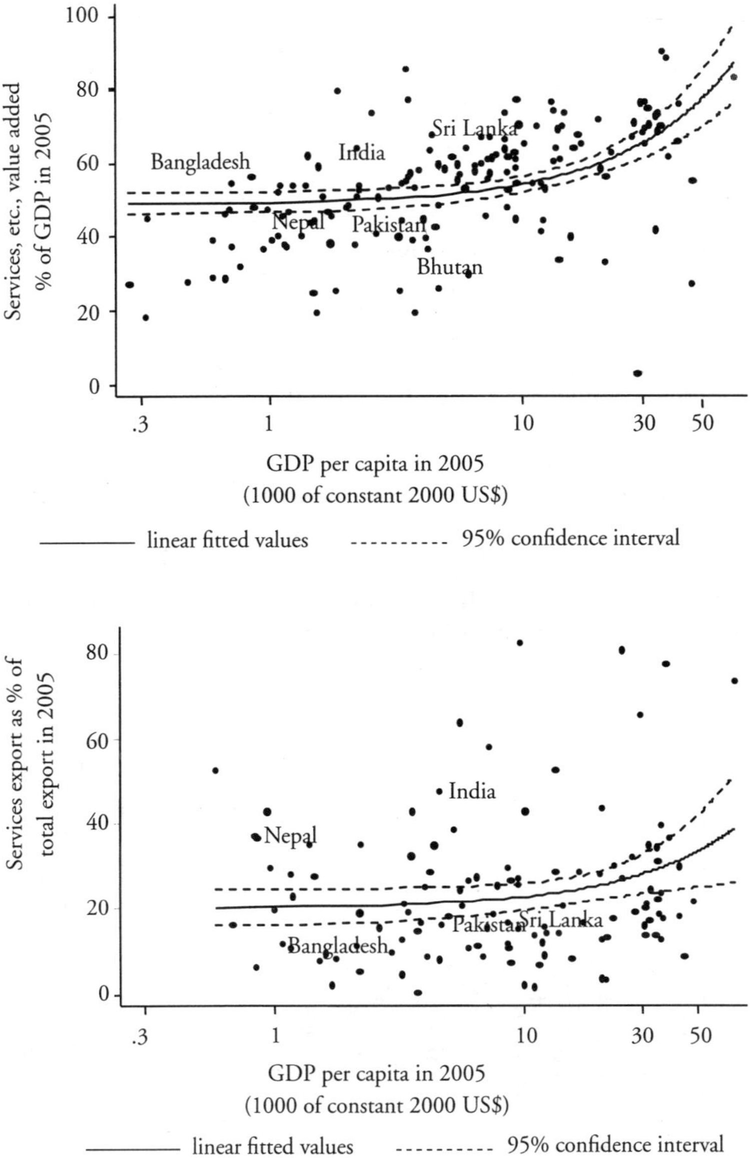

Figure 7.1: Share of Services in GDP and Service Exports in Total Exports against GDP per Capita, 2005

Source: World Bank, *World Development Indicators 2005*.

widening range of professional, research and development, and health services. In 2005, India was the eleventh largest exporter of services, with US$56 billion in exports (8 per cent of GDP). However, not all South Asian countries are participating in service exports: in some, cross-border exports of services stagnated. Figure 7.1 shows that with the exception of Nepal (because of tourism), other South Asian countries have underperformed in exporting services. Even within India, services exports employ only a tiny fraction of the labour force, most of whom are located in a few states.[1]

Today, the entire region wishes to emulate the success of some Indian states (or rather cities) in producing and exporting services. But policy action remains ad hoc—ranging from the creation of IT parks to the granting of tax exemptions—and uninformed by any serious empirical analysis of the determinants of success. Preliminary evidence suggests that the deeper determinants of comparative advantage in services include endowments (especially of human capital), infrastructure (especially relating to telecommunications), and institutions (especially regulatory and contract enforcing). Their evolution can be influenced by current policy choices.

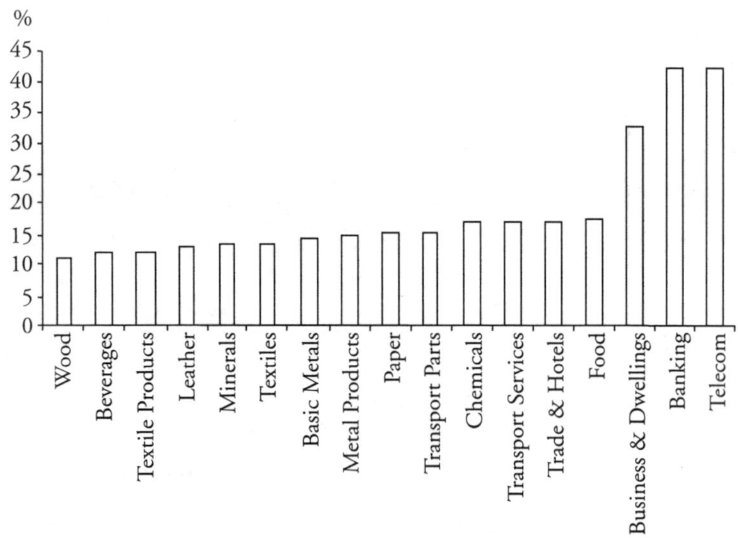

Figure 7.2a: Skill Intensity of Sectors (skilled to total labour ratios)

[1] World Bank (2004), *Sustaining India's Services Revolution: Access to Foreign Markets, Domestic Reform and International Negotiations.*

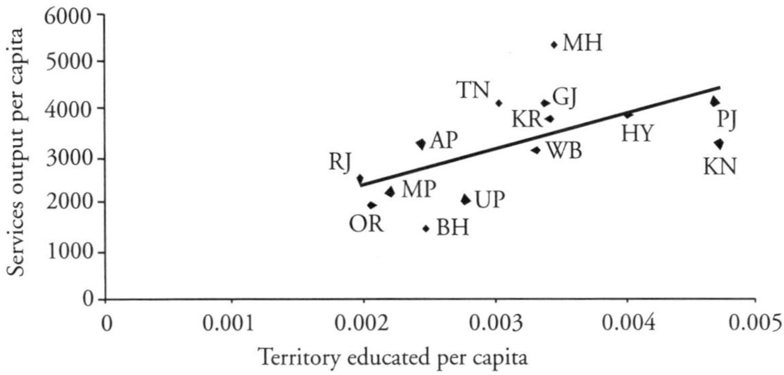

Figure 7.2b: Per Capita Services Output and Tertiary Education across Indian States

Source: Amin and Mattoo (2006).

As services are typically skill intensive (see Figure 7.2a), human capital is a critical source of comparative advantage. As Figure 7.2b shows, across Indian states, services output per capita is strongly associated with the number of people with tertiary education per capita.

Recent research identifies certain types of institutions as sources of comparative advantage in services. First, because it is difficult for consumers to see and inspect services (and all the relevant characteristics of service providers like doctors and banks) before buying and consuming services, consumers rely on regulatory institutions to provide quality assurance through certification and licensing mechanisms. Second, services tend to be customized and require relationship-specific investments by consumers and suppliers, and so the development of services markets is facilitated by contract enforcement institutions (Figure 7.3a—see Amin and Mattoo [2006] for a more detailed discussion). As Figure 7.3b shows, across Indian states, services output per capita is strongly associated with relatively stronger institutions reflected, for example, by the transmission and distribution losses of the public sector electricity providers. Other research finds that the state of telecommunications, itself dependent on the quality of regulatory institutions and policy, has a significant influence on the pattern of services trade.

The aforementioned analysis may help to understand the constraints to the development of services in certain South Asian countries. Some constraints are common to the region,

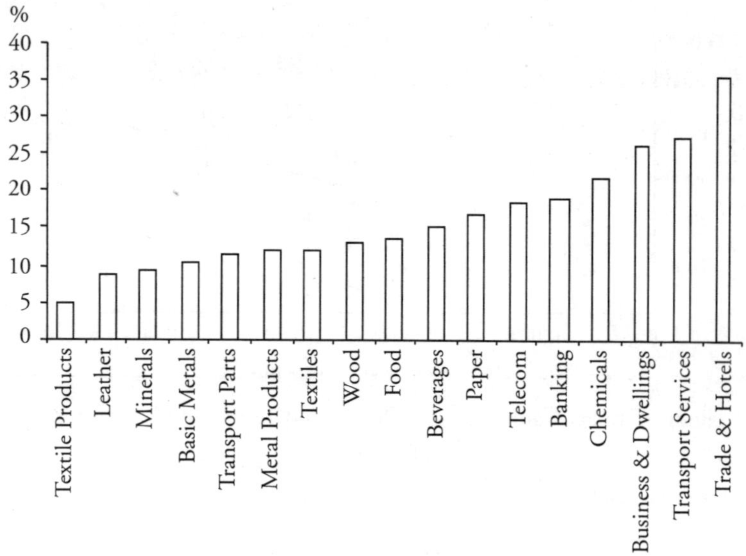

Figure 7.3a: Institutional Dependence of Sectors
(Measured by concentration of upstream and downstream transactions)

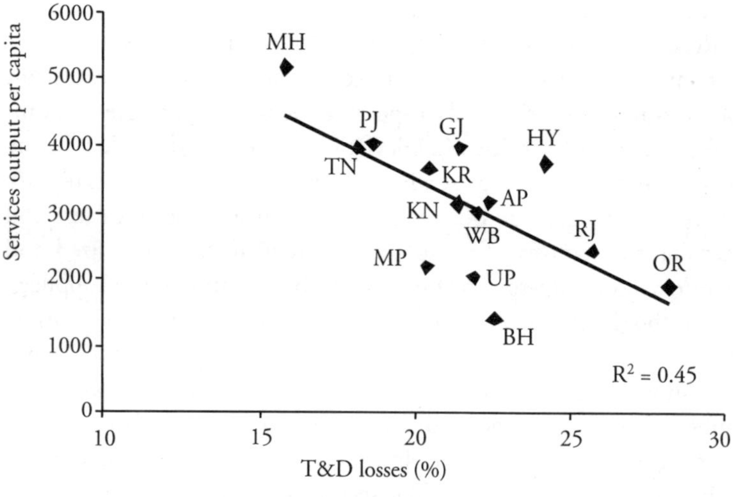

Figure 7.3b: Per Capita Services Output and Institutional Quality across Indian States
(Measured by transmission and distribution losses of public sector electricity undertakings)

Source: Amin and Mattoo (2006).

while others are felt more acutely in specific countries. In each country, including India, overly restrictive regulation has seriously weakened the mechanism for creating human capital—that is, the higher education system (see later). While all countries are seeing improvements in telecommunications infrastructure, impediments to competition in Nepal, Bangladesh, and Sri Lanka create a drag on progress. And political conflict and weak regulatory institutions have deterred foreigners from investing and outsourcing in all but a few locations.

Sri Lanka has nascent exports of information technology-enabled services, with a particular niche in knowledge process outsourcing (KPO). But the industry faces formidable constraints. The most serious is the security situation in the country, which deters foreign investment and outsourcing, and also requires precautionary measures that increase the cost of operation. Another barrier is the high cost of telecommunications services—apparently the cost of a dedicated line is twice as high as in India—because a fully competitive environment still does not exist. The third problem is the scarcity and high cost of skilled workers outside of certain areas like accountancy, both because of limitations of the domestic higher education system and emigration. Finally, space itself has become a constraint in Colombo, where infrastructure and skills are concentrated. The result is that even a company like Amba, which was founded in Sri Lanka, has chosen to expand not locally, but in India and Costa Rica.

After virtual stagnation in the 1990s, Pakistan has seen significant growth of business services exports since 2001, particularly software and IT-enabled services, as shown by data obtained from the State Bank of Pakistan and the Pakistan Software Export Board (PSEB). But exports are still small in absolute magnitude, and originate almost entirely in the three major cities, Islamabad, Karachi, and Lahore. While there have been significant improvements in access to telecommunications, access remains concentrated in urban areas. The high cost of office space (despite subsidies from the PSEB) could be alleviated by a diffusion of economic activity, but this is prevented inter alia by the geographic concentration of telecommunications infrastructure. Steps are being taken to increase the availability of appropriate skills (through reform of higher and vocational education), but the high rates of skilled emigration require an integrated view to be taken of education and emigration. A recurrent theme is the reluctance to outsource to Pakistan because of a supposedly negative external perception of the business and political environment in Pakistan—and there is strong awareness in Pakistan of the benefits of, and constraints to, collaboration with reputable Indian and international companies.

Does International Integration in Services Matter?

The Conceptual Link to Growth

In endogenous growth models, the impact of trade liberalization on output growth can be positive or negative. If the resource allocation effects of trade policy changes promote sectors or activities that generate more long-run growth, the impact is positive, and negative otherwise. For example, if trade liberalization shifts resources into manufacturing and away from agriculture, this will have a positive impact on long-run growth if manufacturing generates greater positive externalities or creates knowledge, that is, if it possesses the attributes necessary for endogenous growth. The impact of trade policy on growth is thus an empirical question.

What about services? It does not seem unreasonable to assume that certain services industries, like certain goods industries, possess growth-generating characteristics (see Box 7.1). In sectors like telecommunications, software, financial services, and transport, there is considerable scope for learning by doing, knowledge generation, expanding product variety, and upgrading product quality, though the precise extent of these possibilities is an empirical question.

A key difference between trade in goods and services in terms of their growth impact is that 'imports' of services often must be locally produced. As long as greater foreign factor participation is associated with increased competition, there will be a larger scale of activity, and hence greater scope for generating growth-enhancing effects. If foreign participation merely substitutes for domestic factors and the sector does not expand, that is, the degree of competition remains unchanged, then there cannot be a positive growth impact on account of the scale effect. Conversely, a larger scale achieved merely by eliminating domestic barriers to entry and attracting domestic resources from other sectors would suffice to generate larger endogenous growth.

Box 7.1: Services and Development

Efficient services not only provide a direct benefit to consumers, but also help shape overall economic performance. An efficient and well-regulated financial sector leads to the efficient transformation of savings to investment, ensuring that resources are deployed wherever they have the highest returns, and facilitates better risk sharing in the economy. Improved efficiency in telecommunications generates economy-wide benefits, because this service is a vital intermediate input and also is crucial to the dissemination and diffusion of knowledge. The spread of the Internet and the dynamism that it has lent to economies around the world is telling testimony to the importance of telecommunications services. Similarly, transport services contribute to the efficient distribution of goods within a country, and are particularly important in influencing a country's ability to participate in global trade.

Although these are the more prominent services, others are also crucial. Business services such as accounting and legal services are important in reducing transaction costs—the high level of which is considered one of the most significant impediments to economic growth in Africa. Education and health services are necessary to build up the stock of human capital. Retail and wholesale services are a vital link between producers and consumers, and influence the efficiency with which resources are allocated to meet consumer needs. Software development is the foundation of the modern knowledge-based economy. Environmental services contribute to sustainable development by helping alleviate the negative impact of economic activity in the environment.

Even without scale effects, and even if services sectors do not possess endogenous growth attributes, the import of foreign factors that characterizes services sector liberalization could still have positive effects because they are likely to bring with them the source of endogenous growth, namely, technology. If greater technology and knowledge transfer accompany services liberalization—either embodied in foreign direct investment (FDI) or disembodied—the growth effect will be stronger. There is evidence demonstrating that technology diffuses through trade in goods and affects total factor productivity growth. At least theoretically, the same should hold true for technology that is diffused through factor flows.

Empirical Evidence

Over the past decade, South Asian countries have made considerable advances in reducing the role of the state in the provision of key infrastructure services and opening service industries to domestic and foreign competition in telecommunications, banking, insurance, business, and health services. There is some evidence from India to suggest that the reforms, combined with access to the global market, seem to have played a role in raising the growth rates of value added and employment in a number of services sectors (Figure 7.4). On the other hand, sectors that have experienced limited opening, like air transport, legal services, real estate, dwellings, railways, post, and storage, have grown less slowly than the rest of the services sector.[2] But these observations should be treated with caution because at this stage we are not in a position to control for other determinants of growth in these sectors.

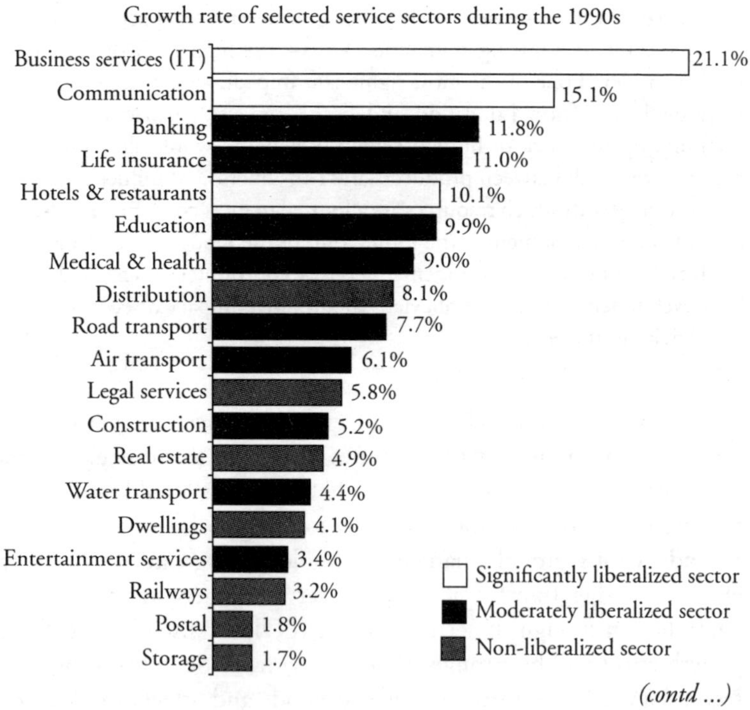

(contd ...)

[2] Some of these sectors have only been liberalized recently and growth may respond after a lag.

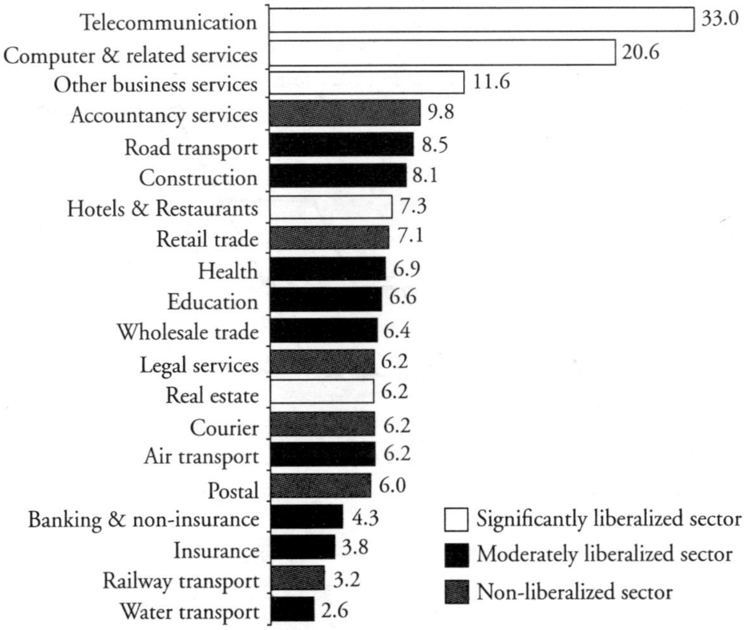

Figure 7.4: Growth Rates of Value Added and Employment in Selected Services Sectors in the 1990s in India

Source: Mattoo, Mishra, and Narain (2007).

In a cross-section, cross-country regression analysis, Mattoo, Rathindran, and Subramanian (2006) find that controlling for other determinants of growth, countries with open financial and telecommunications sectors grew, on average, about 1 percentage point faster than other countries. Fully liberalizing both the telecommunications and the financial services sectors was associated with an average growth rate of 1.5 percentage points above that of other countries.

The positive association between policy reforms in services and inward FDI in services, and between TFP growth performance of downstream firms and FDI is perhaps the most robust finding to emerge from the limited empirical research on the impacts of services reforms. Work in progress by Arnold, Javorcik, Mattoo, and Lipscomb (2007), based on panel data for over 4,000 Indian firms for the 1990–2005 period, examines the link between services sector

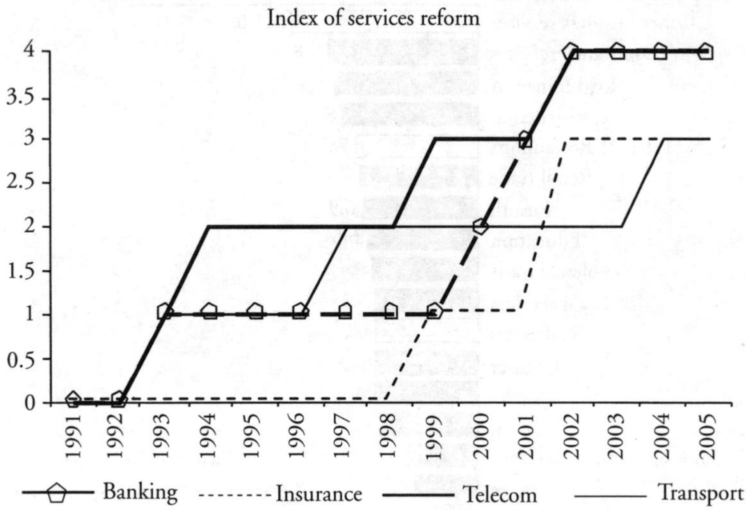

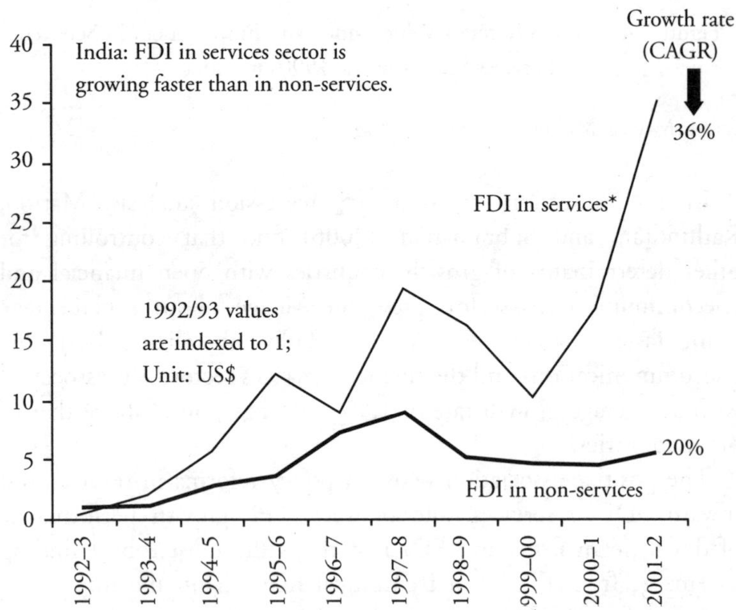

Figure 7.5a: Services Policy Reforms in India, FDI and TFP

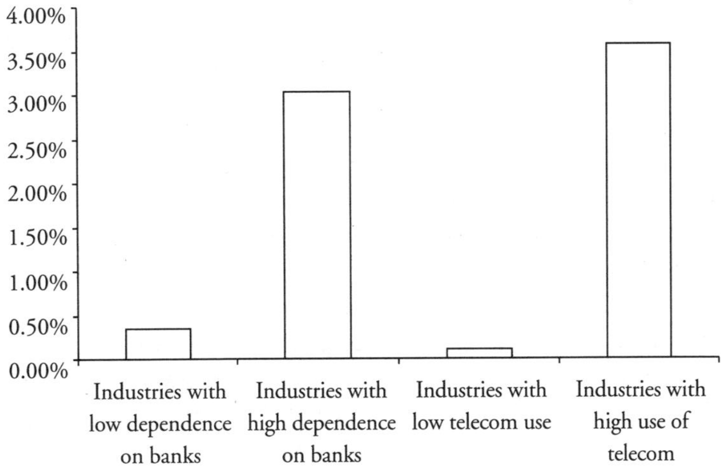

Figure 7.5b: Impacts of Banking and Telecom Reforms on User Industries

Source: Arnold, Javorcik, Mattoo, and Lipscomb (2007).

reforms and manufacturing productivity and export propensity. In recent years, India has radically reformed a number of key 'backbone' services sectors (Figure 7.5a). Barriers to entry by new private firms have been eliminated in telecommunications and freight transport, and are being phased out in insurance and banking—even though restrictions on foreign ownership remain. These reforms are associated with a significant increase of FDI in services, outpacing FDI in goods (panel 2 in Figure 7.5a). There is a significant positive relationship between Indian policy reforms in banking, telecommunications, and transport, and the productivity of firms in manufacturing industries. Enterprises that rely more intensively on services, such as banking and telecommunications, have higher TFP growth rates (Figure 7.5b).

Priorities for Further Reform

As noted earlier, all South Asian countries are today much more open to foreign participation in services. There are signs that FDI in services is beginning to facilitate the diffusion of technology, leading to lower prices, improved quality, and a greater variety of services. Yet there are also concerns about the implications of FDI in services in concentrated and inadequately regulated markets, its impact on employment, and most of all the consequences for access to essential services for the poor. Conflicts between efficiency and equity could arise, for example, as services are liberalized and cross-subsidies become unsustainable, services exports increase, and service standards gravitate towards international levels.

A new World Bank database provides a first view of the state of services policies across five South Asian countries (see appendix Table 7A.1). Even though the countries have moved away from public monopolies in sectors such as communications, finance, and transport, they still restrict new foreign entry in certain ways. Some countries, for example, are unwilling to allow foreigners to acquire majority ownership or full control of firms in certain sectors. Do these restrictions matter? And if they do, how might countries sequence their removal with efforts to improve regulation and implement universal access policies? How do the regulatory preconditions for successful liberalization differ with sector and country? This essay can only provide some examples of reform issues in specific areas and countries, and identify some of the questions that policymakers and analysts must address.

Higher Education

The state of higher education, as we have seen, is a key determinant of the dynamism of the services sector. In each country, higher education has been hobbled by restrictive regulation that does little to remedy market failure and much to inhibit entry and efficiency. Poorly attuned to the needs of the market, educational institutions are seen by many businesses as producing few graduates with relevant skills. With increasing incomes and liberalized foreign exchange regimes, a growing number of the affluent choose to 'import education' by studying abroad—India's spending on education abroad increased exponentially in the last decade—while governments continue to restrict the entry of foreign educational institutions.

In some countries, like Sri Lanka, no private (including foreign) providers are allowed to offer higher education services. Educational institutions are seen by many businesses in Sri Lanka as unresponsive to their needs. The public education system produces a large number of graduates who are apparently suitable only for public employment, with the result that Sri Lanka has an exceptionally large number of bureaucrats per capita. In other countries, like India, there are no explicit barriers, but the regulatory environment (which limits the freedom of institutions to charge fees, admit students on the basis of merit, modify courses, and grant degrees) deters all but the more dubious institutions. A new Foreign Educational Institutions bill has been put before Parliament, but again it is designed more to regulate than to facilitate foreign entry.

All of the countries are also facing a conflict between excellence and access. In India, an increasingly large proportion of places in universities are now reserved for the 'backward castes', even though there has been virtually no serious analysis of what the impact of such reservations has been and would be. Reform in many countries is inhibited by the strength of vested interests, ranging from politicized student bodies that oppose the introduction of fees, to politician-owners of the few incumbent private institutions, who oppose competition.

All countries are in the process of assessing how higher education can serve the needs of the modern economy. Nepal and Pakistan have already begun to implement significant reforms. A central issue is: How can more liberal conditions of entry for domestic and foreign institutions and greater scope for competition exist, without sacrificing quality and while improving access to higher education.

TELECOMMUNICATIONS

Telecommunications growth is the most powerful symbol of the vitality of the services sector, while at the same time being critical for the further development of other services. While there has been a dramatic transformation of this sector, some issues remain: in India, there are still restrictions on foreign ownership; in Bangladesh, a monopoly in international telephony exists; in Nepal, there is an overbearing incumbent and inconsistency between an ostensibly liberal policy and a still-restrictive telecom law; and in Sri Lanka, there is strong suspicion of a cartel of operators, which operates under a regulator who is not independent, but reports to the president.

Nepal has the fifth-lowest teledensity in the world, making it lower than Somalia and much lower than Bangladesh. Again, the handicap of geography has been compounded by the perversity of policy. In addition to a state-owned provider, Nepal Telecom, Nepal has granted exclusive licenses until 2009 to United Telecommunications Limited (UTL) (under majority Indian government ownership) in fixed and Spice Telecom (under majority Kazakhstan ownership) in mobile telephone service. One problem is that the regulator, Nepal Telecommunications Authority (NTA), is self-admittedly powerless to prevent the state-owned incumbent from indulging in anti-competitive practices—which the CEOs of both rival companies blame for their own limited expansion. Second, the exclusive licenses have created duopolies in both fixed and mobile telephony, which are depriving Nepalese of the benefits of meaningful competition in this sector.

Another key issue is the design of universal access policies. India's programme, hitherto focused almost exclusively on fixed line and fixed wireless service, is now providing subsidies for the creation of mobile infrastructure that will be shared among providers. In Bangladesh, given the geography and population density, a universal access scheme is less relevant than the creation of a national backbone. The government is shifting from improving the incumbent's infrastructure to drawing in power and railways to help develop new lines that can be leased to commercial operators like Grameen Phone Ltd. In Sri Lanka it also seems that the creation of a national backbone is a priority; that the incumbent has charged excessively high rates for access to its infrastructure; and that efforts are being made to draw in power providers. In Nepal, a rural telecom development fund exists, but the target of two PCOs per village development committee would not deliver meaningful access.

The priorities, with varying emphasis in each country, are to reform the incumbent operator; strengthen the regulator and enhance its independence from both the incumbent and the government; eliminate barriers to entry other than those dictated by such issues as scarcity of spectrum; and establish an effective universal access scheme that widens access to services in poor and remote areas.

Civil Aviation

A few years ago, a passenger who wanted to travel from Colombo (Sri Lanka) to Karachi (Pakistan) had to go via Dubai, and a passenger who wanted to travel from Colombo to Dhaka (Bangladesh) had to go via Bangkok (Thailand). A liberal agreement with Pakistan made a more direct routing possible for Sri Lankans. In much of the rest of South Asia, little has changed. Restrictive bilateral air service agreements (BASAs) keep regional transport prices high and lead to circuitous routing.

Landlocked countries may be victims of geography, but their isolation is sometimes deepened by their own policies, as well as those of their neighbours. Nepal's unquestioned comparative advantage in tourism is being eroded by the poor state of international and domestic aviation. Apart from the inadequacies in infrastructure, which will take significant resources and time to remedy, there are two major issues for policy: the poor state of the national carrier, Nepal Airlines (NA), and the restrictiveness of bilateral air service agreements that Nepal has concluded with other countries. NA, plagued by poor management and political interference, has seen its financial situation weaken and its fleet shrink to two Boeing 757s and four Twin Otters. Because it is the designated airline, it has a crucial role in BASAs, which it is incapable of exploiting. The BASAs themselves are restrictive, but the poor state of NA means that they are only potentially a binding constraint. The two key hubs are Delhi, India, where the number of seats is limited to 6,000 per week for each side. These are used on the Indian side by the public carrier, India Airlines, and the private carriers, Jet and Sahara, whereas NA uses only 1,300 of the Nepali quota; and Bangkok, where the number of flights is restricted to 10 per week for each side, with seven used by Thai Airlines and three by NA. Japan has refused to grant fifth freedom rights on the Kathmandu–Shanghai–Osaka route, and China may begin restricting flights on the Kathmandu–Lhasa route.

There are three obvious priorities for policy. The first political challenge is to prepare NA for a more competitive environment. Drawing upon the transforming experiences of Kenyan Airways (a joint venture with KLM) and Sri Lankan Airlines (a joint venture with Emirates), serious consideration should be given to a possible joint venture with a foreign airline, which could inject the necessary capital, as well as bring technological and managerial improvements. At the same time, Nepal should push for more liberal BASAs that do not restrict capacity or flight frequency and grant fifth freedom rights, or even for open skies agreements in the South Asian region and more widely. Finally, there is a need for regulatory reforms, particularly to enhance both the independence and capacity of the Department of Civil Aviation.

As noted earlier, a liberal agreement with Pakistan made more direct routing possible for Sri Lankan Airlines. India, too, has allowed Sri Lankan Airlines access to a larger number of destinations (from 4 to 10), and granted fifth freedom rights—but the refusal of other countries such as Nepal to grant similar rights has limited the benefits. In general, restrictive BASAs keep regional transport prices unnecessarily high. Internationally, the unwillingness of certain European destinations (particularly France) to allow more liberal access has also been a problem.

Sri Lankan Airlines has benefited since it was privatized and taken over by Emirates in 1998. But the exclusivity of air traffic rights that Emirates was given may have adversely affected the development of air transport. While these exclusive rights ended in 2004, the airline still has exclusive rights on ground handling and catering, which are perceived to keep prices unnecessarily high. A new Civil Aviation Bill is in the pipeline. This is one of the few areas in which Sri Lanka has an aggressive interest in services in the region.

Surface Transport

Nepal's surface links with the rest of the world are fraught with difficulty. Recently, the president of the Freight Forwarders Association suggested that Nepal should be seen not as landlocked, but as 'land-linked'—that is, as a bridge between India and China, whose relations are improving and trade is growing dramatically. Offering transit facilities to these countries offers Nepal a direct source of income, as well as indirect benefits by helping lower the high costs of transport for its own freight due to its small scale, and imbalances between exports and imports.

Two questions arise. First, what prevents the emergence of a seamless multimodal transport link between Nepal and the rest of the world? Previous studies have focused on inadequacies in infrastructure, cumbersome customs, and other border formalities. We believe that restrictions on the ability of service providers to operate across borders are also to blame, notwithstanding the recent Multimodal Act. Apparently, Indian trucks can carry freight into Nepal, but Nepalese trucks cannot carry freight into India. At the same time, Nepal does not allow foreign investment in transport services. The internal container depot (ICD) created for Nepal with World Bank assistance remains poorly utilized, possibly because of policy restrictions in other areas—revealing, as in basic telecommunications, the need to appropriately sequence softer reforms and assistance for creating hard infrastructure.

Second, if Nepal can offer an efficient link between India and China, what prevents private investment in the creation of the necessary infrastructure? Again, there is a need to identify (and remedy) policy restrictions, as well as other inadequacies in the investment climate and regulatory environment that inhibit investment, before undertaking any public investment.

Surface transport between Bangladesh and India is also impeded by similar policy and regulatory restrictions of both countries, in addition to the hurdles caused by customs red tape and inadequate infrastructure. Questions similar to those cited above also can be raised regarding Bangladesh–India surface transport.

Retail Trade: Assessing the Impact of Liberalization

Reform of retail trade is one of the most contentious issues in India today. This is one of the few areas where FDI is still explicitly prohibited, except under restrictive conditions (single brand stores). These restrictions coexist with domestic regulation, particularly zoning laws, which are outdated and have been haphazardly implemented. Attempts by the judiciary to ensure greater consistency of enforcement by closing illegal retail outlets have met with significant resistance. The government is in the process of developing new 'master plans' that seek to create a more coherent regulatory framework. The forces against liberalization include small incumbent domestic retailers (who are the largest employers in the services sector), and potential large domestic entrants (who are lobbying hard to obtain a first-mover advantage over foreign retailers).

Existing studies, such as the recent World Bank study on Indian horticulture, suggests that there are significant benefits from retail reform. Again, a key issue is the interplay between domestic reform and liberalization of foreign entry. A number of important questions need to be addressed. What are priorities for reform in domestic zoning laws? What are political reasons for reluctance to allow foreign entry and reform zoning laws? How big are gains from full liberalization—including benefits to agriculture? What is the likely impact on employment? How are reforms of domestic entry, regulation, and foreign entry best sequenced?

Professional Services: Regulatory Reform and Liberalization

In both India and Sri Lanka, there are severe restrictions on the entry of foreign individuals or firms into professional services ranging from law to medicine. In the case of India, this policy stance is particularly ironic given the low-cost, highly efficient professionals who have already made significant inroads into the US and EU markets, and given that India has a strong interest in the growth of the export of professional services. As in the services described above, the political feasibility and economic consequences of liberalization will depend on the reform of domestic regulation. For example, rules that prevent domestic firms from exploiting economies of scale (for example, by limiting the number of partners) and scope (for example, by limiting the types of services) make them less able to compete with larger foreign rivals.

In Sri Lanka, the professional associations are most concerned by the threat of Indian competition. There is concern that restrictions on the entry of foreign professionals or firms have been circumvented through exemptions granted by the Board of Investment—for example, to the Indian hospital chain, Apollo, which apparently brings in its own staff for short periods. The representatives of professional associations suggested that Indian professionals offered cheaper services, but were also less well-qualified than their Sri Lankan counterparts, but the absence of a regulatory framework in Sri Lanka enables them to practice. At the same time, many Sri Lankan professionals emigrate to OECD countries. Could it be that Sri Lankan professionals, still trained according to inherited British standards, are 'overtrained' from the perspective of domestic consumers, whereas Indian professionals, trained according to lower national standards, offer the Sri Lankan consumer a more attractive price-quality bundle? How can a stronger regulatory framework in Sri Lanka be created so it protects the interests of the consumer rather than the local professional? How large are the benefits from liberalization regionally and globally? What are the implications for domestic employment? How can the political constraints be overcome?

Emigration: Unilateral Action and Bilateral Cooperation for Development

All countries in the region have a major stake in emigration, but there are big differences in the efforts that each has made to ensure the well-being of the individuals and their communities. Nepal and Sri Lanka are at opposite ends of the spectrum.

One in four Nepalese adult males works outside the country. Most go to India, but an increasingly large number go the Middle

East and South Asia. For a country that is highly dependent on its emigrants, Nepal does surprisingly little to ensure their well-being. There is anecdotal evidence (collected, for example, by the National Institute of Development, NID) of extortion at the departure stage, exploitation overseas, cheating in remittances, and lack of support on return. There is no department in the government that is dedicated to overseas labour issues. The director general of labour is aware of the problems but has few resources; the National Association of Foreign Employment Agencies (NAFEA) self-regulates only in name the 600 different licensed recruiting agencies, but lacks even notional oversight of the numerous unlicensed intermediaries; Nepal became a member of the International Organization of Migration (IOM) only recently and its local office has a staff of one; the World Bank has documented how remittances have led to significant reductions in poverty, but so far undertaken no analysis of policy and provided no support for improving the environment for Nepali migrants.

In contrast, Sri Lanka seems to have made significant efforts to ensure the well-being of emigrants and their communities. The Foreign Employment Act of 1985, and the amendment of 1994, seem to have provided the basis for a relatively well-managed emigration policy. But Sri Lanka resembles the other countries in the region in that it is only just beginning to explore bilateral cooperation with destination countries, such as Jordan and Korea, with which it has concluded agreements within the last year. Countries need to assess how far remedial action can be taken unilaterally, and where there is need to cooperate with destination countries.

Pakistan has a strong interest in exporting services by moving people abroad, which it has done with considerable success, especially in the Middle East. This was evident from preliminary data obtained from the Ministry of Labour, Manpower, and Overseas Pakistanis. On the policy front, while there has been greater difficulty in securing visas abroad since 11 September 2001, Pakistan has just concluded a promising bilateral agreement with Korea on temporary migration (for three years) of unskilled Pakistanis. This agreement improves on earlier agreements with Middle East countries and Malaysia, and may offer a model for similar agreements with other destination countries. Some of the incentives to ensure temporariness include: if the government of Pakistan fails to ensure the return of emigrants, then the quota for Pakistanis shrinks; if emigrants do not return, they lose their deposit (PRs 40,000); and if emigrants return to Pakistan, then they are eligible in six months to reapply for a temporary migration visa.

International Cooperation

To a large extent, South Asian countries can liberalize their markets and strengthen their regulatory institutions unilaterally. But international cooperation has a role, though not necessarily along the traditional lines.

Most countries in the region are active participants in multilateral services negotiations in the context of the General Agreement on Trade in Services (GATS). These negotiations have so far produced disappointing results, both in terms of improved access for the region's services exports, and in terms of galvanizing reforms within the region. The usual mechanism of reciprocal 'concessions' has failed to accelerate the liberalization of services or to produce any meaningful rules for the services trade. South Asian policymakers and negotiators may, nevertheless, be able to devise creative strategies so that multilateral negotiations can lead to further domestic reform and improved access to foreign markets.

South Asia remains the least integrated region in the world, both in goods and services trade. Barriers to intra-regional trade are even more restrictive in services than in goods, resulting in missed opportunities for mutually beneficial trade. Most regional agreements now have a services dimension, and negotiations have focused on preferential liberalization similar to that for goods, but most have been unsuccessful. Experience in other regions of the world suggests that the elimination of explicit barriers to trade in services, such as restrictions on foreign ownership, may be legislatively simpler and economically more desirable on a 'most-favoured nation' (MFN) or non-preferential basis. However, cooperation on services infrastructure and regulation may be more feasible and desirable in the regional context with nearby countries that are at a similar level of development, and with a similar institutional inheritance. Regional cooperation on infrastructure (as in the case of power and transportation) is likely to have large pay-offs, as is regional cooperation on higher education and migration.

The private sector is already taking the initiative in building stronger regional links, for example, the Indian company Reliance is investing in fibre optic links to the Maldives. Key questions for policymakers are: What can be done to facilitate or even encourage such initiatives? What types of regulatory and other cooperation are needed to address the needs of landlocked countries like Afghanistan, Bhutan, and Nepal? Smaller countries could also reap benefits of economies of scale from regulatory cooperation in specific areas, such as trade facilitation, provided they are reassured that such cooperation will not be hegemonic, but mutually beneficial.

Appendix 7A.1

Table 7A.1: Services Trade Policies as of 2007: FDI

Countries	*Retail banking*	*Insurance (life and non-life or automobile insurance)*	*Telecommunications: fixed (basic, domestic, international long distance); mobile*	*Retailing services*	*Air transport: passengers (domestic and international)*	*Maritime shipping: international*	*Professional services: accounting and auditing*	*Professional services: legal advisory services for domestic and international law*
India	OPEN, except for Greenfield investment, entry allowed through only one mode for presence: either through a branch or subsidiary. M&A: FDI limit 74%. Annual limit of 20 applies both to those branches which are the primary form of establishment of foreign banks and to branches of wholly foreign-owned banks.	Foreign entry allowed with restrictions: FDI limit 26%. Licensing subject to conditions of reciprocity. Cession of 20% required.	Foreign entry allowed only through M&A. FDI limit 49% without government approval. FDI limit 74% provided it would divest 26% of equity to public within 5 years of entry. The number of licenses fixed: 4 per service area. Access to international gateway and VOIP* allowed.	Foreign entry allowed only through M&A. FDI 51% subject to operating single brand stores. Government approval required for adding new products and new category of products.	Foreign entry allowed only through M&A. FDI limit 49%. Chairman and two-thirds of the BOD must be of national origin.	OPEN	CLOSED	CLOSED

(contd ...)

Table 7A.1 (contd ...)

Countries	*Retail banking*	*Insurance (life and non-life or automobile insurance)*	*Telecommunications: fixed (basic, domestic, international long distance); mobile*	*Retailing services*	*Air transport: passengers (domestic and international)*	*Maritime shipping: international*	*Professional services: accounting and auditing*	*Professional services: legal advisory services for domestic and international law*
Pakistan	Foreign entry allowed through publicly listed company. Greenfield: FDI limit 50% provided 50% of shares offered to the public within 2 years of entry. M&A: FDI 100%.	Foreign entry allowed only through subsidiary.** FDI 51% subject to bringing at least USD 4 million in foreign exchange. Approval of the regulator required for reinsurance abroad.	Foreign entry allowed only through subsidiary. FDI 100%. The number of licenses not fixed. Access to international gateway and VOIP allowed subject to conditions of the licenses.	OPEN, except entry allowed only through subsidiary. Goods and products made in Israel are not allowed.	Foreign entry allowed only through subsidiary. FDI limit 49%. Must pay income taxes before the repatriation of earnings.	OPEN, except entry allowed only through subsidiary. Must pay income taxes before the repatriation of earnings.	OPEN, subject to bringing a minimum investment of USD 100,000	CLOSED, exceptions can be made if citizenship or reciprocity conditions are met.

(contd ...)

Table 7A.1 (contd ...)

Countries	*Retail banking*	*Insurance (life and non-life or automobile insurance)*	*Telecommunications: fixed (basic, domestic, international long distance); mobile*	*Retailing services*	*Air transport: passengers (domestic and international)*	*Maritime shipping: international*	*Professional services: accounting and auditing*	*Professional services: legal advisory services for domestic and international law*
Sri Lanka	No restrictions on form of legal entry. Foreign banks: FDI 100% subject to approval. Non-bank: FDI 15% of shares with voting rights. Foreign bank branch: repatriation of earnings is limited to 15% of the local operating expenses.	Foreign entry only through subsidiary. FDI 100%. Approval required for the repatriation of earnings, except if dividends are disbursed through Share Investment External Rupee Account (SIERA).	Foreign entry only through subsidiary. FDI 100%. The regulator exercise discretion in making recommendation to the minister who decides the license issuance. Access to international gateway allowed through existing operators. VOIP allowed.	OPEN provided the foreign retailers bring in at least USD 1 million. Approval required for the repatriation of past years' earnings, except if dividends are disbursed through SIERA.	No restrictions on form of legal entry. FDI 49%.	No restrictions on form of legal entry. FDI 40%.	Accounting: OPEN Auditing: Foreign entry allowed only through a partnership with local firm. Partners must be locally qualified.	International law: OPEN. Domestic law: Foreign entry allowed through a partnership with local firm. Partners must pass a local Law College Exam, admitted by the Supreme Court, and pass a local language exam.

(contd ...)

Table 7A.1 (contd ...)

Countries	*Retail banking*	*Insurance (life and non-life or automobile insurance)*	*Telecommunications: fixed (basic, domestic, international long distance); mobile*	*Retailing services*	*Air transport: passengers (domestic and international)*	*Maritime shipping: international*	*Professional services: accounting and auditing*	*Professional services: legal advisory services for domestic and international law*
Bangladesh	OPEN, except no single investor is allowed to own more than 10% of shares. Must be listed publicly within 2 years of entry. Additional licenses required for establishing branch or ATMs.	CLOSED	Fixed telecom: OPEN, except restrictions may apply to international long distance service providers. Licenses granted by the discretionary decision of the regulator. Access to international gateway not allowed. VOIP allowed. Mobile: OPEN except entry allowed only through subsidiary.	OPEN	OPEN	OPEN, except FDI limit 70% and remittances of profits are subject to approval.	Information not available.	Information not available.

(contd ...)

Table 7A.1 (contd ...)

Countries	*Retail banking*	*Insurance (life and non-life or automobile insurance)*	*Telecommunications: fixed (basic, domestic, international long distance); mobile*	*Retailing services*	*Air transport: passengers (domestic and international)*	*Maritime shipping: international*	*Professional services: accounting and auditing*	*Professional services: legal advisory services for domestic and international law*
Nepal	OPEN, except foreign banks are not allowed to establish another financial institution in a form of JV or subsidiary. Additional licenses required for establishing branch or ATM.	OPEN, except licensing is subject to conditions of reciprocity.	Foreign entry is allowed through a JV. FDI 80%. The number of licenses may be limited. Granted by the discretionary decision of the regulator. Majority of BOD must be of national origin.	OPEN, except foreign retailers required to have presence in more than two countries in the world. Additional licenses required for opening new outlets.	CLOSED	Not Applicable (landlocked).	Information not available.	Information not available.

Source: Gootiiz and Mattoo (2008).

Notes: *VOIP—Voice over internet protocol.
**FDI limit reached 100 per cent in insurance sector as of April 2008, according to a source of government.

References

Amin, Mohammad and Aaditya Mattoo. 2006. 'Do Institutions Matter More for Services?' Policy Research Working Paper Series 4032, World Bank.

Arnold, Jens Matthias, Beata Javorcik, Molly Lipscomb, and Aaditya Mattoo. 2007. 'Services Reform and Manufacturing Performance: Evidence from India', Mimeo, World Bank.

Gootiiz, B. and A. Mattoo. 2008. 'Services in Doha: What's on the Table?' Mimeo, World Bank.

Mattoo, A., Deepak Mishra, and Ashish Narain. 2007. *From Competition at Home to Competing Abroad: A Case Study of India's Horticulture*. New Delhi: Oxford University Press.

Mattoo, Aaditya, Randeep Rathindran, and Arvind Subramanian. 2006. 'Measuring Services Trade Liberalization and Its Impact on Economic Growth: An Illustration', *Journal of Economic Integration*, 21: 64–98.

World Bank. 2004. *Sustaining India's Services Revolution: Access to Foreign Markets, Domestic Reform and International Negotiations*. Report. Washington, D.C.: World Bank.

8 IMPROVING SKILLS FOR COMPETITIVENESS

Michelle Riboud and Hong Tan

INTRODUCTION

Globalization and the knowledge economy pose numerous challenges as well as opportunities for developing countries, not least in the area of skills development.[1] Expanding trade and the globalization of production and capital create pressures for economies to restructure, making it imperative to retrain those made redundant in declining industries, and to upgrade the skills of those employed in new industries. In addition, the increased global flow of information made possible by new information technologies creates demand for higher-level cognitive skills and continuous learning over the work life, as the skills people acquire in school and in the workplace become obsolete more quickly, and they need new and more complex skills to respond to accelerating technological change. How education and training systems respond to these sweeping changes and the challenges these changes pose will have far-reaching implications for the economic growth and competitiveness of South Asian countries, and for income growth, employment, job creation, and poverty reduction.

Some effects of globalization and the knowledge economy on the growing relative demand for skills are well-known. Economists have documented diverging changes in earnings distributions by level of education for many developing countries and regions in the late 1980s and 1990s, paralleling similar trends in countries of the Organisation for Economic Co-operation and Development (OECD) that started in the 1970s (Berman, Bound, and Machin 1998). Some have attributed this global phenomenon to skill-biased technological change, whereby the diffusion of skill-intensive,

[1] This chapter draws from Riboud et al. 2007.

advanced technologies developed in OECD countries generates a corresponding, but lagged, pattern of change in relative skills demand in developing countries. How important an influence skill-biased technology has on relative pay by skill level will also depend on supply-side changes in skills, and on the speed of globalization. Education and training policies, as well as policies regarding trade liberalization and market orientation, can offset demand shifts, and thereby mitigate the effects of skill-biased technology on relative pay by skill level.

Policymakers in South Asia are already grappling with the challenges of reforming national education and training systems. For example, the release of a report on the knowledge economy in India (Dahlman, and Utz 2005) has sparked policy interest in how best to reposition education and workforce skills to take advantage of the opportunities afforded by the knowledge economy. Pakistan, recognizing the imperative of expanding access to post-school vocational education and training (VET), has established the National Vocation and Technical Education Commission (NAVTEC), an apex training body, to develop and implement a scaled-up national training strategy for the workforce. The World Bank is also helping the governments of Bangladesh, India, and Sri Lanka with education and vocational training studies and projects.

This chapter seeks to complement and inform these ongoing, but still nascent, initiatives through a cross-country examination of skills development (broadly defined to include both education and post-school training) in the South Asian region. It focuses on Bangladesh, India, Pakistan, and Sri Lanka, four countries for which data on education and training are available for large samples of households and firms from several different surveys.

Trends in Educational Attainment and Returns

We begin by examining several dimensions of education and the economic returns to investing in education in these four SAR countries. We examine the evolution of educational attainment over the past two to four decades as compared to two East Asian countries, estimates of the returns to different levels of education, changes over time in these returns to education, and implications of these trends for education policy in the region.

Stock and Flows of Education

The stock and flow of investments in education can provide insights into the evolution of educational attainment in South Asia over the past two to four decades depending on the country. The stock of human capital at a given time may be characterized by the percentage of the total population aged 15 years and older that has attained the following four levels of education: is illiterate (no education), has completed primary schooling, has completed secondary schooling, or has achieved a level of education above secondary. In all cases, this grouping refers to the highest level of education attained.[2] The flows of human capital, or the speed at which each country is upgrading the skills of its population, is the change over time in the distribution of educational achievement across cohorts of individuals born at different times.

The data for this exercise are based on household surveys. For India and Pakistan, where relatively long time series data are available, we use several rounds of India's NSS and the Pakistan Integrated Household Surveys (PIHSs) for several roughly comparable years. We use secondary data from Barro and Lee (2000) for Bangladesh and Sri Lanka, and for two East Asian comparator countries (China and Malaysia), either because we do not have access to household survey data or because such data are not available for comparable periods. The Barro and Lee classification of education levels is based on criteria adopted by the International Standard Classification of Education in 1976.

The stock of skills at a given point in time reflects past investments in education. When the mean number of years of schooling in a country is low, the distribution of educational attainment resembles a pyramid. The base, which corresponds to the fraction of the

[2] For India, the National Sample Survey (NSS) defines the following education levels: illiterate—not literate, literate through attending NFEC (non-formal education centres)/AEC (alternative education centre), TLC (total literacy campaign), others, literate but below primary; primary—primary or middle school completed; secondary—secondary or higher secondary; above secondary—graduate and above. For Pakistan, the Pakistan Integrated Household Survey (PIHS) education categories are: illiterate—not literate, completed classes 1–4 (less than primary); primary—completed classes 5–9 (primary or middle school completed); secondary—completed classes 10–13 (secondary or higher secondary); and above secondary—BA, BS, and above.

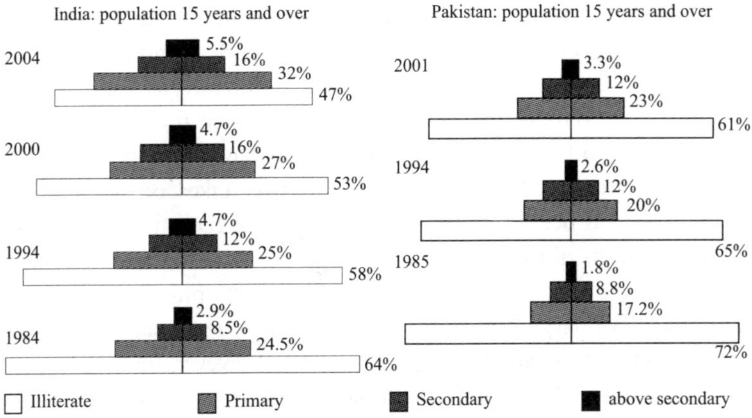

Figure 8.1a: Educational Attainment in India and Pakistan

Source: Authors' calculations based on the NSS and PIHS.

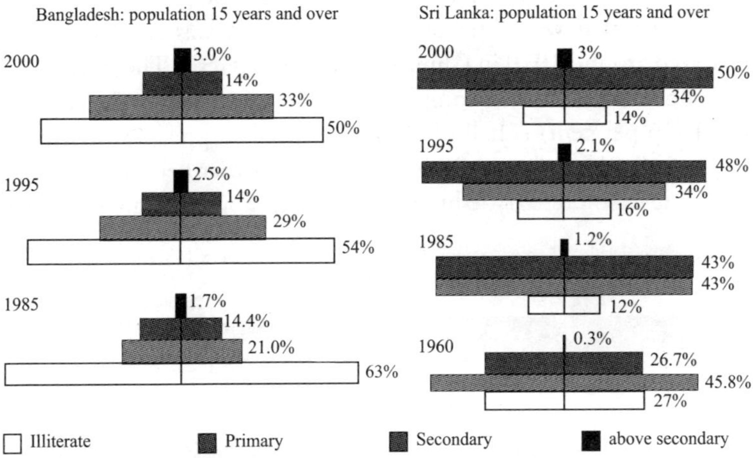

Figure 8.1b: Educational Attainment in Sri Lanka and Bangladesh

Source: Authors' calculations based on Barro and Lee (2000).

population with no education or with less than a primary education, is relatively wide, and the middle and top sections taper off to reflect the smaller shares of the population with higher levels of education.

This pattern has characterized Bangladesh, India, and Pakistan since the mid-1980s (Figures 8.1a and 8.1b). Over time, as these countries have upgraded the education of the population by focusing on the lower education levels, the base has narrowed and the middle sections have become wider. Nevertheless, in both Bangladesh and India, about half the population aged 15 and older is still illiterate, and in Pakistan the figure is even higher. When countries pursue their investments in education to the point where more adults have primary education than are illiterate, the education distribution takes on a diamond shape. This has been the case in Sri Lanka since the early 1960s. The middle sections of the distribution have continued to grow since that time, and by 2000, more than 80 per cent of the population had either completed primary education (34 per cent) or secondary education (50 per cent). Educational progress has not, however, been such that the distribution of education resembles an inverted pyramid.

When looking at how South Asia compares with East Asian countries such as China or Malaysia, which have enjoyed longer periods of economic and total factor productivity growth, Figure 8.2 shows that South Asia is far behind East Asia. The proportion of the population that was illiterate in India in 2004 was similar to that observed around 1970 in China or 1960 in Malaysia. The fraction of the population that had completed secondary education in India in 2004 (16 per cent) is half of the figure that had prevailed in China in 1975. Bangladesh and Pakistan lag even further behind. It is only at the level of tertiary education that the South Asian countries

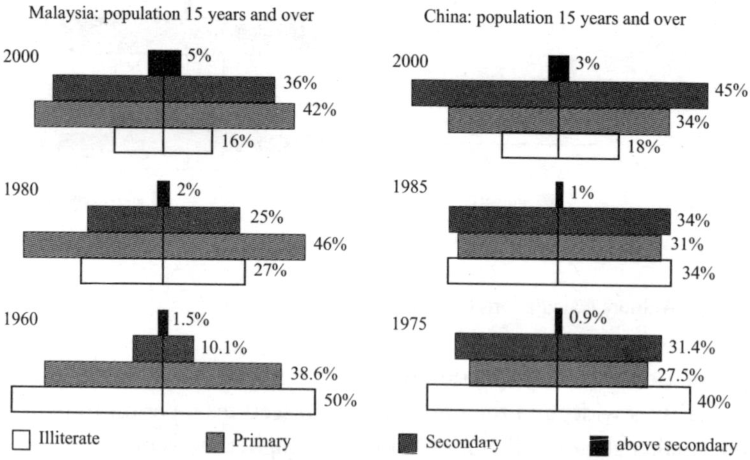

Figure 8.2: Educational Attainment in Malaysia and China

Source: Authors' calculations based on Barro and Lee (2000)

resemble their East Asian counterparts, with India actually having a slight advantage over China and being roughly on par with Malaysia. However, when taking the population as a whole into account, South Asia lags behind East Asia by about 30 years. A comparison with other parts of the world also shows that the distribution of educational attainment in South Asia today is similar to that observed in Latin American countries in the 1960s (de Ferranti et al. 2003). Only Sri Lanka, a clear outlier, did much better, but its comparative advantage has been gradually eroded over time.

While South Asia's stock of education is clearly still low compared with that in other parts of the world, there is evidence of continual upgrading of education in the region over time. The issue is how rapid this progress has been, and whether it is sufficient for South Asia to catch up with other regions. Trends in enrolment rates over time could answer these questions, but the limited availability of household surveys at different points in time for all countries in the region makes the use of enrolment rates to compare trends over time difficult.

To overcome this difficulty, we use data from the most recently available survey and look at the educational attainment of age cohorts of individuals born at different times. For example, individuals aged 50–9 in 2000 were born in the 1940s, those aged 40–9 were born in the 1950s, and so on. With this perspective, we can identify changes in educational investments across different generations and compare the speed at which the human capital stock was upgraded over time. As this only requires using the most recent survey, we were able to add information on additional countries in South Asia, namely, Bhutan, the Maldives, and Nepal. For purposes of comparison across regions, we also add similar data on Malaysia, a rapidly growing East Asian country.

Figure 8.3 shows the share of the population completing at least grade 5 in the countries under consideration. It depicts changes in primary school achievement across different generations, ranging from those now in their fifties to those aged 15–19 at the time of the surveys. Once again, Sri Lanka is the outlier in the South Asian region: more than 70 per cent of Sri Lankans born in the late 1940s had completed at least five years of education, and continuous progress during the next 40 years led to practically universal primary education. For all the other South Asian countries, the starting point was much lower, ranging from 5 per cent for Bhutan to 35 per cent for India. Countries

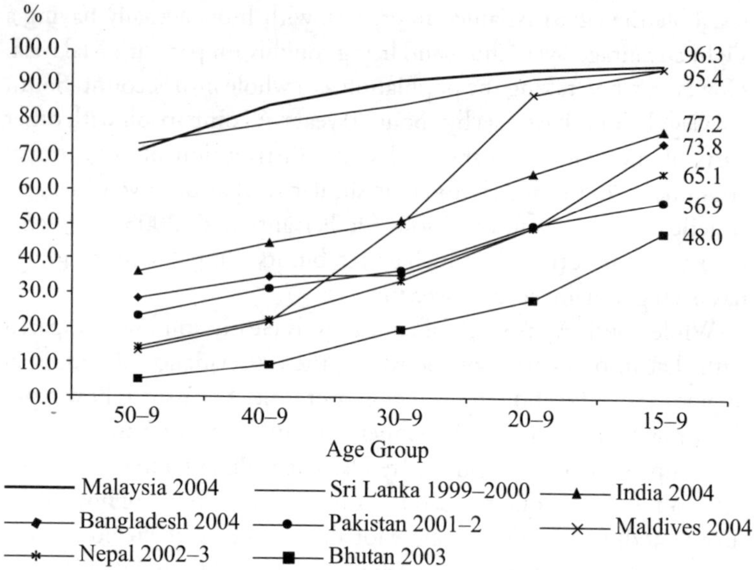

Figure 8.3: Proportion of Population Attaining at least Grade 5

Sources: Leopold R. Sarr and authors' calculations for Bangladesh, India, and Malaysia.

that started with the lowest educational level improved at a more rapid pace. The most spectacular changes took place in Bhutan and in the Maldives. Over a 20-year period, Bhutan moved from a situation where only a tiny proportion of children went to school, to a situation whereby almost half of children spend at least five years in school, and the Maldives was able to increase access to primary education to practically 90 per cent of children and catch up with Sri Lanka. Nepal also stands out, with a 4.5-fold increase in the proportion of children completing at least five years of schooling.

A number of points are notable when we turn to Figure 8.4 and focus on completion of secondary education (grade 12). First, efforts to upgrade skills beyond primary education have been steady in the region. Trend lines in completion of at least 12 years of school are broadly parallel, with the exception of Sri Lanka, India, and the Maldives which have experienced faster progress for the youngest generations than other countries in the region. It is noteworthy that Sri Lanka no longer appears as an outlier in secondary school completion, having concentrated its efforts on basic education

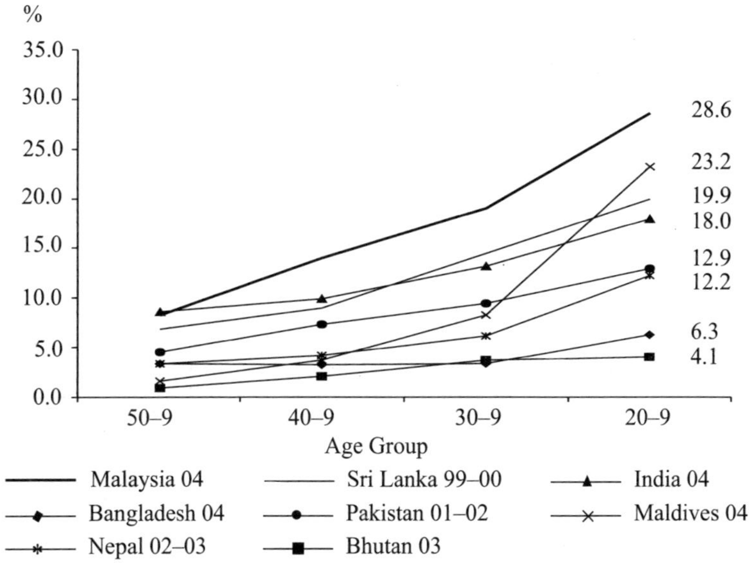

Figure 8.4: Proportion of Population Completing at least Grade 12

Sources: Leopold R. Sarr (unpublished) and authors calculations for Bangladesh, India, and Malaysia

and focused much less on levels of schooling beyond that level. The Maldives now exceeds Sri Lanka in the proportion of children completing grade 12, and India performs almost as well.

The final point that emerges from these figures is that South Asia is unlikely to catch up with East Asia in terms of education, at least in the medium term. With the exception of the Maldives, none of the countries has adopted a path that will, in the near future, enable it to reach the education levels Malaysia has attained if those countries continue to invest in their human capital at the same rate as they currently do. Indeed, differences between South Asian countries and Malaysia are larger for younger than for older generations, suggesting that the gap is widening. Note that India, Malaysia, and Sri Lanka shared almost the same starting point for completion of grade 12 (those aged 50–9 in Figure 8.4), but their trends diverged over time.

Comparisons of enrolment rates at the secondary and tertiary levels across countries confirm this conclusion (Figure 8.5). Even though the proportion of the population with higher education was similar in India, China, and Malaysia, differences in enrolment rates

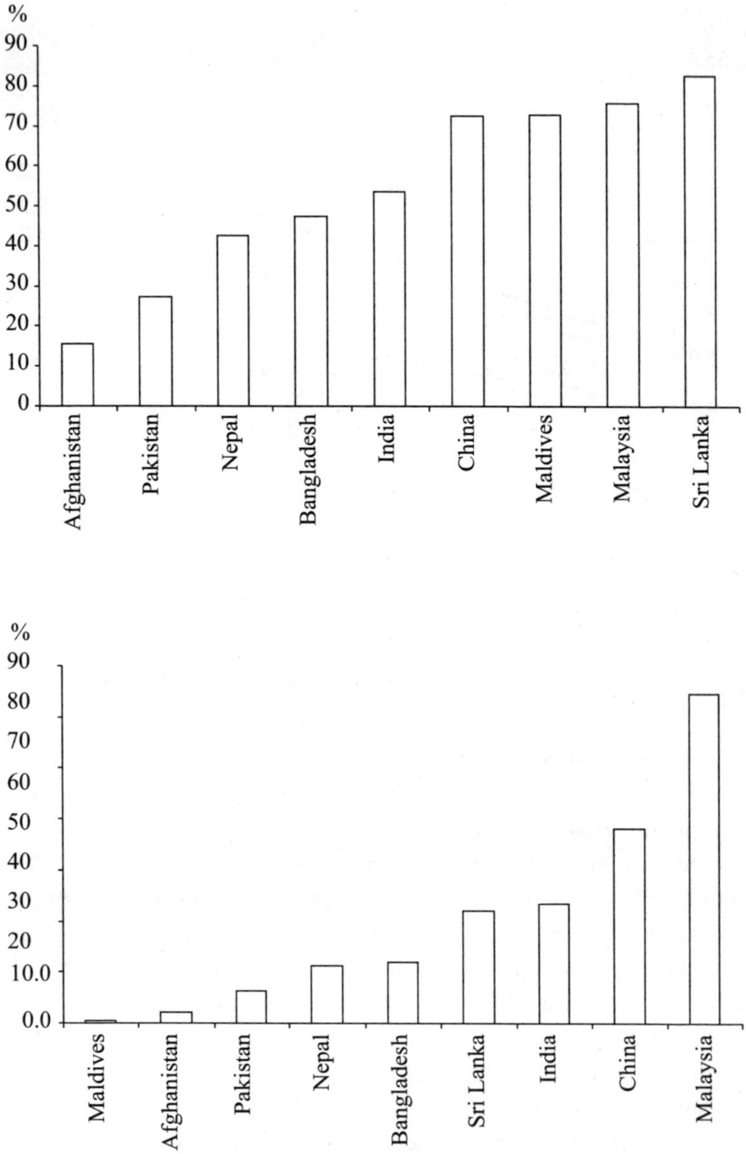

Figure 8.5: Gross Enrolment Rates of Secondary and Tertiary Education, 2004

Source: World Bank, *World Development Indicators*.

suggest that the two regions are not making similar efforts in terms of the flow of human capital. South Asia is clearly lagging behind East Asia, with the implication that levels of attainment of tertiary education are likely to diverge further over time.

Returns to Investments in Education

Has progress in educational investments been adequate to meet the skill needs of the workforce and employers, and the challenges of globalization? To address this issue, we estimate private rates of return to different levels of educational attainment over the past one or two decades for the four countries in our sample. These rates of return can provide useful first insights into the interaction between the demand for and supply of educated workers, and changes over time in the balance of supply and demand.[3]

To calculate rates of returns to education, we use household surveys for Bangladesh (BHIESs), India (NSSs), Pakistan (PIHSs), and LFSs for Sri Lanka. Surveys at different points in time are available that cover about one decade for Pakistan and Sri Lanka, and two decades for India. For Bangladesh, BHIESs were only available for 2000 and 2004, so no comparisons of long-term trends in schooling returns were possible. The focus is on the sample of males and females aged 15–64 who work for salaries or wages. We exclude the self-employed and those for whom compensation for work is not reported.[4] We use information on the sample's wages, salaries, and cash and in-kind payments for their primary occupation or employment to calculate hourly wages, adjusting for the effective hours of work during the preceding week.

Following the standard methodology popularized by Mincer (1974), we estimate the following wage model by ordinary least squares:

$$\log(hourlywage_i) = fn(EDUC_i, EXP_i, OTHER_i, LOCATION)$$

[3] Note that these estimates are private rates of return since they do not capture the full social value of human capital investments for a country, such as non-market benefits and possible externalities. They also do not take into account either government spending on education or direct outlays by families. Investments in education are also crudely measured by the number of years that reaching a given level of education normally takes, and ignores class repetition or the quality of education.

[4] As this section focuses on the returns to human capital, we exclude those earners for whom no wage compensation is reported, as well as the self-employed, whose income also includes a component that reflects returns to capital.

The dependent variable, the logarithm of hourly wage, is a function of the following sets of explanatory variables:

- EDUC consists of five 0,1 indicator variables (six in the case of India) for levels of schooling completed: *literate, below primary* = 1 if the person is literate but has not completed primary education; *primary* = 1 if primary education is the highest level of education completed; *middle* = 1 if middle school is the highest level of education completed; *secondary and higher secondary* = 1 if secondary or higher secondary education is the highest level of education completed; *tertiary* = 1 if any level of tertiary education has been completed; *technical education dummy* (India only) = 1 if any technical education has been completed. In the regression analysis, the illiterate group is omitted.
- EXP measures *years of potential experience,* measured as age–education, 5 (in the case of Pakistan) or 6 (in the case of Bangladesh, India, and Sri Lanka), and its quadratic EXP2[2] or *years of potential experience squared.*
- OTHER is a vector of individual attributes, including *male* = 1 if the respondent is male; *SCST* = 1 if the person belongs to a scheduled caste or scheduled tribe (India only); *regular worker* = 1 for those who receive monthly or annual salaries; and *regular worker* = 0 for casual workers, that is, those who are paid on a daily basis.
- LOCATION controls for place, where *urban* = 1 if the household lives in an urban area and = 0 if it lives in a rural area. The Sri Lankan LFS distinguishes between urban, rural, and estate locations, and to reflect this possibility, both urban and rural dummies are used, with estate as the omitted category.

The underlying human capital model establishes a link between investments in different levels of education, as proxied by foregone earnings while in school, and the value that the labour market attributes to skills thus acquired. The estimated coefficients on the different educational categories allow us to calculate what the corresponding annualized private rates of return are to completing that level of education.

Table 8.1 reports the wage regressions estimated for each of the four South Asian countries, using the most recent data available

TABLE 8.1: Wage Regressions for South Asia

Year	*2004*	*2001/2002*	*2000/2001*	*2004*
Country	*India*	*Sri Lanka*	*Pakistan*	*Bangladesh*
Literate, below primary	0.195 (12.53)	0.057 (2.36)	0.108 (4.69)	0.087 (1.94)
Primary	0.249 (18.38)	0.185 (7.44)	0.225 (12.63)	0.236 (9.29)
Middle	0.461 (34.31)	0.341 (13.52)	0.421 (18.72)	
Secondary & higher secondary	0.717 (52.25)	0.606 (24.08)	0.788 (44.38)	
Secondary				0.443 (10.26)
High				0.585 (12.14)
Tertiary	1.329 (79.64)	0.875 (26.31)	1.397 (61.34)	0.943 (22.90)
Technical education dummy	0.18 (10.87)			
Potential experience (years)	0.056 (53.99)	0.026 (18.63)	0.06 (36.90)	0.024 (6.82)
Potential experience squared	–0.001 (–39.40)	–0.001 (–16.76)	–0.001 (–27.69)	–0.000 (–5.27)
Male	0.446 (47.68)	0.403 (40.72)	1.089 (63.42)	0.601 (17.05)
Urban	0.221 (26.06)	0.271 (12.69)	0.189 (15.73)	0.110 (6.28)
Rural		0.059 (3.03)		
Constant	–0.219 (–13.29)	2.163 (68.73)	0.581 (21.32)	1.103 (16.91)
Number of observations	39,190	20,838	16,200	4729
R-square	0.546	0.292	0.396	0.319

Source: Authors' calculations based on BHIESs, NSSs, PIHSs, and LFSs Surveys.
Notes: Indicator variables included, but not reported, for worker status, caste and scheduled tribes.

(similar regressions were run for all years for which we had data). From empirical evidence based on numerous studies in many countries covering many time periods, we would expect to find that earnings increased with level of educational attainment and, for any given level of education, that earnings increased with the number of years of labour market experience, although at a decreasing rate. Our results are fully consistent with these expectations. Investing in formal education is profitable in all the countries, and additional investment increases earnings substantially. Despite some well-founded concerns about the low quality of primary education, some schooling, even without completion of primary education, results in a significant wage gain. The wage gains from completing secondary and higher levels of education are significantly greater than for primary education. The estimated wage-experience profiles are also consistent with wages increasing with labour force experience, although at a decreasing rate. Finally, the earnings received by men and women differ strikingly, with men, on an average, earning 40 per cent to 100 per cent higher wages than women for a given level of education, and controlling for other attributes.

The wage regression results are broadly similar across all four countries, but some differences are apparent. For instance, in Sri Lanka, the returns to incomplete education are low compared with those in the other countries. Sri Lanka is also noteworthy for the relatively lower return to investment in higher education, as well as its much flatter wage-experience profile, which may reflect the increased supply of those with a tertiary-level education relative to the demand for such workers. Another point that stands out is the large wage premium that men in Bangladesh and Pakistan receive relative to that earned by observationally comparable female workers.

Comparing the profitability of investments in different levels of education and how they vary over time and across countries is greatly facilitated by calculating standardized rates of return to education. Taking into account the years normally required to complete any particular level of education, one can use the schooling coefficients of the regression to calculate standardized rates of return per year of schooling. This is done separately for each schooling level by subtracting the estimated coefficient for that level by the coefficient of the previous level, and dividing by the normal time taken to complete that level of education.[5] The results are interpreted as the rate of return for one additional year of schooling at a given level of education.

TABLE 8.2: Rate of Return to Schooling by Education Level

India	*NSS 1993*	*NSS 1999*	*NSS 2004*
Primary	8.3	8.5	8.5
Middle	9.5	8.4	10.7
Secondary	23.3	22.7	16.8
Higher secondary	11.7	15.0	16.3
Tertiary	12.6	15.2	18.9
Sri Lanka	*LFS 1992/1993*	*LFS 1997/1998*	*LFS 2001/2002*
Primary	5.6	5.0	5.8
Middle	13.2	12.1	11.6
Secondary	10.6	7.8	8.8
Higher secondary	14.4	16.0	18.4
Tertiary	7.1	9.9	9.6
Pakistan	*PHIS 1993/1994*	*PHIS 1996/1997*	*PHIS 2000/2001*
Primary	4.4	4.5	4.8
Middle	5.7	6.4	6.6
Secondary	9.5	9.3	14.2
Higher secondary	10.1	11.4	13.9
Tertiary	13.5	11.5	13.9
Bangladesh		*BHIES 2000*	*BHIES 2004*
Primary		7.0	4.7
Secondary		6.4	4.1
Higher secondary		10.8	7.1
Tertiary		10.1	9.0

Source: Authors' calculations based on BHIESs, NSSs, PIHSs, and LFSs Surveys.

[5] For primary education, we use five years for all countries; for middle, secondary, and higher secondary school, we use three years for India and Pakistan, and four for Sri Lanka; for secondary and higher secondary, three years for India and Pakistan, and four for Sri Lanka; for tertiary, four years for India and Pakistan, and three for Sri Lanka. Because of specifics of the education system in Bangladesh, the normal time used for secondary is five years, two years for higher secondary, and four years for tertiary.

Table 8.2 shows the rates of return to different levels of education. Except for Bangladesh, estimates are calculated at three points in time: the early 1990s, the late 1990s, and the early 2000s. In India, the profitability of each year of primary education averages 8.5 per cent, and the return for each of the following three years of middle education is between 8.4 per cent and 10.7 per cent. Table 8.2 also shows that the profitability of such investments tends to rise with the level of educational attainment, most dramatically in India and Pakistan, and to a lesser extent in Sri Lanka.

The corresponding estimates of the rates of return to education by gender are shown in Table 8.3. They are calculated from wage regressions estimated separately for men and women that control for work experience, location, and type of employment. One finding common to all the countries is the sharp change observed after primary education. While returns to primary education are significantly higher for men than for women in India and Sri Lanka (in the cases of Bangladesh and Pakistan, returns to primary education are higher for women than for men), returns to higher levels of education, especially at secondary and tertiary levels, are substantially higher for women. These results suggest that in countries where access to higher levels of education is more difficult for women than for men, and where labour force participation by women is still low, women who succeed in overcoming these obstacles do relatively well in the labour market. Part of women's high returns to education can be attributed not only to investments in education, but also to the greater motivation and ability of the educated women entering the labour market.

These estimates in Tables 8.2 and 8.3 also indicate that rates of return to higher secondary and tertiary education increased over time in the three countries for which we have time series data. These increased returns were most pronounced for India:[6] between 1993 and 2004, the returns to higher secondary education for males rose from 11 per cent to 15 per cent, and the returns to tertiary education

[6] Patrinos and Sakellariou (2006) analyse 16 East Asian and Latin American countries and obtain similar results. In almost all the countries they look at, returns to university qualifications exceeded returns to all other levels. For evidence from Brazil and Mexico, two countries with long time series data on returns to education, see Blom, Holm-Nielsen, and Verner (2001) and Lachler (1998). Also see Giovagnoli, Fiszbein, and Patrinos (2005) for evidence of increasing returns to higher levels of education in Argentina during 1992–2002.

TABLE 8.3: Rate of Return to Schooling by Education Level and Gender

	Female	*Male*	*Female*	*Male*	*Female*	*Male*
India	*NSS 1993*		*NSS 1999*		*NSS 2004*	
Primary	5.5	8.0	6.9	8.2	6.7	8.2
Middle	14.3	8.7	9.3	8.2	10.3	8.2
Secondary	45.0	20.1	42.0	20.0	31.5	20.0
Higher secondary	13.7	10.8	14.6	14.2	20.7	14.2
Tertiary	9.4	12.8	11.5	15.6	16.8	15.6
Sri Lanka	*LFS 1992/1993*		*LFS 1997/1998*		*LFS 2001/2002*	
Primary	2.6	5.7	1.5	7.1	1.9	7.6
Middle	18.2	12.0	13.7	11.7	17.8	10.0
Secondary	11.5	10.2	9.6	7.1	10.0	8.1
Higher secondary	8.5	17.0	13.6	16.5	14.7	19.6
Tertiary	9.3	5.6	14.2	6.2	11.7	7.5
Pakistan	*PHIS 1993/1994*		*PHIS 1996/1997*		*PHIS 2000/2001*	
Primary	4.3	4.3	12.9	4.0	5.4	4.1
Middle	13.1	5.6	7.2	6.5	17.1	6.2
Secondary	12.1	9.0	17.2	8.1	30.2	12.3
Higher secondary	7.6	9.8	12.8	11.2	18.5	11.9
Tertiary	15.4	13.3	11.2	11.0	18.9	11.9
Bangladesh			*BHIES 2000*		*BHIES 2004*	
Primary			14.1	5.8	13.4	4.2
Secondary			10.7	4.8	11.6	3.3
Higher secondary			15.3	10.0	2.2	7.5
Tertiary			5.0	10.9	10.5	8.9

Source: Authors' calculations based on BHIESs, NSSs, PIHSs, and LFSs Surveys.

for males rose from 12 per cent to 19 per cent. More modest increases in returns were registered for Pakistan and Sri Lanka over the same decade. In Sri Lanka, for example, the corresponding increases in returns were 14 per cent to 18 per cent for higher secondary, and 7 per cent to 9 per cent for tertiary education. These time trends resemble similar increases in the relative returns to higher education reported in other regions, including Latin America, and may reflect the effects of globalization or of skill-biased technological change.

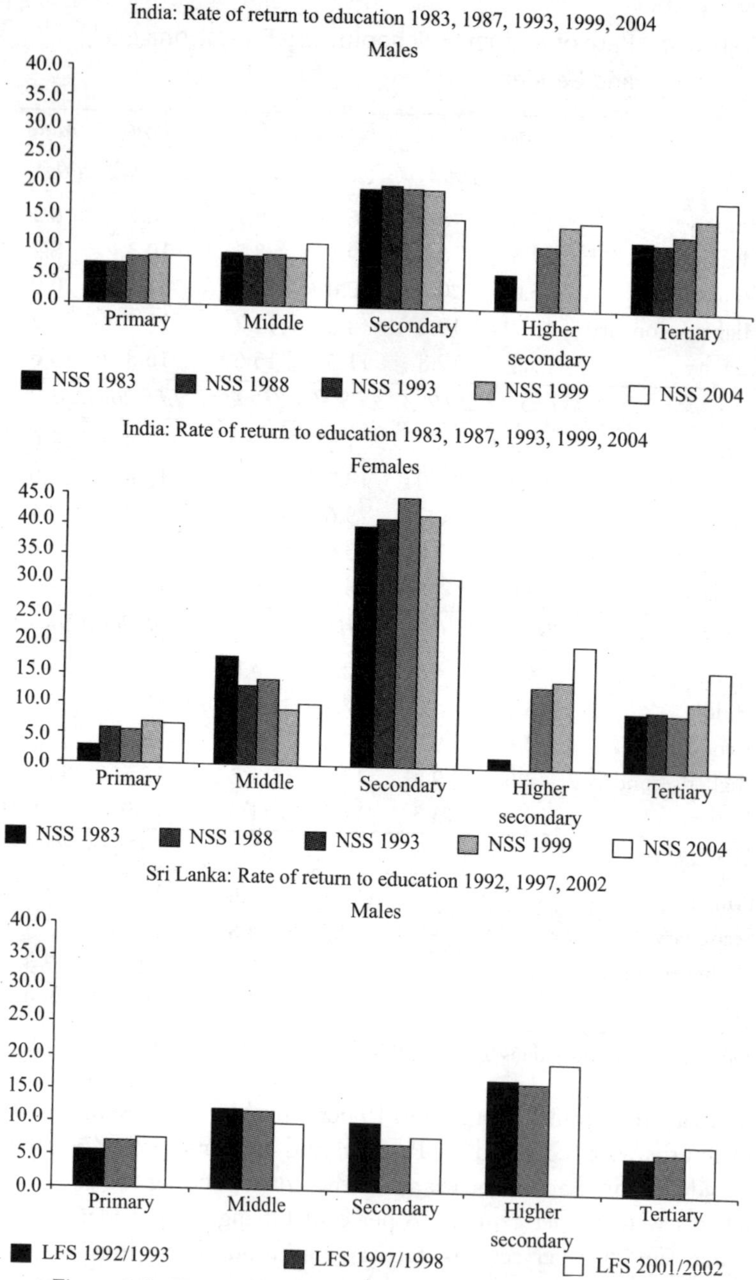

Figure 8.6: Returns to Education over Time by Schooling Level and Gender

(contd ...)

Figure 8.6 (contd ...)

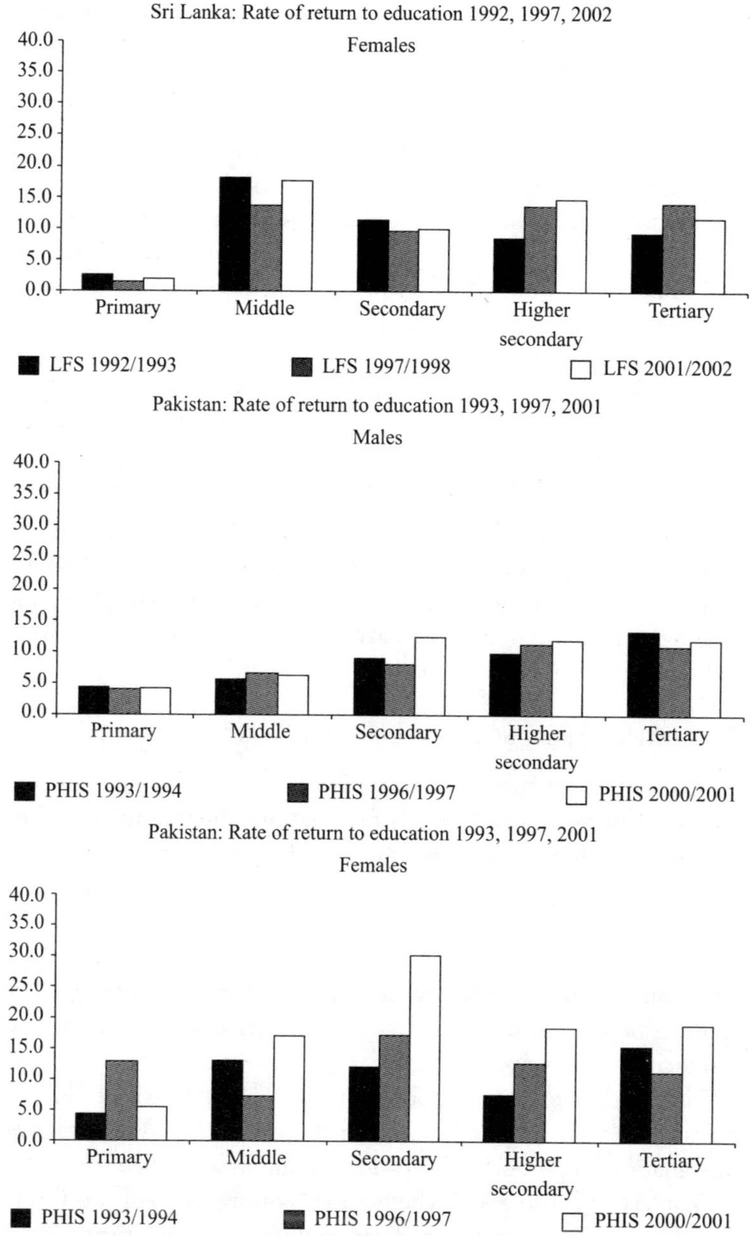

Figure 8.6: Returns to Education over Time by Schooling Level and Gender

Source: Authors' calculations based on BHIESs, NSSs, PIHSs, and LFSs Surveys.

These time trends are more readily apparent when rates of return are presented graphically. Figure 8.6 shows the estimated returns to different levels of schooling for all available years. For each country, the data are shown separately for males and females. The figure confirms the following results. First, returns to education have grown over time, especially for higher secondary and tertiary education. Second, as noted earlier, returns to education are especially high for females, and these, too, have grown over time. Finally, the returns tend to be higher for the high-growth countries (India and Pakistan) and lower for slower growing Sri Lanka.

We conclude from these results that the demand for highly educated and skilled workers is increasing in South Asia, is doing so more rapidly than the supply of graduates, and that this phenomenon coincides with periods of fast growth. This is consistent with the evidence observed in other developing and developed countries, and with the hypothesis that openness to trade, rapid growth, and technological innovations fuel increasing demand for skilled labour relative to those who are unskilled. It makes clear that education and training policies in South Asia have not yet responded to the needs and signals from the labour market.

Post-school Training in the Labour Market

In this section, we turn from education to pre-employment and on-the-job training that individuals may acquire after completing their formal education. Using household and labour force surveys, we provide a broad overview of its incidence among individuals with different levels of education and the effects of training on wages. This is followed by a closer examination of in-service training provided by employers, using firm-level surveys of the manufacturing sector to describe the incidence of training and its impact on firm-level productivity and wages.

Information on post-school training in South Asia is limited. Pakistan and Sri Lanka's Labour Force Surveys (LFSs) have elicited information on post-school vocational training since the early 1990s; Sri Lanka's LFS also asked whether the training received was formal or informal. In other South Asian countries, such information is rarely asked, and if asked, only periodically. In Bangladesh, the 1995 BHIES asked, for just one year, whether respondents had received any vocational training, and if so, the type and length of training, the training institution, and the utility of the training to respondents' current work. In India, the NSS round 60 (2004) asked individuals about vocational training for the first time, and restricted questions to those with at least a middle school education and aged 15–29 years. If respondents had received vocational training, the survey asked about the field of training, the name of the training institution, the duration of the training, and whether respondents had received a degree, a diploma, or a certificate.

Incidence of Post-school Training

Table 8.4 shows the proportion of the population aged 15–64 years reporting that they had received vocational training, broken down by educational attainment and gender in Bangladesh, India, Pakistan, and Sri Lanka. The table is based on the most recent survey available for each country, typically in the early 2000s for India, Pakistan, and Sri Lanka, and 1995 for Bangladesh. The table indicates that the incidence of post-school vocational training is quite low in South Asia. It is lowest in Pakistan (2.4 per cent) and highest in Sri Lanka (12 per cent).

Overall levels aside, the incidence of training in Table 8.4 shows several trends. First, training tends to rise with the level of educational attainment across all the countries, peaking at or after high school. After that it declines, before peaking again after the first degree. These are the times when individuals end their formal education and

TABLE 8.4: Per Cent of Population Aged 15–64 Years Receiving Vocational Training by Education and Gender

Education	*India*		
	All	*M*	*F*
Illiterate	n.a.	n.a.	n.a.
Primary	n.a.	n.a.	n.a.
Middle	0.9	0.7	1.1
Secondary	4.0	4.4	3.4
Higher secondary	8.3	8.9	7.4
Diploma certificate	58.6	62.7	48.4
Graduate	16.8	17.1	16.3
Post-graduate	18.2	18.1	18.3
Total	4.0	4.4	3.6

Source: NSS 60 (2004).

(contd ...)

Table 8.4 (contd ...)

Education	*Bangladesh*		
	All	*M*	*F*
Illiterate	1.5	1.4	2.7
Primary	4.3	4.4	0.0
Secondary VI–VIII	9.2	8.1	49.5
Secondary, class IX	11.1	11.3	0.0
School certificate	13.3	12.5	67.5
Higher certificate	19.7	19.7	18.6
BA general	11.1	11.3	0.0
BA honours	6.7	6.7	0.0
MA and above	27.5	27.5	0.0
Total	4.7	4.6	5.8

Source: BHIES 1995.

Education	*Sri Lanka*		
	All	*M*	*F*
Illiterate	1.2	2.0	0.4
Primary	4.7	6.0	2.0
Lower secondary	9.8	11.4	4.2
Upper secondary	17.4	18.7	13.7
GCE O level	25.0	24.8	25.3
GCE A level	37.4	36.0	39.2
Graduate	34.5	35.1	33.8
Post-graduate	45.1	42.1	48.4
Total	12.0	15.1	9.1

Source: Sri Lanka LFS 2002.

Education	*Pakistan*		
	All	*M*	*F*
No formal	0.9	1.7	0.5
Below primary	2.1	2.6	1.3
Primary	2.5	3.0	1.7
Middle	2.5	3.1	1.4
Secondary	4.3	5.1	3.0
Higher secondary	6.4	7.4	4.7
Degree	8.6	10.7	4.8
Post-graduate	7.6	8.5	5.6
Total	2.4	3.6	1.2

Source: Pakistan LFS 2004.

TABLE 8.5: Per Cent Receiving Vocational Training by Sector of Employment

India, 2004		*Pakistan, 2003/04*		*Bangladesh, 1995*	
Sector	%	*Sector*	%	*Sector*	%
Utilities	23.6	Utilities	17.7	Electricity/gas	39.5
Real estate, renting, business activities	19.4	Finance & business	12.8	Finance/real estate/financial services	17.7
Finance	14.6				
Community, social personal services	10.6	Social services & public administration	8.8	Social/Personal Services	12.9
Public administration	9.0				
Transport	7.2	Transport	6.9	Transport	8.3
Manufacturing	7.1	Manufacturing	10.0	Manufacturing	13.9
Trade	5.5	Trade	2.9		
Construction	4.4	Construction	4.1	Housing, construction	7.4
Hotel & restaurants	3.8			Business/hotel/restaurant	2.5
Mining & quarrying	1.7	Mining	37.7	Mining and quarrying	0.0
Agriculture	1.4	Agriculture	0.9	Agriculture	1.4

Sources: India—NSS 60 (2004); Pakistan—LFS 2003/04; Bangladesh—HIES 1995.

obtain post-school vocational or technical training, either to become skilled workers after high school or to become professionals after completing their tertiary education.[7] Second, Table 8.4 also shows that women are less likely to receive post-school training than their male counterparts with the same level of education. In India, 4.4 per cent of males receive vocational training versus 3.6 per cent of females. The corresponding gender differences are 3.6 and 1.2 per cent in Pakistan, and 15.1 and 9.1 per cent in Sri Lanka. Bangladesh appears to be an anomaly in South Asia, with females being more likely to obtain vocational training (5.8 per cent) than males (4.6 per cent).

The data reveal variations in training incidence across sectors. Table 8.5 tabulates the percentage of the workforce with post-school training by sector of employment in Bangladesh, India, and Pakistan. The utilities sector tends to have the highest share of employees with training, followed broadly by real estate and finance, and public administration and social services. The manufacturing sector occupies the middle ground in terms of percentage of workers with post-school training. The sectors with the smallest shares of workers obtaining vocational training are trade, construction, hotels and restaurants, and agriculture. The mining sector is strikingly different across the three countries, with 37.7 per cent of employees in Pakistan receiving training, compared with 1.7 per cent in India, and none in Bangladesh.

Time Trends in Post-school Training

We exploit the availability of annual time series data from the LFSs in Pakistan and Sri Lanka to look at training trends in the two countries over the past decade. Each country collects, in addition to information training received, unique information about training—Pakistan on the field of training and Sri Lanka on formal (certificated) and informal training. What emerges from the experiences of these two countries is that the incidence of training

[7] In tabulations of training by occupation not reported here, the occupational groups most likely to receive vocational training are professionals, technicians, and clerical personnel. This makes sense, as these are the occupations that tend to include a large number of the highly educated. The occupations with the lowest shares of individuals receiving vocational training are employees in sales, services, and agriculture, where educational requirements tend to be low.

tends to follow cycles of economic growth, with compositional changes in training by demographic groups typically in favour of the more educated.

The Case of Pakistan

Figure 8.7 graphs the time trends in post-school training in Pakistan over the decade between 1993 and 2003. The incidence of training rose from 4.1 per cent of the workforce in 1993 to 4.6 per cent in 1996, then fell to 2.4 per cent in 2001, before rising to 2.5 per cent in 2003. These trends in the proportion of the workforce receiving training appear to mirror the overall growth of the economy. The annual growth rate of the economy rose from 1.8 in 1993 to 5.0

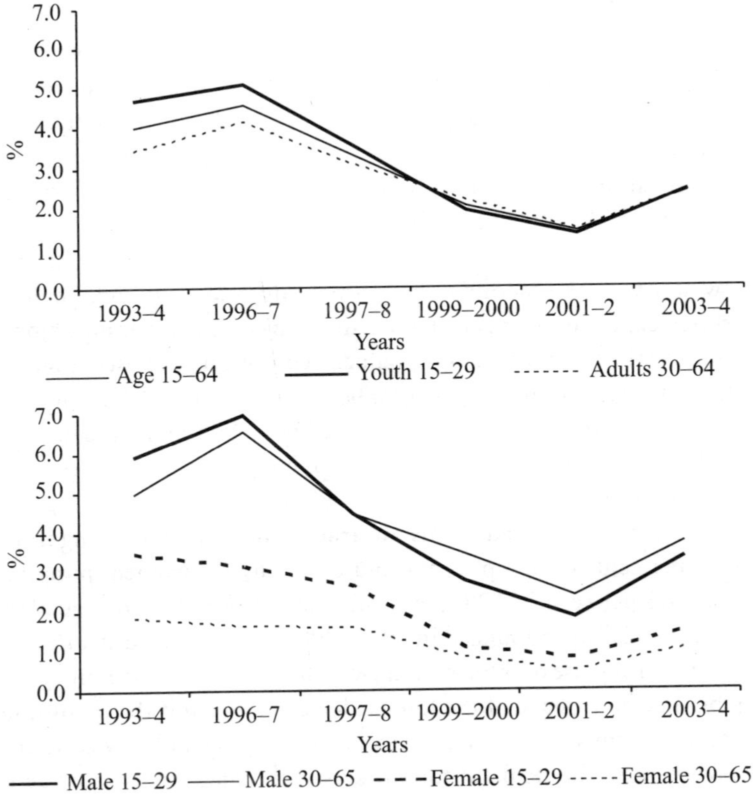

Figure 8.7: Trends in Post-school Training in Pakistan, 1993–2003

Source: Authors' calculations based on LFSs for Pakistan.

per cent in 1995, but slowed thereafter to an annual rate of between 1 per cent and 4 per cent. Sustained growth resumed in 2001, and the economy grew in excess of 6 per cent per annum by 2004. This correlation between growth and training suggests that individuals and employers invest pro-cyclically in training, seeing greater employment opportunities and rising demand for a skilled workforce when the overall economy is growing.

Overall trends aside, Figure 8.7 also shows compositional changes in training by age group and gender. While youth and young adults between the ages of 15 and 29 were more likely to report having received training than adults between the ages of 30 and 64 at the beginning of this period, over time their propensity to get training has become virtually indistinguishable. This is also evident when training incidence is broken down by both age and gender. While young males and females were more likely to receive training than older adults in 1993, by 2003, young and adult females had similar rates of training, but young males were less likely to receive training than older males.

Tabulations of the time series data (not reported here) reveal other trends. First, while the incidence of training declines over time for most groups because of slower economic growth, those with the lowest levels of schooling (no formal education through middle school) experienced the greatest declines. In contrast, training among males with degrees and postgraduate education increased slightly (from 8.3 per cent to 8.6 per cent) between 1993 and 2003, which is consistent with rising skills demand tied to globalization and growth of the knowledge economy. A second point that emerges is the large increase in the proportion of the workforce that reported computer training over this decade. This was true for both men, growing from 12.3 per cent to 17.4 per cent, but especially for women, jumping from 4.4 per cent to 12.6 per cent. The increases for both genders were especially pronounced in 1999–2000, and may be explained by the increasing use of information technology in a growing number of jobs. The emergence of the knowledge economy and the mounting use of information technology in manufacturing and service sector jobs increase the demand for workers with computer literacy and, if this demand is not met by rising supply, will lead to rising wages as well.

The Case of Sri Lanka

In Sri Lanka, the overall incidence of post-school training for the workforce remained unchanged at about 12 per cent during 1992–2002, although this figure conceals considerable compositional changes by education, age, and type of training that took place over that decade.

Figure 8.8 shows trends in the incidence of post-school training in Sri Lanka, separating the information for any training and that for weighted formal or certificated training It also is separated by age category—all ages, youth and young adults aged 15–29, and adults aged 30–65 years. Several trends emerge from the figure. First, training incidence shows a secularly rising trend between 1992 and 1999, a stagnation and marked decline in 2001 in line with negative economic growth, and recovery starting thereafter. Second, the type of training received is increasingly more formal over time: The proportion of the workforce receiving any training rose from 11 per cent to 13 per cent from 1992–2002, but the proportion obtaining formal training climbed from 7 per cent to 10 per cent. Finally, in each year, a higher proportion of youth and young adults aged 15–29 reported training than did adults aged 30–65, and over time, these age-related differences widened.

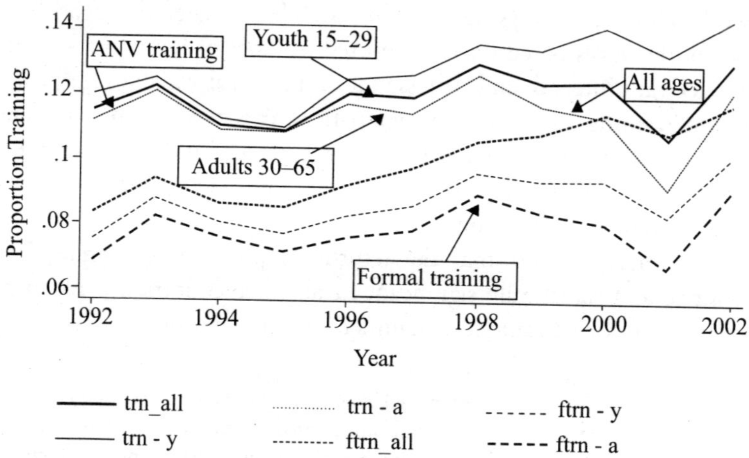

Figure 8.8: Trends in Post-school Training in Sri Lanka, 1992–2002

Source: Authors' calculations based on LFSs for Sri Lanka.

Tabulations (not shown here) reveal several other compositional changes by level of educational attainment in Sri Lanka. First, like Pakistan, the incidence of training fell dramatically between 1992 and 2002 among the least educated—those with primary and lower secondary education. Only the more highly educated—those with GCE A-level qualifications and university graduates—bucked this trend, and their incidence of training rose slightly over levels prevailing in 1992. For post-graduates, however, no clear-cut time trends are apparent. Second, among those who received training, the less educated tended to receive training that was primarily informal (that is, non-certificated), while the more educated tended to receive formal training. Over time, starting with those with lower secondary education, the trend has been toward receipt of formal, credentialed training, especially for males.

Post-school Training and Wages

What are the returns to investments in post-school training, and how do they compare with those from investments in formal education? To address these questions, we estimated broadly comparable wage models for India (2004), Pakistan (2004), and Sri Lanka (2002), using the most recent survey available for each country and including all individuals aged 15–64 who worked for wages and salaries in the week before the surveys were conducted. We calculated the logarithm of hourly wages based on the reported number of hours worked in the relevant interval, and regressed it on indicator variables for post-school training, individual characteristics (years of schooling, gender, a quadratic measure of potential work experience), indicator variables for employment status and caste (India), and geographic location. Table 8.6 reports the results.

The table suggests that the returns to post-school training are positive and statistically significant in all three countries, even after controlling for educational attainment and other worker attributes.[8]

[8] We recognize that the estimated coefficient of training may suffer from selectivity bias (Heckman 1979) from unmeasured productivity attributes of the individual correlated both with the training choice and with the outcome of interest. While econometric techniques exist to address selectivity bias in estimating returns to training (Barnow, Cain, and Goldberger 1981), these are not pursued here because no viable instruments could be identified that were correlated with training but not with earnings.

TABLE 8.6: Post-school Training and Wages—India, Pakistan, and Sri Lanka

Dependent variable: log(hourly wage)	*India*	*Pakistan*		*Sri Lanka*	
Independent variables		Model 1	Model 2	Model 1	Model 2
Years of education	0.084	0.090	0.089	0.079	0.078
	(21.09)**	(63.02)**	(62.82)**	(54.80)**	(53.35)**
Formal vocational training	0.080	0.081		0.170	0.211
	(2.55)*	(2.95)**		(13.68)**	(15.22)**
Computer vocational training			0.186		
			(2.81)**		
Other vocational training			0.061		
			(2.02)**		
Informal vocational/tech. training					0.035
					(1.46)
Male indicator	0.340	0.285	0.285	0.328	0.333
	(14.5)**	(16.26)**	(16.23)**	(33.47)**	(33.89)**
Years of potential experience	0.065	0.060	0.060	0.025	0.025
	(7.83)**	(32.68)**	(32.73)**	(17.67)**	(17.66)**
Experience squared	–0.001	–0.001	–0.001	–0.000	–0.000
	(–2.53)*	(–23.15)**	(–23.21)**	(–14.66)**	(–14.71)**
Constant	0.27	–0.460	–0.462	2.078	2.084
	(4.66)**	(–16.89)**	(–16.93)**	(77.87)**	(78.13)**
Observations	8,299	13,515	13,515	21,328	21,328
R-squared	0.29	0.34	0.34	0.25	0.25

Source: Authors' calculations based on India NSSs, Pakistan LFSs, and Sri Lanka LFSs.
Notes: Indicator variables included (but not reported) for location, caste (India), and worker status.
* statistically significant at i0 per cent; ** statistically significant at 1 per cent.

In India, the returns to formal vocational training are about 8 per cent, almost equivalent to the 8.4 per cent return to an additional year of education. In Pakistan, the returns to formal vocational training are comparable to those in India, and equal 8.1 per cent. This number is slightly lower than the returns to one additional year of education in Pakistan, of about 9 per cent. When vocational training is differentiated by type (see model 2 in the table), the results indicate that the returns to computer training are substantially higher, at 18 per cent, than those from all other types of vocational training combined, at 6 per cent.[9] In Sri Lanka, formal vocational training is associated with relatively high returns of 17 per cent, more than double those of an additional year of formal education. Differentiating between formal and informal vocational training results in statistically significant returns to formal vocational training of 21 per cent, whereas the returns to informal training of 3.5 per cent are not significant.

These estimates of the average returns to training should be treated cautiously, given the caveats about selectivity bias and the paucity of information about the reported training event. Improved estimates of training returns will require more detailed information about when training took place (before employment or as part of in-service training), the duration of the training, and who provided the training (the employer or public or private training institutes). The availability of panel data on individuals and their training and earnings experiences over time would also improve the estimation of training returns, correcting for selectivity bias, and unmeasured ability.

In-Service Training by Employers

The post-school training data analysed previously did not differentiate between pre-employment and in-service training. This distinction is critical since in-service training decisions are typically

[9] The estimated high returns to computer training might plausibly explain both its popularity and its rising incidence among the Pakistani workforce aged 15–65 during 1994–2004. Using a time series of labour force surveys, Savchenko and Tan (2007) show that the proportion of male Pakistani workers who received computer training rose from 12 per cent in 1994 to more than 17 per cent by 2004. This trend was even more dramatic for women: The incidence of computer training among women tripled during this period from 4 to 12 per cent.

made jointly with employers. To obtain insights into the factors that shape employers' demands for skills and their in-service training, we turn to firm-level Investment Climate Surveys (ICSs) to study the in-service training practices of manufacturing firms in our sample of South Asian countries, their determinants, and their consequences for labour productivity and wages.[10]

The ICSs asked employers detailed and comparable questions about their workforce and training practices. These data, together with information about different enterprise attributes and production, allow us to ask not only which firms provide in-service training, who they train, how much training they provide, and the source of the training, but also to examine the productivity and wage outcomes of training. The World Bank has undertaken similar ICSs in many developing countries. Therefore, the in-service training practices of South Asian firms can be compared with those of similar firms in other countries. Such comparisons across countries can provide insights into whether the incidence of in-service training in South

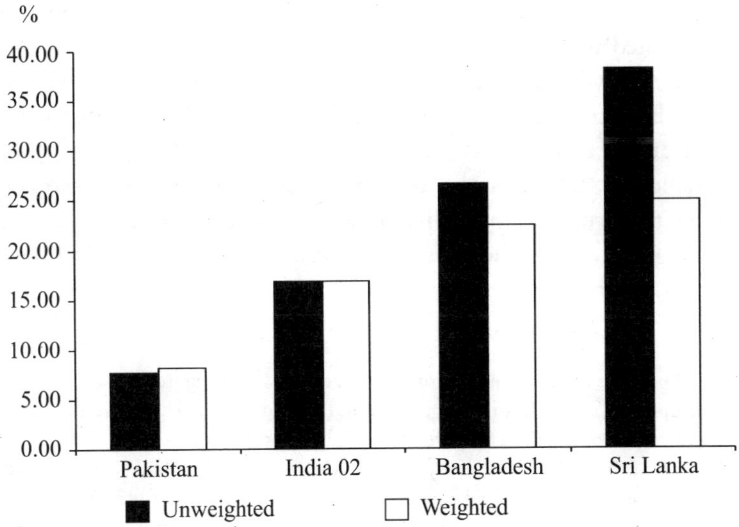

Figure 8.9: Incidence of In-Service Training in South Asia

Source: Authors' calculations based on the Investment Climate Surveys.

[10] This section draws heavily on Tan and Savchenko (2005, 2006).

Asia is low, and if it is, can help policymakers design training policies to remedy identified weaknesses.

Figure 8.9 compares levels of in-service training in Bangladesh, India, Pakistan, and Sri Lanka. Estimates are presented with and without adjustments to reflect differences in the firm size distribution of ICS samples across countries. In particular, the Bangladesh ICS includes a higher proportion of large firms, which tend to train, while the India ICS has a more representative sample of firms of different sizes. The simple, unweighted tabulations suggest that at 37 per cent, the incidence of in-service training is highest in Sri Lanka, followed by Bangladesh (26 per cent), India (17 per cent), and Pakistan (8 per cent). The weighted incidence of in-service training using the size distribution of India as the norm yields the same country rankings, but reduces cross-country disparities.

How does in-service training in South Asia compare with other regions? As Figure 8.10 shows, the incidence of training in South Asia is among the lowest in the world, being almost half the average for Europe and Central Asia, and less than half of Sub-Saharan Africa, East Asia and the Pacific, and Latin America and the Caribbean.[11] If an educated and trained workforce is critical for technological change and the knowledge economy, then low levels of education and this post-school training deficit put South Asia at a distinct competitive disadvantage relative to its neighbours such as East Asia.

Table 8.7 tabulates the percentage of managers, professionals, production workers, and non-production workers receiving in-service training by country. The cross-country rankings of the share of workers trained, or training intensity, vary with per-capita income and years of schooling of the workforce in the country. Sri Lanka has the highest

[11] The cross-country and regional averages shown in Figures 6.2 and 6.3 are based upon ICS data from 35 countries and a total of 17,941 firm respondents. The regional composition is as follows—Sub-Saharan Africa: 2,387 firms in 11 countries (Eritrea, Ethiopia, Kenya, Mali, Mozambique, Nigeria, Senegal, South Africa, Tanzania, Uganda, and Zambia); East Asia and the Pacific: 3,985 firms in five countries (Cambodia, China, Indonesia, Malaysia, and the Philippines); Europe and Central Asia: 280 firms in three countries; Latin America and the Caribbean: 5,112 firms in eight countries (Bolivia, Brazil, Ecuador, El Salvador, Guatemala, Honduras, Nicaragua, and Peru); the Middle East and North Africa: 2,889 firms in five countries (Algeria, the Arab Republic of Egypt, Morocco, Oman, and the Syrian Arab Republic); South Asia: 4,466 firms in six countries (Bangladesh, Bhutan, India, Nepal, Pakistan, and Sri Lanka).

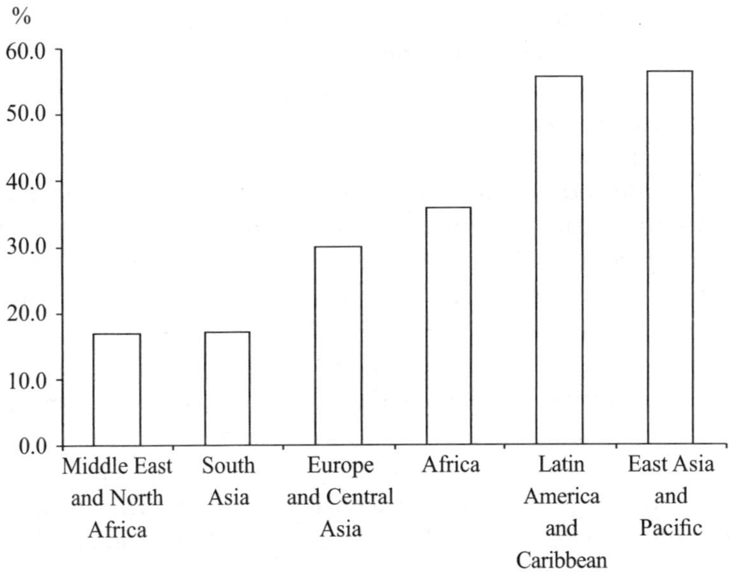

Figure 8.10: Regional Comparisons of In-Service Training in Manufacturing

Source: Authors' calculations based on the Investment Climate Surveys.

training intensity, followed by India, Pakistan, and Bangladesh. In Sri Lanka, 10 per cent of managers, 11 per cent of professionals, 22 per cent of production workers, and 6 per cent of non-production workers received in-service training. In India, the corresponding figures are between 6 and 7 per cent of managers, professionals, and

TABLE 8.7: Share of Workers Trained by Skill Group—South Asia

Country	*Managers*	*Professionals*	*Production*	*Non-production workers*
Bangladesh	1.9	3.0	1.2	0.4
India	6.0	7.3	7.0	2.9
Pakistan	2.0	3.5	3.3	0.4
Sri Lanka	10.4	11.3	22.4	6.0

Source: ICSs for respective countries.
Note: Estimates weighted using the India firm size distribution.

production workers, and about 3 per cent of non-production workers. In Bangladesh and Pakistan, firms extend in-service training to only a small fraction of their workforces, averaging 3 per cent of professionals, 2 per cent of managers, 1.2 per cent of production workers, and less than 0.5 per cent of non-production workers.

How do these estimates for South Asia compare with the level of in-service training in the fast-growing economies of East Asia? A World Bank (1997) study of Malaysian manufacturing estimated that in 1994, the overall proportion of workers receiving formal in-service training was 22 per cent, which included 24 per cent of managers, 32 per cent of technicians, and between 13 and 16 per cent of production workers. South Asian employers are apparently not only less likely to provide in-service training to their workers than employers in other regions, but those that do provide training extend training opportunities to a smaller fraction of their workforce than their counterparts in other regions, especially those in East Asia. This training deficit in terms of the proportion of workers trained is especially significant in Bangladesh and Pakistan.

In relation to the main sources of in-service training in South Asia, Table 8.8 presents information for Bangladesh, India, Pakistan, and Sri Lanka. Conditional on a positive response to the in-service training question, employers were asked whether training was provided through in-house company training programmes, or by external sources such as universities or VET schools. For convenience, these external sources of training may be clustered into two groups: public training providers (universities, VET schools, and government institutes) and private sector training providers (private training institutes and partner firms).

Several points stand out from Table 8.8. First, while enterprises in all four South Asian countries rely on both in-house and external training providers,[12] with the exception of Sri Lanka, in-house programmes are a more common source of training than external training providers. Second, Indian and Sri Lankan firms tend to emphasize both public and private training institutes (between 35 and 60 per cent of firms) as external sources for their in-service

[12] In-house training is training provided on the firm's premises in a specially designated classroom. External training is a training provided outside the firm's premises.

TABLE 8.8: Per Cent of Firms Providing Training by Source—South Asia

Country	*Formal Training*			*External sources conditional on training*				
	Any	*In-house Training*	*External training*	*University*	*Private partners*	*Govt. institute*	*Private institute*	*VET school*
Bangladesh	24.1	17.7	13.1	6.9	25.7	17.6	19.8	31.1
India	16.9	13.8	8.0	10.2	10.2	34.7	53.1	46.3
Pakistan	8.2	6.6	5.0	29.2	18.7	33.9	49.9	34.7
Sri Lanka	25.0	15.7	18.0	7.6	15.9	59.1	41.3	n.a.

Source: ICSs for Bangladesh, India, Pakistan and Sri Lanka.
Note: Estimates are weighted using the size distribution of India as the norm.

training. In contrast, Bangladeshi firms tend to report VET schools (31 per cent) and private sector partner firms (26 per cent) as the most important sources of external training. Pakistani enterprises use private institutes (50 per cent), VET schools (35 per cent) and government institutes (34 per cent) for external training.

What accounts for the relatively low levels of in-service training in South Asia? The literature has suggested two broad sets of hypotheses. First, the business environment may not be conducive to investments of any kind, whether physical or human. On this score, employers in all four countries ranked tax rates, economic and regulatory uncertainty, and access to finance as the top three constraints to doing business, placing relatively little importance on the skills of available workers. This suggests that South Asian employers may not yet recognize the importance of workers' skills for improving productivity and competitiveness. By contrast, Malaysian employers ranked skills availability as their top constraint (World Bank 2005).

A second hypothesis is that specific market failures may inhibit socially optimal levels of worker training. While the South Asian ICSs did not elicit information on why employers might invest little in training, this information is available in the world business environment surveys (WBESs) collected for a broad range of developing countries (Batra and Stone 2004).[13] The WBESs asked respondents to rank a series of statements about what factors influenced their decisions to invest (or not invest) in training workers. Firms cited the following key reasons for not training: use of mature technologies that did not require training or skills upgrading; training was not affordable, suggesting problems with access to finance; high labour turnover of trained staff, an externality that prevents firms from recouping the costs of training employees; and adequacy of informal on-the-job training, which may either imply ready availability of skilled workers or low skill requirements for existing jobs. The small sample of firms from South Asia that participated in the WBESs cited these same key reasons for not training their workforces.

[13] The WBES was an enterprise survey using a standard core questionnaire to more than 10,000 firms in 80 countries between late 1998 and mid-2000 to investigate issues concerning investment climate and firm performance. The analyses reported in Batra and Stone (2004) are based on a special survey module administered in 28 of the WBES countries that focused on competition, trade, technology, and worker training.

What about the factors that increase demand for in-service training, such as globalization and the knowledge economy? Export orientation can motivate firms to provide training so they can produce high-quality products that meet the exacting standards of foreign buyers and also increase their labour productivity to meet competitive pressures (Batra and Stone 2004; Tan and Batra 1995). The effective use of new technology also requires a more skilled and trained workforce (Bell and Pavitt 1992; Enos 1962). Simple tabulations of the ICS data suggest that firms in South Asia that export or are engaged in research and development activities are more likely to report providing in-service training than those that do not. These correlations are most apparent for India, Pakistan, and Sri Lanka.

Regression analysis (not shown here) suggest that employers' demand for training is shaped by firm attributes, the education of the workforce, integration into global markets, and the level of technological sophistication of the firm.[14] First, the incidence of training rises with establishment size, a common finding for all countries for which data are available, and may reflect size-related differences in access to finance, scale economies in training provision, and managerial capabilities. Second, the probability of training rises with the average years of schooling attained by the firm's workforce, a result consistent with the earlier analysis of education and post-school training, and with empirical evidence from many developing countries.[15] Educated workers are not only more productive when performing given tasks, but they benefit more from training than less educated workers. Third, some support is found for the hypotheses that the demand for in-service training is shaped by export orientation and technology. For India and Sri Lanka, both variables are positive and statistically significant; for Bangladesh, exports are positive and marginally significant; and for Pakistan, technology is positive and statistically significant.

[14] A probit model was estimated by regressing a (0,1) indicator variable for 'any formal training' on a set of explanatory variables, including measures of firm size, public sector or foreign ownership, education of the workforce, exports, and level of technology used.

[15] See Tan and Batra (1995) for estimates of the relationship between education and training from five developing countries in East Asia and Latin America, and Tan (2000) and World Bank (1997, 2005) for related training analyses for Malaysia.

Productivity and Wage Outcomes of Training

Providing in-service training only makes sense if employers' investments in training their employees and upgrading their skills yield positive returns in the form of higher productivity and profits.[16] If training results in positive impacts on productivity, employers also need to determine whether, or to what extent, to share these productivity gains with workers in the form of higher wages. This will depend on the transferability of skills gained from training to other potential employers (Acemoglu and Pischke 1998; Becker 1975; Tan 1980). We address these questions using the ICS data for the four countries under review.

For the productivity analysis, we use a production function approach. The dependent variable—the logarithm of value added—is regressed on the logarithms of capital (book value of physical plant and equipment assets), employment, a measure of in-service training, a vector of control variables for worker attributes (mean years of education), location, and industry.

Table 8.9 reports the results of this productivity analysis for the four countries. First, the estimated production function parameters of capital and labour coefficients are positive and statistically significant, and resemble those estimated for many other countries. Second, consistent with the belief that education raises firm-level productivity, the results for Bangladesh and India indicate that increased educational attainment of the firm's workforce by one year is associated with higher levels of firm-level productivity: 3.5 per cent for Bangladesh and 5.8 per cent for India (the results for both Pakistan and Sri Lanka were not statistically significant). Finally, in-service training is typically associated with higher productivity across South Asian countries. The magnitude of the estimated impact on productivity and its significance vary: 67 per cent for Pakistan and 36 per cent for Sri Lanka, both significant at the 1 per cent level; 16 per cent for India, significant at the 10 per cent level; and 7 per cent for Bangladesh, though not significantly different from zero.

[16] Cross-sectional studies have found a strong positive association between in-service training and firms' productivity and wage levels (Batra and Stone 2004; Tan and Batra 1995). Panel studies based on longitudinal firm surveys that elicited repeated information on the training practices of the same firms have also found evidence that training, especially when it is repeated, leads to higher productivity growth and wages (see Dearden, Reed, and Van Reenen [2000] for the United Kingdom; Tan [2000] for Malaysia; Tan and Lopez-Acevedo [2003] for Mexico).

TABLE 8.9: In-Service Training and Productivity

Dependent variable: Log (value added)	*Production function model*			
Country	*Bangladesh*	*India*	*Pakistan*	*Sri Lanka*
Explanatory variables				
Log(capital)	0.247	0.216	0.290	0.162
	(14.05)***	(14.36)***	(8.44)***	(5.31)***
Log (labour)	0.767	0.849	0.700	0.786
	(24.09)***	(27.21)***	(12.59)***	(13.71)***
Mean years schooling	0.035	0.058	0.002	0.017
	(3.93)***	(5.83)***	(1.32)	(1.52)
Formal training	0.066	0.156	0.667	0.364
indicator	(1.03)	(1.78)*	(3.23)***	(2.72)***
Intercept	10.186	11.254	14.026	11.342
	(58.52)***	(49.96)***	(19.89)***	(32.27)***
R-square	0.708	0.662	0.507	0.743
Number of observations	969	1790	892	374

Source: South Asia ICS.
Notes: Control variables included for missing values, location, and industries.
* statistically significant at 10%; *** significant at 1%.

For the wage analysis (not illustrated here), we estimate a wage model relating the logarithm of hourly occupational wages to measures of in-service training and a vector of control variables for firm and worker attributes. Controlling for firm attributes, industry, and location, we failed to find any wage effects from in-service training in India, Pakistan, and Bangladesh; Sri Lanka is the only exception, and in-service training is associated with a statistically significant increase in mean wages of about 20 per cent. Apart from the weak results from training, the regression analysis suggests that employers in all countries pay higher wages for a more educated and experienced workforce (education effects are particularly significant), but tend to pay lower wages when the workforce is predominantly female. Compared with the omitted occupation group (skilled production workers), managers and professionals are paid more, while unskilled and non-production workers receive lower pay; relative wages across these broad occupations appear to be similar across the countries.

Conclusions and Policy Implications

Expanding trade and globalization of production make continuous learning over an employee's work life an imperative, as skills acquired in schools and in the workplace become obsolete more quickly, and new and more complex skills are needed to respond to accelerating technological change. How educational and training systems respond to these challenges will have far-reaching implications for economic growth and competitiveness of South Asian countries, and for income growth, employment, job creation, and poverty reduction.

The findings reported in this chapter suggest that the educational stock of the workforce in South Asia is still low compared to other parts of the world, particularly East Asia. Progress on the educational front has been unequal over time across countries, but none of the countries in the region currently upgrade the education of their populations at a speed that will allow them to 'catch up' quickly with East Asia and the rest of the world. Despite government commitment to and increased investments in education over time in the region, returns to higher secondary and tertiary education have remained high and even increased relative to lower schooling levels, especially in business services as compared to industry. This indicates that the fast-growing demand for skills is outstripping supply from the educational system, and that education policies have not yet responded adequately to this increased demand.

The available data suggest that South Asia invests inadequate resources in skills development after formal schooling. The estimated returns to post-school training are roughly comparable to, or even larger than, those from investing in education. Despite high returns, the incidence of post-school training is low. This is lowest in Pakistan and highest in Sri Lanka, with other countries falling somewhere in between. The low incidence of training is affected in part by slow or erratic economic growth in the region, which reduces demand for skills, and in part by low levels of schooling, which is complementary with training.

South Asia also lags behind other regions in employer provision of in-service training. In fact, in-service training in manufacturing firms in South Asia is among the lowest in the world, being less than half of the average for Europe and Central Asia, East Asia, and Latin America. The deficit is particularly pronounced when South

Asian countries are compared to their competitor countries such as Malaysia (where the incidence is twice as high) and China (where it is three times higher). To the extent that training is associated with productivity growth and is required for technological change, a low incidence of training has negative implications for the industrial competitiveness of countries in the region.

Policymakers in the region are already grappling with the challenges of reforming national education and training systems. All countries are increasingly aware that an educated and trained workforce is critical for technological change, and for creating a knowledge economy, but many countries have yet to put education and training at the top of their priorities, and many education and training policies and programmes have still to respond fully to the needs and signals from the labour market. The challenge for South Asia is to shift emphasis to higher levels of education, without neglecting the unfinished education agenda at the primary level. There is also considerable scope for improving the effectiveness of public VET institutions in the region, including greater partnership with the private sector to develop and deliver skills training demanded by employers and the labour market.

But recent trends are encouraging. In India, for example, the Knowledge Economy report has sparked policy interest in how to reposition education and workforce skills to take advantage of opportunities afforded by the knowledge economy. Pakistan, recognizing the imperative of expanding access to vocational education and technical training, recently established NAVTEC—an apex training body—to implement a scaled-up national training strategy for the workforce. The private sector should take on greater shared responsibility with governments for promoting skills development in the region. Public–private partnerships in the management of VET institutions can help make the training delivery system more responsive to the economy's skill needs. And as employers, it should take the leading role in organizing in-service training programmes for its workers, with the government intervening, when warranted by market imperfections, to promote such efforts.

References

Acemoglu, Daron and Jorn-Steffen Pischke. 1998. 'Why do Firms Train? Theory and Evidence', *Quarterly Journal of Economics*, 113 (February): 79–119.

Barnow, Burt, Glen Cain, and Arthur Goldberger. 1981. 'Issues in the Analysis of Selectivity Bias', in William Stromsdorfer and George Farkas (eds), *Evaluation Studies Review Annual*, pp. 43–59. Beverly Hills, CA: Sage.

Barro, Robert J. and Jong-Wha Lee. 2000. 'International Data on Educational Attainment: Updates and Implications', Working Paper 42, CID Centre for International Development at Harvard University, Cambridge, MA.

Batra, Geeta and Andrew Stone. 2004. 'Investment Climate, Capabilities, and Firm Performance: Evidence from the World Business Environment Survey', World Bank, Investment Climate Unit, Washington, D.C.

Becker, Gary S. 1975. *Human Capital*, 2nd edn. New York: Columbia University Press.

Bell, Martin and Keith Pavitt. 1992. 'Accumulating Technological Capability in Developing Countries', Paper presented at the Annual Bank Conference on Development Economics, World Bank, Washington, D.C.

Berman, Eli, John Bound, and Stephen Machin. 1998. 'Implications of Skill-Biased Technological Change: International Evidence', *Quarterly Journal of Economics*, 113(4): 1245–80.

Blom, Andreas, Lauritz Holm-Nielsen, and Dorte Verner. 2001. 'Education, Earnings and Inequality in Brazil: 1982–1998', Policy Research Working Paper 2686, World Bank, Washington, D.C.

Dahlman, Carl and Anuja Utz. 2005. 'India and the Knowledge Economy: Leveraging Strengths and Opportunities', World Bank, Finance and Private Sector Development Unit, South Asia Region, Washington, D.C.

De Ferranti, David, Guillermo E. Perry, Indermit Gill, J. Luis Guasch, William F. Maloney, Carolina Sanchez-Paramo, and Norger Schady. 2003. *Closing the Gap in Education and Technology*. Latin American and Caribbean Studies. Washington, D.C.: World Bank.

Dearden, Lorraine, Howard Reed, and John Van Reenan. 2006. 'The Impact of Training on Productivity and Wages: Evidence from British Panel Data', *Oxford Bulletin of Economics and Statistics*, 68(4): 305–49.

Enos, John. 1962. 'Invention and Innovation in the Petroleum Refining Industry', in *The Rate and Direction of Inventive Activity*. Princeton University Press.

Giovagnoli, Paula Inés, Ariel Fiszbein, and Harry A. Patrinos. 2005. 'Estimating the Returns to Education in Argentina: 1992—2002', Policy Research Working Paper 3715, World Bank, Washington, D.C.

Heckman, James. 1979. 'Sample Selection Bias as a Specification Error', *Econometrica*, 47(1): 153–62.

Lachler, Ulrich. 1998. 'Education and Earnings Inequality in Mexico', Policy Research Working Paper 1949, World Bank, Washington, D.C.

Mincer, Jacob. 1974. *Schooling, Experience, and Earnings*. New York: National Bureau of Economic Research.

Patrinos, Harry Anthony, Cris Ridao-Cano, and Chris Sakellariou. 2006. 'Estimating the Returns to Education: Accounting for Heterogeneity in Ability', Policy Research Working Paper 4040, World Bank, Washington, D.C.

Riboud, Michelle, Yevgeniya Savchenko, and Hong Tan. 2007. *The Knowledge Economy and Education and Training in South Asia*. Washington, D.C.: Human Development Unit, South Asia Region, World Bank.

Savchenko, Yevgeniya and Hong Tan. 2007. 'Overview of TVET Trends in Pakistan from Labour Force Surveys', Working Paper, World Bank, South Asia Human Development Unit, World Bank, Washington, D.C.

Tan, Hong. 1980. 'Human Capital and Technological Change: A Study of Japanese Wage Differentials in Manufacturing', PhD Thesis, Yale University, New Haven.

———. 2000. *Malaysia Skill Needs Study*. Washington, D.C: World Bank Institute.

———. 2005. *The Skills Challenge of New Technology: Training, Technology, and Productivity Growth in Malaysian Manufacturing in the 1990s*. Washington, D.C.: World Bank Institute.

Tan, Hong and Geeta Batra. 1995. 'Enterprise Training in Developing Countries: Incidence, Productivity Effects, and Policy Implications', Occasional Paper 9, Private Sector Development Department, World Bank, Washington, D.C.

Tan, Hong and Gladys Lopez-Acevedo. 2003. 'Mexico: In-Firm Training for the Knowledge Economy', Policy Research Working Paper 2957, World Bank, Washington, D.C.

Tan, Hong, and Yevgeniya Savchenko. 2005. 'In-Service Training in India: Evidence from the Investment Climate Survey', Background paper for *Skills Development in India: The Vocational Education and Training System*. Washington, D.C.

———. 2006. 'In-Service Training in Bangladesh', in World Bank, *The Bangladesh Vocational Education and Training System: An Assessment*. Washington, D.C.: World Bank.

United Nations. 1976. *International Standard Classification of Education*. Paris: United Nations Educational, Scientific, and Cultural Organization.

World Bank. 1997. 'Malaysia: Enterprise Training, Technology, and Productivity', Country study, World Bank, Washington, D.C.

———. 2005. *Malaysia: Firm Competitiveness, Investment Climate and Growth*. Report No. 26841-MA, East Asia and Pacific Region, World Bank, Washington D.C.

———. 2006. *Malaysia and the Knowledge Economy: Building a World-Class Higher Education System*. Washington, D.C.: World Bank.

9 COMPARING PROPERTY RIGHTS INSTITUTIONS, CONTRACTING INSTITUTIONS, AND GROWTH IN SOUTH ASIA AND EAST ASIA

Ana M. Fernandes

Introduction

While both South Asia and East Asia have experienced strong growth over the last two decades, GDP per capita is still much lower and poverty still much more prevalent in South Asia.[1] It is crucial for policymakers and multilateral development agencies to understand whether South Asia has the necessary factors to achieve East Asian growth rates of 7 to 10 per cent and accelerate poverty reduction. Devarajan and Nabi (2006) identify several key weaknesses of South Asia relative to East Asia, related to the role of the manufacturing sector; export orientation and its technological intensity; the supply of skilled workers; the availability and quality of infrastructure, savings and investment rates; and the costs of doing business. In this essay, we focus on the last factor, specifically on differences in institutional quality between South Asia and East Asia. We examine the impact of those differences on economic performance in the two regions.[2] East Asia is one of the most integrated regions in the world in terms of trade in goods, capital, and ideas, while South Asia is one of the

[1] We use the World Bank's regional grouping of countries. The South Asian region includes Bangladesh, Bhutan, India, Nepal, Pakistan, and Sri Lanka. The East Asian region includes Cambodia, China, Indonesia, the Laos People's Democratic Republic, Malaysia, the Philippines, Thailand, and Vietnam. Due to lack of data, Afghanistan, East Timor, the Maldives, and the Pacific Islands are excluded from our analysis.

[2] This work extends the work of Fernandes and Kraay (2006).

least integrated. Hence, we also assess the validity of the hypothesis that integration has led to convergence in institutional quality across East Asian countries, while South Asia has not (yet) benefited from such convergence.[3]

Researchers have clearly established the importance of institutions, governance, and regulation for economic growth and development.[4] To examine the differences in institutional quality between South Asia and East Asia, we follow Acemoglu and Johnson (2005) in distinguishing between 'property rights institutions', which illustrate the extent to which private property is secure from predation by the state (for example, through expropriation, or from corrupt officials demanding bribes in exchange for favours to firms or individuals), and 'contracting institutions', which illustrate the effectiveness of institutions such as the judicial system, which is used to enforce contracts or mediate disputes between private parties. The former can be viewed as institutions that mediate the 'vertical' relationship between firms or individuals and the state, while the latter mediate the 'horizontal' relationship among firms and individuals, such as debtors and creditors. We use empirical proxies for the quality of property rights and contracting institutions for countries, locations, industries, and firms.

Our findings are as follows. First, after controlling for historical determinants of institutional quality, we find that, with the exception of Sri Lanka, South Asian countries exhibit worse property rights institutions and worse contracting institutions than what those determinants would predict based on the average cross-country relationship. Moreover, South Asian countries perform substantially worse in terms of property rights and contracting institutions than East Asian countries, given the historical determinants. Second, property rights institutions have a large and significant causal impact on per-capita GDP across countries, while contracting institutions

[3] Rodrik, Subramanian, and Trebbi (2004) discuss the hypothesis that international integration can improve institutions.

[4] The literature on institutions and growth has followed either a historical perspective (for example, North and Weingast [1989] and Delong and Shleifer [1993]), or an econometric perspective (for example, Mauro [1995]; Knack and Keefer [1995]; Rodrik, Subramanian, and Trebbi [2004]; Acemoglu and Johnson [2005]). Djankov, McLiesh, and Ramalho find that countries with better regulations exhibit faster growth.

matter much less. Third, property rights institutions and contracting institutions have different effects on performance in South Asia and East Asia, depending on whether macro or micro performance measures are considered. In South Asia, poor property rights institutions have a weak negative effect on per-capita GDP, but poor contracting institutions are associated with higher per-capita GDP, which is counter-intuitive. Poor property rights institutions negatively affect average firm performance, measured by labour productivity, while contracting institutions do not seem to matter. In East Asia, poor property rights institutions have a strong negative effect on per-capita GDP, but poor contracting institutions do not matter. Poor property rights institutions and poor contracting institutions affect firm performance negatively. Considering locations and industries within countries, weak property rights institutions and weak contracting institutions have a detrimental effect on performance both in South Asia as well as in East Asia.

The negative effects are stronger for property rights institutions. Finally, we find evidence of greater differences in institutional quality across countries within South Asia than across countries within East Asia. Within countries, the terms of institutional quality across locations and industries is also higher in South Asia than in East Asia. These findings suggest that pressures for better governance resulting from regional integration in East Asia have led to some convergence in institutional quality. We also find that the variation in the quality of property rights institutions across firms is higher in industries that are less integrated into global markets. However, within countries, these more integrated industries exhibit worse institutional quality according to the micro proxies. This finding may relate to the fact that the micro proxies are partly based on perception, and more integrated firms have better performance and thus are more likely to voice concerns about poor institutional quality.

Several important caveats need to be made. The first is that our analysis is based on imperfect measures of institutional quality, and thus do not allow one to fully understand the causes and consequences of institutional weaknesses. For example, our proxies for property rights institutions related to corruption may also be influenced by non-institutional factors such as the emergence of civil unrest, which has plagued countries in both South Asia (for example, Sri Lanka) and East Asia (for example, Nepal).

We are unable to disentangle such influences. A second caveat is that considering South Asia and East Asia as unitary groups, while useful for policy advice purposes, can be challenging since the countries within those regions differ much in terms of political, religious, cultural, and colonial traditions, which likely influence their institutions and performance. A third caveat is that while our analysis strongly suggests that performance is better when investors feel that their property rights are protected, or when the rule of law is upheld, it is silent regarding the specific rules, legislation, or institutional design that lead investors to feel that way. Bardhan (1997) and Campos, Lien, and Pradhan (1999) argue that the type of corruption existing in a country can affect economic performance. The strength of the central bureaucracy in a country can influence the type of corruption. Thus, more centralized corruption in Indonesia may have made it more predictable and thus less damaging for performance, while a more fragmented and disorganized type of corruption in India has been more damaging for performance. Our measures are unable to capture these crucial nuances. This brings us to our final point, which is that in order to better understand the institutional quality-growth nexus, complementary evidence needs to be gathered through in-depth analysis of country contexts, namely on the nature and functioning of institutions, and how that translates into development. Some steps in that direction have been taken by Lim and Stern (2002) for some East Asian countries, and in World Bank (2006a) for Bangladesh.

Nevertheless, several important policy implications can be drawn based on our findings. In order to achieve East Asian development levels, South Asian countries need to strengthen both their property rights institutions—for example, addressing the prevalence of corruption—as well as their contracting institutions—for example, solving judicial systems' bottlenecks. Stronger regional cooperation and integration across South Asia, following the example of East Asia, can help the sharing of knowledge and the copying of good practices in terms of institutional quality, and consequently reduce the differences in institutional quality across countries. Moreover, South Asian countries need to address the large differences in institutional quality within their borders, which are likely to be due to an uneven enforcement of laws and implementation of reforms at the local level.

Institutional Quality in South Asia and East Asia: Macro and Micro Evidence

We begin by assessing how South Asian countries fare relative to East Asian countries on a general measure of institutional quality: the rule of law index from Kaufmann, Kraay, and Mastruzzi (2005) shown in Figure 9.1.[5] Throughout the chapter, our data is oriented in such a way that *higher* values for measures of institutional quality mean *worse* outcomes. Also, we will refer to the cross-country statistics shown in Figure 9.1 to Figure 9.3 as 'macro' data. A simple ranking of countries according to the rule of law index shows that Bangladesh, Pakistan, and Nepal have fairly poor scores that place them in the bottom quartile of all countries, while India, Sri Lanka, and Bhutan fare much better, close to or above the cross-country median. Interestingly, most East Asian countries do not perform better than their South Asian counterparts on this general measure of institutional quality. Cambodia, China, Laos PDR, Indonesia, the Philippines, and Vietnam fall well below the cross-country median, Thailand exhibits about the median value, and only Malaysia performs better than the median. Not surprisingly, East Asia's four dragons, also shown in the graph, perform substantially better than either South Asian or East Asian countries.[6]

The very general nature of the rule of law index makes Figure 9.1 difficult to interpret. A country may rank poorly on that index not only because its firms and individuals face a high risk of expropriation by the state, but also because they face weak contract enforcement in their private transactions. Thus, we turn to evidence at the macro level on the two dimensions of institutional quality—

[5] The governance indicators compiled by Kaufmann, Kraay, and Mastruzzi (2005) are composite indexes that aggregate a large number of data sources reflecting the perceptions of governance across and within countries: surveys of firms and individuals, assessments of commercial risk rating agencies, non-governmental organizations, and multilateral aid agencies. The rule of law index relates to the protection of property and captures perceptions about the likelihood that property will be expropriated by the state, the likelihood that contracts will be enforced, and the likelihood that property is secure from crime.

[6] Figures 9.1 to 9.3 show data for East Asia's four dragons (Hong Kong, Singapore, Korea, and Taiwan) since these are benchmarks for South Asian and East Asian countries.

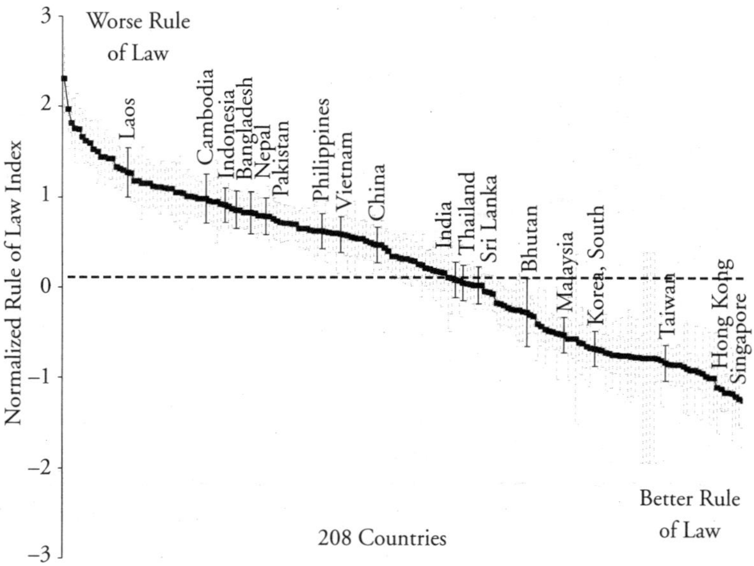

Figure 9.1: Rule of Law Index

Source: Kaufmann, Kraay, and Mastruzzi (2005).
Notes: The dots represent estimates for the 2004 governance indicators. The thin vertical lines represent standard errors around these estimates for each country. The broken line is the cross-country median.

property rights and contracting institutions—for South Asia and East Asia. We measure the quality of property rights institutions using the control of corruption index from Kaufmann, Kraay, and Mastruzzi (2005) shown in Figure 9.2.[7] Perceptions of corruption are clearly not institutions themselves, but the prevalence of corruption is a reasonably good proxy for the absence of well-functioning institutions that limit the arbitrary exercise of power by the state. In particular, since corruption is defined as the misuse of public power for private gain, the taking of bribes by public officials can be thought of as the expropriation of private property by the state. We measure the quality of contracting institutions using an estimate of the length of time required to resolve a dispute over an unpaid

[7] The control of corruption index measures the exercise of public power for private gain, including petty corruption, grand corruption, and state capture.

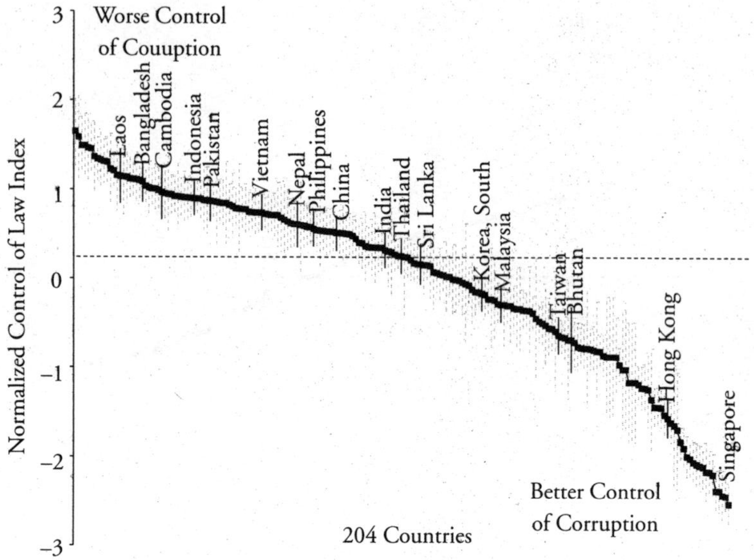

Figure 9.2: Control of Corruption Index

Source: Kaufmann, Kraay, and Mastruzzi (2005).
Notes: The dots represent estimates for the 2004 governance indicators. The thin vertical lines represent standard errors around these estimates for each country. The broken line is the cross-country median.

commercial debt from the World Bank Doing Business Database.[8] Bangladesh, India, Pakistan, and Nepal have poor property rights institutions as shown by the scores on the control of corruption index, all of which fall below the cross-country median in Figure 9.2. Sri Lanka and Bhutan rank much better, around or above the cross-country median. Interestingly, East Asian countries do not fare better than their South Asian counterparts on the quality of property rights institutions, as was the case in Figure 9.1. Cambodia, China, Lao PDR, Indonesia, the Philippines, and Vietnam fall below the

[8] See Appendix Table A9.1.1 for a detailed definition. Note that this measure emphasizes statutory or de jure procedures, but does not measure de facto procedures that are actually followed and that may differ significantly from the de jure ones, particularly in countries where courts are corrupt. The Productivity and Investment Climate Surveys (PICS) data described later provide better measures to proxy for de facto procedures.

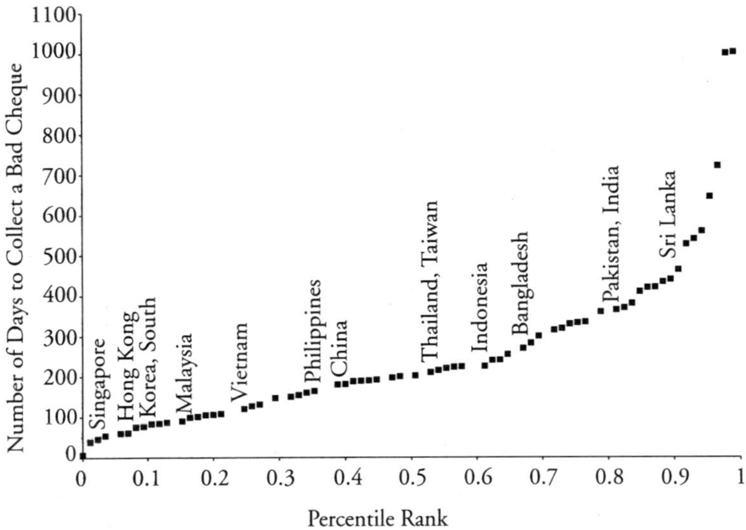

Figure 9.3: Number of Days to Enforce a Contract

Source: World Bank Doing Business database (2004).
Note: On the horizontal axis, the figure shows the ranking of each country according to the measure in the vertical axis, that is, a value of 0.5 in the percentile rank corresponds to the cross-country median number of days to enforce a contract.

cross-country median on the control of corruption index, Thailand has exactly the median value of the index, and only Malaysia performs better than the median. Figure 9.3 shows that all South Asian countries fall well below the cross-country median and below all East Asian countries on the quality of their contracting institutions, as measured by the number of days needed to resolve a dispute over an unpaid commercial debt.

Next we assess the quality of institutions in South Asian and East Asian countries using the World Bank Productivity and Investment Climate Surveys (PICS) firm-level dataset, which we will refer to as 'micro' data. We use three proxies for the quality of property rights institutions—firms' views on the importance of corruption as an obstacle to business, the percentage of firms asked to pay bribes during government inspections, and the average percentage of sales paid by firms in bribes to 'get things done'—and we use firms' assessments of the functioning of the judiciary system in resolving business disputes to proxy for the quality of contracting institutions.[9]

We first investigate the consistency between the micro and the macro data on institutional quality. For this purpose, we average the firm-level data in each country to obtain 'micro-founded' macro measures of institutional quality that we relate to the macro measures of property rights and contracting institutions. Table 9.1 reports the results from regressions of the micro-founded macro proxies for property rights and contracting institutions on the corresponding macro proxies, treating each country as one observation.[10] The results show that the micro and macro data on institutional quality are consistent with one another. Countries with weak property rights institutions according to the control of corruption index also have weak property rights institutions according to the micro proxies. Similarly, countries with poor contracting institutions, based on the number of days taken to resolve a business dispute, also have poor contracting institutions according to the micro proxy.

The regressions in Table 9.1 include dummy variables for South Asian and East Asian countries to capture the extent to which the relationship between macro and micro measures of institutional quality differs for these countries from the average. Bangladesh (Sri Lanka) has clearly worse (better) property rights institutions according to the micro measures than to the macro measures, but the reverse is true for contracting institutions. For Cambodia and India, the micro measures indicate worse quality of property rights and contracting institutions than the macro measures.[11] For Pakistan, the only relevant difference occurs for contracting institutions, which are clearly worse according to the micro measures. For all other East Asian countries, the quality of property rights institutions is higher according to the micro measures than to the macro measures, often significantly so. China is an exception, where the country's ranking according to one of the micro proxies for property rights institutions (the percentage

[9] Detailed definitions and country coverage of the measures are provided in Appendix Table A9.1.1.

[10] Note that the sample of countries for which macro data is available in Figures 9.1–9.3 differs from the sample of countries for which micro data is available, as seen in Appendix Table A9.1.1.

[11] Note that some of these conclusions differ from those in Fernandes and Kraay (2006), given the different sample of countries with PICS data used here.

Table 9.1: Regressions of Micro Measures on Macro Measures of Institutions

	Property Rights Institutions			*Contracting Institutions*
Dependent Variable is:	*Corruption as an Obstacle to Business*	*Perc. of Firms Asked to Pay Bribes in Govt Inspections*	*Percentage of Sales Paid in Bribes to Get Things Done*	*Functioning of Judiciary with respect to Business Disputes*
Control of Corruption	0.511***	0.098***	0.846***	
	(0.117)	(0.036)	(0.161)	
Number of Days to Collect Bad Debt (log)				0.23
				(0.143)
Bangladesh	0.575***	0.397***	0.135	–0.575***
	(0.185)	(0.052)	(0.306)	(0.077)
India	0.354***	0.229***		1.216***
	(0.111)	(0.034)		(0.072)
Pakistan	0.093		–0.155	–0.450***
	(0.163)		(0.275)	(0.079)
Sri Lanka	–0.470***	–0.314***	–1.345***	0.708***
	(0.099)	(0.033)	(0.185)	(0.074)
Cambodia	0.553***	0.081	2.893***	0.574***
	(0.173)	(0.049)	(0.289)	(0.074)
China	–0.207	0.584***	–0.053	–0.874***
	(0.125)	(0.037)	(0.222)	(0.087)

(contd ...)

Table 9.1 (contd ...)

Dependent Variable is:	*Property Rights Institutions*			*Contracting Institutions*
	Corruption as an Obstacle to Business	*Perc. of Firms Asked to Pay Bribes in Govt Inspections*	*Percentage of Sales Paid in Bribes to Get Things Done*	*Functioning of Judiciary with respect to Business Disputes*
Indonesia	–0.021	–0.312***	–0.454	–0.326***
	(0.166)	(0.047)	(0.279)	(0.101)
Malaysia	–0.365***			–0.563***
	(0.080)			(0.074)
Philippines	–0.077	–0.133***	0.017	–0.126*
	(0.132)	(0.039)	(0.233)	(0.071)
Thailand	–0.373***			–0.502***
	(0.093)			(0.073)
Vietnam	–0.870***	0.051	–1.312***	–0.590***
	(0.150)	(0.043)	(0.257)	(0.071)
Observations	71	62	62	64
R-squared	0.31	0.31	0.33	0.33

Source: Author's calculations based on the Productivity and Investment Climate Surveys (PICS).
Notes: Robust standard errors in parentheses. * indicates significance at 10%, ** significance at 5%, and *** significance at 1%. The regressions are estimated by OLS and include a constant. The dependent variables are the average of the firm-level responses in each country.

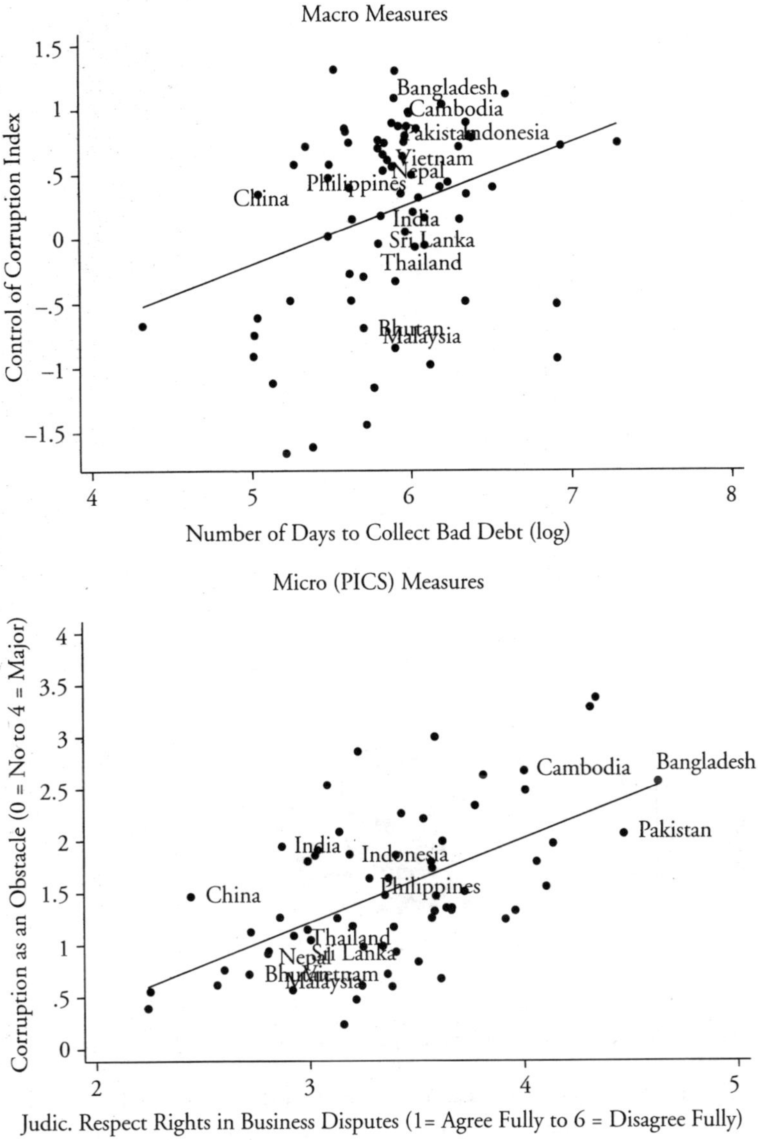

Figure 9.4: Property Rights and Contracting Institutions across Countries

Sources: Kaufmann, Kraay, and Mastruzzi (2005); World Bank Doing Business database (2004); World Bank Productivity and Investment Climate Surveys (PICS).

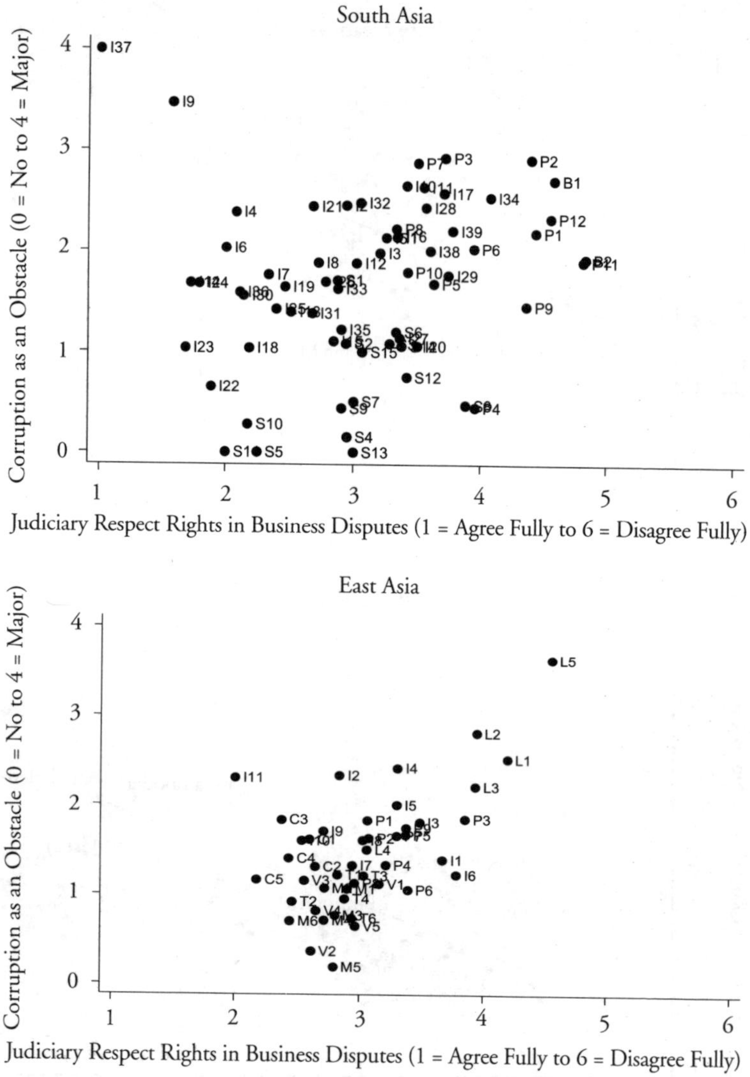

Figure 9.5: Property Rights and Contracting Institutions across Regions within South Asian and East Asian Countries

Source: The World Bank Productivity and Investment Climate Surveys (PICS). In the South Asia graph, B=Bangladesh, I=India, P=Pakistan, S=Sri Lanka. In the East Asia graph, C=Cambodia, CH=China, I=Indonesia, M=Malaysia, P=Philippines, T=Thailand, V=Vietnam. The names of each location in each country are provided in Appendix Table A9.4.

Note: See Table A9.1.4.

of firms paying bribes in inspections) is significantly worse than its ranking according to the control of corruption index. For all East Asian countries except Cambodia, the quality of contracting institutions is significantly higher according to micro measures. These differences in micro and macro measures for specific countries—despite consistency on average—are interesting in light of the fact that macro measures of corruption based on data about perceptions are often viewed with considerable skepticism by local government agencies, particularly in countries that perform poorly on these indicators. Our results here suggest that the macro indicators typically agree quite well with the views of firms operating in those countries. Moreover, firms in Bangladesh, Cambodia, and India view corruption to be even more of a problem than the outside 'expert' assessments that feature prominently in the macro data on corruption. The opposite, however, is found for firms in Sri Lanka, and in other East Asian countries.

Finally, we examine the correlation between the quality of the two types of institutions for South Asian and East Asian countries. Figure 9.4 displays graphs for macro and micro measures where the vertical axis shows the proxy for property rights institutions and the horizontal axis shows the proxy for contracting institutions. We find that countries with poor property rights institutions also tend to have poor contracting institutions, and the correlation is particularly strong for micro measures.[12] However, considering proxies for the two types of institutional quality at the sub-national level, as shown in Figure 9.5, we find that in South Asia, the locations where firms find corruption to be a major problem are not necessarily the same as where firms find a poorly functioning judiciary system to be a major problem. In contrast, the quality of the two types of institutions is highly positively correlated in East Asia.

Institutions and Growth: Cross-Country Evidence for South Asia and East Asia

The preliminary evidence suggests that the quality of contracting institutions is much higher in East Asia than in South Asia, but differences across the two regions are less clear for property rights institutions. In fact, some of the countries in both regions fare

[12] The correlation coefficients corresponding to the graphs shown in Figure 9.4 are 0.32 for the macro measures and 0.57 for the micro measures, and both are significant at the 5 per cent confidence level.

particularly poorly on corruption issues. We now reexamine the differences in institutional quality across South Asia and East Asia after controlling for the deep determinants of institutional quality, and subsequently we link institutional quality to economic development.

The importance of property rights institutions for economic development is suggested by Figure 9.6, which plots our general measure of institutional quality—the rule of law index—against per-capita GDP for a large group of countries. The graph unambiguously shows that countries with worse institutional quality are on average poorer than countries with better institutional quality. All South Asian countries fall below the regression line. In East Asia, Cambodia, and Vietnam also fall below the regression line, while Indonesia, Malaysia, the Philippines, and Thailand fall clearly above the regression line, and China falls exactly on it. Precisely interpreting Figure 9.6 is difficult. However, (*a*) if the graph is read 'horizontally', one concludes that South Asian (most East Asian) countries have much better (worse) institutional quality than expected given their GDP levels (highlighting the fact that the countries fall to the left [right] of the regression line), but the opposite is true for some East Asian countries, and (*b*) if the graph is read 'vertically', one concludes that South Asian (most East Asian) countries have substantially lower (higher) GDP levels than expected given their institutional quality (highlighting the fact that the countries fall below [above] the regression line). The simple correlation in Figure 9.6 between institutions and per capita GDP does not tell us anything about causation: better institutional quality may cause higher incomes, or richer countries may have been able to 'generate' better institutions. Moreover, as noted earlier, the rule of law index combines aspects of property rights and contracting institutions, and these two dimensions of institutional quality may matter differently for development outcomes.

In what follows, we study the causal relationship between property rights and contracting institutions and per-capita GDP.[13] To sort out the direction of causality, we use instrumental variables—sources of exogenous variation—that explain cross-country differences in institutional quality, but do not influence per-capita incomes. We

[13] We follow Hall and Jones (1999) in using per capita GDP levels instead of per capita GDP growth under the rationale that per capita GDP levels were not very different in the distant past; therefore cross-country differences in those per capita GDP levels reflect differences in the countries' very long-run growth performance.

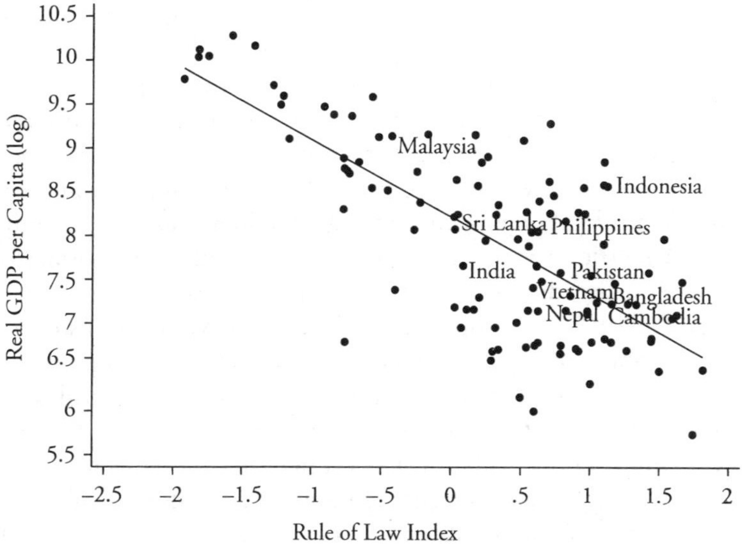

Figure 9.6: Rule of Law and Per Capita Incomes

Source: Kaufmann, Kraay, and Mastruzzi (2005); World Bank, *World Development Indicators*.
Note: Real GDP per capita refers to 1996.

follow Acemoglu, Johnson, and Robinson (2001) and Acemoglu and Johnson (2005) in choosing historical determinants of property rights and contracting institutions linked to colonization to statistically identify the effects of institutions on development. Specifically, we use mortality rates of European settlers around the world in the eighteenth and nineteenth centuries to explain property rights institutions. The rationale for using this variable is that in countries with low settler mortality, colonial powers had interest in erecting solid institutions that protected property rights (at least those of the occupying settlers), and these institutions persist until the present day.[14] In contrast, in countries with high settler mortality, colonial powers were interested only in extracting resources and had no interest in building high-quality formal institutions.[15] In sum, settler mortality rates can help

[14] Acemoglu, Johnson, and Robinson (2001) argue that institutions change only very gradually over time.

[15] We use data on settler mortality compiled by Kaufmann, Kraay, and Mastruzzi, who extend the estimates of settler mortality of Acemoglu, Johnson, and Robinson (2001) to previously uncovered geographically proximate countries with similar climates.

identify which countries acquired good property rights institutions and which did not. We use data on countries' legal traditions to explain contracting institutions. The rationale for using this variable is that countries with British legal origins tend to have much more streamlined and less complex procedures for dispute resolution, relative to the highly formalized and codified procedures in countries with French legal origins. In sum, legal traditions can help identify which countries currently have complex (and are thus more prone to be poor quality) dispute resolution mechanisms and which do not.

In Table 9.2, we show the relationship between the historical determinants and institutional quality today. We regress the control of corruption index and the number of days to collect a bad debt (in logs) on the two instrumental variables: the dummy variable identifying countries with British legal origins and the settler mortality rate (in logs). We also include dummy variables identifying either the countries in South Asia and East Asia, or the South Asian and the East Asian regions as a whole. These dummy variables capture the extent to which these countries and regions differ significantly from the average relationship estimated across 82 countries. The results in columns (1)–(2) show that settler mortality positively and significantly affects the control of corruption index, that is, countries with higher settler mortality 200 years ago have worse property rights institutions today. The results in columns (3)–(4) show that countries with British legal origins have better contracting institutions in that a significantly fewer number of days is needed to resolve a bad debt.[16]

How do countries in South Asia and East Asia stand on these relationships?[17] In column (1), Bangladesh, India, Nepal, and Pakistan exhibit positive and significant residuals, which clearly deviate from the cross-country average relationship. In countries with low settler mortality, one would expect the development of strong property rights institutions. While all South Asian countries belong to the

[16] Note that settler mortality is a good instrument for property rights institutions, but not for contracting institutions, that is, the coefficient on settler mortality is not significant in columns (3)–(4). The opposite is true for British legal origins. This is required for the instrumental variables strategy to be successful, as each instrument helps to isolate the causal effects of only one of the two types of institutions.

[17] China and Thailand are not included in the regressions in Tables 9.2—9.3 since they were never colonized and thus have no information on settler mortality rates.

Table 9.2: First-Stage Regressions for Property Rights and Contracting Institutions

Dependent Variable is:	*Control of Corruption Index*		*Number of Days to Collect Bad Debt (log)*	
	(1)	*(2)*	*(3)*	*(4)*
Settler Mortality (log)	0.342 (0.086)***	0.335 (0.078)***	0.086 (0.060)	0.085 (0.054)
British Legal Origin	–0.249 (0.195)	–0.269 (0.177)	–0.333 (0.161)**	–0.326 (0.147)**
Bangladesh	1.054 (0.191)***		0.264 (0.119)**	
India	0.415 (0.210)*		0.449 (0.124)***	
Nepal	0.708 (0.210)***		0.255 (0.124)**	
Pakistan	1.063 (0.226)***		0.399 (0.129)***	
Sri Lanka	0.136 (0.192)		0.452 (0.119)***	
Cambodia	0.456 (0.091)***		-0.033 (0.090)	
Indonesia	0.321 (0.091)***		0.302 (0.088)***	
Malaysia	0.152 (0.274)		0.187 (0.152)	
Philippines	0.75 (0.207)***		0.037 (0.170)	
Vietnam	0.228 (0.091)**		-0.189 (0.090)**	
South Asia		0.684 (0.252)***		0.359 (0.119)***
East Asia		0.376 (0.141)***		0.062 (0.118)
Observations	82	82	82	82
R-squared	0.34	0.33	0.15	0.14

Source: Author's calculation based on Kaufmann, Kraay, and Mastruzzi (2005); Acemoglu, Johnson, and Robinson (2001); and the World Bank Doing Business database (2004).

Notes: Robust standard errors in parentheses. * indicates significance at 10 per cent, ** significance at 5 per cent, and *** significance at 1 per cent. The regressions are estimated by OLS and include a constant.

group of countries with low settler mortality rates (below median), their performance on the control of corruption index is very poor. An exception should be made for Sri Lanka, for which the relationship between historical determinants and corruption is close to the cross-country average. The results in column (2) confirm that the South Asian region as a whole exhibits particularly poor performance on property rights institutions, even after taking into account the corresponding historical determinants. According to column (1), Cambodia, Indonesia, and Vietnam exhibit even poorer scores on the control of corruption index than what would be expected for the group of countries with high settler mortality rates (above median), to which they belong. The Philippines has low settler mortality rates, but its property rights institutions are weaker than what would be expected given this historical determinant. Column (2) suggests that the East Asian region as a whole has a weaker score on property rights institutions than that predicted by the cross-country average relationship. However, controlling for historical determinants, the quality of property rights institutions is clearly lower in South Asia than in East Asia.

In column (3), the positive dummy variables for all South Asian countries reflect a significant deviation from the average relationship. South Asian countries require substantially more days to resolve a bad debt than other countries with similar British legal origins.[18] Thus, South Asian countries have weak contracting institutions, even after taking into account the historical determinants of this type of institution.[19] This conclusion is confirmed in column (4), where the dummy variable for the South Asian region as a whole is positive and significant. Regarding East Asian countries, the dummy variables in column (3) are positive and significant for Indonesia, and negative and significant for Vietnam. Indonesia, which has a Dutch legal origin, performs poorly in terms of contracting institutions among the group of countries without British legal origin, which are expected to have weaker contracting institutions on average. In contrast,

[18] Among 46 countries with British legal origins, South Asian countries are among the top 14 countries with the highest numbers of days to resolve a bad debt.

[19] Some of the conclusions using the dummy variables for South Asian countries differ from those reached in Fernandes and Kraay (2006), as the regressions here include dummy variables for East Asian countries, thus the comparator relative to which the dummy variables' coefficients are estimated is different.

Vietnam, which has a French legal origin, exhibits relatively strong contracting institutions within that group. Column (4) suggests that the performance of the East Asian region as a whole does not differ from the average relationship regarding contracting institutions.

By making use of only the cross-country variations in institutional quality that are driven by historical determinants, we can statistically identify their causal impact on economic development. We show the results from instrumental variables estimation of the causal impacts of property rights and contracting institutions on per-capita GDP in Table 9.3. The results in columns (1)–(2) show that property rights institutions have a large significant causal impact on development, while contracting institutions matter much less. The magnitude of the effect of property rights institutions on development is very large. For example, an improvement in the control of corruption index by 1.6 standard deviations, which corresponds to the difference between Bangladesh and Malaysia, would result in higher incomes per capita in the long run by a factor of 30.[20] Acemoglu and Johnson (2005) argue that the finding that property rights institutions matter much more than contracting institutions for development can be rationalized by a key feature of contracting institutions. Firms and individuals have the possibility of circumventing contracting institutions such as courts if the services the courts provide are weak. For example, firms may rely on business associations or informal networks to enforce contracts if the courts are ineffective or slow. In contrast, it is much more difficult for firms to 'contract around' a predatory state when property rights institutions are weak.[21] The regressions in columns (1)–(2) include dummy variables to assess how countries or regions differ from the average relationship. Bangladesh, Pakistan, the Philippines, and Vietnam stand out for having very significant positive residuals in column (1), suggesting that they have substantially higher per-capita GDP than that predicted by the average relationship based on their

[20] The figure of 30 is the result of exp((–1.6)* (–2.124)), where –1.6 is obtained as the division of (–1.379), which is the difference in the control of corruption index between Bangladesh and Malaysia, by 0.863 (which is the standard deviation of the control of corruption index for countries included in the regression shown in column (1) of Table 9.3).

[21] Note that our findings of a positive coefficient on the proxy for contracting institutions differ from those in Acemoglu and Johnson (2005) due to the larger sample of countries used here.

weak institutional performance. The other South Asian and East Asian countries fall more or less along the average relationship.

Next, we examine whether property rights and contracting institutions play a different role for development in South Asia versus East Asia. Column (3) of Table 9.3 shows the coefficients from an instrumental variables regression where the effects of the two types of institutions on per-capita GDP are allowed to differ across South Asia, East Asia, and the rest of the world. The results reveal some interesting patterns. Weak property rights institutions have a negative influence on per-capita GDP that is significant in East Asia but insignificant in South Asia. In contrast, contracting institutions significantly impact per-capita GDP in South Asia but not in East Asia. The sign of this impact is counterintuitive, however, suggesting that South Asian countries with poorer contracting institutions (that is, where more days are needed to solve a debt payment) have significantly higher per-capita GDP.

How can we interpret the findings in this section? Focusing on individual countries, Bangladesh and Pakistan are far richer than one would expect based on their weak institutional quality given the average relationship between institutions and economic performance. This pattern is also verified for the Philippines and Vietnam. Focusing on regions as a whole, weak property rights institutions do not matter for per-capita GDP in South Asia, while weak contracting institutions affect it positively. In East Asia, better property rights institutions have a causal positive impact on per-capita GDP, but contracting institutions do not matter. A naive interpretation of these findings could be that institutional quality does not matter for growth in Bangladesh, Pakistan, the Philippines, and Vietnam, as these countries managed to attain quite high per-capita GDP despite poor institutional quality. Moreover, institutions seem unimportant for development in South Asia as a whole. However, this interpretation is too narrow, since it ignores the strong cross-country evidence that property rights institutions typically do matter for economic performance (see Column (1) of Table 9.3). A more nuanced view—which we prefer—is that institutions do in fact matter for development, but in the case of South Asia, particularly India, Nepal, and Sri Lanka, they have not yet delivered their full development impact. The good news in this interpretation is that all three of these countries have room to grow based on the quality of their property

TABLE 9.3: Instrumental Variables Regressions for GDP per Capita

Dependent Variable is:	*GDP per capita (log)*	
	(1)	(2)
Control of Corruption Index	–2.124 (0.595)***	
Number of Days to Collect Bad	2.228 (1.424)	
Control of Corruption Index* South Asia		–1.504 (5.074)
Control of Corruption Index* East Asia		–1.417 (0.440)***
Control of Corruption Index* Rest of World		–1.629 (0.285)***
No. Days to Collect Bad Debt (log)* South Asia		1.417 (0.523)***
Nb. Days to Collect Bad Debt (log)* East Asia		0.378 (2.086)
No. Days to Collect Bad Debt (log)* Rest of World		1.415 (0.022)***
Bangladesh	1.078 (0.397)***	
India	–0.557 (0.345)	
Nepal	–0.012 (0.201)	
Pakistan	0.703 (0.214)***	
Sri Lanka	–0.550 (0.471)	
Cambodia	0.403 (0.242)	
Indonesia	0.635 (0.457)	
Malaysia	0.392 (0.260)	
Philippines	0.709 (0.164)***	
Vietnam	0.571 (0.283)**	
Observations	82	82

Sources: Author's calculation based on Kaufmann, Kraay, and Mastruzzi (2005); and the World Bank Doing Business database (2004).

Notes: Robust standard errors in parentheses. * indicates significance at 10 per cent, ** significance at 5 per cent, and *** significance at 1 per cent. The regressions are estimated by instrumental variables and include a constant.

rights institutions. The bad news is that for Bangladesh and Pakistan, past income gains—whatever their source—may be fragile because they are not supported by commensurately strong property rights institutions. For East Asia, better property rights institutions seem to have delivered high per-capita GDP. The cross-country analysis based on these crude proxies for property rights and contracting institutions has limits in terms of how much understanding it can bring of the causes and consequences of institutional weaknesses. In what follows, we pursue the analysis using the micro data for South Asian and East Asian countries to further probe the links between different types of institutions and economic performance.

Institutions and Growth: Firm-Level Evidence for South Asia and East Asia

In this section, we examine the importance of property rights and contracting institutions for firm performance to assess heterogeneity within a country. In order to assess how institutional weaknesses affect firms in South Asia and East Asia, we need to use proxies for institutional quality that are exogenous to each firm. However, our micro proxies are based on firm perceptions about institutional quality. Hence, there is a potential endogeneity problem that could result in biased estimates of the relationship between institutional quality and firm performance. On the one hand, better performing firms may be more aware of the difficulties that weak institutions cause, and thus may voice stronger concerns. On the other hand, better performing firms may be able to take action to avoid dealing with weak institutions. To circumvent this problem, we average the proxies for institutional quality at the location-industry level and estimate the impact of these averages on firm performance.[22] While institutional quality has an important national dimension, there are several reasons why it may vary at the location or industry level. For example, in large countries such as China, India, Indonesia, or Pakistan, the decentralization of economic policymaking is likely to result in important differences in the enforcement of property rights and contracting institutions across states and cities, depending

[22] A similar approach is taken by Dollar, Hallward-Driemeier, and Mengistae (2005), and Fernandes (2006), when relating firm productivity to various investment climate dimensions.

on the political power, quality, and degree of corruption of local government officials. The dispersion in institutional quality across location-industry cells found in South Asia, but also to a lesser degree in East Asia (see the section 'Dispersion in Institutional Quality in South Asia and East Asia'), allows us to econometrically identify the effects of institutional quality on firm performance.[23] We regress firm-level sales per worker (in logs) on average institutional quality at the location-industry level. Sales per worker is used as a measure of labour productivity, and varies substantially across industries in each country due to differences in capital intensity and production processes.[24] To account for such industry differences, industry fixed effects are controlled for in our regressions. The sample of firms used for the regressions consists of firms that have been in operation for more than 15 years. The rationale behind this choice is to make our measure of sales per worker close to a long-run measure of firm growth, in a similar vein to what is done in the section 'Institutions and Growth: Cross-Country Evidence for South Asia and East Asia', where a country's level of per-capita GDP is used to proxy for that country's long-run growth.[25] To increase the degree of confidence in our results, we impose strict outlier criteria on the sales per worker variable.[26] For ease of interpretation of regression coefficients, we normalize the property rights and contracting institutions to have a mean of 0 and a standard deviation of 1.

The results in columns (2) and (3) of Table 9.4 suggest that weak property rights and contracting institutions have a detrimental effect on firm performance, but the effects are significant only for property rights institutions. According to column (3), firms in a location and industry with a percentage of sales paid in bribes to get 'things done' larger than the average by one standard deviation have

[23] The use of location-industry cell averages has the advantage of providing values for the institutional quality proxies for firms that have missing values for those variables in the survey data.

[24] We use sales per worker rather than value added (sales minus materials costs) per worker to measure firm performance to avoid dropping from the sample 10 per cent of firms that report negative value added.

[25] See note 12 in Chapter 1.

[26] Firms whose sales per worker are in the bottom or top 2 per cent of the sales per worker distribution of their industry and country are considered to be outliers and thus eliminated from the regressions.

TABLE 9.4: Firm-Level Performance, Property Rights, and Contracting Institutions

Dependent Variable is:	*Sales per Worker (log)*					
	(1)	(2)	(3)	(4)	(5)	(6)
Corruption as an Obstacle to Business	0.031					
	(0.049)					
Percentage of Firms Paying Bribes in Inspections		–0.062				
		(0.049)				
Percentage of Sales Paid in Bribes to Get Things Done			–0.138*			
			(0.077)			
Functioning of Judic. in Business Disputes	0.016	–0.003	–0.017			
	(0.050)	(0.064)	(0.083)			
Corruption as an Obstacle to Business* South Asia				–0.043		
				(0.050)		
Corruption as an Obstacle to Business* East Asia				0.321**		
				(0.141)		
Percentage of Firms Bribes Inspections* South Asia					–0.049	
					(0.046)	
Percentage of Firms Bribes Inspections* East Asia					–0.17	
					(0.260)	

(contd ...)

Table 9.4 (contd ...)

Dependent Variable is:	*Sales per Worker (log)*					
	(1)	(2)	(3)	(4)	(5)	(6)
Percentage of Sales Bribes Get Things Done*						–0.113*
South Asia						(0.063)
Percentage of Sales Bribes Get Things Done*						–0.383*
East Asia						(0.201)
Functioning Judic. in Bus. Disputes*				0.065	0.02	0.002
South Asia				(0.054)	(0.069)	(0.099)
Functioning Judic. in Bus. Disputes*				-0.255*	-0.051	-0.002
East Asia				(0.137)	(0.182)	(0.164)
Industry Dummies	Yes	Yes	Yes	Yes	Yes	Yes
Country Dummies	Yes	Yes	Yes	Yes	Yes	Yes
Observations	4859	2943	2675	4859	2943	2675
R-squared	0.83	0.09	0.88	0.83	0.09	0.88

Source: Author's calculations based on the Productivity and Investment Climate Surveys (PICS).

Notes: Robust standard errors in parentheses. * indicates significance at 10 per cent, ** significance at 5 per cent, and *** significance at 1 per cent. The regressions are estimated by OLS and include a constant. The independent variables are the average at the location-industry level of the firm-level normalized measures of property rights and contracting institutions (that is, with a mean of 0 and a variance of 1). The regressions include only firms that are older than 15 years of age. Outliers in the sales per worker distribution for each industry and country (top and bottom 2 per cent) are eliminated from the regressions.

13 per cent lower sales per worker than other firms. In columns (2)–(3), property rights institutions have a much larger negative effect on firm performance than contracting institutions. In column (1), however, the effects of both types of institutions on performance are positive, though insignificant. The differences in results across columns (1) and (2)–(3) of Table 9.4 are likely to reflect a different correlation between the proxy for the quality of contracting institutions (common to all regressions) and each of the proxies for the quality of property rights institutions.

In columns (4)–(6) of Table 9.4, we show the results from regressions that allow for a differential effect of institutional quality on sales per worker for firms in South Asia versus firms in East Asia. In South Asia, weak property rights institutions have a negative effect on firm performance, which is significant in column (3) for the percentage of sales paid in bribes to get 'things done'. However, contracting institutions do not seem to matter for firm performance in South Asia, and, if anything, poor institutional quality in that dimension is associated with better performance. In East Asia, weak property rights institutions have a negative effect on firm performance in columns (2) and (3) but a positive and significant effect in column (1). Weak contracting institutions are associated with worse firm performance, significantly so in column (1). Overall, the effects of institutional quality on performance are much larger in magnitude for firms in East Asia than for firms in South Asia.

The sample size in columns (2)–(3) and (5)–(6) of Table 9.4 is larger than that in columns (1) and (4), since there is no information on payment of bribes during inspections and on bribes paid to get 'things done' for Malaysia and Thailand (see appendix Table A9.1.2). This difference in samples could help explain the different (positive) sign of the coefficient on property rights and contracting institutions in columns (1) and (4). However, that is not the case since estimating the regressions in columns (1) and (4), excluding Malaysia and Thailand still result in positive coefficients for the property rights and contracting institutions proxies, which are significant in the case of property rights institutions.

What summary conclusions can be drawn from the findings in this section, and how do those compare to the cross-country findings in the section 'Institutions and Growth: Cross-Country Evidence for South Asia and East Asia'? First, using both cross-country and firm-level data, the quality of property rights institutions has a stronger effect on performance than the quality of contracting institutions, despite important differences in the samples considered. The cross-country sample includes a large number of developing and developed countries, but the firm-level sample includes only South Asian and East Asian countries.[27] The firm-level evidence is much weaker than the cross-country evidence, likely due to the much lower dispersion in institutional quality across location-industry cells (shown in Table 9.6), which is used to identify the impact of institutions on sales per worker, relative to the dispersion in institutional quality across countries (shown in Table 9.4), which is used to identify the impact of institutions on per-capita GDP. Second, the cross-country and firm-level analyses suggest that (*a*) weak contracting institutions have a counterintuitive positive effect (which is significant) on per capita GDP and sales per worker (though not significant) in South Asia; and (*b*) weak property rights institutions have a negative and significant effect on per-capita GDP and sales per worker (for two of the proxies used) in East Asia. Third, some conclusions differ across the cross-country and the firm-level analyses: (*a*) weak property rights institutions do not significantly affect per capita GDP, but have a negative effect on sales per worker (significant for one of the proxies used) in South Asia; (*b*) poor contracting institutions do not matter for per-capita GDP, but have a significant negative effect on sales per worker (significant in one of the specifications) in East Asia; and (*c*) using firms' perceptions of corruption as an obstacle to business as the proxy for property rights institutions, the effect on sales per worker is positive and significant in East Asia.

Recall that the cross-country analysis relies on instrumental variables estimation of the impact of institutions on per-capita GDP, and hence a causal impact can be safely assumed. The use of location-industry averages of institutional quality measures allows us to argue that the coefficients in the firm-level regressions represent causal impacts of institutional quality on performance, but

[27] As shown in Appendix Table A9.1.2, PICS data for countries outside South Asia and East Asia are used in Tables 9.1 and 9.4, but not in Figures 9.4–9.5 nor Figure 9.5 since the location data needed to measure the average institutional quality at the location-industry level are not available for those countries.

some potential reverse causality problems may still arise.[28] Better performing firms are likely to be much more aware of the bottlenecks that weak institutions generate, and thus express stronger concerns about those. This provides a rationale for why firms' concerns about corruption as an obstacle to business are positively associated with firm performance in our regressions. In this case, one would argue that the causality runs from good firm performance to perceptions of weak institutions. The control of corruption index from Kaufmann, Kraay, and Mastruzzi (2005) used in the cross-country analysis is also partly based on perceptions about corruption. However, since it aggregates information from very different sources, it may better capture the degree of bureaucratic and political corruption across countries than our firm perceptions from the PICS data. This view is not consensual, though, as it is argued in World Bank (2006b) that the control of corruption index may lack specificity, since it combines sources that measure similar, but not identical, phenomena. Also, our firm-level measures related to bribes for inspections and bribes paid to get things done are very specific. They are not perception based, but rather quantitative, and thus may better characterize the problem of corruption at the location-industry level in South Asia and East Asia. Our firm-level measures capture aspects of administrative corruption, which tends to flourish in countries with weak bureaucratic capacity and accountability. We prefer, therefore, to emphasize our findings in columns (2)–(3) and columns (5)–(6) of Table 9.4. Overall, we believe it is valuable to perform the analysis using the two types of data—cross country and firm level—even if some different results emerge.

Dispersion in Institutional Quality in South Asia and East Asia

In this section, we examine the hypothesis that East Asia's higher degree of international integration has led to a convergence in institutional quality across countries, relative to the less integrated South Asia. We first examine the variability of macro and micro proxies for institutional quality *across countries* in South Asia and in East Asia, using coefficients

[28] We would need to use instrumental variables for the location-industry institutional quality measures to be fully confident of the causal interpretation of the regression coefficients. Unfortunately, those are not available.

of variation. According to the macro measures, the evidence of a higher dispersion in institutional quality within South Asia than East Asia is very clear in Table 9.5. The same conclusion is obtained focusing on micro proxies for contracting institutions. However, according to the micro proxies, the dispersion in property rights institutions in higher in East Asia than in South Asia. The presence in East Asia of countries such as Cambodia, with very poor institutional quality, as revealed by the macro—and especially the micro data—is the likely rationale for this finding. Nevertheless, the evidence suggests that the higher degree of integration in East Asia has led to convergence in institutional quality across countries. The greater dissemination of ideas and experience with best practices of good governance that is associated with regional—but also global—integration may be at

TABLE 9.5: Dispersion in Institutional Quality across Countries

Panel A. Macro Measures

	Rule of Law Index	*Control of Corruption Index*	*Days to Collect Bad Debt*
	Coefficient of Variation		
South Asia	1.29	1.61	0.49
East Asia	1.03	0.77	0.32

Panel B. Micro Measures

	Corruption as an Obstacle to Business	*Perc. of Firms Asked to Pay Bribes in Govt Inspections*	*Percentage of Sales Paid in Bribes to Get Things Done*	*Functioning of Judiciary with respect to Business Disputes*
	Coefficient of Variation			
South Asia	0.74	0.82	2.21	0.46
East Asia	1.07	0.86	2.95	0.44

Sources: Author's calculations based on Kaufmann, Kraay, and Mastruzzi (2005); the World Bank Doing Business database (2004); and the Productivity and Investment Climate Surveys (PICS).

Notes: The coefficients of variation shown in panels A and B are calculated across countries in each of the regions. The micro measures are the averages of the firm-level data in each country.

the root of such convergence. So far, such phenomenon has not been verified in the much less integrated South Asia.

Next we examine the variability of micro measures of institutional quality *across locations* within countries in South Asia and East Asia. The horizontal axis of each graph in Table 9.5 shows the proxy for contracting institutions—the judiciary's respect of rights in business disputes. The vertical axis shows one of the proxies for property rights institutions—the importance of corruption as an obstacle to business. Each data point represents a location in a South Asian or an East Asian country, and corresponds to the average at the location level of the firm proxies for the quality of property rights and contracting institutions.[29] Figure 9.5 suggests that the dispersion in institutional quality across locations is higher in South Asia than in East Asia. More precise conclusions are drawn based on Table 9.6, which shows the coefficients of variation for the measures proxying for the two dimensions of institutional quality in the two regions. We focus on two interesting levels of disaggregation: panel A shows the dispersion across locations (corresponding to Figure 9.5), and panel B shows the dispersion across location-industry cells.[30] Panel A of Table 9.6 confirms that the dispersion in institutional quality is higher across locations in South Asia than East Asia. Panel B also shows higher dispersion across location-industry cells in South Asia relative to East Asia, except for the measure capturing the importance of corruption as an obstacle to business. Table 9.6 also shows some dispersion in institutional quality across locations in the more integrated East Asia, suggesting that the pressures for good governance resulting from regional integration in East Asia have faced limits, possibly due to internal barriers within countries.

Finally, we relate the degree of tradability of industries within South Asia and East Asia to the average and dispersion in the quality of property rights and contracting institutions. We test two hypotheses.

[29] In some countries, the location unit in the PICS survey is a city, while in others it is a province or region.

[30] The location-industry cells are constructed by combining the locations in Figure 9.5 with the following industries: auto and auto components, beverages, chemicals and pharmaceuticals, electronics, food, garments, leather products, metals and machinery, non-metallic and plastic materials, paper, other manufacturing, other transport equipment, sporting goods, textiles, and wood and furniture. Appendix Table A9.1.2 shows the industry composition for each country in the PICS dataset.

TABLE 9.6: Dispersion in Institutional Quality across Locations and Location-Industry Cells

Panel A. Dispersion Based on Location-Level Data

	Corruption as an Obstacle to Business	*Perc. of Firms Asked to Pay Bribes in Govt Inspections*	*Percentage of Sales Paid in Bribes to Get Things Done*	*Functioning of Judiciary with respect to Business Disputes*
	Coefficient of Variation			
South Asia	0.50	0.84	1.14	0.27
East Asia	0.45	0.67	0.96	0.18

Panel B. Dispersion Based on Location-Industry-Level Data

	Corruption as an Obstacle to Business	*Perc. of Firms Asked to Pay Bribes in Govt Inspections*	*Percentage of Sales Paid in Bribes to Get Things Done*	*Functioning of Judiciary with respect to Business Disputes*
	Coefficient of Variation			
South Asia	0.59	0.83	4.30	0.39
East Asia	0.64	0.74	1.47	0.25

Sources: Author's calculations based on Kaufmann, Kraay, and Mastruzzi (2005), the World Bank Doing Business database (2004), and the Productivity and Investment Climate Surveys (PICS).

Notes: The measures over which coefficients of variation are calculated in Panel A (Panel B) are the averages of the firm-level data in each location (location-industry cell).

First, and in a vein similar to the argument made above for the integration of East Asia leading to institutional convergence, one can argue that industries that are more integrated into global markets should exhibit less dispersion in the micro proxies for institutional quality. Second, following Rodrik, Subramanian, and Trebbi (2004), one can argue that industries that are more integrated into global markets should exhibit better average institutional quality.

TABLE 9.7: International Integration and Dispersion in Institutional Quality

	Corruption as an Obstacle to Business	*Perc. of Firms Asked to Pay Bribes in Govt Inspections*	*Percentage of Sales Paid in Bribes to Get Things Done*	*Functioning of Judiciary with respect to Business Disputes*
	Coefficient of Variation			
Industries More Integrated into Global Markets	0.88	0.78	2.43	0.47
Industries Less Integrated into Global Markets	0.98	0.93	2.87	0.46
South Asia				
Industries More Integrated into Global Markets	0.73	0.82	2.29	0.46
Industries Less Integrated into Global Markets	0.76	0.82	2.06	0.46
East Asia				
Industries More Integrated into Global Markets	1.03	0.75	2.57	0.45
Industries Less Integrated into Global Markets	1.12	0.97	3.46	0.43

Source: Author's calculations based on the Productivity and Investment Climate Surveys (PICS).
Note: The coefficients of variation are calculated across firms in each industry type.

TABLE 9.8: International Integration and Average Institutional Quality

Dependent Variable is:	*Corruption as an Obstacle to Business*	*Perc. of Firms Asked to Pay Bribes in Govt Inspections*	*Percentage of Sales Paid in Bribes to Get Things Done*	*Functioning of Judiciary with respect to Business Disputes*
	Coefficient of Variation			
Dummy for Industries More Integrated into Global Markets	0.044** (0.020)	0.036* (0.022)	0.049 (0.031)	0.023 (0.019)
Country Dummies	Yes	Yes	Yes	Yes
Observations	9847	5595	4866	10070
R-squared	0.13	0.43	0.04	0.19

Source: Author's calculations based on the Productivity and Investment Climate Surveys (PICS).
Notes: Robust standard errors in parentheses. * indicates significance at 10 per cent, ** significance at 5 per cent, and *** significance at 1 per cent. The regressions are estimated by OLS and include a constant.

Table 9.7 shows how the coefficient of variation for the micro proxies for institutional quality varies, depending on the degree of integration of an industry into global markets. That integration is measured based on the share that such industry represents in a country's total manufacturing exports. [31] The dispersion in measures of property rights institutions across firms is clearly higher for industries that are less integrated into global markets, compared to industries that are more integrated. For contracting institutions, the dispersion is similar in the two types of industries. The findings are verified exactly in East Asia. In South Asia, the coefficient of variation for the proxies related to payment of bribes during government inspections, and the average percentage of sales paid by firms in bribes to get things done are actually higher in industries that are more integrated into global markets. In Table 9.8, we show the results from estimating regressions of each of the proxies for the quality of property rights and contracting institutions on a dummy variable identifying industries that are more integrated into world markets, controlling for country fixed effects. The results suggest that, within countries, industries that are more integrated into global markets exhibit worse institutional quality according to the micro proxies. The hypothesis that international integration leads to an improvement in institutional quality through greater access to ideas and experience with best practices of good governance does not seem to be verified within South Asian or East Asian industries. Alternatively, these results can be related to our earlier finding of a positive effect of firms' perceptions of worse corruption problems on performance. If integration into global markets is associated with better firm performance—as extensive literature suggests (for example, Wagner 2007)—then the results in Table 9.8 simply reflect the fact that better performing firms are more aware and voice stronger concerns about the problems caused by weak institutions.

Conclusion

This chapter analyses the differences in the quality of institutions between South Asia and East Asia, and their impact on economic

[31] Appendix Table A9.1.3 shows which industries in each country are more integrated into global markets. All other industries surveyed and shown in Appendix Table A9.1.2 are less integrated into global markets.

performance at the macro and micro levels. We distinguish between property rights institutions, which capture the extent to which private property is secure from predation by the state or from corrupt officials demanding bribes in exchange for favours, and contracting institutions, which capture the effectiveness of institutions used to mediate disputes between private parties, following Acemoglu and Johnson (2005).

Our findings are as follows. First, the cross-country and firm-level evidence shows that after controlling for historical determinants of institutional quality, South Asian countries (with the exception of Sri Lanka) exhibit worse property rights and contracting institutions than what those determinants would predict, based on the cross-country average relationship. Moreover, South Asian countries perform substantially worse in terms of property rights and contracting institutions than East Asian countries, given the historical determinants. Second, property rights institutions have a large and significant causal impact on income per capita on average across countries, while contracting institutions matter much less. Third, property rights institutions and contracting institutions have different effects on performance in South Asia and East Asia, and depending on whether macro or micro performance measures are considered. In South Asia, poor property rights institutions have a weak negative effect on per-capita GDP, but poor contracting institutions are associated with higher per-capita GDP, which is counterintuitive. Poor property rights institutions affect average firm labour productivity negatively, while contracting institutions do not seem to matter. In East Asia, poor property rights institutions have a strong negative effect on per-capita GDP, but poor contracting institutions do not matter. Poor property rights institutions and poor contracting institutions affect firm labour productivity negatively. Considering locations and industries within countries, weak property rights institutions and weak contracting institutions have a detrimental effect on average labour productivity in South Asia as well as East Asia. The negative effects are stronger for property rights institutions. Finally, we find evidence of higher dispersion in institutional quality across countries within South Asia than East Asia. The dispersion in institutional quality across locations and industries within countries is also higher in South Asia than East Asia. These findings suggest that pressures for better governance resulting from regional integration in East Asia have led to some convergence in institutional quality. We also find that the dispersion in the quality of property rights institutions across firms is higher in industries that are less integrated into global markets. However, within countries, these more integrated industries are associated with worse institutional quality, according to the micro proxies.

Our findings suffer from several caveats, particularly related to the imperfection of the proxies for institutional quality, which do not allow a full understanding of the causes and consequences of institutional weaknesses. Nevertheless, our findings have some important policy implications. In order to achieve East Asian development levels, South Asian countries need to strengthen both their property rights institutions—for example, addressing the prevalence of corruption; as well as their contracting institutions—for example, solving judicial systems' bottlenecks. Stronger regional cooperation and integration across South Asia, following the example of East Asia, can help the sharing of knowledge and the copying of good practices, and consequently reduce the differences in institutional quality across countries. Moreover, South Asian countries need to address the large differences in institutional quality within their borders, which are likely to be due to an uneven enforcement of laws and implementation of reforms at the local level.

Appendix A9.1

Table A9.1.1: Variable Definitions

Variable	*Description*	*Country Coverage*
Rule of law index	Composite index constructed as described in Kaufmann, Kraay, and Mastruzzi (2005)	South Asia: Bangladesh, Bhutan, India, Nepal, Pakistan, Sri Lanka, East Asia: Cambodia, China, Indonesia, Laos, Malaysia, Philippines, Thailand, Vietnam(also included in Figure 9.1 are all countries for which data is available)
Control of corruption index	Composite index constructed as described in Kaufmann, Kraay, and Mastruzzi (2005)	South Asia: Bangladesh, Bhutan, India, Nepal, Pakistan, Sri Lanka, East Asia: Cambodia, China, Indonesia, Laos, Malaysia, Philippines, Thailand, Vietnam (also included in Figure 9.2 are all countries for which data is available)
Number of days to collect bad debt	Measures the number of days needed to complete all legal procedures that must be followed by a plaintiff for him/her to successfully collect on an unpaid debt. More details are available at http://www.doingbusiness.org/	South Asia: Bangladesh, India, Pakistan, Sri Lanka, East Asia: Cambodia, China, Indonesia, Malaysia, Philippines, Thailand, Vietnam(also included in Figure 9.3 are all countries for which data is available)
Settler mortality rates	Compiled by Kaufmann, Kraay, and Mastruzzi, based on the estimates of settler mortality of Acemoglu, Johnson, and Robinson (2001) extending those to previously uncovered geographically proximate countries with similar climate.	South Asia: Bangladesh, India, Nepal, Pakistan, Sri Lanka, East Asia: Cambodia, Laos, Indonesia, Malaysia, Philippines, Vietnam (also included in Table 9.2–Table 9.3 Algeria, Angola, Argentina, Australia, Benin, Bolivia, Botswana, Brazil, Burkina Faso, Burundi, Cameroon, Canada, Central African Republic, Chad, Chile, Colombia, Congo, Costa Rica, Zaire, Dominican Republic, Ecuador, Egypt, El Salvador, Ethiopia, Fiji, Ghana, Guatemala, Guinea, Haiti, Honduras,

(contd ...)

Table A9.1.1 (contd ...)

Variable	*Description*	*Country Coverage*
		Hong Kong, Ivory Coast, Jamaica, Kenya, Lesotho, Madagascar, Malawi, Maldives, Mali, Mauritania, Mauritius, Mexico, Morocco, Mozambique, Namibia, New Zealand, Nicaragua, Niger, Panama, Papua New Guinea, Paraguay, Peru, Rwanda, Sao Tome and Principe, Senegal, Singapore, Solomon Islands, South Africa, Sudan, Tanzania, Togo, Tunisia, Uganda, United States, Uruguay, Vanuatu, Venezuela, Zambia, Zimbabwe)
British legal origin	Compiled from Acemoglu and Johnson (2005)	South Asia: Bangladesh, India, Nepal, Pakistan, Sri LankaEast Asia: Cambodia, Laos, Indonesia, Malaysia, Philippines, Vietnam (also included in Table 9.2–Table 9.3 are same countries as for settler mortality rates)
Functioning of judiciary with respect to business disputes (PICS)	An assessment of the functioning of the judiciary with respect to business disputes based on the rating of the statement 'I am confident that the judicial system will enforce my contractual and property rights in business disputes' ranging 1 = Fully disagree to 6 = Fully agree	South Asia: Bangladesh, India, Pakistan, Sri Lanka, East Asia: Cambodia, China, Indonesia, Malaysia, Philippines, Thailand, Vietnam (also included in Figure 9.4 and Table 9.1 are Albania, Algeria, Armenia, Azerbaijan, Belarus, Benin, Bosnia and Herzegovina, Brazil, Bulgaria, Chile, Croatia, Czech Republic, Ecuador, El Salvador, Estonia, Georgia, Germany, Greece, Guatemala, Honduras, Hungary, Ireland, Kazakhstan, Kenya, South Korea, Kyrgyz Republic, Latvia, Lithuania, Macedonia, Madagascar, Mali, Mauritius, Moldova, Morocco, Nicaragua, Oman, Peru, Poland, Portugal, Romania, Russia, Senegal, Serbia and Montenegro, Slovak Republic, Slovenia, South Africa, Spain, Sri Lanka, Tajikistan, Tanzania, Turkey, Uganda, Ukraine, Uzbekistan, Vietnam, Zambia)
Corruption as an	An assessment of corruption based on 'how	South Asia: Bangladesh, India, Pakistan, Sri Lanka

(contd ...)

Table A9.1.1 (contd ...)

Variable	*Description*	*Country Coverage*
obstacle to business (PICS)	problematic is' corruption 'for the operation and growth' of the firm ranging from 0 = No obstacle to 4 = Major obstacle	East Asia: Cambodia, China, Indonesia, Malaysia, Philippines, Thailand, Vietnam (also included in Figure 9.4 and Table 9.1 are same countries as for functioning of judiciary with respect to business disputes)
Percentage of firms asked to pay bribes inspections (PICS)	The percentage of firms that were asked to pay bribes during inspections by government officials from several agencies	South Asia: Bangladesh, India, Sri Lanka East Asia: Cambodia, China, Indonesia, Philippines, Vietnam (also included in Figure 9.4 and Table 9.1 are same countries as for functioning of judiciary with respect to business disputes)
Percentage of sales paid in bribes to 'get things done' (PICS)	The average percentage of annual sales value that firms answer to be required as gifts or informal payments to public officials to 'get things done' with regard to customs, taxes, licenses, regulations, services, etc., for a typical firm	South Asia: Bangladesh, Pakistan, Sri Lanka East Asia: Cambodia, China, Indonesia, Philippines, Vietnam (also included in Figure 9.4 and Table 9.1 are same countries as for functioning of judiciary with respect to business disputes)
Sales per worker (PICS)	Total sales divided by the total number of workers at the firm transformed into constant 2000 local currency units using a GDP deflator (from World Development Indicators) and then into 2000 USD using the average exchange rate of local currency vis-à-vis the USD (from IMF International Financial Statistics)	South Asia: Bangladesh, India, Pakistan, Sri LankaEast Asia: Cambodia, China, Indonesia, Malaysia, Philippines, Thailand, Vietnam

TABLE A9.1.2: Industry Composition of the PICS Sample of South Asian and East Asian Countries

	South Asia					East Asia						
	Bangladesh	*India*	*Nepal*	*Pakistan*	*Sri Lanka*	*Cambodia*	*China*	*Indonesia*	*Malaysia*	*Philippines*	*Thailand*	*Vietnam*
Auto and Auto-Components		254					611	19	41		145	
Beverages			12					16				9
Chemicals and Pharmaceuticals	85	629	23	139			102	75	31			67
Electronics	91	348		96			934	35	157	117	166	19
Food	147	192	44	148	158	70	71	125	206	271	179	181
Garments	306	508	24	134	139	61	463	155	101	267	168	78
Leather Products	99	65	4	39			62					26
Metals and Machinery		238	35		31		325	2	84		177	192
Non-metallic and Plastic Materials			24		41				248		239	167
Other Manufacturing	11			44								125
Other Transport Equipment								18				
Paper								28				62
Textiles	262	485	39	314	82	2	52	188	30	61	186	79
Wood and Furniture			18					52	4		125	145
Total	1001	2719	223	914	451	133	2620	713	902	716	1385	1150

Source: Author's calculations based on the Productivity and Investment Climate Surveys (PICS).
Note: The table shows the number of observations in each industry for each of the countries in South Asia and East Asia where a PICS survey was conducted.

TABLE A9.1.3: Industries Integrated into Global Markets

	Industries More Integrated into Global Markets
South Asia	
Bangladesh	Garments, leather products, textiles
India	Chemicals and pharmaceuticals, food, garments, textiles
Nepal	Chemicals and pharmaceuticals, food, garments, textiles
Pakistan	Food, garments, textiles
Sri Lanka	Food, garments, non-metallic and plastic materials
East Asia	
Cambodia	Garments
China	Garments, electronics, metals and machinery, textiles
Indonesia	Chemicals and pharmaceuticals, electronics, food, garments, metals and machinery
Malaysia	Chemicals and pharmaceuticals, electronics, food, metals and machinery
Philippines	Electronics and garments
Thailand	Auto and auto-components, electronics, food, metals and machinery
Vietnam	Electronics, garments, leather, wood and furniture

Notes: The selection of industries that account for a larger percentage of a country's manufacturing exports was done based on export data for 2004 from the COMTRADE database. We selected the top five exporting industries of the country, as long as each of those represented more than 5 per cent of total manufacturing exports, and were covered in the PICS survey. For countries where fewer than five industries account for more than 96 per cent of exports, only those industries are considered to be more integrated into global markets.

Appendix Table A9.4: Cities Included in Figure 9.5

			South Asia				
B1	Dhaka	I16	Surat	I33	Hosur	P11	Quetta
B2	Chittagong	I17	Vadodara	I34	Madurai	P12	Peshawar
I1	Ahmedabad	I18	Gurgaon	I35	Ghaziabad	S1	Colombo
I2	Bangalore	I19	Faridabad	I36	Noida	S2	Gampana
I3	Calcutta	I20	Panipat	I37	Shahjahanpur-Lakimpur	S3	Kalutara
I4	Chandigarh	I21	Hubli-Dharwad	I38	Howrah	S4	Kandy
I5	Chennai	I22	Calicut	I39	Mangalore	S5	Matale
I6	Cochin	I23	Palakkad	P1	Karachi	S6	Nuwara Eliya
I7	Delhi	I24	Bhopal	P2	Lahore	S7	Galle
I8	Hyderabad	I25	Gwalior	P3	Sheikhupura	S8	Matara
I9	Kanpur	I26	Indore	P4	Sialkot	S9	Kurunegala
I10	Mumbai	I27	Nagpur	P5	Faisalabad	S10	Puttalam
I11	Pune	I28	Nashik	P6	Gujranwala	S11	Anuradhapura
I12	Mysore	I29	Thane	P7	Wazirabad	S12	Badulla
I13	Vijayawada	I30	Jalandhar	P8	Islamabad/ Rawalpindi	S13	Monaragala
I14	Lucknow	I31	Ludhiana	P9	Sukkur	S14	Ratnapura
I15	Guntur	I32	Coimbatore	P10	Hyderabad	S15	Kegalle
			East Asia				
C1	Phnom Penh	CH13	Hangzhou	I7	East Java	P7	Rizal
C2	Battambang	CH14	Jiangmen	I8	Banten	P8	Batangas
C3	Siem Reap	CH15	Kunming	I9	Bali	P9	NCR
C4	Sihanouk Ville	CH16	Lanzhou	I10	South Kalimanthan	T1	North
C5	Kampong Cham	CH17	Nanchang	I11	South Sulawesi	T2	Central
CH1	Beijing	CH18	Nanning	M1	Central	T3	Bangkok
CH2	Chengdu	CH19	Shenzen	M2	North	T4	East
CH3	Guanzhou	CH20	Wenzhou	M3	South	T5	Northeast
CH4	Shangai	CH21	Wuhan	M4	EastCoast	T6	South
CH5	Tianjin	CH22	Xian	M5	Sabah	V1	Red River Delta
CH6	Benxi	CH23	Zhengzhou	M6	Sarawak	V2	Southern Central Coastal
CH7	Changchun	I1	North Sumatra	P1	Cavite	V3	South East
CH8	Changsha	I2	Riau	P2	Cebu	V4	Mekong River Delta
CH9	Chongqing	I3	Jakarta	P3	Davao	V5	Northern Central
CH10	Dalian	I4	West Java	P4	Laguna		
CH11	Guiyang	I5	Central Java	P5	Manila		
CH12	Haerbin	I6	Jogjakarta	P6	Quezon		

References

Acemoglu, D., S. Johnson, and J. Robinson. 2001. 'The Colonial Origins of Comparative Development', *American Economic Review*, 91: 1369–401.

Acemoglu, D. and S. Johnson. 2005. 'Unbundling Institutions', *Journal of Political Economy*, 113(5): 949–95.

Bardhan, P. 1997. 'Corruption and Development: A Review of Issues', *Journal of Economic Literature*, 35: 1320–46.

Campos, J., D. Lien, and S. Pradhan. 1999. 'The Impact of Corruption on Investment: Predictability Matters', *World Development*, 27: 1059–67.

Delong, J. and A. Shleifer. 1993. 'Princes or Merchants? City Growth Before the Industrial Revolution', *Journal of Law and Economics*, 32: 671–702.

Devarajan, S. and I. Nabi. 2006. 'Economic Growth in South Asia: Promising, Un-Equalizing, Sustainable?' Mimeo, World Bank, Washington, D.C.

Djankov, S., C. McLiesh, and R. Ramalho. 2006. 'Regulation and Growth', *Economics Letters*, 92: 395–401.

Dollar, D., M. Hallward-Driemeier, and T. Mengistae. 2005. 'Investment Climate and Firm Performance in Developing Economies', *Economic Development and Cultural Change*, 54: 1–31.

Fernandes, A. 2006. 'Firm Productivity in Bangladesh Manufacturing Industries', Policy Research Department Working Paper No. 3988, World Bank, Washington, D.C.

Fernandes, A. and A. Kraay. 2006. 'Property Rights Institutions, Contracting Institutions, and Growth in South Asia: Macro and Micro Evidence', in *South Asia—Regional Integration and Growth*. Washington, D.C.: World Bank.

Hall, R. and C. Jones. 1999. 'Why Do Some Countries Produce So Much More Output per Worker than Others?' *Quarterly Journal of Economics*, 114: 83–116.

Kaufmann, D., A. Kraay, and M. Mastruzzi. 2005. 'Governance Matters IV: Governance Estimates for 1996–2004', Policy Research Department Working Paper No. 3630, World Bank, Washington, D.C.

Knack, S. and P. Keefer. 1995. 'Institutions and Economic Performance: Cross-Country Tests Using Alternative Measures', *Economics and Politics*, 7: 207–27.

Lim, L. and A. Stern. 2002. 'State Power and Private Profit: The Political Economy of Corruption in Southeast Asia', *Asian-Pacific Economic Literature*, 16: 18–52.

Mauro, P. 1995. 'Corruption and Growth', *Quarterly Journal of Economics*, 110: 681–712.

North, D. and B. Weingast. 1989. 'Constitutions and Commitment: The Evolution of Institutions Governing Public Choice in 17th Century England', *Journal of Economic History*, 49: 803–32.

Rodrik, D., A. Subramanian, and F. Trebbi. 2004. 'Institutions Rule: The Primacy of Institutions over Geography and Integration in Economic Development', *Journal of Economic Growth*, 9: 131–65.

Wagner, J. 2007. 'Exports and Productivity: A Survey of the Evidence from Firm Level Data', *The World Economy*, 30: 60–82.

World Bank. 2006a. *Bangladesh Strategy for Sustained Growth*. Washington, D.C.: World Bank.

———. 2006b. *Global Monitoring Report 2006 Strenghtening Accountability—Aid, Trade, and Governance*. Washington, D.C.: World Bank.

———. 2004. *Doing Business*. Washington, D.C.: World Bank.

III

REGIONAL COOPERATION FOR GROWTH

10 REGIONAL INTEGRATION AND SMALL COUNTRIES IN SOUTH ASIA

L. Alan Winters

This chapter considers the possible outcome of deepening regional trading arrangements in South Asia. Several papers have done this already—Bandara and Yu (2003), Panagariya (2003), Baysan, Panagariya, and Pitigala (2006)—but the particular slant I wish to take is to focus on the relative size of the member countries and ask, in particular, whether such trading arrangements are likely to benefit the smaller countries in the region. Small countries face a number of challenges (as well as opportunities), and integration with their neighbours is often seen as a key strategy for them. That is correct, but there are two major caveats: integration with neighbours should not involve disintegration with (that is, barriers against trading relations with) the rest of the world; and the policies and circumstances of the larger neighbours will largely determine the effects on the smaller partners. So if these are not appropriate, integration could be harmful. In addition, one must remember that regional integration will usually pose political challenges: it can involve specialization that policymakers feel uncomfortable about—including the movement of people and industry—such that while the economic welfare of individuals and households may improve on average, aggregates pertaining to particular tracts of land—that is, countries—may not. Likewise, achieving integration can involve policy decisions that might appear unpalatable, such as foregoing the right to set its own industrial standards. Unless the political system can cope with such consequences, integration is not likely to get very far.

The chapter proceeds as follows. Section 1 briefly reviews some recent evidence on the private costs of doing business in small countries, and considers possible solutions to them. Section 2 considers the

South Asian region, noting in particular its heterogeneity, its trade policies, and its progress so far on regional integration. Sections 3 and 4 provide brief tours of the economics of regional integration arrangements (RIAs), highlighting issues of pertinence to South Asia, and trying to reach judgements on the question posed at the start of this introduction. I will write of an unspecific South Asian Regional Integration Arrangement (SARIA) in order not to be restrained by the current institutional structures—notably the Singapore-Australia Free Trade Agreement—which have their own histories and objectives. The latter are often less liberal than arrangements elsewhere in the world, and than the clear, analytical assumptions economists frequently have to make.

The bottom line, pulled together in Section 5, is that regional integration in South Asia would be a fine thing, and that some of the many barriers it currently faces should be dismantled. Equally, however, while circumstances vary across countries, it is not such a fine thing that it should absorb a lot of bureaucratic or political energy; the effort required would be massive, and even just restricting ourselves to international trade policy, improving links with the rest of the world would be more important.

Section 1: Small Countries

The supposed problems of small and remote economies have long occupied the economics profession. It is well established that smaller economies have less diversified production structures and are more vulnerable to shocks than others. It also appears that they tend to have larger public sectors, possibly because the fixed costs of government are relatively higher the smaller the economy, according to Alesina and Spolaore (2003), although these authors also argue that the greater homogeneity seen in small economies makes them more efficient at delivering the desired levels of public goods, and more agile in policy terms in responding to changing conditions. For most of the last 50 years, it has been hard to find evidence that small economies either grow less rapidly or have lower incomes per head than others, but over the last decade or so, as the world economy has become more integrated, small economies may be starting to fall behind (Briguglio, Persaud, and Stern 2006). This may reflect changes in technology that make size and agglomeration relatively more important—for example, creating a greater role for innovation and highly skilled workers, both of which appear to benefit from at least moderate scale—or it may arise because advantages that they had previously taken for granted, such as preferential trade access to rich country markets, are starting to erode.

There is another possibility that we consider in this section: namely, that the costs of private business are higher in small, and especially in small and remote economies, than elsewhere. Particularly if these costs afflict trade either within or between countries, they will hinder the division of labour across tasks in producing a single good (the slicing up of the value chain), and as such slicing up becomes more important, render the countries increasingly uncompetitive. Such small economies may be unable to generate acceptable incomes for their residents, and increasingly so if they lose the market privileges they currently have or they find their markets eroded by more fortunate firms.

The economist's stock answer to complaints about the costs of smallness is that international trade allows a very small economy to buy from the most efficient producers in the world (or at the prices defined by them), and to reap at least some economies of scale by concentrating production on a very small number of sectors. But especially when we add remoteness to the equation, this response is attenuated because, even setting aside any risks inherent in specialization, international trade is costly. Once the cost of transporting goods to and from the remote economy is accounted for (a small economy facing given world prices has to pay for both legs of transportation), incomes will necessarily be lower than can be supported in better located and larger economies. Moreover, transport premiums will typically be larger the smaller the economy because consignment sizes will be smaller and infrastructure less developed.

If transportation is prohibitively expensive, the small economy's costs are inflated by the absence of economies of scale, either internal to firms (for example, the technical inefficiencies of very small power plants), or external and arising from the absence of agglomeration economies.

Figure 10.1 illustrates the problem. Suppose we have an industry in which a manufactured good produced in the median-sized economy would require US$ 20 of power, US$ 40 of materials, and US$ 40 of labour. Suppose it sells on the world market for US$ 100. If a small economy pays 50 per cent extra for its power because it lacks scale,

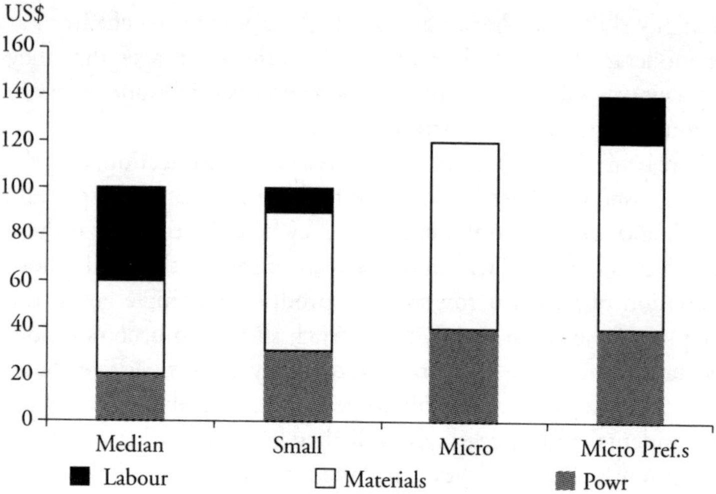

Figure 10.1: Excess Costs Cut Incomes

and 50 per cent extra for its materials because of transport costs, but still has to sell at the same price of US$ 100, it has only US$ 10 left over for labour. If it has the same labour productivity as the median country, that implies wages at one-quarter the median country's rate.

Now consider a micro economy where power and materials cost twice the median country levels: there is nothing left for labour. Even if the wage fell to zero, this industry would still be unviable.[1] What can be done?

Clearly, improving efficiency to reduce the value of inputs could solve the problem, but failing that, the small economy needs higher prices if it is to keep this industry. A niche market—that is, a unique product with high demand—is one source, but more common is a trade preference. If there were a market in the world that imported this good and levied a 40 per cent tariff, its internal price would be US$ 140. If it were to exempt our micro economy from that tariff, the

[1] There is nothing contrary to the law of comparative advantage in this parable. This could easily be the industry in which our country is comparatively most efficient, and hence the one which, if exported, would maximize income. It is just that maximum income is very small or negative: At world prices the country is unviable because of unavoidable excess real costs of doing business. (Imagine it were the moon—in principle you could produce on the moon, but what sort of incomes could that generate?)

latter could also earn US$ 140 per unit on its exports, and suddenly the industry is viable, albeit still with lower returns to labour.

Winters and Martins (2004a, 2004b) investigate the costs of business in small economies and seek to derive estimates of the cost disadvantages they entail. Details are available in the original sources, but they are based on questionnaire responses from mid-2002 for 92 economies, covering air and sea transport costs on exports and imports, the costs of utilities, the wages of different types of labour, taxes, and rents as continuous variables, plus labour shortages, utility reliability, and policy regimes on a categorical basis. There are clearly difficulties in separating the effects of size and isolation, but overall, the results seemed rather robust.

Figure 10.2 illustrates the data on the costs of sending a 20-feett full container from Yokohama, Japan, to the country's capital against population. The fitted line comes from the regression of costs on the logarithm of population that squared, distance, and dummies for OECD countries and for trips where the land distance component exceeds 500 kilometres. Other specifications produced very similar outcomes.

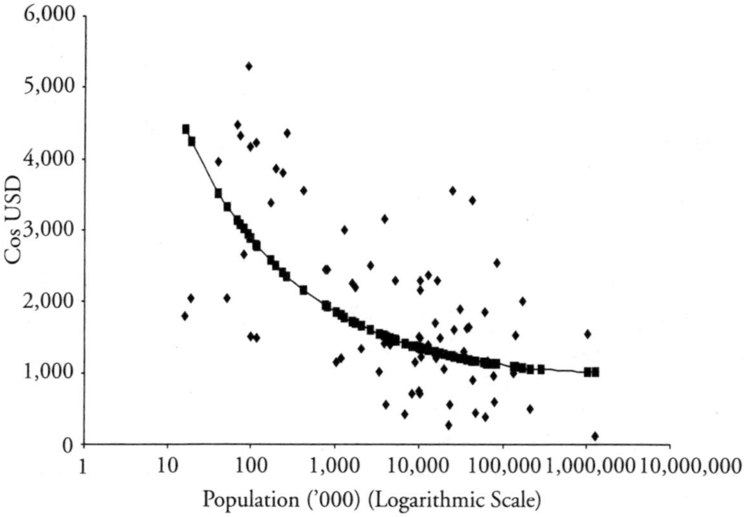

Figure 10.2: Shipping Costs From Yokohama

Source: L. Alan Winters and Pedro M.G. Martins (2005), *Beautiful but Costly: Business Costs in Small Remote Economies*, Economic Paper 67, Commonwealth Secretariat London, 2005.

This procedure was repeated on other cost elements and from the regression results, we calculated the predicted cost disadvantage for four exemplar countries, chosen to represent micro (12,000 inhabitants), very small (200,000), 'threshold' (1.6 million), and small (4 million) economies, relative to the median country, which has approximately 10 million inhabitants.[2]

These calculations suggest that there are significant costs to very small size in most of the areas analysed. Table 10.1 summarizes these estimates for various aggregates of cost. Note the very high cost disadvantages for sea freight and utilities, and the rather lower values for airfreight, water (for which no size effect was evident), and rents, where small countries apparently have an advantage. Once one recalls that rents reflect the value of land in commercial exploitation, however, the negative value reinforces the view that small economies

TABLE 10.1: Summary of Cost Disadvantages

(Percentage deviation of costs in micro, very small, and small economies from those in the median economy)

Area of Cost	*Micro*	*Very small*	*Threshold*	*Small*
Airfreight average*	31.8	4.1	–1.8	–1.7
Sea freight average	219.6	70.5	20.5	9.1
Unskilled wages average	60.1	31.6	13.6	6.6
Semi-skilled wages average	22.4	12.1	5.3	2.6
Skilled wages average	38.0	20.3	8.9	4.3
Telephone average (marginal costs)	98.5	47.2	19.1	9.0
Electricity (marginal costs)	93.1	47.0	19.7	9.4
Water (marginal costs)	0	0	0	0
Fuel average	53.8	28.3	12.3	5.9
Personal air travel average	115.7	56.8	23.3	11.0
Land rent average	–3.5	–17.2	–14.2	–8.9

Source: Winters and Martins (2004a).
Note: *Airfreight average denotes that the reported estimate is the mean of several measures of the costs concerned.

[2] 'Threshold' derives from the now fairly standard threshold for defining small economies of 1.5 million people. The population values used for these representative countries correspond broadly to Anguilla, Vanuatu, Botswana, Singapore, and Hungary, respectively.

are disadvantaged. It is obvious why one would pay more for a plot in Manhattan than in the Marshall Islands.

The second step was to aggregate these cost disadvantage factors into overall cost disadvantages for small economies in three potential export industries (electronic assembly, clothing, and tourism). These suggested that for the manufacturing sectors, a Botswana-sized country faced an excess cost of around 5 per cent, which is not a huge worry. However, for the very small or micro countries (for example, Vanuatu, population 200,000, and Anguilla, population 12,000, respectively), the size disadvantages were large—14 per cent and 36 per cent, respectively. For tourism, in which personal air travel figures large in the cost structure, the disadvantages were larger, but had the same pattern as for manufacturers.

As we noted earlier, if these cost disadvantages cannot be passed onto customers (that is, if small economies have to sell their goods and services at world prices), the only way that very small economies can export is if some input accepts lower payments than it would get in the median economy. Quantifying these penalties requires an assumption about which inputs have unavoidably higher cost and which (the complement of the first set) can be squeezed to accommodate the excess costs elsewhere. For some assumption sets, the illustrative industries could not generate positive incomes in the very small economies in the absence of special conditions, and even for the larger ones, the income penalties could be significant.

Winters and Martins discuss several possible 'solutions' to the costs of smallness, but none is very persuasive. Here we merely note three possible elements. First, one might economize on the costs of economic management or even of statehood by combining small countries to provide various functions of government. We doubt whether such efficiencies are sufficient to overcome large disadvantages, but there is undoubtedly a case for seeking such efficiency gains. They also note that in the European cases in which smallness appears not to have imposed major costs—for example, Luxembourg, Liechtenstein, Andorra—the secret appears to be to integrate extremely closely with the neighbouring large countries. However, combining to produce government services does not mean establishing regional authorities and then maintaining local capabilities to influence and monitor those authorities. It means a genuine pooling of sovereignty with no local shadowing, as, for example, Yorkshiremen and Lancastrians combine in England.

Second, trade preferences allow the small countries to earn higher prices for exports, as do niche markets, for example, for select tourism. Unfortunately, the former are always subject to erosion as global liberalization proceeds, and the latter are vulnerable to swings in tastes.

Finally, we must face the possibility that if the preferences that small countries currently receive are eroded, and with them their income levels, many of their inhabitants will seek to work abroad. Liberalizing the temporary movements of labour within the world economy promises huge economic gains (see Walmsley and Winters 2005). This could be a key factor for very small economies, essentially allowing residents to earn abroad but live and consume at least partly at home. Temporary workers from small countries would still be at a disadvantage relative to those from larger ones: they would face higher transport costs, smaller networks for finding jobs and easing migratory strains, and higher consumption costs at home. However, particularly if they had preferential access—for example, guaranteed quotas like New Zealand offers Polynesia for permanent or seasonal migration—the benefits could be large enough to overcome the disadvantages.

Section 2: The South Asian Economy

This section briefly introduces the economies of South Asia, their trade policies, and their progress towards regional integration to date. In summary, the region is unusually diverse, unusually restrictive in its trade policy, prone to rather ineffective preferential trade agreements, and less well-integrated than one might expect.

Diversity in South Asia

In this chapter, South Asia is treated as comprising seven countries—Bangladesh, Bhutan, India, the Maldives, Nepal, Pakistan, and Sri Lanka—and it is presumed that any regional trading arrangement will include them all. Using this definition, South Asia accounts for around 22.1 per cent of world population and 3.2 per cent of its land area, but accounts only for 2.0 per cent of GDP at current exchange rates and prices, and 7.3 per cent at PPP.[3] It is, by any standards, still

[3] Throughout this section we refer to data averaged over 2000–4 in order to smooth out some of the random shocks in the economic series.

TABLE 10.2: South Asian Countries: A Summary

	Size			GDP/head	Popn. density	Breakdown of GDP (%)				Urbanization	Trade/GDP ratios	
Country Name	*Popn ml.*	*Area km^2*	*GDP $ml*	*$US*	*n/km^2*	*Agriculture*	*Industry*	*Manuf.*	*Services*	*%*	*Exports*	*Imports*
Bangladesh	134.05	130170	49701	371	1029.8	23.0	26.1	*15.7*	50.9	24.0	14.8	20.3
Bhutan	0.85	47000	565	664	18.1	27.1	37.5	*8.0*	35.3	10.2	27.1	42.9
India	1048.23	2973190	548217	523	352.6	21.7	26.4	*15.4*	51.9	28.1	14.8	16.1
Maldives	0.31	300	676	2212	1018.9	n.a.	n.a.	*n.a.*	n.a.	28.3	87.9	70.3
Nepal	25.51	143000	5828	228	178.4	40.3	21.9	*8.6*	37.8	14.4	19.5	30.9
Pakistan	144.99	770880	78953	545	188.1	24.0	23.3	*16.0*	52.7	33.8	15.3	15.5
Sri Lanka	19.15	64630	17383	908	296.4	19.5	26.7	*15.9*	53.8	15.5	37.0	44.7

Source: WDI online, December 2006.
Note: averages 2000–4.

poor as a region, as are its people, with 31 per cent and 78 per cent living below US$ 1 or US$ 2 a day, respectively, in the early 2000s.

For our purposes, the other remarkable feature of South Asia is its diversity compared with almost any other regional integration arrangement (RIA) in the world. Table 10.2 presents some summary statistics for the seven South Asian economies we are considering. They show huge variation—from the island state of the Maldives (population 310,000) to landlocked Bhutan (population 850,000) to India, the second-most-populous country on earth (population 1.048 billion). Sri Lanka and Nepal are small by South Asian standards, and so fall within the ambit of this chapter, but not by the standards of the previous section. Pakistan and Bangladesh are basically large countries (ranked 7th and 8th by population, respectively, in the world). Similar dispersion is evident in land areas and aggregate GDPs, with India's economy nearly 1,000 times larger than the Maldives'.

The variance of GDP per capita is smaller—with a max:min ratio of 10:1—for all South Asian economies are quite poor, and Nepal is very poor. There are also differences in economic structure: Nepal is highly agricultural, whereas Bhutan, with its (relatively) massive electricity sector, very industrialized. Both, however, have small manufacturing sectors. Manufacturing elsewhere in South Asia has a slightly higher share of GDP than in other low-income countries, but at 15 to 16 per cent is not large compared with, say, East Asia. Integration with the rest of the world likewise varies among countries, at relatively low levels. Even the Maldives has an export/GDP ratio of below 100 per cent, which is not huge by the standards of very small states.

In fact, a South Asian RIA—SARIA—would contain a more disparate set of countries than any other major RIA. Table 10.3 presents statistics on the range of population, area, aggregate GDP, and GDP per capita for each of seven RIAs, again using data, so far as possible, averaged over 2000–4. The EU(15) refers to the EU in 1995, before the accession of the 10 new members in 2005, on the grounds that in South Asia we are looking at the creation, not the extension, of an RIA. ASEAN(8) refers only to eight members merely because data were not available on two current members (Brunei Darussalam and Myanmar). Completing either group would increase their diversity, but almost certainly not sufficiently to overtake SARIA.

TABLE 10.3: How Diverse is SAARC?

Bloc	*Population*	*GDP current US$*	*Area km^2*	*GDP pc*
Co-efficient of variation				
EU(15)	1.02	1.07	0.84	0.34
NAFTA	0.78	1.16	0.51	0.55
SACU	1.68	1.80	0.87	0.52
ASEAN (8)	1.08	0.78	1.15	1.78
Mercosur	1.31	1.14	1.22	0.38
Andean Pact	0.60	0.67	0.42	0.27
SAARC	1.80	1.85	1.70	0.79
Maximum/minimum				
EU(15)	185.3	91.9	211.6	4.3
NAFTA	9.2	16.7	4.8	5.8
SACU	41.6	156.3	70.6	7.0
ASEAN (8)	51.1	102.7	2703.8	71.6
Mercosur	52.8	80.0	48.3	4.3
Andean Pact	5.0	10.3	4.6	2.3
SAARC	3,429.4	970.1	9,910.6	9.7

Source: WDI online, December 2006.
Note: Based on data averaged over 2000–4.

The statistics reported are the coefficient of variation and the ratio of maximum to minimum over included countries. In terms of all three measures of size, SARIA is far more diverse than the other blocs, and even in terms of GDP per capita is second only to ASEAN. Of course, these data do not reflect variation over households or firms; only that over the partly arbitrary areas that form sovereign states, but given that states are major players in the creation and management of RIAs, this is not insignificant.

South Asian Trade and Trade Policy

The countries of South Asia have all pursued import substituting development regimes for most of the post-war period, characterized not only by restrictions on international trade, but by intervention, planning, and dirigisme of a high order. In the last decade and a half (three decades for Sri Lanka) this has started to change—quite

TABLE 10.4: MFN Tariffs and Trade Taxes in South Asia

	India	*Pakistan*	*Bangladesh*	*Sri Lanka*	*Nepal*	*The Maldives*	*Bhutan*
Average tariff plus protective duties							
2004							
Total	22.2	16.8	26.5	13.4	16.2		
Agriculture	40.1	18.1	32.1	28.1	16.3		
Non-agriculture	19.7	16.6	25.4	10.7	16.6		
Average tariffs							
2007	10					23	24

Source: World Bank staff estimates.

Note: Average tariff plus protective duties 2004 based on Baysan et al. (2006), table 16.

dramatically in India now—but the legacy remains. Trade is still subject to detailed management and trade agreements replete with reservations, exceptions, and restrictive regulations; see World Bank (2004) for detail.

By world standards, trade is still fairly restricted in the region. Table 10.4 reports average tariffs for 2004–5 from Baysan et al. (2006), plus more recent estimates of tariffs and trade taxes for India, Bhutan, and the Maldives. In addition to these taxes, some trade is subject to quantitative restrictions and other non-tariff barriers (NTBs). Thus, while there has been considerable liberalization recently, especially in India, there are still likely to be significant wedges between world and local prices.

An additional view of trade restrictions is given by the Overall Trade Restrictiveness Indicator (OTRI), by Kee, Nicita, and Olarreaga (2006), as used in the World Bank's *Global Monitoring Report.* This is a theoretically consistent attempt to aggregate tariffs and certain non-tariff barriers (price control measures, QRs, monopolistic measures, and technical regulations) into a single index—the uniform tariff that would have equivalent effect to the actual regime. Like the averages in Table 10.4, it is subject to serious data shortcomings, especially for the NTBs, but it is nonetheless a useful indicator.

Table 10.5 reports OTRIs for South Asian countries in 2004, along with comparisons for other regions. It reports the total OTRI, plus data for manufacturing and agriculture. In terms of tariffs, South Asia is the most restrictive region in the world, albeit with significant variation across the region. Adding NTBs increases the protection estimates, but less in our region than elsewhere. It mainly affects agriculture. Of course, trade liberalization must ultimately be done at a tariff-line level, but these data also suggest that trade is currently seriously restricted, raising the prospect of serious trade diversion if regional integration proceeds.

Table 10.2 shows that South Asian economies are not particularly open in terms of trade/GDP ratios. But what of the direction of trade? Tables 10.6 and 10.7 report the intra-regional shares of total exports and imports, and, from a different source, trade intensity indices (based on export data). Trade intensity indices are calculated as

$$(X_{i,j}/X_{.,j})/(X_{i,.}/X_{.,.})$$

TABLE 10.5: Overall Trade Restrictiveness Indicator, 2004

	OTRI	*OTRI Manufacturing*	*OTRI Agriculture*	*OTRI*	*OTRI Manufacturing*	*OTRI Agriculture*
Restrictions:	(tar+ntb)	(tar+ntb)	(tar+ntb)	(tar)	(tar)	(tar)
Bangladesh	0.188	0.180	0.230	0.152	0.151	0.155
Bhutan	0.254	0.200	0.505	0.218	0.158	0.500
India	0.242	0.203	0.654	0.156	0.129	0.438
Nepal	0.117	0.119	0.107	0.117	0.119	0.107
Pakistan	0.151	0.124	0.348	0.109	0.111	0.096
Sri Lanka	0.075	0.060	0.178	0.074	0.059	0.178
S. ASIA Memorandum:	0.188	0.165	0.345	0.150	0.135	0.257
LAC	0.172	0.151	0.318	0.092	0.086	0.132
ECA	0.106	0.089	0.223	0.063	0.054	0.123
EAP	0.156	0.134	0.401	0.074	0.059	0.244
MENA	0.271	0.237	0.475	0.135	0.116	0.245
SSA	0.232	0.213	0.343	0.143	0.134	0.201

Source: For OTRI see *Global Monitoring Report*, World Bank (various years from 2005).

where $X_{i,j}$ is exports from region *i* to region *j* and a dot (.) denotes summation across the corresponding subscript. Thus the formula expresses the share of *i* in *j*'s imports ($X_{i,j}/X_{.,j}$) relative to *i*'s share of imports into all countries of the world ($X_{i,.}/X_{.,.}$). Thus, an intensity index exceeding 1 implies that *i* is a more important source for *j*'s imports than it is for the world on average. (The intensity index also equals *j*'s share of *i*'s exports relative to *j*'s share of world exports. Hence, a value above 1 indicates that *j* is a more important market for *i* than for source countries on average.) If bilateral trade were random, so that all exports from all countries had an equal chance of ending up in, say, North America, and an equal (albeit different) chance of ending up in, say, Africa, the intensity indices would be unity. If they exceed unity for a bilateral link, they indicate that there is a bias in trade patterns towards that link.

For the large- and medium-sized countries, intra-regional trade shares are generally rather low, although even for them many intra-regional trade intensity indices exceed unity, showing that the share is larger than a purely random allocation of trade across partners throughout the world would indicate. For example, Bangladesh's imports are heavily biased towards India and Pakistan (column 1), and its exports somewhat biased towards Pakistan, although presumably as a result of preferences, Bangladesh's main markets are in the rich countries. Sri Lanka displays stronger interregional intensity, especially with India and Pakistan, but it is Nepal and Bhutan that show the greatest dependence on regional markets. This is consistent with their landlocked status and locations, and in both cases trade is largely with India, with which they have bilateral trade agreements (see later). Even more striking are the intensity indices over 100 for the Maldives and Afghanistan. We are not including the latter in this paper, but the former is interesting. Sri Lanka accounts for 12 per cent of the Maldives' exports and 10 per cent of its imports (WITS data averaged 2002–5), but the intensity index is so high because Sri Lanka is a relatively small trader. In fact, India is as important a source of imports as Sri Lanka, but its greater size renders the intensity index one-twentieth as large.

The data used in this sub-section refer only to official trade, whereas there is at least some informal or unofficial trade across the land borders. World Bank (2004), however, suggests that in aggregate the amounts are not particularly large and that they are roughly in line with recorded trade, so the data reported are not highly misleading.[4] They will, however, be underestimates.

Trade Agreements in South Asia[5]

The most significant bilateral trade agreements in the region are between India and its two smaller landlocked neighbours. The India-Nepal Treaties on Trade and Transit guarantee Nepal access to the sea at Kolkata and Haldia, along with port facilities and procedural concessions for third-country trade. It also defines land routes and customs exit-entry points, and exempts Nepalese goods from all charges in India except for transportation. Exemption from Indian duties is a significant boon, and so the administrative and procedural apparatus to police it are quite heavy, imposing harsh costs on legitimate trade. Nonetheless, Indian firms complain of the leakage of exempt goods into their local economy, while the Nepalese complain about significant losses of goods.

The Indo-Nepal agreement also offers trade preferences: Nepalese exports to India qualify for duty- and quota-free access if accompanied by a suitable certificate of origin,[6] and on the reverse flow, Indian exports receive a 10 per cent to 20 per cent reduction in tariffs. The certificate of origin is basically another restrictive rule of origin. India accepts no reexports from Nepal. As another anti-fraud device, unlike other exports, Indian exports to Nepal have to pay local (Indian) excise duties, which are then offset against Nepalese customs tariffs, with the Indian government subsequently refunding the Nepalese government.

Thus the India–Nepal agreement offers Nepal reasonable de jure access to the Indian market somewhat devalued by bureaucratic procedures, but there is little preferential access the other way. It helps to integrate Nepal into the Indian economy and to facilitate its access to third markets (as littoral countries are required to do by international agreement). The maintenance of Nepalese trade restrictions and the enforcement of administrative rules on trade flows, however, mean that this integration is far from complete.

[4] The significant volume of 'technical' smuggling involves misreporting the products traded to reduce duty payments and so does not affect the aggregate values reported here.

[5] This sub-section draws heavily on World Bank (2004).

[6] A few goods are subject to tariff quotas.

Table 10.6: Average Intra-regional Trade Shares in South Asia—Various Years

	India	*Pakistan*	*Bangladesh*	*Sri Lanka*	*Nepal*	*The Maldives*	*Bhutan*
Share of exports to region %							
2005	4.5	4.6	1.6	9.5	54.3	17.2	95.0
1999	5.5	3.3	2.2	2.6	27.7	16.6	81.9
Share of imports from region %							
2005	0.9	2.8	15.3	22.4	48.0	17.4	n.a.
2001	0.9	2.9	14.4	12.4	19.7	23.7	n.a.

Sources: IMF Direction of Trade Statistics, Bandara and Yu (2003); the World Bank (2004, p. 6); and the World Bank (2004, p. 122), 1998.

TABLE 10.7: Trade Intensity Indices, Average of 2002–4

Exporter	*Importer*																
	BGD	*IND*	*LKA*	*AFG*	*BTN*	*MDV*	*NPL*	*PAK*	*NA rich*	*AP rich*	*EU+ EFTA*	*AP other*	*NA other*	*ECA other*	*LAC*	*MENA*	*SSA*
BGD	0.00	0.97	1.01	3.09	12.87	0.00	0.46	3.42	1.73	0.32	1.37	0.16	0.12	0.17	0.07	0.58	0.63
IND	19.85	0.00	21.87	7.49	63.24	10.94	61.27	2.93	0.99	0.97	0.58	1.27	0.22	0.52	0.66	4.27	3.69
LKA	1.93	6.36	0.00	0.57	0.00	192.61	1.34	4.17	1.88	0.52	0.80	0.13	0.37	0.84	0.27	2.15	0.50
AFG	31.59	24.32	1.07	0.00	0.00	0.00	0.28	154.81	0.80	0.10	0.44	0.11	0.07	1.02	0.79	1.88	0.41
BTN	21.45	108.38	0.00	0.00	0.00	0.04	21.21	6.26	0.06	0.13	0.06	0.14	0.00	0.01	0.19	0.20	0.47
MDV	0.00	0.29	155.20	0.00	0.00	0.00	0.00	0.00	1.50	1.06	0.38	2.11	0.01	0.00	0.11	1.85	0.02
NPL	3.81	62.34	0.88	0.00	40.06	0.22	0.00	1.68	1.41	0.14	0.40	0.24	0.08	0.10	0.01	0.06	0.16
PAK	11.54	0.98	9.93	133.54	1.48	3.40	1.89	0.00	1.27	0.67	0.75	0.53	0.22	0.44	0.45	4.15	3.65
NA rich	0.28	0.67	0.22	0.42	0.07	0.16	0.17	0.72	2.04	1.00	0.45	0.68	5.00	0.19	2.00	0.71	0.55
AP rich	1.82	1.26	1.81	0.70	0.72	2.11	0.86	1.16	1.06	1.73	0.37	3.24	0.41	0.25	0.72	0.76	0.76
EU+EFTA	0.25	0.70	0.44	0.28	0.60	0.34	0.20	0.55	0.51	0.33	1.68	0.30	0.30	1.41	0.51	1.06	1.00
AP other	2.58	1.43	1.84	0.31	0.38	1.51	1.62	2.48	1.07	2.73	0.40	1.17	0.34	0.45	0.55	0.89	1.04
NA other	0.00	0.30	0.01	0.14	0.00	0.00	0.00	0.03	4.55	0.07	0.10	0.05	0.05	0.01	1.42	0.03	0.05
ECA other	0.23	0.57	0.19	1.78	0.02	0.05	0.24	0.53	0.20	0.15	1.42	0.39	0.25	4.53	0.23	1.16	0.39
LAC	0.98	1.03	0.41	0.03	0.01	0.11	0.07	0.36	1.46	0.46	0.56	0.72	1.58	0.37	8.91	0.91	1.00
MENA	0.51	3.36	0.95	7.11	0.05	1.59	0.19	3.21	0.69	2.63	0.61	0.41	0.09	0.46	0.44	2.59	1.14
SSA	0.65	4.24	0.55	2.23	0.10	0.67	0.22	1.93	0.77	0.67	1.02	0.71	0.08	0.19	0.83	0.82	13.39

Source: Author's calculations based on WITS data.

India and Bhutan have a similar bilateral agreement, for similar reasons. In this case, however, trade is free in both directions, and there are no explicit or implicit rules of origin. The only exception is that either side can apply NTBs or third-country goods, and Bhutan can apply NTBs to imports from India to protect local industry. Bhutan's major export is hydroelectricity, all of which goes to India, and the production of which was financed by India using Indian construction services. Overall, Bhutan appears likely to be fairly well-integrated with the Indian economy, and a SARIA would not change the bilateral relationship much.

This is not true to the Bangladesh–Bhutan trade agreement, which offers Bhutan little advantage in the Bangladeshi market, or the India-Bangladesh agreement which refers (not very effectively) to logistics rather than tariffs. In these cases, an effective SARIA would increase market access significantly.

The India–Sri Lanka Free Trade Area, which became operational in 2000, has a slightly more modern feel about it. Although originally conceived to maintain serious restrictions on major trade flows—for example, 15 out of Sri Lanka's top 20 export commodities faced restrictions—it has generated significant trade in products that were barely traded seven years ago (Baysan et al. 2006). I return to this aspect in Section 3 below.

The first step towards broader regional cooperation was the Bangkok Agreement of 1975 which included India, Bangladesh, Sri Lanka, and Korea. It did not create meaningful market access concessions, however, being restricted in coverage and hedged around with tight rules of origin and QRs. A somewhat stronger, and purely regional step, was the formation of the South Asian Association for Regional Cooperation (SAARC) in 1985. This led to the South Asia Preferential Trade Area (SAPTA), which became operational in December 1995. SAPTA had limited coverage and restrictive rules of origin such that for no member did more than 40 per cent of intra-regional imports qualify for preferences (Mukherji 2000).

In 2003, effective plans were agreed to convert SAPTA into a more effective institution, the South Asia Free Trade Agreement (SAFTA), which aimed to reduce tariffs on intra-bloc trade to 5 per cent or less (after eight years), and to institute cooperation in areas such as trade facilitation, transport and communication, and infrastructure and investment, and introduced macroeconomic consultation. There are still exceptions, however, that permit higher barriers on many sensitive goods. SAFTA falls well short of aspirations in other RIAs between developing countries. It indicates a strong deference to established producers and interest groups—which are presumably behind the exceptions lists—and as such misses the chance to introduce a significant increase in competition in the region. In the discussion that follows, focus is on the case in which intra-regional trade is entirely freed, and exceptions and internal restrictions reduced to a very small number, as in the European Union.

Integrating Labour Markets—Migration

A further major component of integration is of labour markets—international migration. In absolute terms, South Asians are among the most mobile people in the world, and there is significant intra-regional mobility. Thus, for example, India and Pakistan were respectively the fourth and eighth largest hosts to migrants in 2000 (the stock in 2000), while India, Bangladesh, and Pakistan were ranked second, third, and eighth, respectively, in terms of the number of people who had been born there who were now residing abroad (Parsons, Skeldon, Walmsley, and Winters 2007: Table 8). The same source (Table 10) shows how strongly these movements reflect intra-regional mobility, with an intra-regional intensity index of 5.67 (see above for details of intensity indices).

Table 10.8 presents migration intensity indices by country using the Parsons et al. data.[7] The top left submatrix refers to South Asian countries, and the remainder to the rest of the world. The large numbers in the submatrix make clear the strong tendency for residents of South Asian countries to migrate among the other countries in the region. The columns report the origins of each country's immigration stock, and show that for most South Asian countries, regional sources are disproportionately favored. Reading along the rows shows where South Asian migrants go. Here again, the predominance of intra-regional movements is obvious, although 'above-expected' stocks are also found in MENA—the Gulf—and Sri Lanka and the Maldives also display positive biases towards certain rich destinations.

[7] Recall from above that the intensity index reports, say, the share of Bangladeshis in India's immigrant total relative to the share of Bangladeshis in immigrants in all countries.

South Asia seems relatively well-integrated in terms of labour markets, but that, of course, is relative to norm that is very restrictive. In fact, given their population sizes, the total emigrant stocks of 9.0 million, 6.6 million, and 3.4 million for India, Bangladesh, and Pakistan, respectively, make a good deal more integration look perfectly feasible.

Section 3: Assessing a SARIA: (I) The Static Analysis

This section and the next are the heart of the chapter. They briefly sketch some of the major analytical approaches to RIAs, and ask how a SARIA would stack up against them. They make no attempt to quantify the various phenomena or to trade one against another. Rather, they identify the components that should enter an applied analysis of a SARIA, and thus essentially lay out an agenda for future applied policy research. This section starts with the simple analysis of RIAs deriving from Viner (1950). It is heuristic and very evidently incomplete, but it has the advantage of simplicity, and many of its messages have turned out to be quite robust. Following that, it deals with a few static extensions to the analysis.

Imports—Theory

The traditional analysis of the welfare effects of RIAs, for small and large countries alike, revolves around the effects that integration has on prices. For small countries, its starting point is that small countries have virtually no effect on the prices faced by large countries, and virtually no influence on the prices they themselves face. Consider Figure 10.3, which refers to the market for a single homogeneous good. Small country *A* has a choice among two suppliers, each of which can supply its full needs of the product at fixed prices: *B*, the potential partners with price P_B, and *R*, the rest of the world, with price P_R. (We assume that *B* and *R* do not trade so their prices are independent.) In the absence of trade, *A*'s price (marginal cost of production) is P_A. Before integration, suppose that tariff t is levied on all imports: since $P_R + t < P_B + t$, consumers in *A* buy from *R*. After offering *B* preferential access under the RIA, *B*'s price, as faced by *A*'s consumers, falls to P_B, and assuming that $P_R + t > P_B$, demand is diverted from *R* to *B*. In terms of welfare, there are losses equal to area $(a + c)$ in terms of tariff revenue, gains to consumers of a because they are paying lower prices for their initial level of purchases, and

TABLE 10.8: Migration Stocks, 2000, Intensity Indices

	Destination Country/Region																		
	Bangladesh	*India*	*Sri Lanka*	*Afghanistan*	*Bhutan*	*Maldives*	*Nepal*	*Pakistan*	*USA*	*Canada*	*EU15+ EFTA*	*Australia+ NZ*	*Japan*	*Hi-inc MENA*	*LAC*	*ECA*	*MENA*	*AFR*	*EAP*
Countries of Origin																			
Bangladesh	0.00	16.07	0.00	11.33	11.31	11.30	0.83	9.41	0.08	0.10	0.23	0.06	0.11	1.08	0.03	0.04	0.59	0.07	0.28
India	19.02	0.00	19.41	3.13	3.12	3.12	0.94	2.80	0.59	1.11	0.47	0.48	0.09	5.62	0.05	0.05	1.87	0.19	0.81
Sri Lanka	0.03	5.66	0.00	4.12	4.12	4.12	0.92	3.60	0.14	3.06	1.29	2.38	0.52	2.30	0.03	0.09	1.17	0.08	0.60
Afghanistan	0.03	0.10	0.00	0.00	0.25	0.25	0.89	0.46	0.09	0.26	0.19	0.16	0.01	1.20	0.03	0.06	14.63	0.08	0.23
Bhutan	0.03	17.34	0.00	12.08	0.00	13.02	0.83	10.12	0.14	0.07	0.32	0.21	0.32	0.05	0.05	0.04	0.08	0.07	0.19
Maldives	0.00	6.37	0.00	4.63	0.00	0.00	0.82	4.02	0.20	0.29	1.76	7.39	2.20	0.06	0.17	0.14	0.26	0.07	0.26
Nepal	0.02	17.73	0.00	12.43	12.41	12.39	0.00	10.30	0.06	0.03	0.10	0.11	0.33	0.29	0.03	0.04	0.11	0.07	0.74
Pakistan	1.07	10.99	0.02	5.66	5.65	5.65	0.99	0.00	0.34	0.76	0.82	0.14	0.19	3.55	0.04	0.07	1.29	0.15	0.47
USA	0.00	0.04	0.04	0.23	0.23	0.22	1.00	0.48	0.00	3.77	1.36	1.09	2.32	0.37	9.56	0.16	0.70	0.23	2.21
Canada	0.00	0.04	0.00	0.25	0.24	0.26	1.07	0.51	3.69	0.00	0.73	0.99	0.74	0.12	0.73	0.09	0.11	0.13	0.31
EU15+ EFTA	0.00	0.02	0.03	0.22	0.22	0.22	1.01	0.47	0.90	2.41	2.34	3.34	0.15	0.18	1.58	0.34	0.23	0.37	0.31
Australia+ NZ	0.00	0.11	0.24	0.30	0.29	0.29	1.04	0.54	0.54	0.96	1.50	15.76	1.21	0.13	0.14	0.12	0.13	0.17	1.17
Japan	0.03	0.03	0.05	0.24	0.23	0.25	1.06	0.49	2.87	0.95	0.65	1.42	0.00	0.07	2.48	0.08	0.16	0.10	1.98
Hi-inc MENA	0.03	0.39	0.00	0.42	0.41	0.39	0.89	0.51	0.47	0.72	0.28	0.28	0.03	1.63	0.13	0.08	11.45	0.09	0.65
LAC	0.00	0.02	0.00	0.23	0.23	0.22	1.08	0.49	3.42	0.73	0.50	0.11	1.19	0.11	3.96	0.06	0.10	0.11	0.18
ECA	0.01	0.01	0.00	0.22	0.22	0.22	1.06	0.48	0.25	0.46	0.96	0.36	0.02	0.57	0.08	3.54	0.23	0.16	0.13
MENA	0.01	0.05	0.00	0.22	0.22	0.22	0.92	0.42	0.32	0.68	1.98	0.49	0.06	3.20	0.15	0.11	4.31	0.44	0.13
AFR	0.00	0.07	0.00	0.22	0.22	0.22	0.94	0.40	0.21	0.38	0.83	0.38	0.03	0.41	0.05	0.06	0.33	8.31	0.06
EAP	0.03	0.17	0.02	0.33	0.32	0.33	1.02	0.56	1.49	1.94	0.50	2.06	6.43	0.68	0.16	0.07	0.22	0.09	6.68

Source: Parsons et al. (2007).

of *b*, which represents the gain from consuming the extra units ($Q_1 - Q_0$), stimulated by the price decline. The net gain is ($b - c$), which could take either sign.

The principal determinant of the net effect of the RIA in this market is the inefficiency of *B* relative to *R*. If *B* were relatively efficient, that is, P_B was only very slightly above P_R, *c* would be small. If it was inefficient, that is, close to ($P_R + t$), *c* would be large. Of course if $P_B < P_R$ (that is, if *B* was very efficient), there would be no problem: *A* would always have imported from *B* and the RIA would have been just like a non-discriminatory liberalization. Alternatively, if *B* was very inefficient, such that $P_B > P_R + t$, *A* would always import from *R*, and the RIA would have had no effect—that is, there would be no trade diversion.

The second key factor is *A*'s tariff, *t*. The lower this is, the smaller the area ($a + c$), and the smaller the revenue that is vulnerable to loses from trade diversion. Similarly, the lower *t* is, the more likely that $P_B > P_R + t$—that is, the trade diversion is avoided. This suggests that lower *t* is better, and that is true, with one partial exception. Suppose that *t* was so high that, in fact, *A* was initially the cheapest supplier to consumers, $P_A < P_j + t, j = B, R$. Then there would initially be no trade and no tariff revenue, and the RIA would potentially create trade by allowing residents to purchase at P_B. This would lead to gains equivalent to *b* in Figure 10.3, although with P_A as the initial price. The gains would be larger if the tariff cut were non-discriminatory—

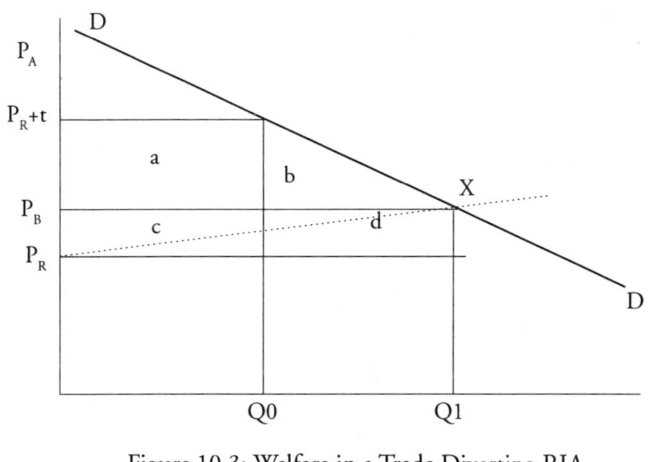

Figure 10.3: Welfare in a Trade Diverting RIA

presuming that $P_R < P_B$—but even preferential trade liberalization would be beneficial.

The final determinant of the welfare outcome is the slope of the demand curve, which we typically represent as elasticity. For policies changing prices the welfare effect is larger, the larger (absolutely) the elasticity.

The conclusion of this excessively simple model is that for a small economy with a RIA, the costs on its imports side are likely to be smaller or the benefits greater, the more efficient its larger partner and the smaller its own tariffs. We shall refine the model considerably, but these conclusions remain fairly robust. The question, then, is how do India and the small South Asian economies stack up on these criteria. The answer once would have been 'pretty badly'. South Asia had high tariffs, which fostered trade diversion and, because tariffs tend to raise production prices (P_B) above world levels (P_R), inefficiency costs that were imposed on partners.

More recently, protection levels have fallen, and given that they have fallen most in India, which would be the principal partner for all other countries and would suffer the greatest absolute losses from trade diversion, the situation is much improved. Having said that, however, there is still a long way to go throughout the region if the dangers outlined here are to fall to negligible levels.

The simple model can be extended in a number of directions, none of which changes the basic story. For example, the area of fiscal loss from the RIA ($a + c$) is not all lost welfare, but if tariffs are important for revenue purposes—as can make sense for very small countries—the adjustment to other sources of funding will be arduous.[8] This is specifically an issue for the Maldives, where customs duties amount to 72 per cent of tax revenue and 21 per cent of total revenues and grants. The standard rate is 15 per cent, but with some higher rates, notably on products such as alcohol, tobacco, and cars, which traditionally attract higher rates of excise duty/consumption taxes. In aggregate, 21 to 24 per cent of the Maldives' imports come from SARIA partners, which suggests that perhaps about 17 per cent of tax revenue or 5 per cent of total revenue is at stake, but detailed

[8] Winters and Martins (2004a, 2004b) argued that for very small island economies, a uniform tariff on imports may be a good approximation to a consumption tax and hence not an irrational way of raising revenue.

calculations relating imports by origin to tariff rates (and exemptions) would be necessary to verify this.

If we model *A*'s production explicitly with a rising supply curve, there will be production as well as consumption effects, and local production may persist after the RIA is signed. None of the basic conclusions is affected, however.

If country *B* is not very large relative to *A*, it is possible that *A* faces a rising supply curve from *B* rather than the horizontal one in Figure 10.3. Two cases exist. First, *B* may still be able to supply the whole of *A*'s market for a price below $(P_R + t)$, so it will still capture the whole market. Diagrammatically, the horizontal supply curve (price line) at P_B would be replaced by the sloped broken line P_RX, and the welfare story would be unchanged. If *B*'s supply curve were lower (rotated counterclockwise through X a little more), there would have been some imports from *B* initially (for the units for which *B*'s price was below P_R), but their price would have been P_R since *R* was the marginal supplier, and they would have faced tariff *t* like *R*'s suppliers did. The analysis would thus still be exactly the same from *A*'s point of view.

Second, it may be that after the RIA, *B* cannot supply the whole of *A*'s market at less than $(P_R + t)$, and that some imports from *R* continue to be made. Since *R* is the marginal supplier, it defines the internal price, which equals $(P_R + t)$ both before and after the RIA. With no price change, neither production nor consumption in *A* changes, but a quantity of imports is diverted from *R* to *B*, and all imports from *B* (new and old) are bought at the internal price. Initially *B* paid the tariff, but now the full tariff-inclusive price goes to producers in *B*, causing a loss of national welfare of *t* per unit of initial imports from *B*. This loss accrues as a benefit to producers in *B* who have been forgiven the tax, but *A* loses unambiguously—the only thing that happens is trade diversion. The size of the most favored nation tariff remains critical as before, and although *B*'s relative inefficiency appears not to matter, that is only because we assume it is too inefficient to supply all of *A*'s needs. That is, the less efficient *B* is (the higher its supply curve), the more likely it is that this 'only losses' case arises. The new critical factor in this story is the initial imports from *B*. The higher these are, the greater the losses from forgiving them the tariff.

The last case is related to a fourth refinement, in which *B's* and *R*'s varieties of the good in question are differentiated. Figure 10.4

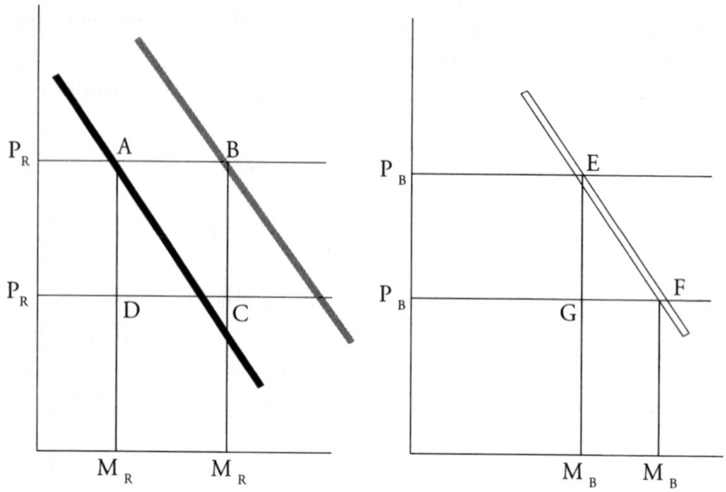

Figure10.4: Differentiated Goods or Services

illustrates this case: it has two related markets, each with a single (geographical) source.[9] Initially, prices and quantities are P_B' and M_B' and P_R' and M_R', respectively. Following the RIA, the equilibrium on *B*'s variety shifts to P_B and M_B, with net benefits EFG. In the other market, the fall in *B*'s price shifts the demand for *R*'s variety leftward, leading to a loss of tariff revenue (trade diversion) of ABCD. The critical factors now are the extent of the tariff and the substitutability between the two varieties. The higher the latter, the greater the diversion, and as it approaches infinity this case converges on the Vinerian case above.

In this case, neither the extent of existing imports from *B*, nor the height of the MFN tariff has direct and obvious implications for the desirability of the RIA. As a rough approximation given the various elasticities, trade creation, EFG, will be proportionate to the square of the tariff removed from *B*'s suppliers. Similarly, if the shift in the demand for *R* supplies is proportionate to the change in the *B*'s price ($=t/1+t$), trade diversion, ABCD, will also be proportionate to t^2. Thus, the size of the effect of the RIA expands with t^2, but to a first order approximation its sign is not affected.

[9] I assume that B producers compete with one another, as do R producers, so that there are no monopoly profits to complicate matters.

To summarize, if we believe that goods and services are fairly homogeneous, we can identify one necessary condition for small countries to gain:

- imports from *R* must cease.

If they do not, the small country will suffer only trade diversion and the transfer of tariff revenue to *B*'s producers. The losses will be larger

- the larger the MFN tariff, and
- the higher the initial level of imports from *B*.

If imports from *R* do cease, trade creation becomes feasible, and as the local price falls below $P_R + t$, tariff revenue starts to be transferred to local consumers rather the *B*'s producers. The critical factor for the sign of the welfare effect then becomes:

- how efficient *B* is relative to global best practice (*R*,),

while those for its size remain as above. If there never were imports from *R*, the RIA is just like a unilateral MFN liberalization, as before.

If we believe that imports are fundamentally differentiated across suppliers, the critical factors are the elasticities of substitution between *B* and *R* supplies, and between *B* and domestic supplies (net of changes in absorption). The height of the tariff affects the size but not the sign of the effects.

Imports—Data

Table 10.9 presents data on the shares of SARIA partners in members' total imports for available recent years derived from detailed UN trade data.[10] The basic data are disaggregated into products according to the Harmonized System (HS) classification at the 6-digit level (with a little over 5,000 headings). For each country, we have isolated every heading reporting positive imports for at least one of the years from 1999–2005, and calculated the intra-regional shares of imports for each year. (In any year for which there are no imports from anywhere, the share is undefined and hence omitted from the statistics reported.) The table reports shares averaged over all the included headings: the weighted average weights each heading's share by total imports for

[10] Thus, these data differ from those in Table 10.6, which stem from aggregate IMF data.

Table 10.9: Intra-regional Shares of Imports from Detailed Trade Data

Country and No. of headings		*Statistic*	*Share of Intra-SAS Imports (%)*						
			1999	*2000*	*2001*	*2002*	*2003*	*2004*	*2005*
Bangladesh		weighted		9.60	12.40	14.82	17.63	14.80	
	4757	unweighted		16.87	17.76	21.26	20.97	22.02	
		median		0.94	1.36	3.69	3.45	3.80	
		exports		*1.45*	*0.80*	*1.09*	*1.33*	*1.99*	
India		weighted	0.80	0.92	1.11	0.83	0.86	0.86	0.91
	4837	unweighted	3.60	4.25	4.45	4.01	5.06	4.64	4.20
		median	0.00	0.00	0.00	0.00	0.00	0.00	0.00
		exports	*3.80*	*4.33*	*4.62*	*5.17*	*6.50*	*5.39*	*5.25*
Maldives		weighted	20.94	23.01	24.00	26.23	24.21	21.24	17.36
	2959	unweighted	14.61	15.24	14.57	15.56	15.49	14.62	21.45
		median	0.00	0.66	0.00	0.58	1.98	1.47	6.23
		exports	*19.57*	*18.13*	*19.67*	*15.49*	*13.89*	*10.45*	*12.97*
Nepal		weighted	47.81	37.76			53.60		
	4456	unweighted	52.64	2.90			53.66		
		median	54.46	0.00			59.37		
		exports	*39.22*	*45.18*			*53.85*		

(contd ...)

Table 10.9 (contd ...)

Country and No. of headings		*Statistic*	*Share of Intra-SAS Imports (%)*						
			1999	*2000*	*2001*	*2002*	*2003*	*2004*	*2005*
Pakistan		weighted					3.08	3.06	2.84
	4437	unweighted					2.73	2.79	3.57
		median					0.00	0.00	0.00
		exports					*3.11*	*3.71*	*4.56*
Sri Lanka		weighted	11.73		13.20	15.48	18.05	18.98	19.08
	4797	unweighted	13.66		14.14	15.73	15.87	16.73	18.98
		median	1.23		1.54	2.40	2.68	3.95	5.06
		exports	*2.83*		*3.37*	*5.42*	*7.06*	*9.09*	*10.43*

Source: WITS (HS-6-digit data).
Note: Data for Bhutan are missing.

that heading (and thus equals the sum of imports from the region as a share of the sum of all imports—equivalent to the data in Table 10.6); the unweighted shares treat all headings equally (and so report the expected share for a heading chosen at random); and the median reports the share for which half the reported shares are larger and half smaller.[11] The complete distributions of shares are given in Figure 10.5. Finally, we report in italics in Table 10.9 the corresponding weighted average for exports.

For Bangladesh in 2004, the expected intra-South Asian share of imports in a typical HS-6 heading was 22 per cent, and the shares of half the headings exceeded 3.8 per cent. Figure 10.5 shows that of the 4,757 headings with positive imports in 2004, 1,184 had no intra-regional trade, while 233 had shares exceeding 99 per cent, and 790 had shares exceeding one-half. In these latter cases, tariff revenue losses could be very significant as partners are exempted from tariffs (it depends on the tariff level and the overall value of trade). In fact, for Bangladesh, the headings with larger shares are typically those with lower total imports, as indicated by the weighted share (that is, share in value) being only 15 per cent rather than 22 per cent. Nonetheless, if one compares the 15 per cent on imports with the 2 per cent intrashare of exports, it is clear that Bangladeshi producers are likely to receive a smaller inward transfer from the tariff exemptions they receive on their exports to partners than the government makes as an outward transfer on the exemptions it grants. And the calculation is even less favourable when one recalls that total imports exceed total exports, so that intra-regional imports at US$ 1,683 million are over ten times greater than intra-regional exports, at US$ 165 million.

Among the other countries, the smaller ones are typically more dependent on intra-regional trade, and where we can trust the data (the Nepalese data seem very unreliable), show excesses of imports over exports. Only for the two largest economies are intra-regional shares of the same magnitude as South Asia's share of world trade, and the share of exports larger than that of imports. Even for Nepal, given that exports to India currently receive full exemptions, whereas imports from India do not, the reallocation of tariff revenue will be unfavourable relative to the status quo. All this suggests that the reallocation of tariff revenues from governments to businesses as a result of a SARIA is likely to harm the smaller South Asian economies.

[11] Readers should be aware of the noisiness of trade data recorded at this level.

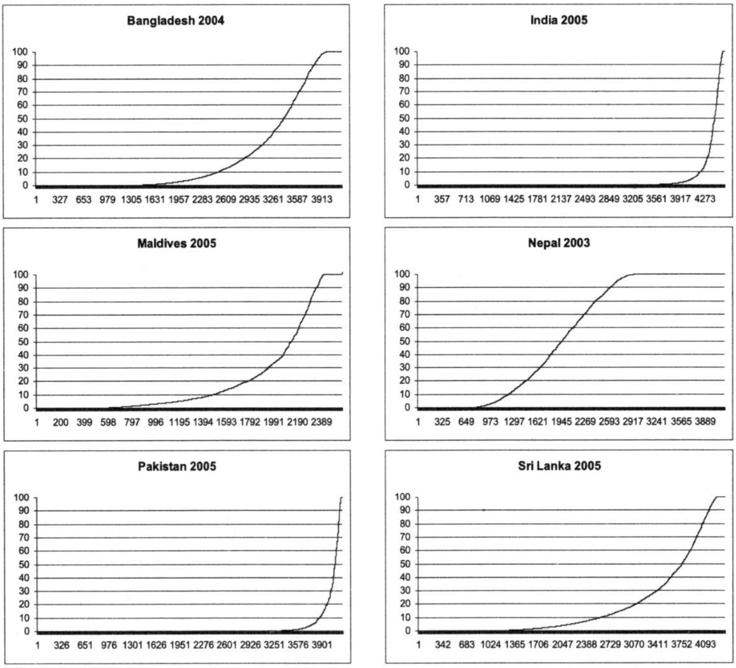

Figure 10.5: The Distribution of Intra-regional Import Shares across HS 6-Digit Heading

Note: HS-6 contains just over five thousand trade headings. Those for which no trade with any country is recorded is excluded from these figures.

Table 10.9 can indicate only presumptions and broad orders of magnitude. A full analysis of the revenue story would need to relate imports by partner at the 6-digit or higher level of the HS to the tariffs actually faced, allowing for any existing preferences for partners, for example, via the India–Sri Lanka FTA.

One interesting feature of the India–Sri Lanka FTA identified by Baysan et al. (2006) is that the resulting increase in trade was mostly in products that previously they had hardly traded with each other. As we noted in Section 2, this was probably because many of the products for which significant trade increases could be anticipated were subject to restrictive exceptions to the liberalization. The products not previously exported from Sri Lanka to India expanded to 37 per cent of total imports over two years, and 83 per cent by 2005 (five years)![12] On the reverse flow, products not previously exported by India increased to 5.8 per cent of the total by 2002, and 7.3 per cent by 2005, while the products comprising the 10 per cent of exports in headings with the smallest positive pre-ISLFTA (India–Sri Lanka Free Trade Agreement) shares of exports to Sri Lanka expanded from 10 per cent to 39.3 per cent by 2002, and to 46.5 per cent by 2005.

However, the simple statistics cited by Baysan et al. do not tell the whole story. Of the headings for which Sri Lankan exports to India were zero in 1999, over 75 per cent of the increase in trade by 2005 (that is, 75 per cent of the 83 per cent) is accounted for by just nine headings. Figure 10.6 illustrates these (as d(SL), they are the only ones for which Sri Lanka's exports increase by US$ 10 million or more), along with total imports in 1999 (M, 1999) and the increase in imports from the rest of the world over 1999–2005, d(RoW). Two of these nine products are edible fats and oils, and five are non-ferrous metals, which clearly raises the possibility of very specific circumstances lying behind the trade increases. In five of the headings, the increases from Sri Lanka clearly outweigh initial trade, and the increases from other countries, which seems consistent with trade creation as very restrictive regimes were breached by the ISLFTA. In one, there appears to be a substitution of Sri Lankan for other countries' exports (wires and bars, copper, unwrought), which shows evidence of diversion, while in the remaining three, RoW exports increase by more than Sri Lankan exports, so that while there may well be some trade diversion (that is, the Sri Lankan share of the increase being larger than warranted), it is not massive. Overall, among these nine commodities, slightly over US$ 80 million of the US$ 368 million of new Sri Lankan exports may be diversionary trade.

Extending the analysis to the 10 initially untraded products with the next largest increases in Sri Lankan exports to India (increases exceeding US$ 3 million) does not change the story much. Non-ferrous metals and electrical parts predominate, and there is only a little evidence of trade diversion.

It is important to remember that trade creation and diversion are

[12] Our data differ very slightly from Baysan et al.'s (2006) because the UN trade statistics have been updated. In particular, the products Baysan identified as accounting for 10 per cent of exports with the smallest flows in 1999 actually account for 10.49 per cent in our data.

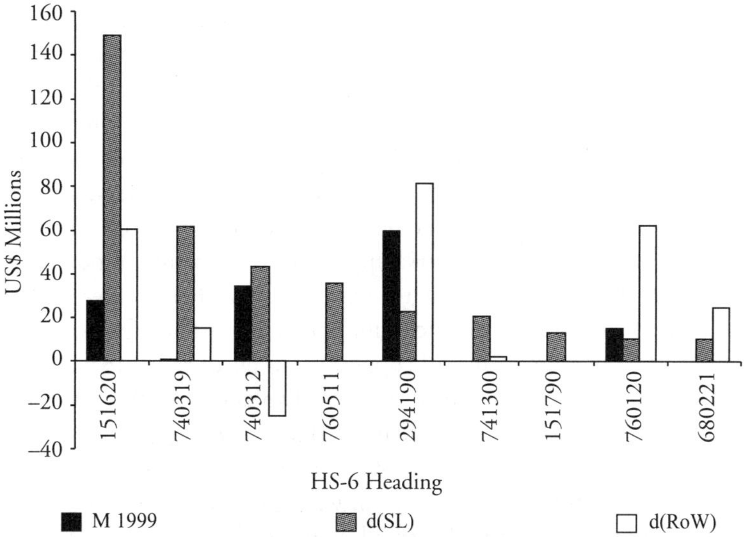

Figure 10.6: India Imports 1999–2005: Headings with Largest Increase from Zero for Sri Lanka

Source: Author's calculations, based on WITS data.

Notes: HS-6 Product description

151620	Vegetable fats and oils and their fractions
740319	Refined copper products, unwrought, nes
740312	Refined copper wire bars, unwrought
760511	Wire aluminium, not alloyed with a maximum cross-sectional dimension exceeds 7 mm
294190	Antibiotics nes, in bulk
741300	Stranded wire, cables, plaited bands and the like, of copper, not electrically insulated.
151790	Other edible mixed/prep. Animal/vegetable fats and oils and their fractions
760120	Aluminium alloys, unwrought
680221	Other monumental or building stone and articles nes, cut or sawn, with a flat/even surface, marble/travertine/alabaster

measured here from the status quo ante, not the potential position under free trade. Thus, for example, the nearly US$ 150 million worth of imports of vegetable fats and oils from Sri Lanka dominated imports in 1999 when total imports amounted to only US$ 28 million, and is quite consistent with there being trade creation; however, this does not mean that India is not incurring excess costs by importing from Sri

Lanka rather than from the rest of the world. The significance of this is heightened by observing first that in none of the 'top nine' commodities and only one of the 'next 10' does Sri Lanka export significantly to the rest of the world, and second that Sri Lanka's margin of preference in India exceeds 13 per cent for all these products. Moreover, only for two commodities is there evidence of significant increases in Sri Lankan imports from the rest of the world, which could indicate trade deflection. Thus, Sri Lanka appears to be devoting resources to producing these goods in which it has only an artificial rather than a real comparative advantage, including importing inputs (for example, waste and scrap aluminum and copper) to support production.[13]

The increases in Indian exports to Sri Lanka over 1999–2005 are also concentrated, but in a different fashion. Among products with zero trade in 1999, 31 per cent of the increase is due to petroleum (HS 270900) and 19 per cent to unwrought aluminum (760110), while among those with the smallest positive shares in 1999, 50 per cent of the subsequent increase is due to refined petroleum (271000), followed by maize (100590) with 6 per cent. Non-ferrous metals and vegetable oils also figure in both lists, but so do plenty of other products, and beyond the first couple, the concentration is not great. There are certainly signs of trade diversion even relative to 1999—falling imports from the rest of the world and rising imports from India—including, for example, headings in foodstuffs, textiles, and electrical equipment. However, one needs more structure than I have here to analyse the situation completely. By enlarging the set of preferred partners, a SARIA might reduce such diversion, but in fact, given the products concerned and Sri Lanka's geographical location, such efforts may not be strong.

The use of FTAs to foster export diversification—an objective for many developing countries—seems *prima facie* attractive. However, the more detailed analysis here suggests that it is not as strong an effect as previously suggested for the ISLFTA, and that it poses dangers of trade diversion. Whether trade increases within a SARIA are similarly restricted to initially small items will depend on the negative lists, exceptions, quotas, and Rules of Origin (ROOs) incorporated in

[13] One note of caution: The data in this paragraph are based on Sri Lankan data rather than Indian, as was true of the previous paragraphs, and the two sources do not entirely agree on Sri Lankan–Indian trade.

the SARIA. If these are not overly restrictive, 'traditional' flows will probably expand while 'non-traditional' ones may fail to do so. Lest this appear an obvious cause for jubilation, however, recall that trade diversion is perfectly possible in traditional sectors as well, and that where there is existing trade, revenue effects will be important for the distribution of the benefits.

Exports

The analysis of exports for a small country entering an RIA is even more straightforward than that for imports. Assuming it to be too small to influence the prices it receives on either *B's* or *R's* markets, *A's* aim is to receive the highest possible price net of trading costs. Suppose that *B* initially imposed a tax of t' on *A's* exports. When this is removed, *A's* producers receive t' per unit more on their initial sales to *B*. In addition, they may either switch sales from *R* to *B*, or produce more for sale in *B*. In the first case, the price they receive increases from P_R to $P_B + t'$, where P_R and P_B were the prices they initially received on sales to *R* and *B* (before tariffs) and where, after the RIA, because they are too small to affect *B's* internal price, they now receive the entire amount of the tax they have been forgiven. In the second case, assuming that *A* had an increasing marginal cost curve and that total sales increased, some of the extra revenue received per unit (t') would be dissipated in increased costs, production increasing until marginal costs had increased from P_B to $P_B + t'$. (If $P_R > P_B + t'$, there would be no sales to *B*, and the RIA would be irrelevant; and if *B* were open to trade with *R*, $P_B = P_R$ except to the extent that transactions costs differed on the two sales flows.)

The simple model in this case suggests that the benefits of the RIAs are positively related to the height of *B's* tariff and the extent of existing sales to *B*, the extent to which $P_B + t'$ exceeds P_R (that is, the higher prices are in *B* anyway), and the elasticity of supply of the product.

If we move to differentiated products, the basic story on exports remains the same, but *A* may well export to both *B* and *R* and the pass-through of t' to *A's* producers would be attenuated.

From the export perspective, regional trade looks rather attractive to South Asian countries because its tariffs are relatively high and, at least in some cases, existing trade flows are quite thick (see Table 10.9). The poverty of South Asia relative to much of the rest of the world is, of course, a disadvantage, but the analysis above ignores it by assuming that there is demand enough for *A*'s product at a fixed local price in *B*. It is important to recall, however, that the transfers of tariff revenue from governments in one partner to firms in another are just transfers. The extra costs (relative to world levels) entailed in producing extra goods for partner markets are deadweight losses. That is, the transfers affect only the distribution of benefits around the RIA, but the production losses impose costs on the RIA as a whole relative to optimal policies.

One important wrinkle should be noted at this point. If *A*'s firms can suddenly earn a lot more from exporting to *B*, they will presumably divert sales from *A* itself. Indeed, in the limit the domestic price in *A* could rise to $P_B + t'$, which might impose high costs on consumers. Here the distinction between a free trade area (FTA) and a customs union (CU) becomes important. The latter entails a common external tariff, so that if *B* levied t' on its imports, A would have to do the same, and the internal price would indeed equal $P_B + t'$ (except perhaps for transactions costs). An FTA, on the other hand, allows each partner to levy its own external tariff (with rules of origin to prevent goods entering the member with the lowest tariff and then transshipping to the others from there). In that case, *A*'s optimal policy would be to export all its output to *B* for $P_B + t'$ and meet its own needs from *R* at P_R, although this may not be optimal for the RIA (*A* and *B* together).

General Equilibrium

Putting the export and import sides together requires, in principle, considering all these factors in all these markets, allowing for interactions between them, and calculating the net effects. For *ex ante* analyses of prospective policies, this is usually achieved via computable general equilibrium (CGE) modeling. This is almost always based on the differentiated products assumption, which, I have argued (in Schiff and Winters 2003), tends to paint a rather favourable picture. Nonetheless, the most recent CGE study of South Asian integration that I know of, by Bandara and Yu (2003), suggests losses for one country and only very small gains for the rest—at most one-fifth of a per cent of GDP.[14]

At first sight, it is surprising that Bandara and Yu's analysis

[14] The study omits Bhutan and the Maldives, however.

has India gaining most and a small country losing. After all, one expects the predominant economy to feel little effects on its prices and the peripheral ones to feel much. The result appears to derive from India's higher tariffs (the study uses a 1990 base) and the fact that the intra-regional share of its exports is the second highest in the region, while the intra-regional share of its imports is by far the lowest. That is, the country has a larger interest in markets where it will gain than in those (imports) where it will lose. In addition, India's high tariff and resulting low efficiency mean that it imposes larger losses on the others via trade diversion. Other distortions also figure in the explanation, with the increase in ostensibly subsidized exports imposing costs on Sri Lanka. Clearly, given the changes in trade policy that have occurred since 1990, reworking this exercise could dramatically change the results.

Economies of Scale

The analysis so far has assumed constant returns to scale and perfect competition. A major theme of the RIA literature emanating from Europe over the last two decades has been to relax these assumptions. The initial attempts to incorporate economies of scale into integration theory by Corden (1972), were not very persuasive, but when we combine *internal* economies of scale with the monopoly pricing power they confer on firms, the model becomes much more fruitful. Essentially, fixed costs for firms, plus segmented markets, restrict the number of firms operating in a market, and hence curtail sales, raise prices, and create rents. Opening up to trade, even just regionally, might dramatically change market structure by permitting more firms to compete in any market. Especially for small economies, which in the restricted initial position have few firms, this could generate large gains, especially if we appeal to competition to eliminate production inefficiencies as well as allocative ones (for example, eliminating x-inefficiency or stimulating innovation).

This attractive story was the backbone of the analysis of the European Single Market Programme (SMP) starting with Smith and Venables (1986) and continuing through Gasiorek, Smith, and Venables (1992), and Haaland and Norman (1992). These papers did indeed forecast major gains to small entrants to an RIA (European Free Trade Association [EFTA]) countries in the latter case). However, the assumptions necessary to generate their results, especially for aggregates as opposed to specific sectors, were so heroic as to leave a good deal of uncertainty about their applicability (Winters 1992). These include assumptions about the nature of competitive game (for example, Cournot vs Bertrand models of oligopoly), the extent to which integration lowered trading costs, and whether the new RIA market was fully integrated over all members. In particular, it became clear that, even within Europe, transactions costs and residual differences in standards and tastes conspired to keep many markets fairly segmented even after the SMP was implemented. Extending these doubts to SARIA—especially those on the likely degree of market integration—should cause a good deal of caution in predicting the benefits that will emanate from economies of scale. On the other hand, given the dirigiste history of South Asian manufacturing, one suspects that if there were a genuine commitment to increase competition, it would generate considerable benefits.

Section 4: The Dynamic Case for Integration in South Asia

Much of the enthusiasm for RIAs has been grounded in so-called dynamic gains. Following European integration, it was observed that incomes per head in the smaller and poorer members converged towards those in the larger and richer. Some of the mechanisms involved may be relevant in South Asia, but not others. Among the latter, for example, it was frequently argued that joining an RIA was a way of acquiring credibility for economic reform programmes: maybe because, in the absence of continuing reforms, the sunk costs in adjusting the RIA would be wasted, or because RIA partners may offer an external agent of restraint. Fernandez and Portes (1998) and Schiff and Winters (2003) find some virtue in these arguments, but they do not seem very likely to apply in South Asia at present. So far, no country has invested heavily in reforms specifically for the RIA. Similarly, no member would effectively restrain India's policy discretion, none would welcome Indian pressure on its own policymaking, and it is not clear that India would seek to apply such pressure.

A related but long-run argument is that an RIA would help cement peace and security in the region, as is argued plausibly to have happened in Europe. In the long run, increased intra-regional trade would increase contacts, which in turn would increase trust and mutual understanding and help to promote peace. However, the parallel with Europe is weak. France and Germany had fought violently three times in a century, and were prepared to do almost anything to avoid doing so again. They tried several things before settling on the European Economic Community (EEC) (for example, a defence community and political community), so that the latter was almost the last remaining option. The resulting commitment to the EEC made it feasible politically to undertake adjustment and surrender sovereignty sufficiently to make European integration deep and dynamic. This, in turn, fed back into support for the European ideal as a means to secure peace. Less strongly bound RIAs may dissolve—sometimes in violence—with rivalries exacerbated rather than assuaged by increased contacts. For example, the American Civil War was arguably as much about tariff policy as about slavery, while the break-up of East and West Pakistan and the East African Common Market were substantially caused by income divergence within groups that were expected to induce convergence (see World Bank 2000).[15]

Among the more plausible dynamic elements in South Asia are technology transfer, accumulation, and agglomeration. Technology transfer has generally been seen as a North-North or North-South phenomenon, but it is certainly plausible that innovations from one part of South Asia—quite possibly in terms of the adaptation and the application of existing knowledge, rather than wholly new techniques—will spread elsewhere in the region. And if markets become more open, and especially if labour movement is permitted, an RIA could help that process. The current dynamism of Indian entrepreneurs seems a potential boon to the rest of South Asia, and since India is the regional market of most interest, that will increase the likelihood of transfer.

Accumulation

Closely related is capital accumulation. If creating an RIA increases rates of return to capital investment, capital stocks will increase and output per worker will rise. Under a purely factor endowment view of trade, however, it is far from clear that South Asian integration would increase such rates of return, although if one believes that tradables are more capital intensive than non-tradables and receive a relatively

[15] Schiff and Winters (1998) analyse the security case for RIAs in more detail.

greater impetus from integration, then it is possible. And this could be supplemented by induced improvements in TFP (see above), in financial integration (which reduces investment costs), and possibly reductions in barriers to trade in capital goods. All told, then, an RIA could increase capital accumulation above what would happen in its absence, although such effects mainly serve to magnify other beneficial effects rather than substitute for them if they are missing. That is, accumulation effects seem unlikely to be strong if the RIA does not generate other benefits.

A small but important element of investment is FDI, and, as Lane and Schmukler (2007) show, it is much smaller in India than one might expect (see Table 10.10). Among South Asian economies, only two have FDI inflows exceeding 1 per cent of GDP, compared with an average of 1.4 per cent for low-income countries (including South Asia) and 2.8 per cent for lower-middle-income countries. Given South Asia's modest share of world GDP, this translates into very small absolute flows of FDI.

There is circumstantial evidence that some RIAs have been followed by booms in FDI. Ethier (1998) argues that this is, indeed, the objective of many North–South arrangements and I would speculate that his arguments could also apply in asymmetric South-South arrangements such as SARIA. One might expect FDI to increase in

TABLE 10.10: FDI Flows (2000–4 Average)

		As % of total for	
	As % of GDP	*Low income*	*World*
Bangladesh	0.44	1.7	0.0
Bhutan	0.08	0.0	0.0
India	0.91	36.7	0.6
Maldives	1.95	0.1	0.0
Nepal	0.04	0.0	0.0
Pakistan	0.78	4.5	0.1
Sri Lanka	1.15	1.5	0.0
South Asia	0.86	44.5	0.8
Low Income	1.39		1.8
Lower-middle	2.84		12.0

Source: WDI online 29/12/06.

India anyway as regulation relaxes—Lane and Schmukler (2007)—so in a sense the question is whether an RIA would allow the smaller partners to pick up some of that. An RIA is unlikely to render South Asian countries easier locations for serving third markets—indeed, possibly the opposite if it results in inward-looking policies and policy-attention—so this question in turn becomes one of serving the large and growing Indian market.[16] This seems possible but will depend on SARIA delivering genuine improvements in market access. Again, FDI effects are icing on the cake, not the cake itself: they will tend to enlarge the standard trade effects of an RIA rather than create new ones. This applies equally to positive and negative impacts, as, for example, we saw in Mercusor with FDI into the auto industry exacerbating the costs of protection and trade diversion in that sector. In addition, of course, given the modest size of GDP and current inflows it seems unlikely that a SARIA would have a dramatic effect on global investment flows.

New Economic Geography

One of the intellectual products of the study of RIAs was the new economic geography in which Paul Krugman and Tony Venables sought to explore the question of whether European integration would be good for the peripheral regions (Krugman and Venables 1995). Combining (external) economies of scale and transportation (transactions) costs between regions, their insight was that with infinite transactions costs, firms would locate in both the centre and the periphery in order to serve both markets, and that with zero costs they would choose the periphery, with its lower production costs. But at intermediate values it may be that industry would agglomerate in the centre. This is because its higher factor and congestion costs may be offset by the benefits of being located in the major market and hence having to pay no trade costs on sales there, while being able to serve the minor one from there with only finite additional costs.

Figure 10.7, based on Venables (2006), offers an accessible view of this subject area, and summarizes the consequences of this sort of story in terms of income levels in two identical countries (regions). In this case, the benefits of agglomeration arise only from the need for

[16] If a SARIA had dramatic agglomeration effects—see later—it might increase competitiveness, but in truth this seems rather unlikely.

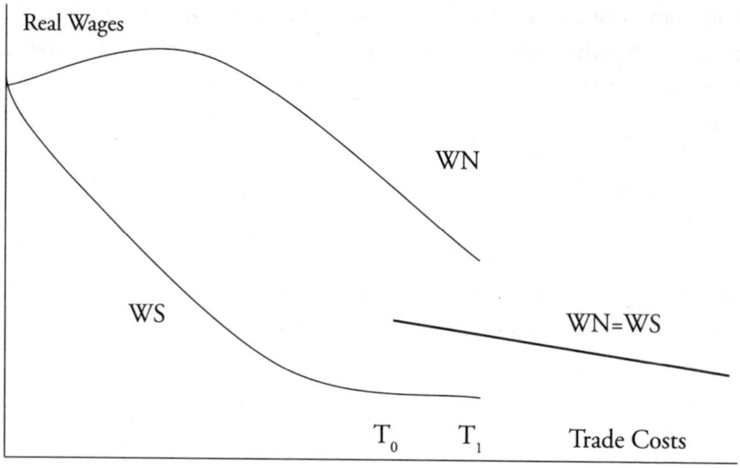

Figure 10.7: Geographical Divergence

Source: Venables (2006).

produced intermediate inputs, which require transportation which, in turn, is assumed to be higher across borders than within them. Starting at the far right, consider successive reductions in trade costs. At very high trade costs, industry locates in both countries to serve the local markets, and, because they are identical, the two countries support identical real wages (incomes). As trade costs fall toward $T_{1,}$ incomes can rise slightly because internal efficiency increases slightly. Looking now at the far left of the figure, at zero trade costs, costs become independent of location so far as trading is concerned and so arbitrage on factor costs will again divide industry equally between locations and result in equal real wages.

With trade costs between *0* and T_1, however, bifurcated equilibria are possible, with one country (*N*) maintaining a higher proportion of industry which, because of economies of agglomeration, can afford to pay higher wages. There is still scope for some industry in the other country (*S*), which has lower costs and lower productivity, but it is essentially de-industrialized once trade costs fall below T_0. (Between T_0 and T_1, both sorts of equilibria are stable. Which one exists depends on history.)

In a world of falling transactions costs or trade liberalization, the question on policymakers' minds is 'how do we get to be *N* rather than *S*'. History and luck may matter in establishing a small advantage in industrialization: a few firms choose N and agglomeration economies cause most of the rest to follow. The improved market access of an RIA might be one such bit of 'luck', as, for example, Hanson (1997) argued occurred for northern Mexico with the North American Free Trade Agreement (NAFTA), and for which Overman and Winters (2005) find some evidence for the Southeast of England following UK accession to the EEC in 1973.[17] An important implication of this model is that to the extent that one area flourishes through agglomeration, others will suffer as they lose economic mass—they may become poorer than they would have been in the absence of the RIA.[18] Puga and Venables (1997, 1998) demonstrate these possibilities clearly for various types of integration arrangements, showing that the ideal situation for a small (Southern) country is to have an RIA with a larger, richer, Northern partner, *while others do not.* If several Southern partners have such an RIA, the resulting hub and spoke pattern is rather disadvantageous for them, although good for the North, and the policy imperative becomes getting trade costs between themselves to create an area of integration covering both all of themselves and the North. For a SARIA, the question of a formal hub and spoke arrangement does not arise, but it is still desirable to avoid one growing up 'naturally'—because topography and infrastructure lead every partner to focus mainly on trade with India—or via regulation—such that rules of origin or standards or exceptions to the liberalization prevent integration among the smaller partners.

The geography model also sheds light on city formation and growth, so that particular cities become hot spots while other, less fortunate ones, languish. Part of this could reflect enlarged hinterlands for cities located near the borders within an RIA. For example, Kolkata may benefit from better trading conditions with Bangladesh. Venables (2006) argues, however, that cities can easily expand beyond optimum size.

Lall and Chakravorty (2005) offer evidence for these kinds of effects in the location of Indian industry. They show, first, that firms in locations

[17] In both cases, the shift in industry is plain. The difficulty is showing that the process had an agglomeration component on top of the obvious and direct benefits of locating close to a growing market.

[18] This rivalry is different from the implication of neoclassical constant returns to scale models in which one country's good fortune is shared with others via increased demand and terms-of-trade changes.

with diverse industrial bases—typically the larger agglomerations—have significant cost advantages relative to other firms. Diversity effects seem to be better identified than those of market access, own-industry concentration, and inter-industry linkages, although all three show some beneficial effects on costs. Second, they show that private firms do respond to these sorts of cost advantages in their location decisions, particularly favouring coastal areas and regions that have a history of strong (private sector) investment and whose neighbouring districts have strong current investment. As with all research on economic geography, it is difficult to isolate causation perfectly in these exercises, but the general tenor of the results is strongly toward the hypothesis that agglomeration and clustering effects matter in India.

Transactions Costs

Absolutely central to the new economic geography are transactions costs. These include transport costs, financial transaction costs such as payments and insurance, time delays, losses and damages, bribes and informal payments, re-engineering and redesign to meet different standards in different markets, etc. These costs absorb resources and profits directly, but they also increase uncertainty and segment markets and thus reduce competition. The latter effect is arguably the most important consequence and the most difficult to overcome.

India is notorious for the poor quality of its infrastructure, and there is evidence that this leads to internal market segmentation. Mattoo, Mishra, and Narain (2007) document the 'logistical tax' on Indian exports of horticulture, and the large variation in prices of apparently homogeneous goods over space. Thus, an important area of future study should be to consider such segmentation with a view to exploring its costs and ways of reducing it.[19] Economically, the best that a SARIA can do for the region is to be equivalent to adding a few extra states to the Indian economy. If domestic markets are already highly segmented, the effect is likely to be quite muted. Nonetheless, there is evidence that the transactions costs on South Asian's intra-regional trade are egregiously high, so there is scope for reducing them and increasing international competition, even without tackling internal inefficiencies.

[19] Even the United States, the most integrated continental economy, has significant geographical segmentation reflected in price dispersion (for example, Engel and Rogers [1996, 2001]).

One route that has been fairly carefully studied is Indian exports to Bangladesh (see Das and Pohit 2006, World Bank 2006). These authors studied consignments flowing from Kolkata, through the Indian customs post at Petrapole to its Bangladeshi twin, Benapole, where they are unloaded and their truck driven back to the Indian soil. The total distance is about 100 km, excluding all distances beyond the border into Bangladesh. The study documents the poor infrastructure, unhelpful regulation, inefficiency and corruption of the journey, and attempts to put values on it in terms of both time and money (Table 10.11).

The column 'ideal' in Table 10.11 reflects local ideas of what might be reasonable, and because it is provided by traders is liable to underestimation; however, even allowing for this, the overall cost of over 12 per cent of the *average* consignment value is clearly large. Section (A) of the table shows that most of the excess time (and hence the transport/customs figure in section (B)) arises from inefficient customs formalities and unnecessary unloading in Bangladesh.[20] In addition, the authors note the universality of having to pay 'speed money' to avoid even longer delays. The financing cost is also notable for such a simple and essentially localized trade.

TABLE 10.11: Indian Exports to Bangladesh via Kolkata and Benapole

(A) Cumulative Time (hours)	*Actual*	*'Ideal'*
Loading/unloading/returning empty	17.80	5.90
Transportation	3.20	2.40
Parking/customs/crossing on export	7.80	21.30
(B) Costs (as % of average shipment value)		
Transport/customs	7.44	1.71
Speed money	2.50	0
Time to receipt of payment	2.15	0.22

Sources: World Bank (2006); and Das and Pohit (2006).

[20] The value under transport/customs reflects the opportunity cost of the trucks and drivers for the times reported.

The estimates in Table 10.11 are certainly subject to wide margins of error, but they are not obviously biased. Hence, individual consignments may face far larger delays or costs—a source of serious risk for traders, which in itself would reduce trade. Moreover, the data refer to trade in only one direction. Since trade is two way and the World Bank (2006) suggests at least as many inefficiencies with Bangladesh's exports to India, we could imagine average relative price wedges of nearly 25 per cent between Indian and Bangladeshi prices before trade arose to arbitrage them away.[21] In these circumstances, one might wonder how effective removing trade policy barriers would be.

Taneja, Sarvananthan, and Pohit (2003) document the same sort of issues for trade between India and Sri Lanka, including delays in receiving export licenses even before goods start to move. India and Pakistan do not permit goods trade by land, and so costs are very high indeed, relying on informal connections and circuitous routes.

Deep Integration

Deep integration is, loosely speaking, conscious or positive integration designed to break down barriers between markets in order to foster competition. As well as transportation and trading costs, deep integration can occur in areas such as product standards, so products designed for one member of an RIA are usable and saleable in another, both de jure and de facto, that is, without excess testing, registration, etc. It might also reside in process standards and regulatory harmonization so firms within an RIA compete on a level playing field. This is likely to be particularly important for services, where barriers to trade are more often regulatory than anything else.

Two related but different questions arise with deep integration: what standards to adopt and with whom to integrate. Within an RIA, it seems sensible to aspire to common standards, and indeed, mutually acceptable standards are necessary if one is to achieve a truly integrated market. But if the RIA is with a minor trading partner, and if the minor partner's standards are inappropriate or perhaps significantly different from those of a major market, it might not

[21] Imagine India exports X and imports M from Bangladesh. If Indian prices were PX and PM , respectively, local prices in Bangladesh would be PX (1 + 0.121) and PM/(1 + 0.121), respectively.

make sense to integrate in this way.[22] Certainly such integration is costly to achieve and politically very sensitive.

There is also a question of cost in designing and enforcing standards. Briguglio et al. (2006) argue that one of the economies that small countries can make is to combine in standard setting, or delegate it to a larger entity. Korea, for example, decided early in its development to base all its industrial standards on Germany's, which had the effects of both facilitating access to other markets (which accepted German standards), and avoiding the skilled-labour costs (and potential interest-group struggles) of designing its own. Similarly, if one considers the very small European landlocked states, for example, Luxembourg, Liechtenstein, and Andorra, they appear to have overcome the costs of smallness by integrating seamlessly with their larger neighbours.

The actual and political cost of achieving meaningful deep integration should not be underestimated, and indeed very few RIAs have attempted it seriously. The United States tends to require its partners to conform to its own standards and procedures, but has still found progress very slow—witness, for example, the ongoing disputes over standards for Mexican-registered trucks entering the United States under NAFTA.

In Europe, the SMP was mainly about deep integration. It was bolstered by a new streamlined approach to defining standards; a dedicated bureaucracy (within the European Commission); political commitment, including the constitutional innovation of allowing single-market measures to be determined by qualified majority voting in the European Council rather than unanimity; and by the full force of the European Court of Justice, which can overrule European Union member governments.[23] And yet European Commission staff still write, 'It is somewhat disappointing that fifteen years after the so-called "completion of the Single Market" multiple barriers continue to hinder cross-border activities within the EU' (Ilkovitz et al. 2007).

[22] Some standards are easy to vary according to the market one is selling in, and in those cases, firms can easily meet several sets of standards, such as for the plug fitted to an appliance, but others are impossible to vary, such as production process requirements or rules of origin specifying the origins of inputs.

[23] See Winters (1997) for a brief account of the constitutional components of European integration, and Molle (2006) for a fuller account.

The political and administrative challenges of achieving deep integration in South Asia are formidable. True, a SARIA is less symmetric than Europe, and so India might be able to shepherd the process along more effectively than the core European countries could, but the political tensions are greater, and no significant bureaucracy or court structure is planned for SARIA. Thus, it is not realistic to expect great progress on deep integration per se. Rather, South Asian governments should better focus on 'negative' integration—removing policy and physical barriers to regional trade than on harmonization, etc.

SECTION 5: A CONCLUSION

The case for increasing integration among the South Asian states is very strong. There are almost certainly major efficiencies to be reaped via increased trade and competition. But this is not the same as saying that increasing regional integration should become a focus of policy-making effort. Rather, focus should be on increasing international integration in general and allow this to foster 'normal' amounts of regional integration.

The regional agenda clearly should include the removal of additional barriers to regional trade, such as the prohibitions on Indo-Pakistani trade and the border bottlenecks on Indian–Bangladeshi trade. Services reforms could foster trade by allowing trucks to operate on both sides of a border, reducing the need for transshipment. Even these simple things would greatly increase competition, and, almost certainly, efficiency.

It seems impossible to envisage the creation of a customs union which (*à la* Europe) would allow the elimination of most border inspection activities, and highly improbable that deep integration would proceed far enough to allow really seamless integration of specific markets. Thus, at least for the foreseeable future, goods and people are likely to be stopped on most international borders within the region. Given this, the case for abolishing tariffs at these borders is at best a second-best one. There may be some trade creation, and there will almost certainly be some trade diversion. Moreover, given the obvious tendencies for South Asian policymakers to try to manage the liberalization process, and the understandable tendency for management to favour diversion over creation (Grossman and Helpman 1995, Schiff and Winters 2003), liberalization of a traditional South Asian type seems likely to yield only minor net benefits, or worse. Thus, unless we can jump to simple, transparent, rules-based liberalizations with no exceptions (or perhaps a handful of exceptions), the suspicion probably remains that effort would be better directed at MFN liberalizations. For sure, these would be managed too, but India has shown progress is possible, and at least with MFN tariff and NTB cuts, one avoids the temptations of trade diversion.

Suppose we achieved strong intra-regional tariff liberalization. What would this imply for production? There clearly would be changes in the sourcing of purchases, but there is doubt that these would be large enough to have major effects on economic geography. Some agglomeration of export activity in the smaller partners around the Indian border might occur, but the absence of genuinely deep integration and high *internal* costs of transactions would limit these. For every country other than the two landlocked ones, the rest of the world is likely to remain a more important market than the region, and thus should be the major focus of policy attention.

Among the smaller countries, Bhutan has already achieved a reasonable degree of integration with India, its predominant neighbour, while the Maldives is separated from the mainland and is fairly reliant on the rest of the world. Neither has much to gain directly from further regional integration. Nepal would probably benefit from a genuine increase in competition. Much of this would be with India, and so could be handled unilaterally or under the cooperation agreement, but a SARIA may provide an alternative route. Sri Lanka could benefit from an increase in access to regional markets, and so may gain somewhat from a far-reaching integration arrangement. Probably the most important effect, however, would be indirect. All of South Asia, but particularly Nepal and Bhutan, would gain from greater efficiency in India, on which they, to different degrees, are dependent. Whether a SARIA is the best route to this goal, however, is debatable. Many would argue that a multilateral and unilateral trade policy would be a better one.

References

Alesina, A. and E. Spolaore. 2003. *The Size of Nations.* MIT Press.

Bandara, J.S. and W. Yu. 2003. 'How Desirable is the South Asian Free Trade

Area? A Quantitative Economic Assessment', *The World Economy*, 26(9): 1293–323.

Baysan, T., A. Panagariya, and N. Pitigala. 2006. 'Preferential Trading in South Asia', Policy Research Working Paper No. 3813, World Bank, Washington, D.C.

Briguglio, L., B. Persaud, and R. Stern. 2006. 'Toward an Outward-Oriented Development Strategy for Small States: Issues, Opportunities, and Resilience Building', A Review of the Small States Agenda Proposed in the Commonwealth/World Bank Joint Task Force Report of April 2000.

Corden, M. 1972. 'Economies of Scale and Customs Union Theory', *The Journal of Political Economy*, 80(3): 465–75.

Das, Samantak and Sanjib Pohit. 2006. 'Quantifying Transport, Regulatory and Other Costs of Indian Overland Exports to Bangladesh', *The World Economy*, 29(9): 1227–42.

Engel, C. and J. H. Rogers. 1996. 'How Wide is the Border?' *American Economic Review*, 86(5): 1112–25.

———. 2001. 'Deviations from Purchasing Power Parity: Causes and Welfare Costs', *Journal of International Economics*, 55(1): 29–57.

Ethier, W.J. 1998. 'The New Regionalism', *The Economic Journal*, 108(449): 1149–61.

Fernández, R. and J. Portes. 1998. 'Returns to Regionalism: Analysis of Nontraditional Gains from Regional Trade', *World Bank Economic Review*, 12(2): 197–220.

Gasiorek, M., A. Smith, and A.J. Venables. 1992. 'Trade and Welfare-A General Equilibrium Model', in L.A. Winters (ed.), *Trade Flows and Trade Policy after 1992*, pp. 35–61. Cambridge University Press.

Grossman, G.M. and E. Helpman. 1995. 'The Politics of Free-Trade Agreements', *American Economic Review*, 85(4): 667–90.

Haaland, J.I. and V. Norman. 1992. 'Global Production Effects of European Integration', in L.A. Winters (ed.), *Trade Flows and Trade Policy after 1992*. Cambridge University Press.

Hanson, G. H. 1997. 'Increasing Returns, Trade and the Regional Structure of Wages', *Economic Journal*, 107(440): 113–33.

Ilkovitz, F., A. Dierx, V. Kovacs, and N. Sousa. 2007. 'Steps Towards a Deeper Economic Integration: The Internal Market in the 21st Century. A Contribution to the Single Market Review', Economic Papers No. 271. European Economy, European Commission, Directorate-General for Economic and Financial Affairs.

Kee, H.L., M. Olarreaga, and A. Nicita. 'Estimating Trade Restrictiveness Indices', Policy Research Working Paper, No. 3840, World Bank.

Krugman, P. and A. J. Venables. 1995. 'Globalization and the Inequality of Nations', *The Quarterly Journal of Economics*, 110(4): 857–80.

Lall, S. and S. Chakravorty. 2005. 'Industrial Location and Spatial Inequality: Theory and Evidence from India', *Review Of Development Economics*, 9(1) (Special Issue): 47–68.

Lane, P.R. and S. Schmukler. 2007. 'International Financial Integration of China and India', in L. A. Winters and S. Yusuf (eds), *Dancing with Giants: China, India and the Global Economy*. Washington, D.C.: World Bank, and Singapore: The Institute of Policy Studies.

Mattoo, A., D. Mishra, and A. Narain. 2007. *From Competition at Home to Competing Abroad: A Case Study of India's Horticulture*. Oxford University Press.

Molle, W. 2006. *The Economics of European Integration: Theory, Practice, Policy*, 5th edn. Aldershot, England; Burlington, VT: Ashgate.

Mukherji, I.N. 2000. 'Charting a Free Trade Area in South Asia: Instruments and Modalities', Paper presented to the Second Conference of the South Asia Network of Economic Research Institute (SANEI), Kathmandu, 28–29 August.

Overman, H.G. and L. A. Winters. 2005. 'The Port Geography of UK International Trade', *Environment and Planning Series A*, 37: 1751–68.

Panagariya, A. 2003. 'South Asia: Does Preferential Trade Liberalisation Make Sense?' *World Economy*, 26(9): 1279–91.

Parsons, C., R. Skeldon, T. Walmsley, and L. A. Winters. 2007. 'Quantifying International Migration: A Database of Bilateral Migrant Stocks', Policy Research Working Paper 4165, World Bank, Washington, D.C.

Puga, D. and A. J. Venables. 1997. 'Preferential Trading Arrangements and Industrial Location', *Journal of International Economics*, 43(3–4): 347–68.

———. 1998. 'Trading Arrangements and Industrial Development', *World Bank Economic Review*, 12(2): 221–49.

Schiff, M. and L. A. Winters. 1998. 'Regional Integration as Diplomacy', *World Bank Economic Review*, 12: 271–95, reprinted in H. Singer, N. Hatti, and R. Tandon (eds), *Regional Trading Arrangements*, vol. 22 of New World Order Series. B.R. Publishing: Delhi.

———. 2003. *Regional Integration and Development*. World Bank and Oxford University Press.

Smith, A. and A.J. Venables. 1986. ' Trade and Industrial Policy under Imperfect Competition', *Economic Policy*, No. 3, pp. 621–60.

Taneja, N., M. Sarvananthan, and S. Pohit. 2003. 'India–Sri Lanka Trade: Transacting Environments in Formal and Informal Trading', *Economic and Political Weekly*.

Venables, A. J. and A. Smith. 1986. 'Trade and Industrial Policy under Imperfect Competition', *Economic Policy*, 1(3): 621–72.

Venables, A. J. 2006. 'Shifts in Economic Geography and Their Causes', Paper presented at the Jackson Hole Symposium on The New Economic Geography: Effects and Policy Implications, A Symposium Sponsored by The Federal Reserve Bank of Kansas City, 24–26 August.

Viner, J. 1950. *The Customs Union Issue*. New York: Carnegie Endowment for International Peace.

Walmsley, T. and L. A.Winters. 2005. 'Relaxing the Restrictions on the Temporary Movement of Natural Persons: A Simulation Analysis', *Journal of Economic Integration*, 20(4): 688–726.

Winters, L. A. 1992. 'The Policy and Welfare Implications of the International Trade Consequences of "1992"', *American Economic Review Papers and Proceedings*, 82: 104–8.

———. 1997. 'What Can European Experience Teach Developing Countries about Integration?' *World Economy*, 20(7): 889–912.

Winters, L. A. and P. M. G. Martins. 2004. 'When Comparative Advantage is not Enough: Business Costs in Small Remote Economies', *World Trade Review*, 3(3): 347–83.

———. 2005. 'Beautiful but Costly: Business Costs in Small Remote Economies', Economic Paper 67, Commonwealth Secretariat, London, UK.

World Bank. 2000. *Trade Blocs*. New York: Oxford University Press.

———. 2004. 'Trade Policies in South Asia', Three Volumes, Report 29949, South Asia Region, World Bank.

———. 2006. 'Studies on India–Bangladesh Trade: Trade Policies and Potential FTA', Poverty Reduction and Economic Management Sector Unit, South Asia Region, the World Bank.

11 REMOVING THE ENERGY CONSTRAINT TO GROWTH THROUGH REGIONAL COOPERATION

Vladislav Vucetic and
Venkataraman Krishnaswamy

ENERGY CONSTRAINT TO ECONOMIC GROWTH

South Asia has become one of the fastest-growing regions in the world during the last several years as result of the first-generation reforms relating to the correction of macroeconomic imbalances; the adoption of more liberal regimes relating to trade, investments, and exchange rates; and the generally increasing economic openness and integration into the global economy. India is targeting an annual growth rate of 10 per cent, with Pakistan, Bangladesh, and Sri Lanka following closely behind. Such buoyancy of growth is expected to continue through 2015, halving the regional poverty levels.

Such dynamic growth in the past had been driven by global, rather than regional, integration. The intra-regional trade in South Asia was only about 2 per cent of its GDP, compared to more than 20 per cent in East Asia in 2005. Per-capita income in the region was still less than US$ 700 in 2005, and in order to sustain growth with job creation, the region's growth has to encompass not merely the services sector (in which remarkable progress had been registered), but also the industrial and agricultural sectors, and should be supported by improved delivery of health and educational services. The key impediment to achieving and sustaining such broad-based growth at the targeted rates is the lack of adequate infrastructure, which is especially acute in the energy sector, not only in the larger countries of India, Pakistan, Bangladesh, and Afghanistan, but also in smaller ones, such as Nepal, Bhutan, and Sri Lanka.

Lack of adequate and reliable energy is proving to be a major constraint to growth in production and productivity. Relieving this constraint through the sustainable provision of secure energy supply at affordable prices remains a significant challenge that deserves the attention of governments and businessmen on a priority basis.

Regional Energy Trade to mitigate Energy Shortages

After decades of insignificant volumes of cross-border electricity trade and absence of any cross-border trade in natural gas through pipelines among the countries in South Asia, political leaders and businessmen of the region have recently evinced a great deal of interest and enthusiasm in cross-border electricity and gas trade, not only within South Asia, but also with its neighbours in the west (Central Asia and Iran) and east (Myanmar) as a measure for mitigating the energy shortages in the region.

Such a public policy choice provides a win-win situation to all the participants and is considered logical and rational because of:

- *The mismatch between energy demand growth and energy resource endowments.* Relatively smaller economies (Tajikistan, the Kyrgyz Republic, Nepal, Bhutan, Myanmar, and Turkmenistan) have hydropower or gas resources and Iran has hydrocarbon resources far in excess of their energy demands. The remaining countries (India, Pakistan, Bangladesh, Sri Lanka, and Afghanistan) have energy demand growth far outstripping domestic supply, and in the foreseeable future the demand-supply gap will become wider unless the domestic supplies are supplemented by imports (see Appendix A11.1).
- *Implications of trade to energy security.* Reliance on energy trade for meeting a part of the domestic demand can actually enhance national energy security by diversifying energy forms and supply sources and lowering the cost of energy supply.
- *The substantial benefits to the smaller exporting economies.* Energy exports could make dramatically significant contribution to the GDP growth of economies like Bhutan, Nepal, Myanmar, Tajikistan, and the Kyrgyz Republic, and enable their export-led growth. For example, Bhutan's electricity export in fiscal 2007

was expected to constitute nearly 25 per cent of its GDP, and 60 per cent of its state revenues (see Appendix A11.2 for data on some illustrative benefits).

- *The significant relief from energy constraints to rapid economic growth.* This is especially true in the importing economies, India, Pakistan, and Afghanistan. For example, in India alone, the volume of unserved electricity in fiscal 2007 is estimated at 54,916 gigawatt hours (GWh) and valued at US$ 12.1 billion on the basis of the short-term marginal costs in the Indian grid. The value of the corresponding industrial production foregone would be several times more.
- *The environmental imperatives.* This is especially relevant for India, which relies very heavily on domestic coal. Its carbon dioxide emissions will rise from 4 per cent of the world total today to about 13 per cent by 2030 unless low-carbon strategies are adopted. Imported hydropower and natural gas would help in moderating this increase to some extent.
- *Climate change imperatives.* Carbon emissions are increasing and Himalayan glacial resources are shrinking. The management of regional water resources and the use of other primary energy sources have to be optimized for the benefit of the region as a whole, and trade enables such optimization for the benefit of all.
- *Reduction of supply costs.* Trade could reduce system development costs and enable lower-cost supply. Nepal, for example, could dramatically reduce its cost of power supply (compared to its attempt to meet its demand by the expensive all-hydro generation option) by optimizing its power system with sale of hydropower to, and import of thermal power from, India.
- *Cash-flow implications.* Often energy import options improve cash flow and enable postponement of lumpy and large domestic capital investment needs, to avoid crowding out other important investment needs (the classic make or buy choice).

Mismatch between Resource Distribution and Demand Growth Distribution

The region currently has installed power generation capacity of about 152 gigawatts (GW), an annual generation of the order of 740 terawatt hours (TWh), and the demand is expected to grow annually in the range of 6.6 per cent to 11.5 per cent during the next 15 to 20 years, if supply growth can keep pace with growing demand.[1] Bhutan, Nepal, Myanmar, and the Central Asian economies (such as Tajikistan and the Kyrgyz Republic) have energy resources far in excess of their domestic needs. Total hydropower potential of these five countries exceeds 170,000 megawatts (MW), of which less than 6 per cent has been developed. The combined peak demands of their systems amount to no more than 60 per cent of the developed capacity. The development of even a part of their undeveloped resources for export would enable export-led growth of these relatively smaller economies.

India and Pakistan had a total annual gas consumption of the order of about 2.5 tcf (in fiscal 2006), divided approximately equally between them. Gas demand in India and Pakistan is forecast to grow annually at the rate of 8 per cent and 7 per cent, respectively, in the next 25 to 30 years. In Pakistan, supply shortfall is projected to be about 4 per cent to 10 per cent till fiscal 2010, and thereafter widen to 20 per cent or more. India's import dependency for gas is expected to increase from the present level of 7 per cent, to the 49 per cent to 58 per cent range by fiscal 2032. Total gas reserves of Turkmenistan, Iran, and Myanmar exceed 1000 tcf. Bangladesh is also believed to have significant potential for export of gas or gas-fueled electricity.

India and Pakistan could provide the major import markets for the surplus energy from these countries as well as from Iran and Turkmenistan and secure additional energy supplies to relieve shortages and sustain economic growth.

Existing Level of Trade

Currently there is no cross-border pipeline or trade in natural gas. Cross-border electricity interconnections and electricity trade are insignificant except for the following:

- Bhutan's export of 5,664 GWh in fiscal 2007 to India from three hydropower projects with total generating capacity of 1,416 MW, constructed with substantial grant assistance from India;
- Import of about 430 GWh (or about 28 per cent of the total supply) by Afghanistan from Iran, Turkmenistan, Uzbekistan, and Tajikistan;

[1] The region, with its share of more than 20 per cent of world population, is estimated to produce only 4 per cent of the world's total electricity generation and have annual per capita electricity consumption at about one-sixth of the world average.

- Nepal's import from India of 266.23 GWh (or 9.6 per cent of its total supply) and its export of 101 GWh (or 5 per cent of its total sales) to India; and
- Pakistan's import of about 25MW of power from Iran to the isolated grid of Baluchistan near the Gwadar deep sea port.

FACTORS WHICH INHIBITED TRADE IN THE PAST

The most important among the factors that inhibited regional energy trade in the past relate to political tensions, security issues, and past economic policy choices. These factors include:

- Prolonged political tension between India and Pakistan over Kashmir; war-like conditions in Afghanistan; internal armed conflicts in Sri Lanka and Nepal; as well as the political turmoil in Bangladesh.
- Past pursuit of inward-looking, import substitution-based policy approaches aimed at the elusive goal of national self-sufficiency. This approach regarded energy imports as diluting energy security.
- Lack of cross-border transmission links and adequate transmission infrastructure, even for transferring power among the various regions within the large countries such as India, Pakistan, and Bangladesh. The dilapidated and war-damaged infrastructure in the key transit country of Afghanistan was a major constraint to trade between Central Asia and South Asia.
- Poor operational efficiency and lack of creditworthiness (arising from inadequate tariffs, high system losses and poor collections) of most power utilities in the region, which did not encourage trade with them, as payment risks with them were perceived as unmanageable;
- Pervasive state ownership of the utilities, their poor earnings, and the lack of resources to invest for their own domestic needs, let alone the investments for export.
- Low levels of private sector investments and participation in the energy sector.

In addition, in a large country like India, progress in sector restructuring, open access to transmission systems, and fair and transparent sector regulation, at least at the level of national and regional grids, as well as the emergence of licensed power trading firms, were needed even for stimulating internal trade among the various regions of the country.

EMERGING FAVOURABLE FACTORS

Since the late 1990s, several new factors favourable to trade have emerged. The most important is the change in the political mindset of the politicians away from inward-looking, import substitution-based development strategies relying on controls on trade, investment, and exchange rate regimes. Newer approaches to growth, led by liberalized trade and investment regimes, and with an expanding role for the private sector and the markets have come into vogue, resulting in a greater degree of global integration and significant growth dynamism, and increasing foreign exchange earnings and reserves, which in turn enable further liberalization. Increasing growth rates translate into rapidly increasing energy demand and the urgent need for timely supply augmentation to meet such demand both from internal and external resources. Other key factors include:

- Emergence of national transmission companies in India, Pakistan, and Bangladesh paying special attention to increasing the inter-regional transfer capacities within each country. In India, such transfer capacities have nearly doubled during fiscal 2002 to 2008 to reach about 17,000 MW, and are expected to reach 37,000 MW by fiscal 2012. This would effectively enlarge the markets for imports by giving the exporter a substantially broader physical access to the market and a wider choice of buyers.
- Emergence of national and regional power markets in India enabled by the new Electricity Law of 2003. The law has enabled the creation of regulatory bodies, the phased open access to the national and regional transmission grids, and the emergence of licensed and regulated energy trading companies. The adoption of availability based tariffs (ABTs) with a frequency-linked Unscheduled Interchange (UI) charge in the national and regional grids has led to the emergence of lively electricity trade and a market sending reliable price signals to the participants (see Appendix A11.3 for details). Trade in electricity in fiscal 2007 amounted to about 15,000 GWh, or about 3 per cent of the total volume handled by the national grid. Traded prices

ranged from 12.5 cents/kWh (off-peak) to 13.7 cents/kWh (peak) in the third quarter of 2006. Such trade became possible, in part, by the special steps taken by the government and the central bank to reschedule the past debts of provincial power utilities and to enforce payment discipline.

- Increasing role of the private sector. The private sector has a total generation capacity of nearly 24,000 MW (or about 16 per cent of the total installed capacity) in the region. Distribution systems in Delhi, Orissa, Mumbai, Kolkata, Surat, and Ahmedabad in India, and Karachi in Pakistan, are in the private sector or have recently been privatized. The privately owned tiny distribution system in the city of Ghazni (Afghanistan) and the rural electric cooperatives in Bangladesh are the heart-warming examples in an otherwise bleak environment of the sector in these countries. The 400 kilovolt (kV) transmission link between eastern and western regions of India (enabling the absorption of Bhutan power imports) has been constructed by a joint venture between a private investor and the Power Grid Corporation of India. There are more than 20 private sector licensed power trading companies in India besides the PTC Limited (in which both the public sector and private sector hold shares). Indian private investors are actively looking for opportunities to invest in export power projects in Bangladesh, Bhutan, and Nepal. Majority state-owned NTPC of India is considering investing in a large thermal power plant in Sri Lanka. The Tata Group is pursuing investment in a 1,000 MW plant in Bangladesh.
- Commercialization of the distribution segment, through enterprise reform, privatization, and regulatory prodding, is proceeding, though often frustratingly slowly, in India, Pakistan, and Bangladesh.
- Structural changes involving the separation of transmission from generation and distribution functions, open access to transmission and creation of independent regulatory bodies, are progressing at different speeds, with India leading the pack and Pakistan and Bangladesh closely following.
- Political tensions between India and Pakistan are being lessened through a series of high-level talks and confidence-building measures. Internal conflicts in Nepal have subsided and that in Afghanistan still seems to be under control.

- There is an increasingly serious interest in discussing energy-related cooperation, cross-border energy investments, and trade possibilities in a range of regional organizations such as SAARC, ECO and BIMSTEC.

Evolution of the Regional Trade

The nascent bilateral energy trade is expected to increase among the countries in the region and their neighbours. India, Pakistan, and possibly Bangladesh, would emerge as major importers, while Central Asia, Iran, Nepal, Bhutan, and Myanmar could emerge as significant exporters. Afghanistan would be both an importer and the important transit country. Experience and confidence gained through bilateral trade are expected to help the evolution of regional energy markets with multiple sellers and multiple buyers. It is envisaged that initially trade would be clustered around two energy markets—a Western Energy Market (in which Central Asia and Iran would sell electricity and gas to Afghanistan and Pakistan, and possibly to India) and an Eastern Energy Market (in which Nepal and Bhutan would export hydropower to India, and Myanmar would export both natural gas and hydropower to India. Bangladesh could also export gas or gas-based power and could import some hydropower from Nepal, Bhutan, and Myanmar. Eventually, interconnection of the grids of India and Pakistan would integrate the two markets and create the fully integrated single regional electricity and gas market serving a population of 1.5 billion people. This market would be one of the largest in the world, whose sheer size would make it easier to mitigate the various risks, bear external shocks, reduce cost, create additional and more profitable trading opportunities, and attract investments.

Opportunities in the Western Energy Market

Energy trade opportunities currently being discussed or pursued include:

- *Power imports to Afghanistan*. Afghanistan's power demand is expected to grow to the level of 905 MW by 2020, and agreements in principle have been reached to import 300 MW each from Tajikistan, Uzbekistan, and Turkmenistan. Arrangements for the reinforcement of transmission links with Tajikistan and Turkmenistan are in place, and that for the link to Uzbekistan is being reviewed and is likely to be pursued in the context of projects to decongest the Uzbek grid. Imports from Iran of 60 MW to 100 MW to serve the Herat and Nimroz provinces would continue, and adequate transmission links for this have already been constructed. Funding is in place and construction is in progress for the North East Power System in Afghanistan to transmit the imported power to various load centres.

- *Power import from Iran to the Gwadar port area in Pakistan.* These will increase from about 25 MW now to about 100 MW when the proposed 220 KV link is completed. Arrangements for this are in place.
- *Hydropower import from Central Asia to Afghanistan and Pakistan.* This prominent multilateral trade project is currently being discussed and formulated with the help of multilateral and bilateral development partners led by the World Bank. It relates to the export of about 1,000 MW of power from Tajikistan and the Kyrgyz Republic to Pakistan and Afghanistan. A World Bank study (2004) showed that the completion of the partially constructed Central Asian hydropower projects (including new transmission links) would enable Tajikistan and the Kyrgyz Republic to supply power to Afghanistan and Pakistan at a delivered cost lower than the marginal cost of generation in Pakistan (see Appendix A11.4 for the comparative advantages of the Central Asian republics). Pakistan's present power demand at the generation level of about 14,000 MW is expected to reach 20,000 MW by fiscal 2010 and 44,700 MW by fiscal 2020. Among the several options to meet such growing demand, import of power from Central Asia has a prominent place.[2] A memorandum of understanding (MOU) among the four governments had been signed and a council of ministers and multi-country working group have been set up to coordinate

[2] The 670 MW Sangtuda I hydropower plant is under construction by a joint venture between RAO UES of Russia and the Tajik government. The plant will increase the surplus power available in Tajikistan during the summer months. Tajikistan is currently experiencing severe power shortages in winter months, which strengthens the argument for better regional integration, which would enable Tajikistan also to import electricity during winter from thermal-based power systems of Central Asia to alleviate the shortages. The revenues earned from summer season electricity exports could help pay for the winter imports.

further efforts. Studies for the dedicated transmission line and other technical, legal, commercial, and risk mitigation related studies are ongoing under the technical assistance provided by the World Bank and the Asian Development Bank. Private participation in the transmission component is also envisaged. Should this initial project prove cost effective and reliable, Pakistan is expected to increase its import from Central Asia to about 4,000 MW in the second stage.

- *Natural gas import by India and Pakistan from Iran (IPI gas project).* This project, which is in an advanced state of negotiation, is for importing annually (for 30 years) 33 bcm of gas by India and 21.7 bcm of gas by Pakistan from Iran in two phases. In the first phase, one pipeline with a diameter of 56 inches would be built to annually transport 21.7 bcm of gas. This would be shared equally between India and Pakistan. In the second phase, the pipeline capacity would be doubled to increase the total volume of supply to 54.3 bcm per year. Of this, 21.7 bcm per year would go to Pakistan and the remaining 32.6 bcm would go to India. Iran would build the pipeline up to the Pakistan border, and Pakistan would build it further to the Indian border. Pakistan would buy all the gas at the Iran–Pakistan border and transport it across its territory and sell it to India, and the latter's share price would include Pakistan's transmission charges and transit fees. The total distance involved is about 2,670 kilometres. Total pipeline costs are believed to be about US$ 7 billion. Many private investors appear to be interested in participating in the project. Russian Gazprom has also expressed interest in investing in this pipeline. Completion of the first phase is expected by 2013. There is considerable popular support for this project in India and Pakistan, since to a certain degree it is regarded as a 'peace project' like the Egypt–Turkey pipeline project. However, it appears that there are still considerable hurdles to be overcome, related to ensuring sufficient production of gas in Iran and to the pricing of gas exports and transit.
- *Natural gas import by Pakistan from Turkmenistan via Afghanistan (TAP gas project).* This project involves the construction of a 1,680-kilometre-long, 56-inch diameter pipeline, at a cost of about US$ 5.3 billion, to supply about 30 bcm of gas per year from Turkmenistan to Pakistan via Afghanistan. India has also

TABLE 11.1: Summary of the Prospects for Trade in the Western Energy Market

Importing countries	*Exporting countries*					
	CARs	*Turkmenistan*	*Iran*	*Afghanistan*	*Pakistan*	*India*
CARs	x	Some gas exports are possible; mutual electricity support*	Unlikely (uncompetitive)**	No scope**	Limited (some emergency support possible)*	No scope**
Turkmenistan	Mutual electricity support*	x	Unlikely (similarity of resources—gas; little scope in electricity)**	No scope**	No scope**	No scope**
Iran	Limited power exports possible*	Power exports are ongoing#	x	No scope**	No scope**	No scope**
Afghanistan	Power exports are ongoing and should grow#	Power exports are ongoing and should grow#	Power exports are ongoing and may grow#	x	Small cross-border power export possible*	No scope**

(contd ...)

Table 11.1 (contd ...)

Importing countries	*Exporting countries*					
	CARs	*Turkmenistan*	*Iran*	*Afghanistan*	*Pakistan*	*India*
Pakistan	Potential for power exports##	Significant potential for gas exports##	Significant potential for gas export; cross-border electricity trade could grow##	No scope for trade; transit of electricity and gas##	x	Mutual short-term trading support in power*
India	Gas and power exports possible*	Significant potential for gas exports##	Significant potential for gas exports##	No scope; Transit of gas*	Mutual short-term trading support in power; transit of gas*	x

Notes: # denotes that trade prospects are significant and are either being exploited or can be brought to fruition in the short-to-medium term. ## denotes that prospects of the trade are good and may materialize in the medium term. * denotes that prospects for the trade are more limited and may materialize in the medium-to-long term, and ** denotes that the prospects for the trade are weak.

been invited to join this venture and it has attended the steering committee meetings as an observer. Further progress would depend on the robustness of the gas reserves data, certification of the reserves, extent of possible private interest, ability and willingness of Turkmenistan to fulfil its commitments to Gazprom of Russia and still supply Pakistan and India, and finally on gas pricing.

The overall prospects for energy trade in the Western Energy Market in the near term are summarized in Table 11.1.

Opportunities for Trade in the Eastern Energy Market

The Indian power market is large, and the demand growth is constantly outpacing supply growth. In fiscal 2007, India faced a capacity deficit of 13,727 MW (or 11.9 per cent) and an energy shortage of 54,916 GWh (or 7.6 pecent). Within India, only the Eastern region had an energy surplus of 8,500 GWh (or 12.2 per cent), and all other regions had shortages of capacity and energy. Internal trade induced by the availability based tariff (ABT) and unscheduled interchange charge (UI) rate regime in the national grid amounted to about 15,000 GWh, or 3 per cent of the total volume handled in the national grid. The deficit is expected to widen in the foreseeable future. The average traded price ranged from Rs[i] 5.5 (12.5 cents/kWh) (off-peak) to Rs[i] 5.75 (13.7 cents/kWh) (peak) in the third quarter of 2006. Bids under ICB for large power stations based on indigenous coal from captive mines indicate a levelized price of Rs[i] 1.196/kWh (2.99 cents/kWh), and such bids for plants based on imported coal show a levelized price of Rs[i] 2.29/KWh (5.72 cents/KWh). Gas-based power with gas prices of $7 per million British thermal units (mmbtu) is expected to cost Rs[i] 3.7.KWh (9.25 cents/KWh). Prices from large hydro projects constructed or under construction range from 3.5 to 6 cents/KWh. While domestic coal will continue to play an important role in India, it will be insufficient to meet the entire demand for power in the country because of difficulties related to the expansion of coal mining and transport bottlenecks. The need for imported fuels (coal, liquefied natural gas, and piped gas) and imported electricity will remain significant. Thus, India is an attractive power market from the point of view of volume and power prices.

Indian policymakers envisage import of hydropower from Bhutan,

Nepal, and Myanmar, and gas-based power from Bangladesh, as well as import of gas from Myanmar and Bangladesh. Key opportunities for trade in the eastern market include:

- *Hydropower exports from Bhutan.* Bhutan's unexploited hydropower potential exceeds 23,000 MW and there is a wide shelf of projects from which to choose. Bhutan's power system master plan envisages the construction of six new hydropower projects with a total capacity of 4,484 MW through 2024. The government has also signed an umbrella agreement with the Government of India for the preparation of projects and feasibility studies for several hydropower projects, and many of the studies are ongoing. Most large Bhutanese projects are run-of-the-river type, with little firm energy and with substantial wet season energy and tend to have high capital costs and modest internal rates of return not likely to be attractive to private investors. However, the evolution of the power trading market in the Indian grid provides an opportunity for Bhutan to choose that part of India which has a demand pattern matching its supply pattern and marginal costs exceeding its supply cost. Major increases in Bhutan's power exports to India in the medium to long term could materialize, mostly in the context of the continuation of the present financing arrangement, under which the Indian government provides a grant to cover 60 per cent of the capital cost and soft loans for the remaining 40 per cent. Modest increases through medium-sized projects could come through investments by private investors.
- *Hydropower exports from Nepal.* Construction of two 220 kV links between India and Nepal[3] would help increase the present modest level of power exchange between the two countries, and would also enable many of the privately owned IPPs in Nepal to export their surplus power to India. Nepal's unexploited hydropower potential exceeds 43,000 MW, and it has a large shelf of proposals for run-of-the river and storage projects of large and medium sizes, which have been studied over the last several decades. They have not made much progress, as intergovernmental agreements were not easy to reach. The

[3] 220 kV single or double circuit links: Butwal–Ghorakpur and Dhalkebar–Muzaffarpur.

situation has dramatically changed with the emergence of private sector investors with keen interest in investing in Nepal projects for exports to India. The government has recently invited RFPs in respect to three hydropower projects (Upper Karnali, Arun III, Buri Gandaki) totalling about 1,300 MW, and several major Indian investors—some, in collaboration with international investors—have responded. The focus, which is mainly on the simpler run-of-the-river projects, needs to shift to storage hydropower projects to realize better values in the Indian market. In this context, it is heartening to note that after efforts lasting over 12 years, the 750 MW West Seti Storage Hydropower project, sponsored by SMEC of Australia, appears likely to achieve financial closure in the next few months, with equity participation from Australian, Chinese, Indian, and Nepalese investors and debt substantially from China. Ninety per cent of the electricity output (2,970 GWh) had already been contracted for export to India at a price of 4.95 cents/KWh.

- *Grid interconnections.* Interconnection of the grids of India, Nepal, Bhutan, and Bangladesh through the junction of the borders of these four countries has been shown by studies to be beneficial for all four parties to improve the reliability of their systems. Similar benefits are expected from the proposed interconnection between the Indian and Sri Lankan grid across the sea, for which preliminary intergovernmental agreement has recently been reached.
- *Export of hydropower from Myanmar.* Myanmar has unexploited hydro potential of about 39,000 MW and is developing about 10,400 MW of new capacity through joint ventures with Thai and Chinese businessmen and utilities, mainly for export to Thailand. Indian and Myanmar governments have a history of cooperation in designing and building hydropower projects in Myanmar, and are again collabourating in the design and formulation of the Tamanti multipurpose project located near the Indian border, with an initial power component of 1,200 MW, essentially for export to India. This is likely to be developed as a joint venture between Myanmar and Indian power entities.
- *Power and gas exports from Bangladesh.* Several proposals have been made by public and private sector entities of India and other countries for establishing large gas-fired combined cycle

TABLE 11.2: Summary of prospects of Trade in the Eastern Energy Market

Importing countries	*Exporting countries*					
	India	*Bhutan*	*Nepal*	*Bengladesh*	*Sri Lanka*	*Myanmar*
India	x	Significant quantities of hydropower (H)#	Significant hydropower export possible#	Significant amounts of gas or power possible. Some resource uncertainty##	Some peak power support possible##	Significant gas and power supply possible##
Bhutan	Dry Season Support#	x	Unlikely, similarity of resources and seasonal shortages**	Small amounts of thermal power and gas; connection via India (L)*	No scope**	Unlikely (far off; too small market)**
Nepal	Thermal power support. Dry season support#	Unlikely, similarity of resources and seasonal shortages**	x	Small amounts of thermal power and gas; connection via India (L)*	No scope**	Unlikely**

(contd ...)

Table 11.2 (contd ...)

Importing countries	*Exporting countries*					
	India	*Bhutan*	*Nepal*	*Bengladesh*	*Sri Lanka*	*Myanmar*
Bangladesh	Sharing reserves; electricity swaps##	Some hydropower; connection via India (L)*	Some hydropower; connection via India (L)*	x	No scope**	Unlikely (although some potential in hydropower)**
Sri Lanka	Dry season and thermal power support##	Unlikely (far off)**	Unlikely (far off)**	Unlikely (far off)**	x	Unlikely (far off)**
Myanmar	No scope**	Uncompetitive**	Uncompetitive**	Uncompetitive**	No scope**	x

Note: # denotes that trade prospects are significant and are either being exploited or can be brought to fruition in the short-to-medium term. ## denotes that prospects of the trade are good and may materialize in the medium term. * denotes that prospects for the trade are more limited and may materialize in the medium-to-long term, and ** denotes that the prospects for the trade are weak.

power projects in Bangladesh, mainly for export to India, but perceived uncertainties about the volume of gas reserves in Bangladesh have led its government to hesitate to concur. Recent discoveries and development of coal in Bangladesh, and the expected changes in the political condition of the country, could perhaps lead to a concurrence. Most observers believe that Bangladesh has abundant gas reserves, and that it has the potential for significant gas exports to India. However, the Bangladesh government is not yet fully convinced about the adequacy of its reserves.

- *Gas exports from Myanmar.* Oil and Natural Gas Corporation of India (ONGC) and Gas Authority of India Limited (GAIL) have invested in successful gas exploration in two blocks in Myanmar. In order to transport gas from those blocks to India, they have designed alternative gas pipelines from Myanmar's offshore fields to India—one passing through Bangladesh and the other bypassing that country. Depending on the outcome of discussions with Bangladesh, one of these pipelines is expected to be selected. Meanwhile, the Myanmar government is also considering piping gas to China and exporting gas as LNG. Final decisions would be taken after the evaluation of the reserves in both the blocks during the next several months.

The overall prospects for energy trade in the Eastern Energy Market are summarized in Table 11.2.

What the Governments Need to Do to Promote Energy Trade?

Trade is a corollary to the availability of opportunities for arbitrage. Energy trade can take place under a wide range of sector policies, structures, and conditions, and their levels of development and sophistication. The regional governments should make use of the present political consensus on the need for developing regional energy trade, in light of the strong commitment expressed at the highest levels at the recent SAARC conference (April 2007) and SAARC energy ministers' meeting (March 2007). Some of the trade opportunities described in the earlier sections should be within reach. Based on their state of preparation, the priority deals for such immediate action would include: (*a*) Central Asia–South Asia 1,000

MW electricity trade project; (*b*) West Seti Hydropower project in Nepal; (*c*) Iran-Pakistan-India gas pipeline project; (*d*) strengthening transmission interconnections between Nepal and India; and (*e*) the 'four-borders' transmission interconnections linking the power systems of India, Bangladesh, Bhutan, and Nepal. These projects could jumpstart regional energy trade and lead the way for more active regional cooperation, whose benefits would spill over into other economic areas.

While these and possibly other energy trade projects could be implemented under the present circumstances, to facilitate a more vigorous pursuit of regional trade opportunities, the governments may have to focus in the *near term* on a number of measures:

- Further articulating and strengthening public support for the emerging policy approach, treating energy imports as enhancing energy security in the major importing countries such as India, Pakistan, and Bangladesh, and energy exports as driving rapid economic growth in the exporting and transit countries.
- Encouraging both national and international private sector investors to play a major role in the form of PPP structures in cross-border investments in export projects, to take advantage of their financial capacity, technical and commercial expertise, and reputation. The involvement of private investors would also help depoliticize the trade better than arrangements that solely involve state-owned entities.
- Subscribing to, and becoming members of, the Energy Charter Treaty (see Appendix A11.5 for details of this treaty), as Pakistan has done, in order to place cross-border energy trade on firmer multilateral footing in relation to investment protection, regulation of cross-border energy infrastructure and flows; to provide additional comfort and confidence to all participants; and to minimize the political risks to prospective investors.
- Reducing political tensions within and across the countries, with special attention to the integrity of transit countries (such as Afghanistan) and the viability and operational stability of their energy systems. Trade flourishes under peaceful conditions.
- Adopting a sustainable commercial approach to trade (rather than a political ad hoc approach) and using standard commercial contracts, which allocate risks fairly. Letting the private investors

and market forces play a major role in actual buying and selling.

- Creating the capacity in smaller economies such as Afghanistan, Bangladesh, Kyrgyzstan, Nepal, and Tajikistan to prepare, negotiate, monitor, and enforce such commercial contracts. Solvent and properly regulated energy traders would have a very useful role to play.
- Keeping the price expectations realistic, based on reliable market signals, and ensuring that both the buyer and seller see advantages in the trade.
- Letting the momentum of political commitment built by the recent SAARC summit drive the prioritized available opportunities towards the conclusion of intergovernmental agreements and trade contracts.

To sustain and expand energy trade and minimize trade risks, and to enable the evolution of a more integrated and more efficient regional energy market in the medium to long term, governments have to deepen and advance sector reforms aimed at creating appropriate sector structures, financially viable entities, and an environment of predictable and neutral regulation. The governments may have to focus on the following initiatives:

- Reviewing and reoptimizing the least-cost power and gas development plans of the individual countries, with energy trade as an explicit option to meet part of the demand, minimizing carbon emission, and identifying—on the basis of such reoptimization—priority regional energy projects to be constructed and operated.
- Carrying out detailed feasibility studies for such projects, inter alia, to quantify trade benefits and to proceed with implementation.
- Constructing the essential transmission links to move the imported energy to the demand centres, including the essential transborder links, and facilitating the technical coordination of interconnected systems and harmonization of grid codes and operational practices, making the best use of the Energy Working Group of SAARC and its Energy Center, securing for this purpose technical assistance and cooperation with the Union for the Co-ordination of Transmission of Electricity (UCTE), if

needed (see Appendix A11.6 for details of UCTE). The same forum could be used to harmonize the regulatory practice and the evolution of a regional regulatory body.

- Completing the ongoing energy sector restructuring process, particularly in separating the transmission systems (from generation and distribution) and ensuring their open access, and enabling the evolution of national energy markets in which the distribution entities, large consumers, and energy traders, could choose their suppliers and negotiate contracts with them. The Indian lead in the power sector in this regard is noteworthy. Similar reforms in the gas sector in India, Pakistan, and Bangladesh would be very helpful.
- Improving the operational and commercial efficiency and financial viability of the distribution entities through enterprise reform, inter alia, making the best use of technology, such as remote or smart metering and GPS technologies, and through privatization and concessions.
- Adjusting tariffs and cross subsidies to enable financial sustainability of the sector, shifting subsidies from the utility to state budgets, and developing sustainable and targeted social protection schemes. This needs to be done both in exporting and importing countries to sustain trade.
- Making the best efforts to conclude international river basin agreements on a priority basis as storage hydropower projects are badly needed in the region to provide firm power and meet peak demands. These agreements, which have a broader focus than mere power generation, have to take into account the concepts of benefit sharing, and the imperatives of global concerns such as climate change and the need to adopt low carbon strategies, as well as regional concerns such as integrated river basin management involving the regional optimization of the use of water and primary energy resources.

Possible Role for Multilateral and Bilateral Development Partners

Neutral parties such as the international financial institutions (IFIs) and their development partners could play a significant role as an honest broker in facilitating cross-border investments for export and associated trading arrangements. This is illustrated by the current efforts to establish the 1,000 MW transmission interconnections between Central Asia (Tajikistan and the Kyrgyz Republic) and South Asia (Afghanistan and Pakistan), supported by the World Bank, the Asian Development Bank, the Islamic Development Bank, and other development partners.

The multilateral agencies have a key role in the structuring of PPP-type projects and their financing arrangements, and also in devising ways for mitigating a wide range of risks faced in such projects based on their worldwide experiences. They could help the smaller low-income exporting countries to participate with some equity in the PPP arrangements. The presence of multilateral agencies in the projects as equity holders and lenders (even with small amounts) encourages the parties to abide by their contractual obligations, helps resolve potential disputes, and thus provides a source of comfort for the parties involved. They can also use their guarantee instruments to reduce a range of risks for the investors.

The multilateral agencies could use their lending and non-lending services to

- build capacity in the governments and the public and private sector energy entities of smaller economies (such as Tajikistan, the Kyrgyz Republic, Nepal, Bangladesh, and Sri Lanka) to negotiate, implement, monitor, and enforce energy export contracts;
- promote the separation of transmission (from generation and distribution) and its operation under an open access regime;
- help expand the inter-regional transmission capacity in large markets such as India, Pakistan, and Bangladesh, and promote the evolution of national markets;
- help the regulatory regimes to mature;
- encourage pricing reforms and support the enterprise reform and privatization of distribution entities; and
- help the SAARC Energy Working Group and its Energy Center secure UCTE or other suitable assistance for technical coordination of regional power systems, and also to develop regional regulatory oversight of the interconnected grids.

The multilateral and bilateral agencies need to give adequate priority to regional trade initiatives in their assistance strategies, and to fully coordinate among themselves to improve the synergy of their operations. The regional trade agenda should be appropriately integrated into the country strategies and country programs. Regional energy projects, as a rule, have higher risk profiles and may benefit from the involvement of international agencies, which have complementary instruments that can collectively cover wider ranges of risks, as well as help spread the risks over a large number of participants.

Conclusions

Given the mismatch between the energy resource endowments and the national energy demand outlook in the region and its neighbours on the west and the east, and the imperatives of relieving the energy constraint to growth, focus on regional energy trade is a logical public policy choice, which is receiving increasing attention from political and business leaders of the region. The political mindset is changing, and has started viewing energy trade as enhancing energy security. The private sector is emerging as a key player in the construction and operation of export project facilities and in trading functions. Various energy trade-related projects are being formulated and discussed. Decisions on the most advanced and feasible ones need to be taken urgently, so as to not lose the momentum generated at the recent SAARC-related events.

India, with its geographic position and the size and the buoyancy of its economy, plays a unique and critical role in regional integration in South Asia, including in the energy sector. Bilateral energy trade between India and its neighbours is a key building block of the integrated regional energy market. While it would be useful and perhaps necessary to develop an upfront understanding at the regional (SAARC) level as to how such region-wide energy systems (electricity and gas grids) and trade could evolve, the pace of regional integration will be in large part determined by the pace of development of energy trade with India, especially on the eastern side of the region. In this context, it is very encouraging to see the reforms that are taking place in the Indian energy sector and the efforts India is taking to strengthen its domestic electricity transmission grid. It is also encouraging to see that similar reforms are either under way or being planned in other countries in the region. Pakistan could develop into a regional gas trading hub, gathering gas from Iran and Central Asia and transshipping it to India and the countries in the east. These developments, with increased political consensus among the countries on the need to encourage regional integration in general, and regional energy trade in particular, should bode well for development of regional energy trade.

Reduction of political tension is usually considered a key requirement for cross-border investment and trade. Conversely, the world experience appears to demonstrate that cross-border investments and trade and associated business interests help to lower political tensions. Entrepreneurial investment initiatives with imaginative financing and risk mitigation strategies—possibly with the involvement of multilateral financing institutions in some projects as neutral parties to help build confidence and mitigate risks—could help to start and strengthen the virtuous circle of regional peace and cross-border trade and investment.

Appendix A11.1

Table A11.1.1: Selected Indicators of Electricity Sector Dimensions

Country	*Installed generation capacity (MW)*	*Peak demand (MW)*	*Electricity generation (GWh)*	*Imports and/or exports (GWh)*	*Past annual demand growth rate (%)*	*Forecast annual demand growth rate (%)*	*Access to electricity*
Afghanistan	Total 475 MW (of which hydro is 261 MW). Available capacity 270MW	215MW (Suppressed Demand) 363 MW (Unsup_ pressed demand estimate)	839 GWh	323 GWh import	n/a	6.6% through 2020	26% of the population
Bangladesh	Total 4120 MW (of which hydro is 218 MW)	3,592 MW (FY 2005)	21,162 GWh (FY 2005)	None	9% (1996–2003)	About 8.2% per year through 2020	38% by area and 20% by population
Bhutan	Total 481 MW (of which hydro is 469 MW)	105 MW (2003)	2,355 GWh (FY2005)	Imports 25GWh Exports 1764 GWh	7.3% (FY 19 98 to FY 2003)	11.5% through 2012	40% of the population
India	Total 124,287 MW (of which hydro is 32,300 MW)	93,255MW (FY 2006) Actual Peak demand met: 81,792MW	617,510 GWh (FY 2006)	Imports 1764 GWh (Bhutan) Export 241 GWh (to Nepal)	4.2% during FY 2000 to FY 2004.	6.7% to 7.5% through 2032	55.8% of the households (Census of 2001)

(contd ...)

Table A11.1.1 (contd ...)

Country	*Installed generation capacity (MW)*	*Peak demand (MW)*	*Electricity generation (GWh)*	*Imports and/or exports (GWh)*	*Past annual demand growth rate (%)*	*Forecast annual demand growth rate (%)*	*Access to electricity*
Nepal	Total 684 MW (of which hydro is 627 MW)	557 MW (FY 2005)	2,643 GWh (FY 2005)	Import 241 GWh Export 111 GWh)	11% FY 1997–FY 2005	7.6% through FY 2020	40% of households (2001 census)
Pakistan	Total 19,505 MW of which hydro is 6,500 MW	14,091 MW (FY 2005)	87,114 GWh (FY 2005)	Import 25 MW (from Iran)	About 5% (FY 1994–FY2003)	7.9% through 2025	55% to 60% of the population.
Sri Lanka	Total 2,426 MW of which hydro is 1,247 MW	1,516 MW (2003)	7,662 GWh (2003)	None	5.1% 1999 to 2003	7.8% through 2024	73.4% of the population.
Region	Total 151,978 MW of which hydro is 41,622 MW	113,479 MW	739,285 GWh				

Source: Mostly country profiles and updated data from utility websites.
Note: It is estimated by the CEA that India had a capacity shortage of 12.3 per cent and energy shortage of 8.4 per cent in FY 2006. Since data may relate to different years for the member countries, the regional totals, while not accurate, are taken to be indicative of the order of magnitude. Regional peak demand is an arithmetical total of the peak demand of the countries, and thus may tend to overstate the peak demand.

Table A11.1.2: Energy Resource Endowments of the Region

Country	*Oil reserves (Mt)*	*Oil production (Mt/y)*	*Gas reserves (bcm)*	*Gas production (bcm/y)*	*Coal reserves (Gt)*	*Coal production Mt/y)*	*Hydropower potential (MW)*	*Hydropower developed (MW)*
Afghanistan	10–15/ 100	0.025	28.3/142	0.114	0.1	0.044	745	262
Bangladesh	7.8	0.340	580/810	13.8	2.2	n/a	755	230
Bhutan	0	0	0	0	0	0	23,760/ 30,000	468
India	786 (2005)	33.000	948	32.680	25/285	409.000	84000/ 150,000	32,300
Nepal	0	0	0	0	modest	0	43,000/ 83,000	600
Pakistan	105	3.100	1300/5700	28.000	185	3.300	54,000	6,500
Sri Lanka	14–18	0	0	0	0	0	9,100	1,250

Source: World Bank internal documents.

Notes: Under oil and gas reserves, proven/probable reserves are shown where available. Under hydro, economically viable potentials/technical potential are shown. Production data relates to the most recent year data available during 2003–5. With the commissioning of all units of the Tala hydropower project, hydro capacity developed in Bhutan will be 1,488 MW in 2006. Coal data includes lignite.

Table A11.1.3: Energy Resource Endowment of the Region's Neighbouring Countries

Country	*Oil*	*Natural Gas*	*Coal*	*Hydropower*
Kazakhstan	Reserves: 29 billion bbl Production: 1.3 million bbl/day	Reserves: 65 to 70 trillion Cubic feet (tcf) Production: 0.570 tcf/yr	Reserves: 37.5 billion tons Production: 95 million tons (2004)	Potential: 20,000 MW Developed: 2000 MW
Turkmenistan	Reserves: 546 million bbl. Production: 260,000 bbl/day	Reserves: 71 tcf Production: 2.1 tcf/year	Modest or negligible	Potential: Modest
Uzbekistan	Reserves: 594 million bbl. Production: 150,000 bbl/day	Reserves: 66.2 tcf Production: 2.07 tcf/year	Reserves: 4 billion tons Production: 2.8 million tons	Potential: Modest Developed: 1700 MW
Tajikistan	Modest or negligible endowment	Modest or negligible Endowment	Reserves: 3.6 billion tons Production: 32,000 tons (2002)	Potential: 40,000 MW Developed 4000 MW
Kyrgyz Republic	Modest or negligible endowment	Modest or negligible Endowment	Reserves: 0.8 billion tons Production: 400,000 tons (2003)	Potential: 26,000 MW Developed: 3000 MW
Iran	Reserves:132.5 billion bbl Production: 4.2million bbl/Day	Reserves: 971 tcf Production: 3.5 tcf/year	Reserves: 461million tons Production: 1.1 million tons	Potential: 42,000 MW Developed: 2,000 MW
Myanmar	Reserves: 3.2 billion bbl Production: 7.3 million bbl (During 11 months of 2005–2006)	Reserves: 18 tcf Probable: 89.7 tcf Production: 362 bcf (10.53 bcm) Exports: 0.28 tcf (8.06 bcm) (During 11 months of 2005–6)	Reserves: Modest Production: Modest	Potential: 39,720 MW Developed: 747 MW

Source: World Bank documents and US Department of Energy/Energy Information Administration Country Briefs.

Note: An Australian company exploring the Fergana valley area in Uzbekistan believes that area itself may have reserves of 1.2 billion barrels of oil and 5.5 tcf of gas.

Appendix A11.2: Benefits of Electricity Trade at a Glance, Some Illustrative Numbers

Country	*Details*
Afghanistan	Imported 430.12 GWh of electricity, or 27 per cent of total supply, in FY 2006. Marginal cost of electricity was 22 cents, while the average import cost was 2 cents. Savings to economy amounted to US$ 86.02 m (or 1.2 per cent of GDP in 2005 of US$ 7.3 billion).
Bangladesh	Bangladesh shed loads at around 694 MW in FY 2004. Unserved energy amounted to 3,900 GWh valued at US$ 171 million on the basis of the system AIC of 4.38 cents/KWh and substantially more when valued at the system marginal costs. Marginal price during the peak period is estimated at Tk2.03/KWh (2.8 cents) in the east zone (EZ) and Tk 11.642 (16 cents) in the west zone (WZ). By linking WZ with the eastern regional grid of India, which has an energy surplus, Bangladesh can hope to lower the marginal cost in WZ substantially. Conversely, gas supply to WZ could be stepped up across the Jamuna River to set up large plants (1,000 MW) in the WZ, partly to meet the demand in WZ (600 MW) and to lower the marginal cost there (from16 cents to about 4 to 5 cents or even lower) and to export power to India (400 MW or 2,453 GWh at 4.7 cents/KWh and earn US$ 115.3 million annually.
Bhutan	Exports in FY 2007 amounted to 5,664 GWh at 4.65 cents/KWh. Export receipts at US$ 263.4 million would be equal to about 25 per cent of GDP. Tala Hydropower Project capital cost was US$ 1,082 million, or a little over 100 per cent of the country's GDP.
India	The energy shortage in FY 2007 was 54,916 GWh, valued at the marginal cost of Rs[i] 9.3 or (22 cents), which is equal to US$ 12.082 billion (valuation by CERC). If it gets imported electricity at 6 cents to 7 cents , and imported gas-based electricity at 8 cents to 9 cents, the savings would be of the order of US$ 7.7 billion. On the basis of recently received bids in the ICB for ultra mega projects, the levelized cost of power from the new 3,500–3,800 MW power stations using domestic coal from captive coal mines would be 2.85 cents/KWh and the cost of power from a similar-size power station based on imported coal would be 5.45 cents per KWh. Cost of power from most large hydro projects recently constructed or under construction is around 3.5 to 6 cents/KWh. Gas-based generation using gas at US$ 7/mmbtu will cost 9.25 cents/KWh. These figures give a flavour of the attractiveness of the Indian market for exporters and the likely volume of benefits to India from trade.

(contd ...)

Appendix A11.2 (contd ...)

Country	*Details*
Nepal	West Seti HPP: Capital cost US$ 1,098 million, exports to India 2,970 GWH (90 per cent of production) at 4.95 cents/KWh, valued at US$ 147 million (or 2 per cent of GDP). Upper Karnauli, Buri Gandaki, and Arun 3 HPPs with a total capacity of 1,302 MW could possibly export 4,562 GWh (at 40 per cent PLF) at 6 cents/KWh. Value US$ 274 million or 4 per cent GDP. All four projects will yield export earnings of 6 per cent of GDP. WS HPP costs alone amount to 15 per cent of GDP of the country. This would be a significant investment benefit.
Pakistan	Unserved energy in FY 2007 amounted to 17,704 GWh and may rise to over 27,000 GWh by FY 2010 and to 35,000 GWh by FY 2011 if no capacity is added. When valued at the assumed Pakistan system average incremental cost of about 7 cents/KWh, the cost of these shortages are of the order of US$ 1.9 billion for FY2010, rising to US$ 2.5 billion for FY 2011. Power and gas imports could help reduce these shortages significantly. In general, new IPP projects are expected to have a levelized tariff of 5.9 cents to 13.8 cents/KWh based on the fuel they use. Use of domestic gas results in the lowest, and high speed diesel in the highest levelized tariffs. The gas price to IPPs in 2007 is US$ 4.23/mmbtu and as it rises to match import parity prices of around US$ 6.8 to US$ 7/mmbtu, the levelized power tariffs would be higher.

Appendix A11.3: Availability Based Tariffs and Unscheduled Interchange Charge in the National Grid of India

Central government-owned generating companies (such as NTPC and NHPC) own and operate about 39,900 MW, or about 32 per cent, of India's total installed generation capacity. The capacities of their various large generating units are allocated to the relevant state electricity boards at the time of their construction. The tariff for the sale of this electricity in the past used to be designated in terms of a composite KWh charge only, and billing was on the basis of monthly net energy drawn from the national grid. This did not discourage the electricity boards from drawing substantially more or less than the allocated capacity. They could overdraw during peak hours and underdraw during off-peak hours without any financial consequences. This greatly interfered with the merit order dispatch and adversely affected the frequency in the grid. Also, it provided no incentive to the states to trade the unwanted portion of their allocated capacity.

To overcome these problems, the concept of Availability Based Tariff (ABT) was introduced in mid-2002. This involves: (*a*) a fixed capacity charge/kW/

month payable by the electricity board, based on the capacity allocated to it and linked to the availability of the plant; (*b*) a regulated variable energy charge based on the actual scheduled consumption; and (*c*) a special unscheduled interchange (UI) charge for deviations from schedule.

The UI charge is linked *inversely* to the frequency in the grid and is high at Rs 6.00/KWh (or 14.3 cents) when the frequency goes down to 49.02 hertz (Hz) (high demand situation) and becomes zero when the frequency is at 50.5 Hz or higher (low demand situation). For this purpose the energy is metered in 15-minute blocks, and the average frequency is taken into account. In the range 50.5 Hz to 49.02 Hz, the UI charge increases from 0 by Rs 0.08 for each reduction in frequency by 0.02 Hz in a linear fashion.

Since the states pay a fixed capacity charge based on the capacity allocated to them, they have a strong incentive to draw the allocated energy or to sell the unwanted portion of such energy to other buyers. Overdrawing during high demand periods (frequency lower than 50.5 Hz) penalizes them heavily through a high UI charge. Similarly, generators get high UI charges for extra generation during periods of high demand and have no incentive to generate extra energy during periods of low demand since the UI charge becomes zero.

The introduction of ABT has greatly improved the frequency conditions of the national grid, promoted intelligent load management on the part of electricity boards, enabled a more meaningful merit order dispatch and above all, facilitated the emergence of a significant volume of energy trade in the national grid (which grew from 1,617 GWh in fiscal 2002 to greater than 15,000 GWh in fiscal 2007).

The maximum UI charge at 49.02 Hz was fixed in fiscal 2003 at Rs 4.2/KWh based on the cost of electricity from generating sets using high speed diesel (with a fuel cost of Rs 13.33/litre) as representing the short-term marginal cost.

With changes in high speed diesel prices, the UI charge went up to Rs 6/KWh, and then came down to Rs 5.7 in 2004. On the same basis, the UI charge should be Rs 9.3 (23.25 cents) for fiscal 2008, but to avoid too steep a revision, the Central Electricity Regulatory Commission has fixed it at Rs 7.5/KWh (18.75 cents), with effect from 30 April 2007, as an interim measure, based on the cost of generation from combined cycle power stations using naphtha as fuel.

Sources: Bhanu Bhushan, *ABC of ABT, A Primer on Availability Based Tariff*, 27 June 2005, and CERC order dated 5 April 2007, in Petition No.15/2007, available at www.cercind.gov.in

Appendix A11.4: Comparative Advantages of Central Asian Republics in Electricity Exports

Kazakhstan, the Kyrgyz Republic, Uzbekistan, and Tajikistan, which currently constitute the Central Asian Power System (CAPS),[4] have a combined generation capacity of about 38,000 MW and an annual generation in excess of 135 TWh. Their comparative advantage in terms of electricity exports arises from the factors summarized below.

- Dramatic decline in electricity demand upon the dissolution of the Soviet Union rendered their generating capacity excessive. Annual generation of electricity, although increasing currently, still lags considerably behind the pre-1990 level.
- Tajikistan and the Kyrgyz Republic have huge hydropower potential. They operate predominantly hydroelectric power systems, have large surplus generation available for export in spring and summer, and face supply deficits in winter due to lack of thermal generation capacity or lack of fossil fuels.
- Generating facilities, including those whose construction had been initiated during Soviet rule but stopped after the break-up of the Soviet Union, were designed or optimized on the basis of large regional markets within the Soviet Union, and became excessive for the needs of newly independent republics.
- There were a number of large power projects that commenced construction during the Soviet regime and later were suspended after incurring considerable amounts of sunk cost, for want of funds to complete them. When completed, their outputs would be far in excess of the needs of the host countries, and thus their completion would make economic sense only if export markets could be found. Because of the large sunk costs already incurred in the Soviet era, the marginal cost of generation based on incremental investments could be attractive to prospective importers.
- Similarly, the incremental generation costs from the mothballed thermal generating assets in Kazakhstan (upon their rehabilitation) would also be attractive.[5] Export of surplus thermal power from

[4] Turkmenistan's power system also used to operate synchronously with the system of the other four Central Asian countries. During the time of the Soviet Union, the power systems of the five countries were developed as an integrated system, and operated from a regional dispatch centre in Tashkent, Uzbekistan. Since May 2003, the Turkmenistan system has been operating synchronously with that of Iran and not with the rest of the CAPS.

[5] AES, the owner of Ekibastuz Thermal power plant in Kazakhstan and related coal fields estimates power generation costs of 1.0 to 1.2 cents per kWh upon

Kazakhstan, Turkmenistan, and Uzbekistan (with significant and developed fossil fuel resources) could complement the hydropower exports from Tajikistan and the Kyrgyz Republic to make part of the supply firm year round.

- In these countries, practically 100 per cent of the households have access to electricity. Based on present high per-capita consumption levels, income elasticity, and effective price elasticity, the demand for electricity in these four countries during 2005–25 is expected to grow at a very modest annual average rate of about 2 per cent only, if the tariffs are to increase to full cost recovery levels and commercial discipline is strictly enforced.[6]
- Supply options such as system loss reduction, rehabilitation of generating units, and completion of the large projects currently languishing for want of funds, could produce enough electricity to meet the forecast demand and leave substantial surpluses for export.
- Currently the surpluses are of the order of 11 TWh, but almost the entire surplus is in the spring and summer months. In winter there is actually a shortage of about 1 TWh. The total annual surpluses could exceed 30 TWh in the next five years and 50 TWh in the next 10 years if the envisaged investment programme is implemented. The major portion of the surpluses would continue to be in spring and summer, while surpluses in fall and winter would be lower by about 10 TWh.

Appendix A11.5: Energy Charter Treaty

International trade is carried out under the framework of the treaty, rules, and regulations of the World Trade Organization (WTO), which supplement and influence the national rules. In order to accede to WTO, each country has to harmonize its laws, rules, and regulations with the WTO framework. A similar organization to provide the multilateral framework specifically for energy sector cross-border trade and investment came into existence in 1991 when the Energy Charter Declaration was made. The Energy Charter Treaty provides a broad multilateral framework of rules governing energy cooperation. The fundamental aim of the Energy Charter Treaty is to

---

rehabilitation of units 3–7 (300 MW) (2005–7), less than 2.0 cents/kWh upon rehabilitation of unit 8 (500 MW) (2009), 2.0 to 3.0 cents/kWh upon rehabilitation of unit 2 (500 MW) by 2011 and unit 1 (500 MW) by 2013 (Presentation by Dale Perry of AES in Istanbul conference 'Electricity Beyond Borders', on 13 June 2006).

[6] Price increases and substantial improvements in metering, billing, and collection systems, and procedures to enforce payments, reduce theft and other commercial losses, should limit demand increase.

strengthen the rule of law on energy issues by creating a level playing field of rules to be observed by all participating governments, thus minimizing the risks associated with energy-related investments and trade.

The treaty's provisions focus on five broad areas: (*a*) the protection and promotion of foreign energy investments, based on the extension of national treatment, or most-favoured nation treatment (whichever is more favourable); (*b*) free trade in energy materials, products and energy-related equipment, based on WTO rules; (*c*) freedom of energy transit through pipelines and grids; (*d*) reducing the negative environmental impact of the energy cycle through improving energy efficiency; and (*e*) mechanisms for the resolution of state-to-state or investor-to-state disputes.

The Energy Charter Treaty and the Energy Charter Protocol on Energy Efficiency and Related Environmental Aspects were signed in December 1994 and entered into legal force in April 1998. To date the treaty has been signed or acceded to by 51 states plus the European Communities (the total number of its signatories is therefore 52). The treaty was developed on the basis of the Energy Charter Declaration of 1991. Whereas the latter document was drawn up as a declaration of political intent to promote energy cooperation, the Energy Charter Treaty is a legally binding multilateral instrument, the only one of its kind dealing specifically with intergovernmental cooperation in the energy sector.

The treaty is open for accession by any country that wishes to participate, that is ready to take on the obligations in the treaty, and whose application is accepted by the Energy Charter Conference. In order to join the Energy Charter Treaty, a country has to take the first step of signing the 1991 Energy Charter Declaration, thus committing itself to the principles of the charter. By doing this, it becomes an observer to the Energy Charter, with access to all its meetings and documents. The next step is the actual accession for which the country and the Energy Charter Secretariat must assess the compatibility of a country's domestic legislation with the provisions of the treaty. Once the assessment reports are found satisfactory by the Energy Charter Conference, the country is invited to accede to the treaty and become a full member.

While the Central Asian Republics are already members, Afghanistan, Iran, Pakistan, and China are observers.[7] India is believed to have initiated action to become an observer. Bangladesh, Bhutan, Nepal, and Sri Lanka are not yet associated with this treaty. Since they have substantial potential for energy trade and the need for cross-border investments and for attracting capital for such investments to enable and sustain trade, it would be advantageous for them to become members of the Energy Charter Treaty. In particular, the membership of the regional countries in the treaty would

[7] Pakistan has recently been made a member of the Energy Charter Treaty.

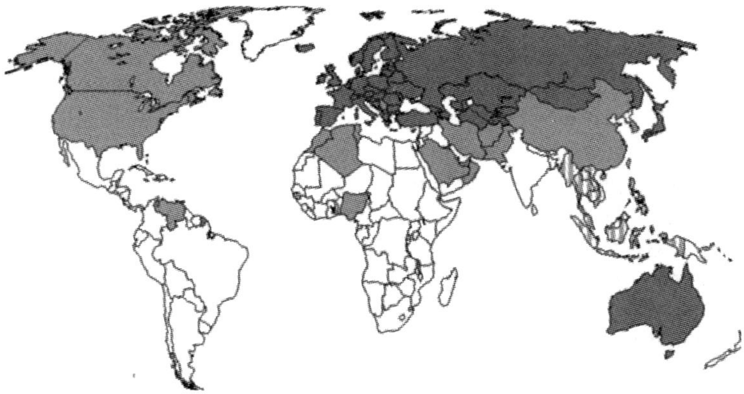

Figure A11.5.1: Participation in the Energy Charter Treaty

Source: www.encharter.org

Notes:
- ■ Signatories of the Energy Charter Treaty, and members of the Energy Charter Conference.
- ■ Observers
- ▥ Countries of ASEAN

greatly facilitate the private investors in the region making investments at home and abroad to create regional energy import or export opportunities.

APPENDIX A11.6: TECHNICAL COORDINATION OF INTERCONNECTED GRIDS

In the regional energy trade, there is always a need to coordinate the technical conditions and interconnected operation of two or more systems and the associated transit issues (Box A11.6.1).

Box A11.6.1: Interconnection Options for Electricity Trade

Bilateral electricity trade between two adjoining countries is the least complicated option from the technical point of view. If a relatively small part of one country has power shortage and needs import, that part of the grid is disconnected from the main country grid and connected in the 'island mode' to the grid of the exporting country. The frequency of the interconnected grid is then regulated by the exporting country grid. This is referred to as the 'synchronous island mode operation'. Trading here would be governed by bilateral trade contracts.

(contd ...)

Box A11.6.2 (contd ...)

When the grids of the two adjoining countries are compatible and fulfil certain technical criteria (such as principles of voltage and frequency regulation, level of reserve capacities, quality standards of supply to customers, communication, and protection systems), they can be fully synchronized and operate on the same frequency and submit themselves to the unified common rules of system operation and control. This is referred to as fully synchronized operation, which maximizes the benefits of interconnection. Trading here would be governed by contracts and the bilateral agreement on grid operation and discipline.

Interconnection of two non-adjacent countries through a transit country, or interconnection among more than two countries, would call for synchronizing all the connected grids with all the discipline accompanying such synchronous operation, and would thus become more complicated as common criteria for system operation and control would have to be agreed among several parties and observed continuously. Trading here would be governed by contracts and multilateral agreements on grid operation and discipline.

When the systems to be interconnected are electrically incompatible, then they could be interconnected by direct current (DC) transmission. Converters in the exporting country convert the alternating current (AC) into DC, and it is then transmitted through the DC line. In the receiving country, converters convert DC back to AC for normal supply. Such DC options used to be expensive, but in recent years costs have come down due to cost-effective technology upgrades. Nonetheless, the DC interconnection options are more expensive and would require a much larger volume of electricity transmission to become economic than in the case of AC interconnection.

The Union for Co-ordination of Transmission of Electricity (UCTE) is a well-known example of an arrangement for technical coordination of the operation of a number of power systems in Europe. Fifty years of joint activities laid the basis for the leading position in the world that the UCTE holds in terms of the quality of synchronous operation of interconnected power systems. Through the networks of the UCTE, about 450 million people of Europe are supplied with electric energy. Annual electricity consumption totals approximately 2,300 TWh. It is an association of transmission system operators (TSO) in continental Europe, providing a reliable market base for electricity trade by efficient and secure electric 'power highways'. Each TSO is individually committed: (*a*) to a common set of rules for the operation of the interconnection, its development and reliability standards; and (*b*) to support the principles of the common electricity market. There is no supra-regional 'UCTE control centre' governing the whole system. Rather, the integrated, synchronously connected grids are operated in a decentralized way, with adherence to strict technical and organizational rules and standards by all UCTE members (for more details, see www.ucte.org).

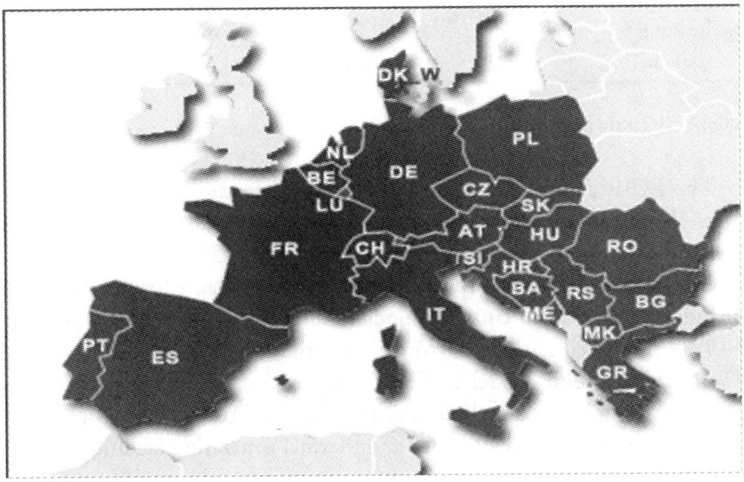

Figure A11.6.2: UCTE Area of Operation in Europe

Source: www.ucte.org

The volume of electricity exported and imported in relation to domestic generation in respect tof a few select European countries is given in Table A11.6.1.

Table A11.6.1: Imports/Exports (TWh) in Selected European Countries in 2005

Country	*Net generation*	*Imports*	*Exports*	*Net exchange as % of avail. energy*
Austria	63.9	20.4	17.4	4.5
Belgium	82.3	14.3	8.0	7.1
Czech Rep.	76.2	12.4	24.9	–19.6
Denmark	34.3	12.9	11.6	3.7
Finland	67.7	17.9	0.9	20.1

(contd ...)

Table A11.6.1 (contd ...)

Country	*Net generation*	*Imports*	*Exports*	*Net exchange as % of avail. energy*
France	547.8	7.2	67.6	–12.4
Germany	533.7	53.4	61.8	–1.6
Hungary	32.3	15.0	8.8	16.1
Italy	300.2	49.8	1.0	14.0
Netherlands	96.0	23.7	5.4	16.0
Switzerland	57.9	43.9	39.4	7.2

Source: Monthly Statistics of UCTE (available at www.ucte.org).

The EU is currently considering whether there should be a regulatory oversight of the operation of the interconnected system at the EU level in light of some of the problems recently emerging. UCTE is not the only model available for this purpose. Other models available for consideration include the reliability councils models followed in North America, the NORDEL model followed in Nordic countries, the Greater Mekong Power Trade Organization model in East Asia, the South African Power Pool model enabling multilateral trading, and the West Africa Power Pool model enabling the optimal use of hydro and thermal generating facilities.

12 SUPPORTING GROWTH THROUGH BETTER CONNECTIVITY

ROLE OF REGIONAL TRANSPORT

Simon Thomas

PERCEPTIONS OF TRADE–TRANSPORT IN SOUTH ASIA

The South Asian region is perceived as having complex, cumbersome, and costly trade procedures operated by unresponsive and sometimes venal bureaucracies; and systems that might include demand for informal payments for smooth passage. The perception of low productivity, delays, and cost pervades all modes of transport. Not surprising, studies have shown that South Asia, as a region, has the greatest to gain from improvements to trade facilitation and its external transport systems.

Published data tend to support such perceptions. The World Bank has just reported the results of *Doing Business*, which considered the costs and complications of participating in trade (Table 12.1).

TABLE 12.1: Trading across Borders: Procedures, Delays, and Costs

	EXPORTS				*IMPORTS*			
	Documents	*Signatures*	Days	*US$/TEU*	*Documents*	*Signatures*	Days	*US$/TEU*
East Asia								
Cambodia	8	10	36	736	12	18	45	816
China	6	7	20	335	12	8	22	375
Malaysia	6	3	20	481	12	5	22	428
Thailand	9	10	23	848	10	10	22	1042
Vietnam	6	12	35	701	15	15	36	887
Average[+]	*6.3*	*8.0*	*23.9*	*488*	*11.9*	*8.2*	*22.6*	*484*

(contd ...)

Table 12.1 (contd ...)

	EXPORTS				*IMPORTS*			
	Documents	*Signatures*	Days	*US$/ TEU*	*Documents*	*Signatures*	Days	*US$/ TEU*
South Asia								
Bangladesh	7	15	35	902	16	38	57	1287
India	10	22	27	864	15	27	41	1244
Nepal	7	12	44	1599	10	24	37	1800
Pakistan	8	10	24	996	12	15	19	1005
Sri Lanka	8	10	25	797	13	15	27	789
Average+	*9.4*	*19.1*	*17.3*	*886*	*14.5*	*25.6*	*38.6*	*1197*
G8								
Germany	4	1	6	731	4	1	6	750
Japan	5	3	11	789	7	3	11	847
UK	5	5	12	676	4	5	12	756
USA	6	5	9	625	5	4	9	625
Average+	*5.0*	*3.2*	*8.8*	*703*	*4.9*	*3.3*	*9.0*	*704*

Source: *Doing Business*, 2006 (www.doingbusiness.org).
Notes: Transport and transaction costs within the country. + Weighted by the level of merchandise trade.

South Asia performs poorly on all the measures in comparison with both the rich industrialized countries and countries in East Asia, which are South Asia's main competitors in core sectors such as garments. The comparisons between South Asian countries and China are particularly stark. It is, however, almost inevitable that China has a cost advantage as its industries were established for exporting, and thus located close to the coast. In South Asia, industries were primarily supplying the domestic market and mainly located inland. But the better performance of China spans all the indicators. Other sources show rather less difference between East and South Asia. In terms of Trade Facilitation Indicator rankings,[1] Malaysia performs well but there is no difference, on average, between Sri Lanka and Thailand (both ranked 45), little difference between China (57) and India (59), or between Bangladesh (70) and Vietnam (71).

[1] Wilson, Mann, and Otsuki database: World Bank Working Paper 3224.

The external sectors in South Asia are changing rapidly, and much of the older information and databases reflect a situation that was left behind in the late 1990s and early 2000s. As governments have moved from import substitution and the protection of domestic industry to export orientation and acceptance of greater competition, they have accorded far higher priority to streamlining trade procedures and enhancing the competitiveness of the export sectors. Indifferent external transport systems and cumbersome trade procedures, designed to control trade and maximize trade-related government revenues, simply reinforced the effectiveness of inward-looking economic policies, adding non-tariff to tariff and quota barriers. Indifferent external transport and cumbersome procedures are antithetical, however, when promoting export-based growth, especially if the export products are, at least, partly dependent on imported inputs.

The Status of International Trade-Transport in South Asia

This section provides a very broad review of the developments in the main sectors that affect the quality of trade transport in the South Asia region. The review concentrates primarily on continental South Asia; Sri Lanka's trade with the rest of South Asia is overwhelmingly by sea and is thus broadly covered by the review of ports and shipping, and the main land transport corridors. In terms of its quality of access to inter-regional trade, Sri Lanka has, perhaps, the most favourable position in the region, with Colombo being a main hub port. Sri Lanka has thus frequent feeder services to the ports in the region, and access to the mainline container services, offering the cheapest and quickest services to Asian, European, and the US markets.

Ports and Shipping

Both India and Pakistan have container terminals that operate at international levels of productivity. The main container terminals in both countries are, with one exception (JNPT) privately managed, and it is accepted that future terminal development will be largely financed by the private sector. Bulk cargo handling generally meets international standards and ship charter rates are comparable to those charged elsewhere. However, the ports in the Bay of Bengal have very much lower levels of productivity: shallower drafts, smaller vessels, public sector management, and less productive equipment. Indeed,

Chittagong, Bangladesh, is among the least productive container ports in the world and at the bottom of the list for ports handling similar volumes of containers.

While the handling productivity at many South Asian ports is at international levels, container dwell time remains well above average, although it has been declining recently. Customs clearance is no longer a major source of general delay, although inadequate documentation may delay some containers. Long free storage periods, inadequate inland transport, and lack of direct delivery from the berth may all contribute to the delays. Some traders keep their containers in the ports until the contents are sold, only then getting customs clearance. Unfortunately, such delays can have significant economic costs—congested container yards feed through to reduced port productivity, and thus additional terminal investment, despite low berth occupancy.

Until the late 1990s, South Asia, other than Sri Lanka, depended on container feeder services connecting with hubs such as Colombo, Singapore, and Salalah in Oman. Increased traffic and higher port productivity has led to the introduction of direct services to several ports. At Nhava Sheva in India, less than 15 per cent of containers are now shipped by feeder vessels. The Pakistan ports are now served by a combination of direct (mainly to Asia, but some to Europe) and feeder services (mainly for Europe and the United States). Until recently, Chennai, the main container port on India's east coast, was served by feeder vessels despite having the traffic, draft, and productivity that normally justify direct services. This is beginning to change, with direct services to Asia and, very recently, direct services to both Europe and the United States have been announced.

In terms of freight rates and delivery times, South Asia is reasonably well served (Table 12.2).

South Asia has a time and cost advantage over China for destinations in Europe and the US East Coast, but a substantial disadvantage on the US West Coast routes. Bangladesh faces the highest freight rates to Europe and the US East Coast, and longest shipping times. Chittagong is only served by feeder vessels, and the very poor port performance means that the shipping lines do not run service on a timetable. Consequently, exporters have to build in slack time in their plans to ensure that containers connect with the mainline services at the hub ports.

TABLE 12.2: Container Shipping Rates and Times

Destination		*Pakistan*	*India*		*Bangladesh*	*China*
			West Coast	*East Coast*		
Europe	US$/ TEU	1150–1350	1050–1250	100–1300	1200–1400	1650
	Days	19	17	21	22–30	19–21
US East Coast	US$/ TEU	2700–2750	2600	2700	2800–3200	3100
	Days	19–22	19–21	23	27–35	24
US West Coast	US$/ TEU	2750	2500	2600	2400	1800
	Days	22–29	26	24	19–28	15

Source: World Bank staff.

There is little domestic coastal container shipping in South Asia, but services have been established within the last two years between India's west coast ports and Pakistan's ports, and between Vizag, on India's east coast, and Kolkata and Chittagong. These direct services have reduced the need for routing intra-regional sea trade through hub ports. The revisions to the Shipping Protocol should help to strengthen India–Pakistan shipping links.

While, in general, ports and shipping can be considered as reasonably satisfactory, Chittagong being the exception, the sector could make a greater contribution to the region's competitiveness if the following factors are addressed:

- *High port charges*. While cargo handling charges are not substantially different from international levels, the charges on vessels are extremely high. Such high charges result in higher freight rates and reduced service frequency; both reduce international competitiveness. Though financially self-sustaining ports may be desirable, excessively high profits are a tax on trade.
- *High port costs*. Many of the public sector port trusts have not fully adjusted their employment to containerization and mechanized handling. Port employment has fallen, but further substantial reductions are possible. Pakistan is now addressing the Karachi Dock Labour Board and the unnecessary labour practices that it maintains.
- *Port capacity*. Container traffic is growing in South Asia by 11 to

15 per cent annually, and there is little prospect of the growth levels declining in the near-medium term. New container terminals are being constructed (a third berth at JNPT has recently started operations) and others are planned, but it will be essential that investment in the port sector maintains capacity in line with demand growth.

- *Port drafts*. Container vessels are becoming larger as shipping lines seek further economies of scale and lower costs. With the growth in container traffic to the region, the shipping lines are using larger vessels; between 2001 and 2005, the average vessel to Europe increased from 2,281 TEU to 3,070 TEU, while on routes to the Far East, it increased from 1,962 TEU to 2,307 TEU. Most of the main container ports in South Asia have limited draft, and vessels are restricted to about 4,000 TEU (Nhava Sheva can provide restricted access to 4,500 TEU vessels). As the shipping lines increase the size of their vessels (increasingly, vessels in excess of 7,500 TEU are being delivered and one 10,000 TEU vessel is already operating), the ports in South Asia will have to deepen their drafts to 13.5 metres or even 14.5 metres, or risk being reduced to feeder port status.

In the short term, however, the ports and shipping sector is not a major constraint to the trade transport competitiveness of South Asia, with the exception of Chittagong, which is probably the single greatest infrastructure constraint to Bangladesh's economic growth.

Highway Infrastructure

Bangladesh, India, and Pakistan have extensive road networks, much of them paved, which provide access for most of the population. The more mountainous countries, Afghanistan, Bhutan, and Nepal, have much smaller road networks and much lower levels of motorized access. The problem of infrastructure in South Asia is less the size and coverage of the networks, and more the quality and capacity in the face of rapidly growing traffic. Until the last few years, South Asia's main road network consisted of, at best, two-lane roads. with motor vehicles competing for road space with tractors, non-motorized transport, and pedestrians. Much of the road network has one-lane (3.5 metres) or intermediate (5.5 metres) width.

For years, South Asia under-invested and under-maintained its main arterial highway networks. Consequently, service standards were very low, vehicle speeds slow, and travel times high. The railways were supposed to move long-distance freight and passengers, but road transport became the dominant transport mode. The Indian and Pakistan governments began to invest in major inter-urban highways in the mid-1990s, but progress has been slow. Pakistan expects to complete the multilane highway from Peshawar to Karachi in fiscal 2008, and India's four-laning of the Golden Quadrilateral (connecting Delhi, Kolkata, Chennai, and Mumbai) is approaching completion. Overall, however, there are less than 10,000 km of multilane highways in South Asia, and many of these are widened two-lane roads without substantially improved alignment or access control.[2] Bangladesh is addressing critical bottlenecks, including on the Dhaka–Chittagong corridor, but not yet providing a high-speed, high-capacity network.

Though in total network terms the achievements have been limited, the investments have had a marked impact on some of the key trade corridors. Average truck trip times between Delhi and Mumbai have been reduced, for example, from five to six days to two to three, though, international standards for this length trip might be 24 hours to 30 hours. Trip times in South Asia are not only constrained by road conditions, but also by the types of trucks and the gross vehicle overloading.

Substantially greater investment in the highway network will be necessary to provide South Asia with that which is needed to support sustained high levels of economic and traffic growth. Pakistan proposes investments of about US$ 3.6 billion to upgrade the North-South Corridor, under the National Trade Corridor Improvement Program (NTCIP), and India's National Highway Development Plan envisages the completion of the Golden Quadrilateral and the North–South and East–West Highways, four-laning of a further 10,000 km, six-laning of 6,500 km, and two-laning of 20,000 km, and 1,000 km of expressways, at a total cost of about US$ 50 billion.

Unfortunately, at even the present, relatively modest levels of highway investment (though significantly higher than previously), the programmes are facing major constraints in terms of:

[2] This may be compared with highway development in China, where 50,000 km of multilane roads were constructed, including 25,000 km of expressway, in a 10-year period.

- public sector financing, and thus expected reliance on private sector funding;
- planning and implementation management capacity; and
- construction sector capacity.

These constraints, if not suitably addressed, have the potential to restrict both economic and trade growth.

Road Transport

Trucks account for about 95 per cent of total ton-km in Pakistan, 70 per cent in India, and 60 per cent in Bangladesh. The other countries in continental South Asia are entirely dependent on road transport as they have no domestic rail networks. The quality and cost of road freight has, therefore, an important impact on the region's overall trade-transport costs; domestic transport costs can often equal those of long-distance ocean freight. In most regions, long-distance road freight is now carried in large, multi-axle tractor/semi-trailer units. These units are expensive, but unit costs are low because of their high capacity and high utilization. Until recently, the trucking sectors in South Asia were dominated by two-axle trucks. These remain predominant in Bangladesh, and are important elsewhere, but three-axle rigid trucks have become much more common, and the multi-axle, semi-trailers are entering the market in greater numbers. The shift to multi-axle trucks is more advanced in Pakistan, but with the entry of Tata into the market, they will become increasingly important in India[3] (Tata has also recently opened an assembly plant in Karachi).

Road freight rates in India and Pakistan are perhaps the lowest in the world, especially for bulk cargo. Rates for bagged cargo on very long distance hauls in Pakistan can be below the equivalent of US1 cent/ton-km. Rates are higher for containers, but in Pakistan in 2005, for example, they were still only about US2 cents per ton-km for the forward movement, and slightly lower for the backhaul. Such low rates are the result of: (*a*) a highly competitive market; (*b*) low-cost trucks; (*c*) low crew costs; (*d*) relatively low fuel prices; (*e*) relatively high vehicle utilization (much higher than Africa, but

[3] Sales of multi-axle trucks in India increased by over 100 per cent in 2006, to 22,000 units, but overall sales were still dominated by three-axle trucks, with 111,000 units.

lower than North America). However, despite the low freight rates, the economic costs are much higher (road damage, impacts on other road users, and adverse road safety) due to inadequate regulations and overloading.

The service levels are also poor—long transit times, unpredictable delivery, no cargo insurance, etc. Trucks can carry the overloads because they are specially modified and are driven very slowly, even on roads in good condition.[4] But in general, users are getting the standards for which they are prepared to pay; the emphasis is on low costs rather than high quality. The market is beginning to change as the economies become more diversified and higher value, and more time-sensitive products are being shipped. In India, for example, more shippers are moving from using transport agents and the spot market to longer-term contracts with transport companies, with the contracts incorporating performance standards and penalties. A similar pattern is happening in Pakistan: the normal arrangements for delivery of a container from Lahore to the Karachi ports are 48 hours at a rate of US$ 280 per /FEU, but a premium service is also available, with delivery in 28 hours (three drivers and continuous operation) at a rate of US$ 417/FEU.

Transport is a derived demand, and will adapt to changing requirements from the shippers. As distribution and supply changes become more complex, and the demand for shorter transit times and strict delivery schedules become more important, more integrated logistics will develop and this will lead to major changes in some segments of the trucking industry. The modernization of the sector, and the facilitation of more advanced trucking operations, particularly the shift to multi-axle vehicles, would be encouraged by control of overloading, the setting of road user charges to reflect vehicle road damage costs, and the completion of a high-speed highway network, which would allow modern trucks to be utilized in their most economic manner.

Rail Transport

Though rail transport has lost considerable market share in the freight sector, it remains very important in India for the movement of low-value, bulk commodities, and has the potential throughout South

[4] Overloading is assisted in Pakistan by the main trade route being along the Indus Valley, with no appreciable gradients.

Asia to play a much greater role in trade transport, particularly for the movement of containers to and from ports. Major changes in the South Asian railway sector are now underway or are proposed. Very significant improvements in operational and financial performance have already been brought about in Indian Railways (IR), and restructuring of both Bangladesh Railways (BR) and Pakistan Railways (PR), giving a greater emphasis to freight, are at the beginning stages of implementation. Unfortunately, both BR and PR have to overcome decades of underinvestment in their freight sectors, which has left them with fleets of four-wheeler wagons more suitable to the museum or scrap yard than to modern freight operations.

The railway sector in Bangladesh has the major disadvantage of two-track gauges, broad gauge in the west and meter gauge in the east, and limited links between the two systems. While rail's freight role has diminished very substantially, demand for container transport on the Chittagong–Dhaka corridor exceeds demand, and shippers have to wait, on average, three to five days for wagons. The demand for rail on such a short haul (the road distance is only 220 km) is surprising, but reflects low road service standards, the lack of tractor-trailers, the difficulties of sending uncleared containers by road, and the faster and cheaper customs clearance at the Dhaka ICD compared with the Chittagong port. Capacity on the link is limited by track capacity and the priority given to passenger trains, the lack of container wagons, and the limited space at the ICD.

The financial and operational performance of BR is grossly inadequate, and a major programme of investment and reform has just started, supported by the ADB and the World Bank. The objective is to turn BR into a market-oriented enterprise with improved governance, financial management, human resources, and operational systems, with the eventual aim of creating a government-owned corporation. The investment programme will ease track capacity constraints and begin to re-equip the railway with modern wagons.

Unlike the other railways in South Asia, IR's freight traffic has consistently increased, though its overall market share has declined. IR made the decision to abandon wagon-load general cargo and concentrate resources on train-load bulk traffic, which now accounts for well over 90 per cent of its total freight traffic. Container traffic has, however, increased very rapidly; the container sector is managed by the Container Corporation of India (Concor), a listed company with minority private shareholders. Concor's traffic rose from 700,000 TEU in fiscal 1997 to over 1.9 million TEU in fiscal 2006, and it has established a nationwide network of ICDs. Concor is a major player on the key route from Mumbai to Delhi, but faces problems in meeting the growing demand, too few wagons and too few train paths on the congested track.

Indian Railways' financial position deteriorated to the early 2000s, with the operational ratio approaching 100 per cent and under-provisioning for depreciation. However, in the last few years, the situation has improved. Traffic has increased rapidly (reflecting the growth in the economy), operational performance has improved significantly, and financial results have shown a rapid turnaround. The better financial results reflect both increased traffic and a far more commercial approach to pricing. To raise capacity in the container sector, IR made the decision to end Concor's monopoly, and has licensed an additional 13 operators on the same basic 'hook and haul' arrangement under which Concor operates. The new operators are presently sourcing wagons to start their operations. With the increasing number of operators, track capacity is becoming a major constraint on IR's main commercial routes, and the decision has been taken to construct a network of freight-only corridors, which will provide a major increase in freight capacity, as well as allowing faster services and heavier—and thus more economic—loads.

The railway sector in Pakistan failed to respond to the development of the highway network and the emergence of a highly competitive trucking industry. PR has become a medium-sized passenger railway, which also carries some freight. As with BR, one of the basic limitations has been the lack of modern wagons but, with some new fast-speed container flat wagons, PR has commenced a scheduled container service between Karachi and Lahore, and its container traffic increased from 8,000 to 28,000 TEU over the period fiscal 2001–5. There is, however, a much larger potential demand; PR is only carrying some 5 per cent of the containers handled at the ports.

The NTCIP gives high priority to the rail freight business, with the objective of raising freight traffic and revenues very substantially through the provision of more scheduled, fast freight services between the ports and the main production and consumption centres. The draft business plan foresees a total investment of about US$ 1.7 billion, excluding major new lines, with the investment designed to modernize the train control systems, as well as providing additional locomotive power and modern rolling stock. Key to the success of the programme will be the creation of effective freight and passenger business units in order to redress the lack of managerial and operational priorities currently given to freight traffic, and overcoming the entrenched legacy of priority given to passengers within PR and the Ministry of Railways.

Customs

The customs sector is changing very rapidly in South Asia, at least in India and Pakistan. The region has the reputation of having immensely complex and cumbersome customs procedures with a large number of procedures, documents, copies, and signatures. Such complex systems required traders to use the services of customs agents (sometimes termed customs house agents), who understood both the formal and informal complexities of the systems. One diagnostic study by Transparency International at Chittagong found that informal payments had to be made at 35 different steps in the import clearance process.

In the mid- to late 1990s, the situation began to change with the introduction of computer systems into the customs business. The pace of change has accelerated in recent years, and some countries are now approaching a paperless system, and follow the principles of the Revised Kyoto Convention. All the countries in the region have computerized customs systems.

- Afghanistan,[5] Bangladesh, and Nepal have adopted UNCTAD's ASYCUDA.
- Bhutan employed contractors to develop BACS.
- Indian customs developed ICEGATE.
- Pakistan developed PRAL, but recently introduced PaCCS for the clearance of containers at the port terminals and the Lahore ICD.

In addition to the computerized systems, several countries have been simplifying and reducing the number of procedures required

[5] Afghanistan is having to rebuild almost its entire customs service and infrastructure after the many years of strife; ASYCUDA is currently being implemented, and the transit module, for movement from the border to inland destinations, has been successfully implemented.

for both exports and imports. There has also been a move away from 100 per cent physical examination of cargo to the use of risk management systems. However, the process of streamlining customs has proceeded much further in some countries than in others. For example, India has moved to an almost paperless system, with the last remaining step being the electronic signature on the customs declaration, while Nepal has only really adopted the revenue and statistic modules of ASYCUDA, and the clearance system itself remains largely manual.[6]

Some impressive results have already been achieved, with customs clearance times at the main gateway ports falling markedly, and customs clearance now no longer being the major cause of extended cargo dwell time at the ports in India and Pakistan. Documentation, numbers of copies required, etc., remain excessive, but this partly reflects the complexity of the trading system, with numerous incentives schemes under which goods can be manufactured and exported, as well as the growing number of trade arrangements with different countries and trading blocs. The frequent changes to tariffs and tariff exemptions further complicate system maintenance.

While the recent progress has been marked and very rapid, further work is required to complete the overall modernization of the customs' regimes. In some countries, like Bangladesh and Nepal, the systems have to be extended to more customs functions, moving more to the paperless system, and further reducing the personal interface between the trader and the customs official; in other countries, the systems need to be rolled out from the gateway ports and main ICDs to the other customs stations; the risk management systems have to be developed in a systematic fashion to provide the data and intelligence required for them to be effective; electronic signatures and payment systems have to be developed and accepted; and, generally, further streamlining of procedures and reduced supporting documentation is both possible and desirable.

Overall, however, the progress made in the last few years has been almost remarkable, and if Pakistan succeeds with the integrated trade community system for which it has recently advertised, a really major advance in trade facilitation will have been achieved.

[6] One component of a recently started ADB funded programme is designed to extend the scope of ASYCUDA application in Nepal.

The Logistics Industry

The supply chains for most internal and external transactions are still relatively simple, and this is reflected in the logistics sector. Most imports are delivered C&F or CIF and most exports are shipped free on board (FOB). The South Asian logistics sector is confined, therefore, to arranging customs clearance and inland transport for imports and delivery to port, inland ICD or buyers' warehouses for exports. Logistics have yet to reach the standards found elsewhere. South Asia produces a very significant share of the world's fruit and vegetables, but the region's participation in world trade for these perishable commodities is still very limited, largely confined to supplying ethnic communities in the Middle East and the United Kingdom. The exceptions are commodities with long shelf lives, like grapes and kinnows, which do not require the tightly controlled time and quality supply chains that more perishable commodities require.

In the smaller economies, the logistics sector has moved little beyond basic activities with the exception of India, where the industry is beginning to change, paralleling the increasing complexity of production and distribution. The development of the Indian economy and its very rapid growth has generated considerable interest from the international logistics companies, which are now entering the market. All the major express carriers have a major presence, and many other logistics providers are either establishing subsidiaries or are buying into local companies. The flow of international participation is not one way, as a number of Indian companies are also establishing overseas offices to widen the scope of their services.

The development of the automotive and parts industry in India has generated the need for much more sophisticated logistics to meet the just-in-time production schedules. The logistics sector has responded by either going into joint venture with overseas companies (such as the Transport Corporation of India) or developing indigenously (such as TVS). National networks are developing, and the replacement of state taxes by VAT should be a major impetus to the streamlining of supply and distribution systems, as will a reasonably fast national arterial highway network. The development of organized retail chains, especially with international companies such as Wal-Mart, participating in the wholesaling activity, will result in further major changes, which are likely to have substantial spin-off effects in the logistics arrangements for other sectors. For example, establishing the supply networks for perishable commodities destined for domestic retail chains could be adapted relatively quickly to provide the types of logistics necessary to break into the higher-value sectors of the export market for fruit and vegetables.

The logistics sector is developing as demand changes and becomes more logistics intensive, although the proportion of South Asian companies using logistics companies is still relatively low. It is important that governments facilitate the development of the sector by minimizing regulation and allowing the participation of international logistics companies that will bring in the technology and management practices that have proved successful in other countries and are needed in the rapidly growing 'new' sectors in South Asia. Both India and Pakistan have adopted an open approach to the participation of international operators, but Bangladesh has been more restrictive, with financial requirements that are likely to deter international participation. If experience in other sectors is a guide, once domestic companies appreciate the benefits of modern logistics, there will be a rapid growth in domestic logistics companies, allied with the IT sector, which will then themselves expand internationally. To an extent, this is already happening.

Trade and Transport Facilitation in Intra-regional Trade

While there have been substantial advances in trade transport facilitation in South Asia in recent years, these advances have been largely confined to inter-regional trade and the main trade transport corridors. The priority given to facilities and facilitation for inter-regional trade by the larger economies reflects the importance of such trade in their overall trade (Table 12.3).

Intra-regional trade is a very small proportion of the region's overall trade. In contrast, inter-regional trade accounts for over 95 per cent of all trade. The importance of intra-regional trade is large for the smaller economies in the region, but is almost trivial for India, although it accounts for well over half of the region's total intra-regional trade.

In some cases, such as between Afghanistan and Pakistan, intra-regional trade uses the main inter-regional trade corridors, and some other intra-regional trade will have benefited from the improvements in the port sector. However, much of the intra-regional trade is carried by truck on routes outside the main trade corridors. Some investments

TABLE 12.3: South Asia Trade, 2005

	Imports from SAARC		*Exports to SAARC*	
	US$ million	*% total exports*	*US$ million*	*% total exports*
World	145,155		134,871	
SAARC	5,897	5.1	5,621	3.20
Afghanistan	112	20.0	1,208	37.8
Bangladesh	196	2.1	1,907	13.8
Bhutan	90	30.0	100	25.0
India	3,469	3.5	837	0.60
Nepal	385	46.4	867	46.6
Pakistan	1,645	10.3	702	2.80
Inter-regional	139,258	94.9	129,250	96.8

Source: World Bank staff.

have been made, such as rehabilitation and upgrading of the N34 and the SH1 and SH10 under the West Bengal Corridor Development Project, which will help to raise transport standards for Bangladesh–India trade. The investments in the ICDs in Nepal will facilitate Nepal's bilateral trade with India, as well as its transit connections for inter-regional trade. Nepal's trade links should also benefit from the construction of the East–West Highway. In general, these routes have received much lower priority in terms of infrastructure development and provide much lower levels of service.

Much of the trade uses the relatively unimproved parts of the road network, consequently trucks' speed are very slow. Prior to the ongoing improvements to the roads in West Bengal, truck transit times between Kolkata and Petrapole, at the border with Bangladesh, have been estimated as between six and 10 hours, for a distance of under 100 km Truck transit time between Nepal and Kolkata is four days, for a distance of under 700 km. Excessive loading of trucks is partly the cause of the slow speed, but roads in poor condition with inadequate capacity are also a major factor. Nepal has to use the road networks in Uttar Pradesh and Bihar to reach the main trade corridor routes, and truck speed on these state networks may be less than 20 km per hour, especially in Bihar.

Major advances have been made in computerizing customs clearance and streamlining procedures. These advances have, however, been very largely confined to the gateways for inter-regional trade.

The computerized systems have been rolled out to some of the most important land customs stations, but they may not be applied to all trade (for example, Indian Customs has installed ICEGATE at Raxaul, the main border crossing with Nepal, but the system only handles exports; other trade has to use the old manual systems) or may not be functional because of poor communications or power supplies (such as at Petrapole). Consequently, much of the intra-regional trade is still cleared through manual systems, which require considerable personal interface between the trader, or agent, and the customs official. Risk management and linked green channel systems for the expedited clearance of consignments from traders who are either authorized or have a good compliance record are not yet applied to the land border crossings.

Unlike ports or airports, the land crossings require the consecutive clearance through two sets of officials. Most land border stations operate restricted hours and are not open at night; some customs authorities do not work a seven-day week (Bangladesh customs is closed on Fridays). The time window for processing customs and other formalities at a land border crossing may thus be reduced to a few hours per day, and not on every day. Land borders face not only the issue of customs control, but also of security. These concerns are important along most borders in South Asia, reflecting the legacy of years of fraught relations between neighbouring countries. Even along the India–Nepal border, traditionally an open border, security is becoming a greater concern. However, even where security is tight, informal trade flourishes within groups that straddle the border areas.

While all the continental South Asian countries are now members of SAARC, some of the formal trade transport links are still subject to restriction. Pakistan, for example, operates a positive list of goods that can be traded with India, and Bangladesh has restricted some goods from crossing the land borders. Partly as a consequence of these trade restrictions, partly as a consequence of tariffs and other import-related taxes, and partly as a consequence of the high cost of trading through formal channels, there are significant flows of either informal or misreported trade in the region. These flows may equal the levels of formal trade on some of the trade links. Reducing the costs of formal trade, improving customs clearance, and upgrading the infrastructure, may shift some informal trade to formal channels, but are unlikely to eliminate informal channels unless accompanied by the removal of trade barriers and reduction in import-related taxation levels.

The present pattern of intra-regional, formal trade flows is outlined in Table 12.4.

TABLE 12.4: SAARC Region: Intra-regional Formal Trade Flows, 2005–6 (US$ million)

	Destination Country						
Origin	*Bangladesh*	*India*	*Nepal*	*Pakistan*	*Bhutan*	*Afghanistan*	*Total*
Bangladesh	–	157	4	51	4	7	223
India	1636	–	859	943[7]	84	147	3669
Nepal	6	347	–	4	1	0	358
Pakistan	228	284	3	–	0	832	1347
Bhutan	0	88	1	1	–	*	90
Afghanistan	9	66	0	53	*	–	128
Total	1879	942	867	1052	89	986	5815

Source: World Bank staff.
Note: * denotes that data is unavailable.

India dominates trade within the region and has major trade surpluses with all the other countries, most strikingly with Bangladesh. The trade imbalance with Pakistan would be considerably larger if informal trade was also included. A recent report on informal and misreported trade between the two countries estimated Indian exports to Pakistan of US$ 514 million and imports of only US$ 10 million. There is relatively little trade between non-neighbouring countries; such trade has to face the complexities of transit, as well as intra-regional trade documentation.

CONSTRAINTS TO INTRA-REGIONAL TRADE

Restrictions on Trade

The countries in the South Asian region have a number of restrictions in place that either reduce or complicate and shift formal trade into informal channels:

[7] Indian exports to Pakistan have increased rapidly over the last three years. Much of the increased trade in FY06 was sugar, totalling US$ 339 million.

Bangladesh

Certain commodities, such as yarn and textiles, are not allowed to be imported across the land border with India and have to be shipped to Chittagong. This increases the import time and cost considerably for imports from India, as all containers have to be routed via a hub port such as Singapore. The regulation was implemented to protect Bangladesh yarn and textile producers. These restrictions were one of the reasons for the failure of the inland water transport (IWT) service that Concor developed in 2005, in association with Bangladesh and Indian shipping companies. They found that two of the target commodities, textiles and rice, could not be transported by IWT. With the development of a direct container shipping service between India and Pakistan, the time and cost penalties will have been reduced quite considerably, but the road route would offer the quickest and lowest-cost routing for much of this traffic. Thus, the trade barrier remains, though it may have been somewhat lowered.

Pakistan

The positive list approach to trade with India results in a significant level of misreported trade. Exports from India are routed to Dubai, where the goods are relabeled and then shipped to Pakistan under a different certificate of origin. Alternatively, the bill of lading may be switched once the goods are on the vessel and are then shipped directly to Pakistan. Such 'switch' bills of lading are illegal, but are reported to be obtained at a relatively modest cost. The misreported trade enters into Pakistan as legal trade, but from an incorrect origin. This trade is different from the exports from India that are routed via Dubai, Iran, and Afghanistan, and then cross the border into Pakistan by camel or donkey as informal trade. Such routing is designed to avoid high Pakistani import-related taxes—the importers are prepared to pay considerably higher transport costs as well as Afghan customs duties in order to evade Pakistan's taxation. The flow of informal trade from India into Pakistan is reported to have diminished somewhat in recent years, with corresponding growth in informal trade from China.

India

The 1996 Indo-Nepal Trade Treaty gave duty-free access to goods manufactured in Nepal and removed the value addition norms of the previous treaty. Nepalese exports to India grew rapidly, but India claimed that some of the exports were effectively only the reexport of third-country imports into Nepal. The revised treaty, signed in 2002, reimposed eligibility criteria and established quotas for four products, exports beyond which would be subject to MFN customs duties. The Federation of Nepalese Chambers of Commerce and Industry normally does not issue certificates of origin under MFN status, apparently fearing that such trade would endanger duty-free access for other products.

Constraints to Cross-Border Rail Transport

Rail transport often offers easier customs clearance procedures than road transport. This may be due, in part, to the lower unit value of much of the rail cargo, but it may also be due, in part, to the public ownership of the railways. The advantages are most manifest with respect to transit traffic for which bonds and other restrictions are often not required if the goods are moved by rail. Given the inadequacies of much of South Asia's highway infrastructure, rail should offer potential for intra-regional trade, especially over longer distances. Unfortunately, the realization of that potential in South Asia is constrained by the deficiencies in the asset base of some of the regional railways, as well as the freight priorities of Indian Railways.

Afghanistan-Pakistan

There is currently no direct rail link from Pakistan to Afghanistan, though there are plans to extend the Quetta–Chaman line across the border. The Afghan Transit Trade Agreement (ATTA) required that commercial trade in transit through Pakistan had to use PR, but this has been somewhat relaxed and the National Logistics Cell is now authorized to carry such cargo by road and to subcontract to other truckers. Pakistan's trade with Afghanistan that originates in the Karachi area should find rail attractive given the very long haul, but PR's inadequate capacity and service standards mean that almost all bilateral trade is carried by truck.

Bangladesh-India

There is quite a considerable flow of low-value exports from India to Bangladesh by rail. The traffic can only be carried in IR wagons as few BR wagons meet the technical standards (brake systems and wagon running speeds) required on IR. BR locomotives haul the wagons inside Bangladesh, but as IR trains are longer and heavier than those operated on BR, the trains have to be reconfigured at the border.

Intra-regional rail traffic cannot reach the main markets in Bangladesh. The broad-gauge wagons from India cannot cross the Jamuna Bridge, despite the availability of a broad-gauge track, as it does not have the capacity to handle fully laden IR wagons. One study reported that wagons carrying containers would meet the loading standards, but containers are currently not allowed to cross the land border and, in any case, the broad-gauge track does not yet extend down to Dhaka and Chittagong, the main centres. Rail cargo has thus to be transshipped at some point to BR wagons, trucks, or barges for final delivery, diminishing the attractiveness of rail.

Bhutan-India

Bhutan is currently not connected to the IR network, although lines are relatively close to the border. Bhutan's level of foreign merchandise trade is limited, and its level of trade with countries other than India even smaller (possibly 6–8 TEU/day). IR is only interested in running train-load traffic, and the demand for such services from Bhutan would be very limited, and thus the likely economics of extending the rail network across the border is poor.

India-Nepal

Raxual, the main Indian border crossing into Nepal is now connected by broad-gauge railway. The line was extended across the border in the late 1990s to a rail-based ICD at Birgunj. The line and the ICD were opened in 2004, after considerable delay in awarding the management concession for the ICD and negotiating the rail operating agreement. The ICD was designed primarily to handle transit traffic to Nepal, and Concor operates about three unit trains week from Kolkata to Birgung. This level of traffic is only about half of the levels forecast in the feasibility study; consequently, the ICD is underutilized, and its revenue is seriously below the concessionaire's expectations, raising problems with regard to payment of the concession fees. Export traffic from Nepal continues to use road transport; rail does not provide scheduled service, but operates when a trainload has been assembled. This pattern of service does not provide the reliability that exporters require to meet delivery deadlines and shipping dates.

To increase utilization of the ICD, it has been agreed to open the ICD to both non-containerized traffic and bilateral trade. Raxual is reported to receive about 13 trainloads of traffic for Nepal each month, but relatively little of this traffic has been attracted to the ICD. This may be partly the result of the Indian government's refusal to allow open wagons to cross the border—traffic is restricted to container flats, covered wagons, and tanker wagons. Truck operators have also resisted the transfer of edible oils from road to rail for the movement from Kolkata.

India-Pakistan

Both IR and PR are now essentially broad-gauge railways with the same permissible axle-loads and maximum speeds.[8] There should be little infrastructure constraint to major freight flows between the two countries. There are currently two rail links connecting the countries, but the link in Sindh only carries passenger trains, the Thar Express. The freight link is through Wagah-Attari. PR locomotives haul trains to the border, where IR locomotives take over. Wagons are interchanged on a balance system—the wagons balances have to be cleared every 10 days. This form of interchange can give rise to wagons not being available when required and traders having to wait until wagon balances have been reestablished. Most railways elsewhere have much more flexible interchange arrangements, which minimize the delays. It is presumed that the wagon balance approach is designed to minimize the costs to each railway if the border was to close again and wagons were stranded in the adjoining country.

While the infrastructure standards are similar, there are major differences in the quality of the wagons. PR has few modern, bogie wagons, and the available fleet is concentrated on the main Karachi to Lahore corridor. PR's wagons for transport to India are largely confined to the old four-wheeler stock, except for the 10 bogie parcel vans attached to the passenger trains. These uneconomic four-wheeler wagons have been almost entirely scrapped by IR, and IR would not want to operate long-distance freight trains with old PR stock. The availability of wagons was not a major issue when trade was low, but, with the recent increases, capacity has become

[8] IR still has quite an extensive network of metre-gauge lines, but these now carry very little freight traffic. All the main metre-gauge lines have been converted to broad gauge under IR's Unigauge Programme. PR has a very small and little used network of metre-gauge line.

a constraint, leading to long delays (especially for nonperishable goods), informal payments for wagon allocation, and the diversion of trade to the sea route via Mumbai to Karachi. Goods traded between the two Punjabs may, as a consequence, travel more than 3,000 km rather than a land route of less than 300 km. Indian sugar exporters recently complained bitterly about the lack of rail capacity when Pakistan imported substantial quantities.

There are few reports of major customs clearance or other formality problems with the rail movement, though cargo is inspected and is often trans-shipped to truck once the border is crossed.

Constraints to Cross-Border Truck Transport

Rail transport often offers easier customs clearance procedures than road transport. This may be due, in part, to the lower unit value of much of the rail cargo, but it may also be due, in part, to the public ownership of the railways. The advantages are most manifest with respect to transit traffic for which bonds and other restrictions are often not required if the goods are moved by rail. Given the inadequacies of much of South Asia's highway infrastructure, rail should offer potential for intra-regional trade, especially over longer distances. Unfortunately, the realization of that potential in South Asia is constrained by the deficiencies in the asset base of some of the regional railways, as well as the freight priorities of Indian Railways.

Afghanistan-Pakistan

There is currently no direct rail link from Pakistan to Afghanistan, though there are plans to extend the Quetta–Chaman line across the border. The Afghan Transit Trade Agreement (ATTA) required that commercial trade in transit through Pakistan had to use PR, but this has been somewhat relaxed and the National Logistics Cell is now authorized to carry such cargo by road and to subcontract to other truckers. Pakistan's trade with Afghanistan that originates in the Karachi area should find rail attractive given the very long haul, but PR's inadequate capacity and service standards mean that almost all bilateral trade is carried by truck.

Bangladesh-India

There is quite a considerable flow of low-value exports from India to Bangladesh by rail. The traffic can only be carried in IR wagons as few BR wagons meet the technical standards (brake systems and wagon running speeds) required on IR. BR locomotives haul the wagons inside Bangladesh, but as IR trains are longer and heavier than those operated on BR, the trains have to be reconfigured at the border.

Intra-regional rail traffic cannot reach the main markets in Bangladesh. The broad-gauge wagons from India cannot cross the Jamuna Bridge, despite the availability of a broad-gauge track, as it does not have the capacity to handle fully laden IR wagons. One study reported that wagons carrying containers would meet the loading standards, but containers are currently not allowed to cross the land border and, in any case, the broad-gauge track does not yet extend down to Dhaka and Chittagong, the main centres. Rail cargo has thus to be transshipped at some point to BR wagons, trucks, or barges for final delivery, diminishing the attractiveness of rail.

Bhutan-India

Bhutan is currently not connected to the IR network, although lines are relatively close to the border. Bhutan's level of foreign merchandise trade is limited, and its level of trade with countries other than India even smaller (possibly 6–8 TEU/day). IR is only interested in running train-load traffic, and the demand for such services from Bhutan would be very limited, and thus the likely economics of extending the rail network across the border is poor.

India-Nepal

Raxual, the main Indian border crossing into Nepal is now connected by broad-gauge railway. The line was extended across the border in the late 1990s to a rail-based ICD at Birgunj. The line and the ICD were opened in 2004, after considerable delay in awarding the management concession for the ICD and negotiating the rail operating agreement. The ICD was designed primarily to handle transit traffic to Nepal, and Concor operates about three unit trains week from Kolkata to Birgung. This level of traffic is only about half of the levels forecast in the feasibility study. Consequently, the ICD is underutilized, and its revenue is seriously below the concessionaire's expectations, raising problems with regard to payment of the concession fees. Export traffic from Nepal continues to use road transport; rail does not provide scheduled service, but operates when a trainload has been assembled.

This pattern of service does not provide the reliability that exporters require to meet delivery deadlines and shipping dates.

To increase utilization of the ICD, it has been agreed to open the ICD to both non-containerized traffic and bilateral trade. Raxual is reported to receive about 13 trainloads of traffic for Nepal each month, but relatively little of this traffic has been attracted to the ICD. This may be partly the result of the Indian government's refusal to allow open wagons to cross the border—traffic is restricted to container flats, covered wagons, and tanker wagons. Truck operators have also resisted the transfer of edible oils from road to rail for the movement from Kolkata.

India-Pakistan

Both IR and PR are now essentially broad-gauge railways with the same permissible axle-loads and maximum speeds.[9] There should be little infrastructure constraint to major freight flows between the two countries. There are currently two rail links connecting the countries, but the link in Sindh only carries passenger trains, the Thar Express. The freight link is through Wagah–Attari. PR locomotives haul trains to the border, where IR locomotives take over. Wagons are interchanged on a balance system—the wagons balances have to be cleared every 10 days. This form of interchange can give rise to wagons not being available when required and traders having to wait until wagon balances have been re-established. Most railways elsewhere have much more flexible interchange arrangements, which minimize the delays. It is presumed that the wagon balance approach is designed to minimize the costs to each railway if the border was to close again and wagons were stranded in the adjoining country.

While the infrastructure standards are similar, there are major differences in the quality of the wagons. PR has few modern, bogie wagons, and the available fleet is concentrated on the main Karachi to Lahore corridor. PR's wagons for transport to India are largely confined to the old four-wheeler stock, except for the 10-bogie parcel vans attached to the passenger trains. These uneconomic four-wheeler wagons have been almost entirely scrapped by IR, and IR would not

[9] IR still has quite an extensive network of metre-gauge lines, but these now carry very little freight traffic. All the main metre-gauge lines have been converted to broad gauge under IR's Unigauge Programme. PR has a very small and little used network of metre-gauge line.

want to operate long-distance freight trains with old PR stock. The availability of wagons was not a major issue when trade was low, but, with the recent increases, capacity has become a constraint, leading to long delays (especially for non-perishable goods), informal payments for wagon allocation, and the diversion of trade to the sea route via Mumbai to Karachi. Goods traded between the two Punjabs may, as a consequence, travel more than 3,000 km rather than a land route of less than 300 km. Indian sugar exporters recently complained bitterly about the lack of rail capacity when Pakistan imported substantial quantities.

There are few reports of major customs clearance or other formality problems with the rail movement, though cargo is inspected and is often transshipped to truck once the border is crossed.

The Landport Philosophy

Seaports and airports are necessary misfortunes; the interfaces between ocean or air transport and land transport. There is nothing that can be done other than to minimize the cost and disruption that they impose on the transport chain. Land borders are very different, being a political rather than a geographical barrier. The same forms of transport can and do operate on both sides of a land border, and while a political interface exists, there is no reason why a transport interface needs also exist. The transport interface, if it exists, is a political creation.

Unfortunately, there seems to be a growing trend in South Asia to view land borders as seacoasts and to create the land equivalent of seaports at the frontiers. Bangladesh has moved the farthest down this path with the establishment of a Land Port Authority, which is seeking public–private partnerships to develop facilities at the frontier—cargo handling facilities, storage facilities, and ancillary infrastructure and services. India has recently announced that it is going to establish a similar authority, with a plan to construct 13 integrated check posts (ICP) along its borders at a cost of Rs 853 crore (US$ 190 million). These ICPs would house all the regulatory agencies like immigration, customs, and border security, together with support facilities like parking, warehousing, banking, and hotels in a single complex.

Improved border facilities are very much to be welcomed, especially if they include reliable power supply and telecommunications. The need for border crossing formalities, covering both people and vehicles, is likely to remain for the foreseeable future, and efficient facilities would help to reduce their costs. The danger is that the investment in cargo handling and storage facilities would create major impediments to the streamlining of freight movement across the borders by generating vested interests in maintaining present procedures and the resulting revenues. Customs and other border control officers may already have interest in maintaining slow and cumbersome procedures as they provide opportunities for 'speed' payments; a Transparency International study at Benapole identified 30 separate points in the cargo clearance process where informal payments had to be made, with payments going to both customs and land port officials. Private investors, and the people employed by them, are likely to have no interest in the through movement of cargo and vehicles.

Once constructed, there is the danger that these land ports will become permanent blocks on the economic landscape of South Asia. On the other hand, the present freight arrangements at many of the borders are so poor, and the costs so high that improved handling and storage facilities could undoubtedly provide significant benefits. Unfortunately, such short-term benefits could well result in continuing long-term costs. It is a question of whether there is a reasonable prospect of introducing the types of cargo and vehicle arrangements that exist elsewhere in the world, which obviate the need for the border transshipment of trade.

Streamlining Intra-regional Trade

South Asia has the lowest level of intra-regional trade of any region, even lower than Sub-Saharan Africa and the Middle East and North Africa (Table 12.5).

The economic size of India, in comparison with the other countries in South Asia, is clearly one factor underlying the low percentage level of trade, but a comparable situation exists in East Asia with China, though the intra-regional trade is almost six times larger. The similarity of the production patterns and main exports may also be a contributory factor, as well as the legacy of the past political difficulties in the region. However, the importance of the difficulties attached to trade within the region, and its time and costs, should not be underestimated. For enterprises in many South Asian

TABLE 12.5: World Intra-regional Trade Flows, 2005

	Trade with Own Region	
	% total exports	*% total imports*
South Asia	4.7	3.1
East Asia and Pacific: low income	9.6	18.4
Europe and Central Asia	21.1	22.9
Middle East and North Africa	2.2	6.6
Sub-Saharan Africa	6.8	6.8
South and Central America	20.8	25.2
East Asia and Pacific: high income	19.1	16.5
EEC15	58.2	54.7
NAFTA	59.0	34.0

Source: World Bank staff.
Notes: Data for South and Central America exclude Mexico. EEC15 are the more recent EU members included in Europe and Central Asia.

countries, inter-regional trade may well be easier than trading within the region.

While each of the important intra-regional trading links has particular characteristics and issues, there are some common features that need to be addressed if intra-regional trade is to grow to the levels achieved in other regions, such as:

- allowing cross-border movement of road transport;
- improving the capacity of regional rail links; and
- upgrading the levels of customs and trade facilitation reform for those at the gateway ports.

Achieving these objectives would provide the trade transport facilitation basis for substantially increased trade. Whether such trade develops would then depend more upon modifications to trade regimes, as in the case of India-Pakistan, or political attitudes to trade, as with Bangladesh-India.

Cross-Border Trucking

With limited exceptions, trucks cannot cross borders in South Asia, but neighbouring countries in all other regions of the world have developed procedures and safeguards to allow cross-border truck movement and direct delivery of freight. There are various potential ways that such a desirable outcome might be achieved in South Asia.

- *Limited-time entry for cargo delivery.* This is the practice between India and Nepal; extending this approach to the rest of South Asia, even for 72 hours, would encompass significant potential trade links, such as between northern India and Pakistan's Punjab province. Ideally, however, the time allowed within the neighbouring country should be adjusted to reflect the transport reality; for example, it may take longer than 72 hours for trucks to reach Dhaka and then return to cross the Indian border.
- *Route licensing for foreign trucks.* A broader solution would be the provision of specific route licenses for foreign truckers without the time restriction. This would solve the problem of the lack of effective reciprocity that might exist with the fixed-time approach, that is, major cargo destinations in only one of the trading countries may be reached within the allowable time, as is possibly the case between India and Nepal. An issue for route licensing, important in the case of highly imbalanced traffic flows, is that the trucking industry of the exporting country might dominate the business. Though customers in the importing country would benefit from reduced costs and faster delivery, dominance by the trucks of the exporting country is likely to raise objections, both legal and non-legal, from the truckers of the importing country. The power of the trucking lobbies can be strong, especially in some of the border areas. It may be essential, therefore, that truckers on both sides of the border perceive the potential for financial gain.
- *Dual-country vehicle registration.* Vehicles would be registered in both countries, obtaining the relevant licenses and paying the applicable taxes. To an extent, this already happens between Afghanistan and Pakistan. To protect national interests, a first step might be to have the number of trucks with such dual registration limited by quota to ensure an equal or equitable distribution of the traffic between the truckers of the different countries.

It is conceivable that security concerns might be raised regarding foreign nationals driving trucks in the country (though this seems acceptable elsewhere in the world). This could be addressed by the dual registration of semi-trailers—the semi-trailer would be delivered to the border by the tractor unit of one country, and then hauled by a tractor unit from the neighbouring country. Such arrangements often take place at sea crossings, such as between England and France, so as to avoid the cost of shipping the tractor unit. However, such an arrangement would require a level of trust between trucking enterprises that might currently not exist. It is also a solution more applicable to organized, formal sector enterprises, which comprise a relatively small proportion of the trucking industries throughout South Asia.

- *Joint-venture trucking companies.* This would be a more restrictive form of the dual-vehicle registration. It would reduce the flexibility and possibly the capacity of the system, but it could be a major improvement upon the present transshipment. In effect, the formal requirement of a domestic-only trucking system would be preserved. Unfortunately, the drawback of the approach is the possibility that governments would see an opportunity for the creation of public sector trucking enterprises to operate such services, and public sector trucking enterprises have an almost universal record of low service standards, as well as financial and operational failure.
- *Containerization and swap bodies.* If, for political or quasi-security reasons, it is not possible for vehicles to cross borders, then an alternative would be allowing the cross-border movement of containers or other forms of swap bodies, which could be shifted quickly and cheaply from one vehicle to another, avoiding the costs of manually unloading and reloading trucks. Containerization has many advantages in trade logistics, and its use on intra-regional routes would help avoid the unnecessary costs imposed by the present system. Domestic containers from India are already used in intra-regional trade with Nepal, and specific customs procedures have been developed for the movement.

It would require the investment in a pool of regional containers as well, perhaps, as deposits to ensure their return. It would also be necessary to invest in limited container yards at border crossings and suitable container handling equipment. However, such costs would be well below the requirements for warehousing to store cargo, etc.

- *TIR or similar.* The possibilities outlined above do not include the TIR system, which is now such a feature of cross-border transport in Europe and Central Asia. Certainly, TIR or a similar regionally based equivalent system would be very desirable, but such systems address a customs rather than a transport issue, and would allow the clearance of cargo away from the border, providing a guarantee for the payment of customs duties if cargos were diverted to the domestic economy prior to clearance. Certainly some such system would need to accompany the potential solutions, if the full benefits of cross-border trucking are to be achieved. Much of the benefit of such movement would be negated if the trucks had to be offloaded even partially for customs inspection at the border. Similarly, containers would be little improvement to the present system if they have to be stripped at the border for customs examination.
- *Vehicle standards*, While TIR addresses a rather different issue, it does raise the problem of appropriate vehicle standards for cross-border trucking. In theory, Iran allows Afghan trucks to operate inside its territory but, in practice, Afghan trucks cannot operate because they do not meet the vehicle standards required and enforced. Such problems may seem of less consequence in South Asia, where there is little enforcement of any vehicle or trucking regulation. However, unless vehicle standards are rather precisely established and trucks certified as meeting these standards, vehicle safety standards may well be used as a barrier to participation by the trucks of a neighbouring country. Perhaps the real key is whether the governments see liberalizing movement as a zero-sum game or one in which both countries benefit.

Regional Rail Links and Services

In terms of intra-regional trade, rail has the advantages of lower costs, easier border formalities, and often, in South Asia, faster transit times compared with road transport. There is currently some intra-regional trade moved by rail, but the flows are limited by critical capacity and infrastructure constraints.

Bangladesh, India, and Pakistan

The potential benefits for intra-regional trade from direct rail transport are very considerable.

- To move a 40-foot container from Delhi to Lahore, via JNPT and Karachi, currently costs about US$ 2,400; direct rail movement between Delhi and Lahore would cost less than US$ 1,000.
- To move a 20-foot container from Ludhiana, India, to Dhaka via JNPT costs about US$ 2,200 and takes 30 to 40 days; direct rail transport of the container would cost about US$ 1,400 and take 9 or 10 days.

The issue is how to realize the potential. Both BR and PR require modern wagon fleets; their present four-wheeler wagons are incompatible with modern railway operations. BR has also to address infrastructure constraints. In view of the fact that the Jamuna Bridge can probably already accommodate trains loaded with containers, the initial priorities for intra-regional linkages may be: (*a*) agreement on the cross-border movement of containers; and (*b*) completion of the broad-gauge connection to Dhaka.

The physical infrastructure and operating assets must be accompanied by appropriate cost-effective interchange agreements that allow the wagons of one country to move on the network of the neighbouring railway. Such agreements need to provide both flexibility and compensation for wagon use. The present wagon balance system between IR and PR is too restrictive, but no railway wants to see its wagons accumulate within the system of a neighbouring railway. Some form of wagon rental is necessary, perhaps with an escalating price, depending upon the length of wagon detention. It is also possible that some form of payment guarantee system might be necessary to build confidence in the initial stages of such interchange systems. But no system will survive an environment in which wagons are detained for extended periods or payments are delayed. Wagon tracking systems might also be desirable both commercially, so that shippers know where their consignments have reached, and operationally, so that wagons do not get lost on the system of the neighbouring railway.

The first priority should be to raise the capacity and efficiency of cross-border rail freight movement. The second priority would be to improve rail's competitive position. Initially, it might be expected that the railways would each raise their own freight bills—rail users would thus be faced with two freight bills. In the longer term, a more commercial and competitive approach would be a through-freight bill, with the revenue shared between the railways. Joint marketing and pricing, however, might well be beyond the present levels of cooperation between the railway systems in the region.

There is, however, the need to resolve some commercial and operational aspects of joint rail operations; for example:

- whether the trains would be operated as fixed rakes from each railway or in a pool arrangement, which would add flexibility to the arrangement;
- how to market the potential of rail for less than train loads on which Indian railways now concentrates its activities; and
- should there be some intermediary between the customer and the railway to market and consolidate individual consignments to trainload traffics for the railways to haul.

The real question, however, is whether the railways in the region see intra-regional trade as a priority. IR, in particular, faces a growing domestic market, which it finds hard to satisfy. As a result, it may view cross-border traffic as a difficult and complicated market, not worth the management time. An alternative approach to overcome might be some form of cross-border concessionaire to market and manage the traffic, operating on a hook and haul contract with the neighbouring railways.

Afghanistan, Bhutan, and Nepal

Neither Afghanistan nor Nepal have domestic rail networks, but they do have cross-border spur lines. These spur lines allow trains to be originated and terminated within domestic territory which can provide some important advantages. It allows:

- the country to develop the level of infrastructure appropriate to the traffic (storage, processing, repackaging, etc.) and also possibly as the basis for a logistics hub. Such investment and activities rarely occur at railheads on the other side of the border.[10]
- cross-border movement by rail, which often is less cumbersome and time consuming than movement by road; and
- conceptually at least, the country to have its own rail wagon fleet, though such wagons would be hauled by the locomotives of the neighbouring country.

[10] The World Food Programme does have storage facilities for bulk cargo in Peshawar, from which it supplies Afghanistan.

Overall, such spur lines should make rail more attractive, especially if cargo transshipment between trucks is required. The real issue is then whether the quality of service provided by the neighbouring railway makes rail a commercial alternative. IR provides efficient trainload services, but the potential for cross-border movement may be limited by the restrictions on the type of wagon that can cross the border. Such restrictions should be removed as quickly as possible. PR's capacity and service quality is much more limited, and the benefits of a proposed rail spur into Afghanistan may be limited until the restructuring of PR delivers results.

Both Afghanistan and Nepal have levels of trade that may justify rail freight services. Bhutan, with much lower trade flows, is in a more difficult position, given IR's policy on running only trainloads. Bhutan would generate few such services, making investment in spur lines and associated facilities difficult to justify. Low traffic would mean infrequent service, leaving truck transport with important service advantages.

Upgrading Customs and Trade Facilitation

The basic priority actions to enhance intra-regional trade facilitation are to extend the reforms being implemented at the major inter-regional trade gateways to the land border crossings, replacing the manual systems for trade processing and customs clearance by automatic computerized systems. Such a rollout may require investment in more reliable power and data transmission and communications networks. The nature of intra-regional trade may be rather different from inter-regional trade through the major gateways, with smaller traders and smaller consignments. This may necessitate a rather different approach to risk assessment, and perhaps also a rather higher level of examination. As customs reforms and streamlining proceed at the main trade entry and exit points, they should also be applied to intra-regional, land-based trade flows. Reducing the complexity of customs procedures and minimizing the personal interaction between the officials and traders would also help to reduce the levels of corruption said to be prevalent at the land border crossings.

Streamlining customs procedures and reducing the costs of formal trade should help to shift some of the present informal trade to documented channels, as would the normalization of trade relations, most particularly between India and Pakistan. However, they are unlikely to eliminate informal trade where there is a conducive environment and large profits to be made by avoiding formal trade routes and import duties and taxes. Reducing the profits from informal trade by shifting the burden of government revenue generation away from import-related sources may be the ultimate solution, but improved customs enforcement would also assist by increasing the costs of informal trade. Such enforcement has to address corruption among border officials on both sides of the border, and perhaps also the lack of cooperation between these officials.

Greater cross-border cooperation and coordination between customs authorities should be encouraged within the region at both the national and border levels. This is not to suggest that one eliminate customs facilities or similar joint border processing of trade, which is being tried elsewhere. Such developments might have significant benefits, but they seem unlikely any time soon in the region. Rather, close working relations and the sharing of intelligence and data would facilitate the work of customs and other authorities on both sides of the land borders. Even basic telecommunications links between customs offices at the borders would be a step forward. Clearly, history and political and economic differences have resulted in intra-regional relationships with particular characteristics, but customs authorities elsewhere manage good working relationships, despite governmental differences.

Container Movement and Inland Customs Clearance

Modern logistics for nonbulk international trade is founded on: (*a*) the use of containers; and, (*b*) clearance of cargo at or near the importers' premises, rather than at the initial point of entry. Containerized inter-regional trade is commonplace throughout the region, although shipping lines require special arrangements for containers going to Afghanistan. All the countries have procedures to allow customs clearance at an inland destination, away from the entry seaport. But the use of containers for land-based intra-regional trade is very limited (some trade between India and Nepal), and cargo has to be cleared at the border rather than at the destination (Afghanistan is the exception).

The issue of cross-border container movement has to be resolved. A difficult issue is that at some borders there may be security as well as customs concerns. However, if substantially larger flows of intra-regional trade are to develop in South Asia, and trade is to move up the value chain, some means of allowing cross-border container land movement has to be devised. Stripping containers at the borders for customs examination cannot be the answer. Some other solution is required, even if this necessitates the use of scanners to check containers for illicit or nondeclared cargo.

There is also the need to introduce procedures that will allow customs clearance away from the border. Such systems already operate from most gateway ports. Similar systems need to be developed and introduced at the land customs stations, especially if and when through-movement of trucks and containers is allowed. Afghanistan is already moving in this direction, and other countries with ASYCUDA could also use the transit module. Such systems would allow countries to avoid the unnecessary investment, operating costs, and delays associated with land port facilities. Customs bonding systems are in place for the movement of cargo from seaports to inland destinations, and the same systems should be possible from the land border to an inland destination. A regional or international duty guarantee or bond system, like TIR, would be preferable, as duty insurance is often required in both the exporting and importing countries.

Regional Trade Corridors

The approach to improving trade transport facilitation in South Asia has generally been rather fragmented, with each separate institution undertaking reforms, making investments, etc., according to its own priorities. While the actions have raised the overall levels of performance, they have probably been less effective than a more integrated and comprehensive approach to trade facilitation taking into account the key linkages between the links in the trade transport chain. Investments at the ports, for example, will be less effective if the delays caused by customs or other official procedures are not also addressed. Some major improvements are being made to the highway networks, but these could provide a greater stimulus to trade and economic activity if the other constraints to modern truck operations were simultaneously removed or reduced. Reducing the transit time to the border by a few hours is welcome, but the greatest problem may be the days that the trucks wait at the border, rather than the hours that they spend on the road.

While national trade facilitation committees and task forces have been established, they have tended to concentrate rather narrowly upon issues relating to customs and other trade-related documentation. These issues, while extremely important, are only a subset of the total issues that have to be addressed if South Asia is to develop international standard trade transport corridors, providing the region with the increased potential to compete in the global market. Infrastructure, transport operations, transport regulation, and other trade transport issues must also be addressed. Some of these issues may be national, but many may be more corridor specific. To provide a more inclusive approach to raising the levels of trade transport performance, many countries have moved toward a corridor approach, addressing the issues and constraints on a corridor as an integrated problem requiring multifaceted solutions.

Pakistan has adopted this approach with the National Trade Corridor Improvement Program (NTCIP), which includes highway infrastructure, modernization of the trucking, railway, port, customs, and trade logistics sectors. A similar approach on the other main trade corridors, such as Delhi–Mumbai and Dhaka–Chittagong, could well provide greater benefit than the fragmented initiatives of individual ministries and departments. The concept of integrated approaches is attractive, but it requires strong leadership to ensure that the component parts do not simply continue following their more narrow interests.[11] It also requires the integration of all the stakeholders in the corridor: the providers of the infrastructure, the providers of the transport and related services; and the users. This necessarily means a full public-private partnership approach, and this may not be the normal style for policy formulation and decision making in South Asia.

Establishing the corridor approach within a country is not easy; establishing the approach when the corridor connects two countries is even more difficult. But other countries have demonstrated that it is achievable, if there is the underlying belief that trade brings benefits and that efficient trade transport encourages such trade. The Northern Corridor Transport Agreement in East Africa harmonizes the customs procedures and transport regulations of five countries, and finances a secretariat to monitor performance and identify further

[11] NTCIP in Pakistan has the very great advantage of the very committed leadership of the prime minister.

improvements. The Trans-Kalahari Corridor has similarly linked South Africa, Botswana, and Namibia, and the approach has made major improvements to performance along the corridors through Southeastern Europe.

Establishing such corridor-based approaches to improving the trade transport arrangements for intra-regional trade within South Asia may offer a promising alternative to the present unilateral and departmental management of trade transport. Certainly, there are key issues that require a common and coordinated approach if real advances are to be achieved. For example, the issue of customs procedures related to movement of trucks and inland clearance of cargo almost demands an integrated approach. Developing corridor arrangements will certainly be a challenge in the South Asian environment, but the rewards could be very considerable and little else seems likely to provide the desired transformation in intra-regional trade transport.

References

Wilson, John, Catherine Mann, and Tsunehiro Otsuki. 2004. 'Assessing the Potential Benefit of Trade Facilitation: A Global Perspective', World Bank Policy Research Working Paper 3224, February.

World Bank. 2007. *Doing Business in 2006: Creating Jobs*. Washington D.C: World Bank.

ANNEXURE A1

STATISTICS ON GROWTH AND EMPLOYMENT

Kaushik Basu and Annemie Maertens

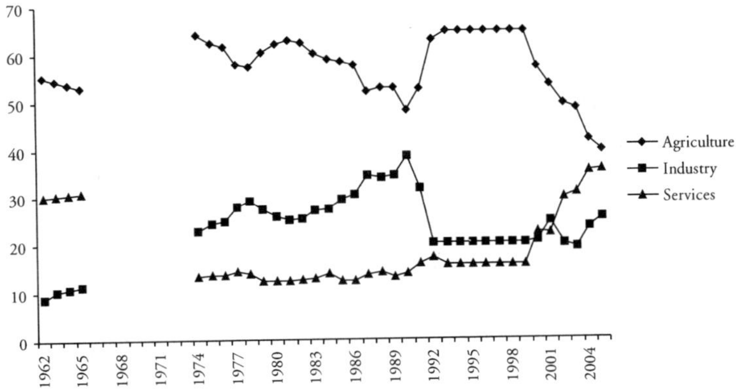

Figure A1.1: Structure of the Economy—Afghanistan

Sources: 1962–5: Key Indicators ADB (January 1973) series; 1974–5: Key Indicators ADB (July 1988); 1976–87: Key Indicators ADB (July 1990); 1988–93 Key Indicators ADB (1996); 1994–2003: UNESCAP Statistical Yearbook of Asia and the Pacific (1994); 2004 and 2005: Key Indicators ADB 2007.

Note: 1962–5 GDP market price by industrial origin in percentage; 1974–5 calculated from GDP by industrial origin at 1978/79 prices; 1976–87 calculated from GDP by industrial origin at 1978/79 prices; 1988–93 calculated from GDP by industrial origin at 1978/79 prices; 1994–2003 calculated from GDP by origin at constant 1990 prices.

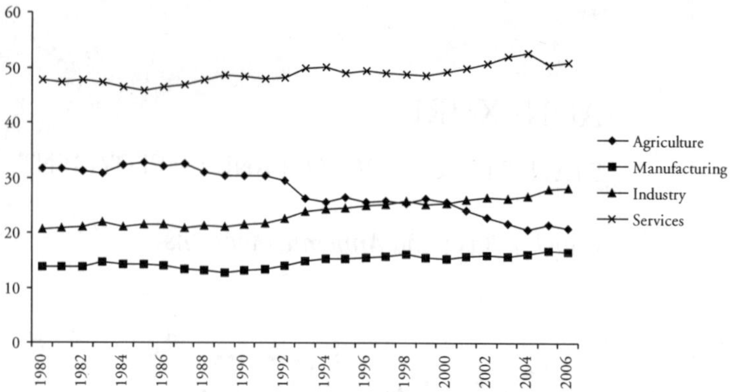

Figure A1.2: Structure of the Economy—Bangladesh

Source: *WDI 2007*.
Note: The *WDI* covers data from 1980–2006. Pre-1980 data is not available from the *WDI*.

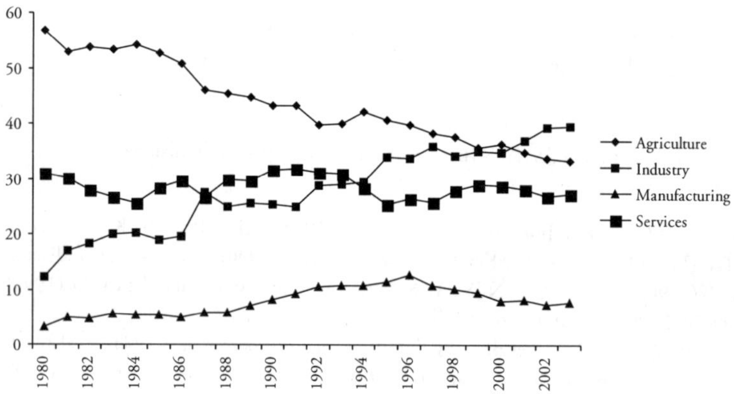

Figure A1.3: Structure of the Economy—Bhutan

Source: *WDI 2007*.
Note: The *WDI* are available up to 2003. *The Statistical Yearbook of Bhutan* also reports data on the sectoral division of the GDP, but the data are not comparable to the *WDI* series and hence are omitted here. Even though the 1977–9 data are available from *ADB Key Indicators* (1984) (series GDP by industrial origin at current market prices from April 1984), we have opted not to show these as there is large sector called 'others' that is not identified.

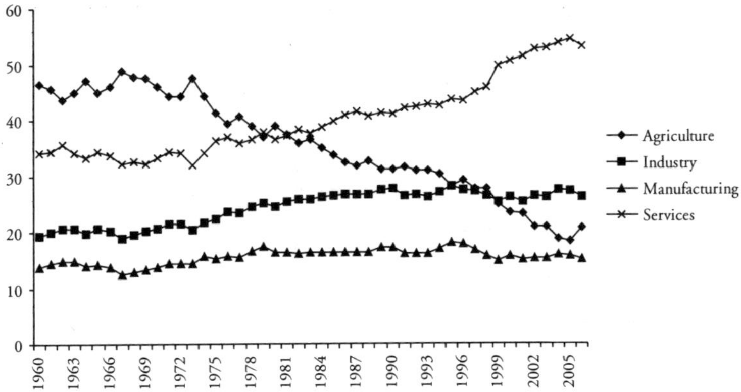

Figure A1.4: Structure of the Economy—India

Source: *WDI 2007*.

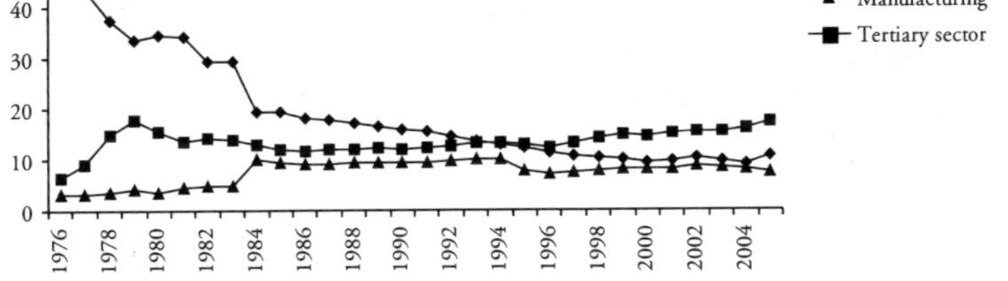

Figure A1.5: Structure of the Economy—The Maldives

Sources: ADB Key Indicators (1990), 1976–83: ADB Key Indicators (1990) calculated from GDP by industrial origin at constant 1985 prices; 1984–2003: The 25 Years of Statistics–the Maldives; 2004–2005: *Statistical Yearbook 2006*.
Note: The series do not match up perfectly.

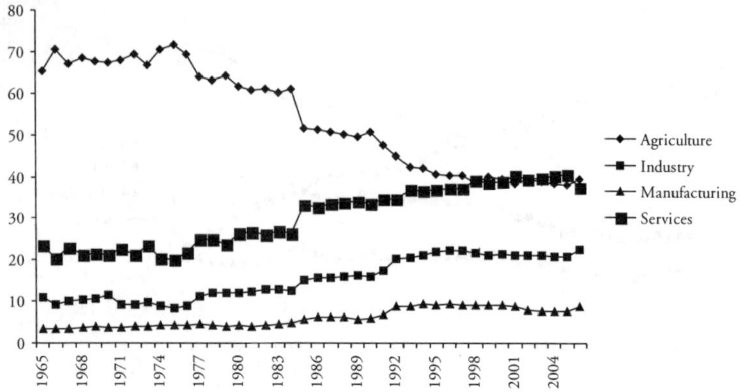

Figure A1.6: Structure of the Economy—Nepal

Source: *WDI 2007*.

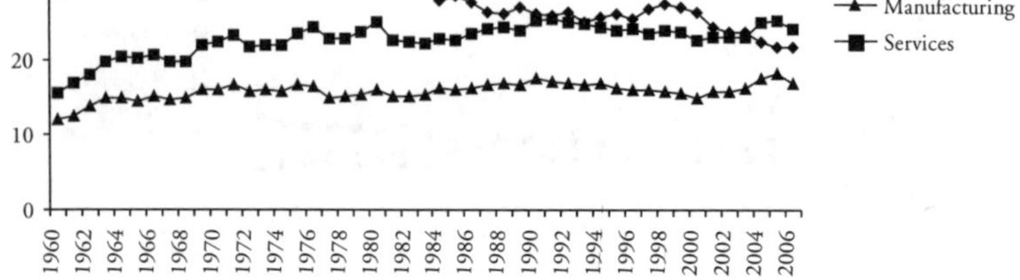

Figure A1.7: Structure of the Economy—Pakistan

Source: *WDI 2007*.

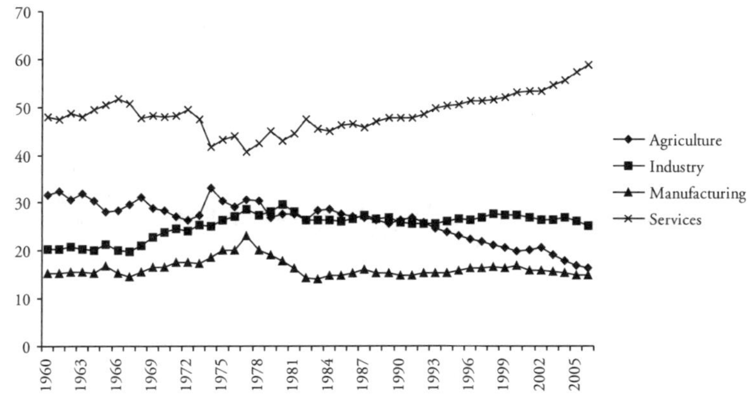

Figure A1.8: Structure of the Economy—Sri Lanka

Source: *WDI 2007.*

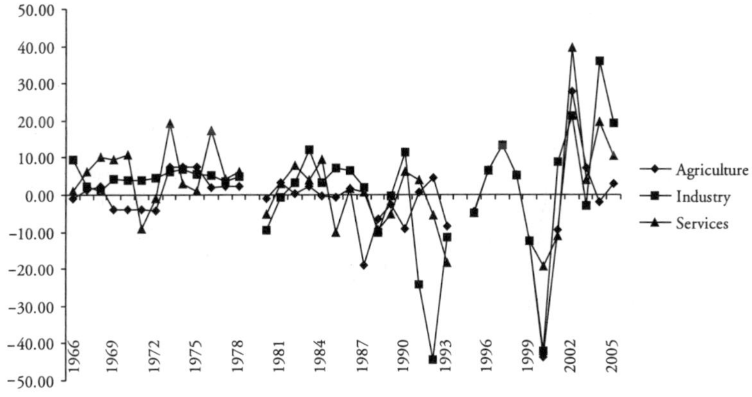

Figure A1.9: Annual Growth Rate by Sector—Afghanistan

Sources: 1966–78: WDI 2007; 1980–4: ADB Key Indicators (1990); 1985–93: ADB Key Indicators (1996); 1995–2001: ADB Key Indicators (2004); 2002 from ADB Key Indicators (2006); 2003–4 from ADB Key Indicators (2007).

Notes: No separate data on manufacturing is available from any (English-medium language) source, other than for the last few years.

1966–78 was calculated from GDP by industry at 1978 constant prices; 1985–93 was calculated from GDP by industry at constant 1978 prices; 1995–2001 was calculated from GDP by industry at 2001 constant prices.

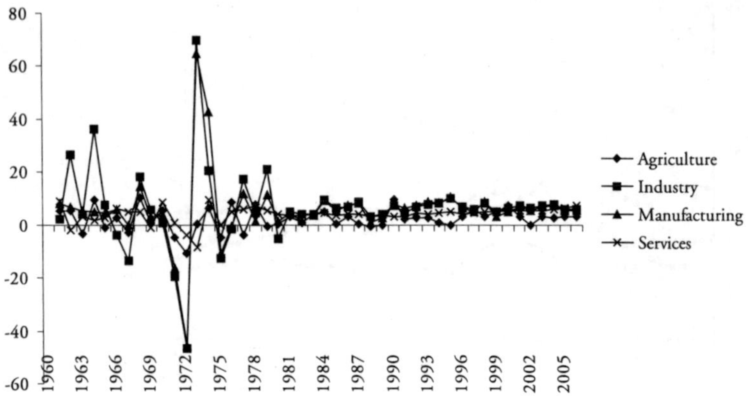

Figure A1.10: Annual Growth Rate by Sector—Bangladesh

Source: *WDI 2007*.

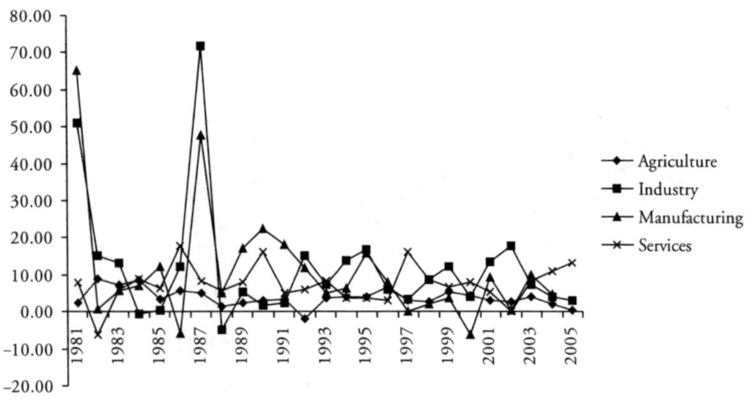

Figure A1.11: Annual Growth Rate by Sector—Bhutan

Sources: 1981–2003: WDI 2007; 2004–5: ADB Key Indicators (2007); 2004 Manufacturing: Bhutan Statistical Yearbook 2005.

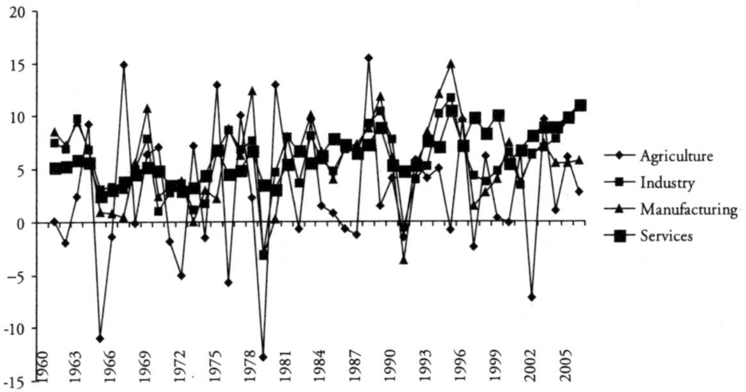

Figure A1.12: Annual Growth Rate by Sector—India

Sources: WDI 2007; 2005–6: ADB Key Indicators 2007; Manufacturing data 2005–6: WDI 2007.

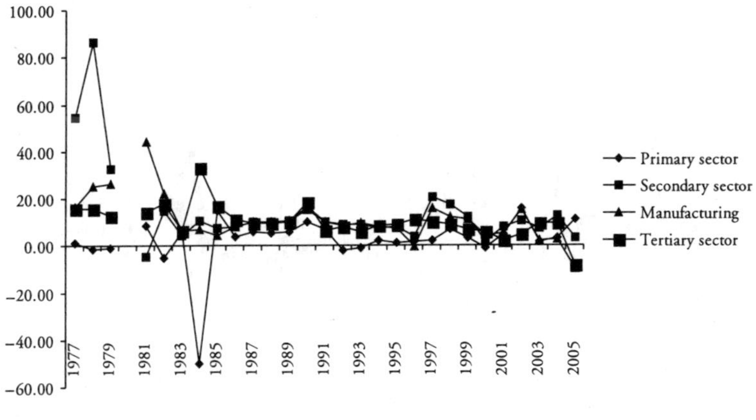

Figure A1.13: Annual Growth Rate by Sector—The Maldives

Sources: 1977–9: ADB Key Indicators (1990) calculated from GDP at 1980 Constant Prices; 1981–4: ADB Key Indicators (1990) calculated from GDP at 1984 Constant Prices; 1985–2003: The 25 Years of Statistics–the Maldives; 2004–2005: Statistical Yearbook 2006. Year 1980 is missing due to change in base year ADB series.

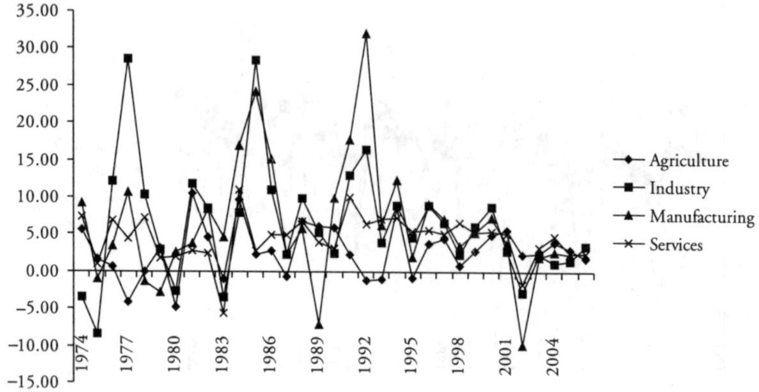

Figure A1.14: Annual Growth Rate by Sector—Nepal

Sources: 1974–2003: WDI 2007; 2004–6: ADB Key Indicators (2007); Manufacturing 2004 (2004–5) and 2005 (2005–6): Nepal Rastra Bank Annual Economic Report (2005). Pre-1974 data is in ADB books only available at current prices.

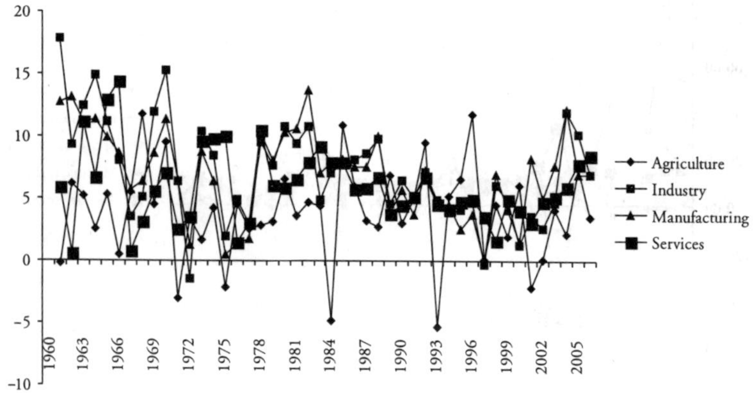

Figure A1.15: Annual Growth Rate by Sector—Pakistan

Source: *WDI 2007.*

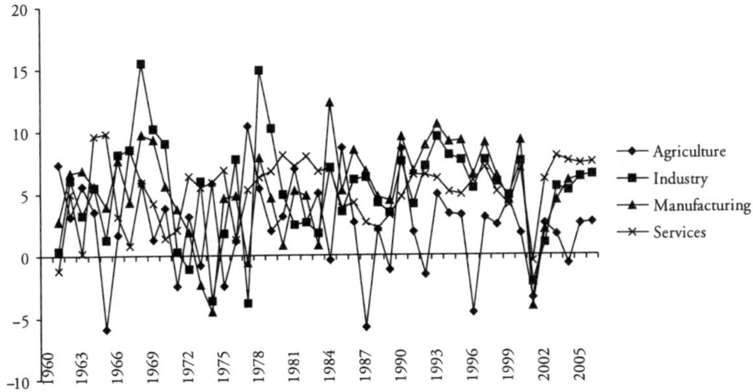

Figure A1.16: Annual Growth Rate by Sector—Sri Lanka

Source: *WDI 2007*.

Table A1.1: Annual Growth Rate by Sector—India, Pakistan, Sri Lanka, Bangladesh (1961–2006)

	Agriculture				*Industry*				*Manufacturing*				*Services*			
	Bangla-desh	*India*	*Pakistan*	*Sri Lanka*	*Bangla-desh*	*India*	*Pakistan*	*Sri Lanka*	*Bangla-desh*	*India*	*Pakistan*	*Sri Lanka*	*Bangla-desh*	*India*	*Pakistan*	*Sri Lanka*
1961	5.2	0.1	–0.2	7.3	2.0	7.5	17.8	0.4	8.2	8.5	12.8	2.8	9.2	5.3	5.9	–1.2
1962	5.3	–2.0	6.2	3.1	26.7	7.0	9.3	6.1	7.0	7.3	13.2	6.7	–1.8	5.4	0.5	5.0
1963	–3.4	2.3	5.2	5.6	3.9	9.9	12.4	3.3	5.5	9.5	11.2	6.9	2.9	5.9	11.2	0.2
1964	9.5	9.2	2.5	3.5	36.1	6.9	14.9	5.5	4.9	6.9	11.4	5.6	1.6	5.8	6.7	9.6
1965	–1.1	–11.0	5.3	–5.9	7.9	3.1	11.2	1.2	4.3	0.9	9.9	4.0	2.7	2.5	13.0	9.9
1966	2.6	–1.4	0.5	1.7	–4.0	3.3	8.0	8.1	6.1	0.8	8.6	7.6	6.4	3.1	14.5	3.1
1967	–2.7	14.9	5.5	8.5	–13.3	3.1	3.6	8.5	0.0	0.4	5.7	4.3	5.0	3.9	0.7	0.8
1968	10.3	–0.2	11.7	5.9	18.4	5.0	5.1	15.5	14.7	5.5	6.4	9.7	4.9	4.6	3.1	5.9
1969	1.0	6.4	4.5	1.3	6.0	7.9	12.0	10.2	3.2	10.7	8.6	9.3	–0.9	5.2	5.6	4.2
1970	5.4	7.1	9.6	3.8	0.7	1.0	15.3	9.0	3.6	2.4	11.3	5.6	8.4	4.9	7.0	1.4
1971	–4.5	–1.9	–3.1	–2.4	–19.6	2.7	6.4	0.3	–16.3	3.3	6.4	3.7	0.6	3.6	2.5	2.1
1972	–10.7	–5.0	3.5	3.1	–46.7	3.7	–1.5	–1.1	–45.5	3.9	1.3	1.8	–4.0	3.0	3.6	6.3
1973	0.3	7.2	1.7	–0.8	69.7	1.1	10.4	6.0	65.0	4.45	8.7	–2.4	–8.6	3.3	9.6	5.5
1974	6.4	–1.5	4.2	5.8	20.6	1.7	8.4	–3.6	42.6	2.9	6.4	–4.5	9.7	4.5	9.8	5.9
1975	–4.6	12.9	–2.1	–2.4	–12.6	6.6	2.0	1.8	–10.9	2.1	0.5	4.6	0.1	6.8	10.0	6.8
1976	8.4	–5.8	4.5	1.2	–1.6	8.7	4.9	7.7	–0.7	8.8	1.4	4.8	4.83	4.6	1.5	1.3

(contd ...)

Table A1.1 (contd ...)

	Agriculture				*Industry*				*Manufacturing*				*Services*			
	Bangla-desh	*India*	*Pakistan*	*Sri Lanka*	*Bangla-desh*	*India*	*Pakistan*	*Sri Lanka*	*Bangla-desh*	*India*	*Pakistan*	*Sri Lanka*	*Bangla-desh*	*India*	*Pakistan*	*Sri Lanka*
1977	–3.7	10.0	2.5	10.4	17.2	6.9	3.0	–3.9	11.7	6.2	1.8	–0.6	6.0	5.0	3.0	5.3
1978	7.8	2.3	2.8	5.4	4.6	7.6	9.5	14.9	1.2	12.4	10.2	7.8	7.1	6.8	10.5	6.3
1979	–0.7	–12.8	3.1	2.0	21.1	–3.1	7.6	10.2	11.2	–3.2	8.0	4.6	5.3	3.6	6.1	6.8
1980	0.2	12.9	6.6	3.1	–5.2	4.7	10.8	4.9	1.5	0.2	10.3	0.8	4.1	3.1	5.9	8.0
1981	3.3	5.3	3.7	6.9	5.1	8.0	9.4	2.5	4.4	8.0	10.6	5.2	3.6	5.4	6.6	7.1
1982	1.0	–0.7	4.7	2.6	3.9	3.7	10.7	2.7	1.3	6.6	13.8	4.8	3.4	6.7	7.9	7.9
1983	3.9	9.6	4.4	5.0	4.1	8.1	4.9	1.8	3.4	10.1	7.0	0.8	4.1	5.6	9.2	6.7
1984	4.9	1.5	–4.8	–0.4	9.3	5.8	7.1	7.1	8.9	6.6	7.9	12.3	4.4	6.3	7.9	7.0
1985	0.3	0.8	10.9	8.6	6.1	4.8	7.8	3.5	5.6	3.9	8.1	5.2	3.7	7.9	7.9	3.9
1986	3.3	–0.7	6.0	2.6	6.7	6.9	8.1	6.1	7.3	7.0	7.6	8.4	4.1	7.4	5.8	4.2
1987	0.1	–1.3	3.3	–5.8	8.5	6.6	8.7	6.3	8.0	7.3	7.5	6.8	4.0	6.5	5.9	2.7
1988	–0.6	15.5	2.7	2.1	3.2	9.2	9.8	4.2	0.7	8.8	10.0	4.7	3.1	7.3	6.8	2.2
1989	–0.3	1.5	6.9	–1.1	3.9	10.3	4.7	3.4	2.8	11.8	4.0	4.4	3.4	8.9	3.8	3.2
1990	9.4	4.1	3.0	8.5	7.0	7.7	6.4	7.5	7.7	6.1	5.7	9.5	3.3	5.3	4.5	4.7
1991	2.2	–1.6	5.0	1.9	4.6	–0.6	5.1	4.1	6.4	–3.7	3.8	6.8	3.3	4.8	5.2	6.4
1992	2.5	5.8	9.5	–1.6	6.9	4.0	7.2	7.2	7.4	4.1	7.2	8.8	4.4	5.4	6.8	6.4

(contd ...)

Table A1.1 (contd ...)

	Agriculture				*Industry*				*Manufacturing*				*Services*			
	Bangla-desh	*India*	*Pakistan*	*Sri Lanka*	*Bangla-desh*	*India*	*Pakistan*	*Sri Lanka*	*Bangla-desh*	*India*	*Pakistan*	*Sri Lanka*	*Bangla-desh*	*India*	*Pakistan*	*Sri Lanka*
1993	2.5	4.1	–5.3	4.9	7.8	5.2	4.9	9.6	8.6	8.5	4.4	10.5	3.9	7.7	4.6	6.2
1994	0.9	5.0	5.2	3.3	8.2	10.2	3.9	8.0	8.2	12.0	4.6	9.1	4.3	7.1	4.2	5.1
1995	–0.3	–0.9	6.6	3.3	9.9	11.6	4.1	7.6	10.5	14.9	2.5	9.2	4.9	10.5	4.8	4.9
1996	3.1	9.6	11.7	–4.6	7.0	7.1	4.7	5.4	6.4	9.7	3.7	6.5	4.0	7.2	5.0	6.0
1997	6.0	–2.4	0.1	3.0	5.8	4.3	–0.3	7.6	5.1	1.5	–0.1	9.1	4.5	9.8	3.6	7.1
1998	3.2	6.2	4.5	2.5	8.3	3.8	6.1	5.9	8.5	2.7	6.9	6.4	5.0	8.4	1.6	5.1
1999	4.7	0.3	2.0	4.5	4.9	4.8	4.9	4.8	3.2	4.0	4.1	4.4	5.2	10.1	5.0	4.0
2000	7.4	–0.1	6.1	1.8	6.2	6.6	1.3	7.5	4.8	7.4	1.5	9.2	5.5	5.5	4.2	7.0
2001	3.1	6.5	–2.2	–3.4	7.5	3.4	3.6	–2.1	6.7	3.6	8.2	–4.2	5.5	6.8	3.1	–0.5
2002	0.0	–7.2	0.1	2.5	6.5	6.4	2.7	1.0	5.5	6.3	5.0	2.1	5.4	8.1	4.8	6.1
2003	3.1	9.6	4.2	1.63	7.3	7.0	4.7	5.5	6.8	7.3	7.7	4.4	5.4	8.9	5.2	7.9
2004	2.7	1.1	2.2	–0.7	7.7	7.8	12.0	5.2	7.4	5.5	12.1	6.0	5.7	8.9	6.0	7.6
2005	3.0	6.0	7.5	2.5	6.0	9,59	10.2	6.3	5.5	5.5	7.0	6.3	6.3	9,83	7.9	7.3
2006	3.0	2.7	3.5	2.6	6.0	10,92	7.0	6.5	5.5	5.7	7.0	6.5	7.4	11.02	8.5	7.5

Source: Based on Figures A1.9–A1.16.

TABLE A1.2: Annual Growth Rates by Sector—Afghanistan, Nepal, Maldives, Bhutan (1966–2006)

	Agriculture				*Industry*				*Manufacturing*			*Services*			
	Afghanistan	*Nepal*	*Maldives*	*Bhutan*	*Afghanistan*	*Nepal*	*Maldives*	*Bhutan*	*Nepal*	*Maldives*	*Bhutan*	*Afghanistan*	*Nepal*	*Maldives*	*Bhutan*
1966	–1.0				9.6							0.9			
1967	1.4				2.2							6.3			
1968	2.4				1.1							10.1			
1969	–3.9				4.3							9.6			
1970	–3.9				4.1							10.8			
1971	–3.8				3.9							–9.2			
1972	–4.2				4.7							–1.0			
1973	7.4				6.3							19.3			
1974	7.5	5.6			6.8	–3.5			9.1			2.9	7.4		
1975	7.4	1.7			5.6	–8.4			–1.0			0.9	1.0		
1976	2.0	0.6			5.3	12.1			3.4			17.3	6.8		
1977	2.2	–4.2	1.2		3.6	28.5	54.3		10.6	16.2		4.4	4.5	15.6	
1978	2.1	0.0	–1.6		4.8	10.4	86.6		–1.4	25.3		6.3	7.2	15.7	
1979		3.0	–0.7			2.9	32.5		–2.9	26.3			1.7	12.8	
1980	–0.8	–4.8			–9.4	–2.6			2.6			–5.2	2.0		

(contd ...)

Table A1.2 (contd ...)

	Agriculture				*Industry*				*Manufacturing*			*Services*			
	Afghanistan	*Nepal*	*Maldives*	*Bhutan*	*Afghanistan*	*Nepal*	*Maldives*	*Bhutan*	*Nepal*	*Maldives*	*Bhutan*	*Afghanistan*	*Nepal*	*Maldives*	*Bhutan*
1981	3.1	10.5	8.2	2.4	–0.6	11.8	–4.3	51.0	3.8	44.1	65.1	3.1	2.8	14.4	7.9
1982	0.5	4.6	–5.3	8.8	3.2	8.5	14.8	15.3	8.4	21.9	0.9	7.7	2.4	18.1	–6.1
1983	2.2	–1.1	5.8	7.2	12.1	–3.4	4.6	13.1	4.6	6.3	5.5	3.9	–5.6	6.2	6.0
1984	–0.5	9.7	–50.2	8.7	3.3	7.9	10.4	–0.5	16.9	7.2	6.8	9.5	11.1	33.0	8.9
1985	–0.6	2.2	14.7	3.4	7.0	28.4	7.6	0.5	24.1	4.4	12.2	–10.1	2.8	17.1	6.4
1986	1.6	2.7	3.7	5.7	6.6	11.0	7.8	12.3	15.2	7.8	–5.8	1.6	4.9	11.1	17.8
1987	–19.0	–0.7	6.1	5.1	1.9	2.3	10.0	71.9	2.3	10.0	47.9	0.5	4.8	9.3	8.3
1988	–6.7	6.7	5.4	1.5	–10.2	9.9	9.9	–4.8	5.7	9.8	5.1	–9.5	6.8	9.4	5.7
1989	–2.5	6.1	5.8	2.5	–0.5	5.2	10.5	5.4	–7.1	10.6	17.1	–5.2	3.9	10.0	7.8
1990	–9.2	5.8	10.2	3.1	11.5	2.5	16.2	1.8	9.8	15.4	22.4	6.1	3.1	18.6	16.1
1991	0.5	2.3	6.7	3.2	–24.1	12.9	10.1	2.4	17.7	10.1	18.1	4.1	10.0	6.4	4.9
1992	4.7	–1.1	–1.9	–2.0	–44.5	16.4	9.0	15.1	32.0	8.7	11.8	–5.6	6.4	7.8	5.8
1993	–8.6	–1.0	–0.7	3.6	–11.4	4.0	9.2	7.3	6.2	9.5	4.8	–18.2	7.1	6.0	8.4
1994		8.5	2.3	3.9		8.8	7.3	13.9	12.3	8.0	6.4		7.3	8.5	3.6
1995	–4.7	–0.9	1.2	4.0	–4.7	4.6	8.0	17.0	2.0	7.6	15.8	–4.9	5.5	8.9	3.7
1996	6.5	3.8	1.8	6.5	6.6	8.8	3.7	5.8	9.0	–0.4	8.1	6.7	5.6	11.0	3.0

(contd ...)

Table A1.2 (contd ...)

	Agriculture				*Industry*				*Manufacturing*			*Services*			
	Afghani-stan	*Nepal*	*Maldives*	*Bhutan*	*Afghani-stan*	*Nepal*	*Maldives*	*Bhutan*	*Nepal*	*Maldives*	*Bhutan*	*Afghani-stan*	*Nepal*	*Maldives*	*Bhutan*
1997	13.3	4.4	2.1	3.1	13.3	6.5	20.5	3.5	7.1	16.0	0.2	13.3	5.0	10.0	16.1
1998	5.3	0.9	7.0	2.8	5.3	2.3	17.2	8.6	3.4	12.0	2.0	5.3	6.5	8.9	8.6
1999	–12.4	2.8	3.5	5.2	–12.3	6.0	12.4	12.2	5.3	11.0	3.7	–12.3	5.3	6.8	6.6
2000	–43.7	4.9	–0.7	4.5	–42.1	8.8	1.6	4.0	7.2	4.5	–6.2	–19.4	5.4	6.0	7.9
2001	–9.4	5.5	5.1	3.2	8.7	2.7	8.1	13.7	3.8	5.4	9.4	–11.0	5.0	2.4	5.4
2002	27.7	2.2	15.9	2.5	21.1	–2.8	10.4	17.9	–10.0	15.6	0.3	39.5	–1.7	4.7	0.2
2003	7.1	2.5	1.9	4.1	–2.8	2.3	7.5	7.3	2.0	2.0	10.1	4.0	3.2	9.6	8.3
2004	–2.1	3.9	3.1	2.1	35.8	1.1	12.9	4.1	2.6	2.7	4.6	19.6	4.8	9.7	11.0
2005	2.8	3.0	11.3	0.4	19.3	1.5	3.0	3.0	2.2	–9.9		10.4	2.4	–8.1	13.2
2006		1.7				3.5							2.4		

Source: Based on Figures A1.9–A1.16.

TABLE A1.3: Annual Growth Rates by Sector—Afghanistan (1980–2003)

	1980	*1981*	*1982*	*1983*	*1984*	*1985*	*1986*	*1987*	*1988*	*1989*	*1990*
Mining, manufacturing, electricity, gas, and water	–6.2	–2.1	4.6	10.2	2.2	8.7	5.0	–1.6	–12.1	8.5	13.5
Construction	–22.4	6.8	–3.2	21.3	8.1	0.0	13.8	16.5	–3.8	–29.4	1.4
Trade	–4.9	3.1	9.9	0.9	10.7	–2.4	4.1	–4.8	–11.7	–6.6	6.1
Transport	–7.7	0.0	4.2	10.0	7.3	–27.1	–7.0	22.5	–6.1	–4.4	6.8
Finance	0.0	11.1	5.0	4.8	9.1	–8.3	4.6	–8.7	–4.8	0.0	5.0

	1991	*1992*	*1993*	*1995*	*1996*	*1997*	*1998*	*1999*	*2000*	*2001*	*2002*	*2003*
Mining, manufacturing, electricity, gas, and water	–27.7	–51.0	–14.0	–4.6	6.5	13.3	5.2	–12.3	–42.0	8.6	2.8	12.0
Construction	–4.1	–17.1	–5.2	–5.0	6.9	13.2	5.3	–12.3	–42.2	8.8	3.5	11.7
Trade	5.7	–5.4	–3.8	–4.8	6.6	13.4	5.3	–12.4	–19.3	–11.0	73.4	19.4
Transport	2.1	–6.3	–55.6	–5.3	6.7	13.5	5.5	–12.2	–19.8	–11.1	73.6	20.0
Finance	0.0	–4.8	–10.0	–4.7	7.4	12.6	5.1	–11.7	–19.8	–11.0	73.9	19.5

Sources: Authors' calculation based on UNESCAP Statistical Yearbook for Asia and the Pacific.

Note: 1980–4 based on series GDP by industry at constant 1978 prices of 1990 yearbook, 1985–93 based on series GDP by industry at constant 1978 prices, 1994–2003 based on series GDP by industry at constant 1990 prices.

Table A1.4: Annual Growth Rates by Sector—Bangladesh (1979–2006)

	1979/ 80	*1980/ 81*	*1981/ 82*	*1982/ 83*	*1983/ 84*	*1984/ 85*	*1985/ 86*	*1986/ 87*	*1987/ 88*	*1988/ 89*	*1989/ 90*
Mining and quarrying		–0.8	100.0	–50.0			–25.0	33.3	–50.0	50.0	..
Large-scale manufacturing	0.0	7.3	0.7	–4.9	4.3	4.3	3.8	13.6	0.7	2.7	10.6
Small-scale manufacturing	4.9	3.0	2.8	2,82	2.8	3.0	1.3	1.3	0.5	2.9	2.9
Construction	–21.3	13.4	5.6	1.1	20.1	5.5	1.7	6.8	12.3	4.9	3.2
Power, gas, water, and sanitary services	16.6	11.1	18.4	53.0	7.1	14.2	12.5	21.8	16.4	28.8	15.3
Transport, storage, and communication	2.2	2.8	0.1	7.7	2.2	2.2	3.2	11.1	3.7	4.3	4.3
Trade	8.4	1.3	–8.7	2.6	5.7	4.2	1.5	2.6	3.2	4.8	3.0
Housing	2.2	2.2	2.4	2.3	2.3	2.4	3.1	3.3	3.2	3.3	3.3
Public administration & defence	7.5	75.8	6.6	–0.4	20.7	15.5	20.5	7.8	7.9	6.9	2.6
Banking & insurance	23.3	21.3	–6.9	–5.7	5.8	5.0	26.3	5.5	1.4	1.1	1.1
Professional & misc. services	5.7	5.9	6.4	6.5	6.8	6.7	8.0	6.9	11.1	6.3	6.3

	1990/ 91	*1991/ 92*	*1992/ 93*	*1993/ 94*	*1994/ 95*	*1995/ 96*	*1996/ 97*	*1997/ 98*	*1998/ 99*	*1999/ 2000*	*2000/ 01*	*2001/ 02*
Mining and quarrying	21.2	17.5	13.9	5.2	9.7	7.8	3.6	5.8	1.3	9.5	9.8	4.5
Large-scale manufacturing	2.4	7.3	9.1	8.2	10.5	6.4	5.1	8.5	3.2	4.8	6.7	5.6
Small-scale manufacturing	2.0	10.5	13.3	8.3	11.4	5.7	4.0	9.3	4.2	4.4	6.6	4.6
Construction	2.9	2.9	2.9	7.9	8.1	8.3	7.8	6.8	0.8	5.8	7.0	7.7
Power, gas, water, & sanitary services	4.5	4.5	4.8	9.3	9.6	8.5	8.6	9.5	8.9	8.5	8.7	8.6

(contd ...)

Table A1.4 (contd ...)

	1990/ 91	*1991/ 92*	*1992/ 93*	*1993/ 94*	*1994/ 95*	*1995/ 96*	*1996/ 97*	*1997/ 98*	*1998/ 99*	*1999/ 2000*	*2000/ 01*	*2001/ 02*
Transport, storage, and communication	20.6	17.5	13.4	6.5	5.3	5.4	1.9	2.0	6.0	6.8	7.4	7.6
Trade	3.1	4.1	4.8	4.0	5.0	5.2	5.5	5.7	5.9	6.1	7.9	6.6
Housing	3.9	4.0	4.3	5.6	8.0	4.6	5.5	6.0	6.5	7.3	6.4	6.6
Public administration & defence	3.4	3.4	3.8	3.3	3.5	3.4	3.5	3.8	3.8	3.8	3.4	3.4
Banking & insurance	9.7	8.3	8.5	5.6	4.5	4.2	5.5	5.9	5.7	6.0	5.9	5.9
Professional & misc. services	2.4	2.5	3.0	5.0	5.1	4.9	5.1	5.3	5.4	5.5	5.5	6.7

Sources: *Statistical Yearbook of Bangladesh*, various editions. 1979–84 from yearbook 1984–85, 1985/86–1988/89 from 1990 yearbook, 1989/90–1992–93 from yearbook 1994; and 1993/94 to 2001/02 from yearbook 2002.

Note: Professional & misc. services data from 1993/94 onwards are missing since it is unclear which categories belong to that sub–category.

(contd ...)

Table A1.4 (contd ...)

	2003–04	*2004–05*	*2005–06*
Mining and quarrying	10.1	10.9	14.9
Natural gas and petroleum	9.8	10.0	11.9
Other mining and coal	10.5	12.1	18.8
Manufacturing	12.5	14.1	17.2
Large- and medium-scale manufacturing	12.3	14.2	17.9
Small-scale manufacturing	12.9	13.8	15.6
Electricity, gas, water	10.9	11.0	9.8
Electricity	11.0	10.4	9.6
Gas	9.7	10.8	11.7
Water	12.0	19.3	9.9
Construction	10.4	14.4	12.9
Wholesale and retail trade	12.8	14.0	13.3
Hotel and restaurants	13.3	14.1	13.6
Transport, storage, communication	10.7	11.2	12.8
Land transport	11.5	9.4	11.8
Water transport	3.3	3.8	4.8
Air transport	4.5	6.5	7.2
Support transport and services	3.3	9.5	7.6
Post and telecommunications	15.3	34.2	27.7
Financial intermediation	10.2	14.2	12.6
Monetary intermediation (banks)	9.9	14.5	12.2
Insurance	11.2	13.3	13.6
Other	10.1	13.4	15.6
Real estate renting and business activities	7.5	7.8	8.1
Public administration and defence	10.8	11.8	14.5
Education	11.5	11.6	13.0
Health and social work	9.0	12.6	11.3
Community, social, and personal services	12.5	12.8	13.0

Source: Bangladesh Bureau of Statistics—online—updated July 2007.

TABLE A1.5: Annual Growth Rates by Sector—Bhutan (1981–2004)

	1981	*1982*	*1983*	*1984*	*1985*	*1986*	*1987*	*1988*	*1989*	*1990*	*1991*	*1992*
Mining	30.9	36.0	–26.5	77.5	–20.3	76.2	–2.7	–12.0	14.2	–11.1	42.0	–14.2
Manufacturing	65.1	0.9	5.5	6.8	12.2	–5.8	47.9	5.1	16.2	23.3	18.1	11.8
Electricity	8.0	14.8	93.6	–13.3	15.4	906.7	279.1	–1.7	2.8	–11.8	–1.8	4.8
Construction	48.0	20.4	17.4	–6.3	–2.6	–16.1	7.4	–15.3	3.7	2.2	–15.1	34.8
Trade	15.5	–5.9	–7.6	1.2	7.3	8.3	–0.7	–9.3	3.4	0.8	7.7	10.8
Transport	14.6	4.6	12.9	2.5	19.6	5.7	8.8	33.7	16.6	20.9	5.8	5.7
Finance	14.4	–4.1	18.3	20.1	0.6	14.6	7.5	3.9	16.0	29.8	–1.6	3.2
Government services	0.9	–16.0	10.8	15.2	–3.3	33.8	18.6	5.0	3.3	2.9	4.4	7.9
	1993	*1994*	*1995*	*1996*	*1997*	*1998*	*1999*	*2000*	*2001*	*2002*	*2003*	
Mining	11.5	13.7	9.7	41.3	–5.4	11.9	14.5	–14.3	18.8	14.0	10.8	
Manufacturing	4.1	2.9	14.0	23.2	3.6	6.2	–10.6	–6.2	9.3	0.3	10.1	
Electricity	10.5	–1.0	3.0	44.7	3.2	2.0	11.2	–0.8	12.3	21.9	2.0	
Construction	16.1	53.9	8.6	–20.0	6.6	14.7	34.3	19.1	17.1	25.0	9.8	
Trade	1.9	3.9	3.0	15.9	7.4	1.0	5.3	2.2	7.2	–5.5	3.3	
Transport	16.2	3.4	3.0	15.4	14.0	13.5	7.6	6.0	8.6	0.5	11.1	
Finance	10.5	3.1	9.4	–4.6	24.9	9.3	–3.0	24.2	8.8	–7.0	8.5	
Government services	5.9	10.9	6.6	6.2	7.8	0.7	13.0	2.0	5.5	1.8	6.2	

Source: Authors' calculation based on GDP by industrial origin data at constant 1980 factor cost for 1980–9 from ADB Key Indicators 1992, 1990–5 from ADB Key Indicators 1996, 1996–8 from ADB Key Indicators 2000, and 1999–2003 from ADB Key Indicators 2004. Pre–1980 data are unavailable from ADB.

(contd ...)

Table A1.5 (contd ...)

Sectors	*2000*	*2001*	*2002*	*2003*	*2004*
Agriculture, livestock, forestry	4.6	5	3.1	2.7	2.5
Agriculture	4.7	4	2.8	3	2
Livestock	5.1	8	2.9	2	1.8
Forestry	3.9	3	4.2	3.3	4.3
Mining	–2.8	16.9	10.4	5.8	–8.7
Manufacturing	4.3	2.3	2	6.8	4.6
Electricity, gas, water	–9.8	1.7	10.5	–0.6	9.9
Construction	24.4	29.9	27	5.3	8.5
Wholesale & Retail Trade	15.7	14.4	8	23.9	19
Hotels & restaurants	1.8	27.9	3	11.3	32.8
Transport, storage, communication	6	7.4	4.6	4.6	18.9
Financing insurance, real estate	18.5	1.3	11.9	20.6	5.7
Finance	17.5	7	14.7	16.4	9.6
Real estate	19.8	–5.4	–8.1	25.9	1.2
Community and social services	1.6	1.8	10.1	7.5	0.2
Public administration	1.6	2.2	10	7.5	–0.3
Education & health	1.6	–3.2	12.7	7.5	8.2
Private social, personal, & recreational services	1	3.2	9.2	9.5	

Source: *Bhutan Statistical Yearbook 2003–2006*.

Table A1.6: Annual Growth Rates by Sector—India (1981–2006)

	1981–82	*1982–83*	*1983–84*	*1984–85*	*1985–86*	*1986–87*	*1987–88*	*1988–89*	*1989–90*	*1990–91*	*1992–93*
Agriculture, forestry, fishing	5.3	–0.7	9.6	1.5	0.8	–0.7	–1.3	15.5	1.5	4.1	5.8
Agriculture	5.6	–0.5	10.3	1.4	0.7	–0.6	–1.4	16.8	0.7	4.4	6.2
Forestry & logging	2.8	–2.6	–3.1	–0.5	0.6	–1.8	–2.4	–1.3	9.5	–1.8	–2.6
Fishing	1.4	–0.9	19.8	7.3	3.2	0.8	3.1	8.6	11.0	5.3	7.8
Mining & quarrying	13.5	11.5	2.7	1.4	5.5	13.5	3.4	15.0	7.3	10.7	1.2
Manufacturing	8.0	6.6	10.1	6.6	3.9	7.0	7.3	8.8	11.8	6.1	4.1
Registered	7.7	9.6	14.7	8.4	2.3	5.8	7.1	10.6	13.9	5.0	3.2
Unregistered	8.5	2.5	3.3	3.5	6.7	8.9	7.7	5.9	8.2	7.9	5.9
Electricity, gas, water supply	9.5	6.7	7.1	11.7	8.4	10.5	7.7	10.9	11.5	7.4	7.0
Construction	5.5	–7.0	5.4	3.5	5.7	2.4	5.7	7.0	7.0	11.8	3.5
Trade, hotels, restaurants	6.4	5.4	5.3	4.3	8.2	5.8	4.3	6.8	7.8	5.1	6.1
Trade	6.4	5.2	5.5	4.3	8.4	5.8	4.3	6.6	7.6	5.0	6.0
Hotels & restaurants	6.6	9.6	1.7	5.3	4.5	5.4	5.8	9.1	11.5	5.4	6.6
Transport, storage, communication	5.7	3.0	4.1	6.8	7.3	6.2	7.0	4.4	6.6	4.6	4.6
Railways	10.0	1.7	–1.5	1.5	13.5	9.2	4.6	–1.3	4.8	5.3	–2.9
Transport by other means	3.5	3.0	5.9	8.2	6.5	5.0	8.5	6.7	7.5	3.7	5.4
Storage	7.2	1.7	3.6	8.2	5.5	3.8	–0.4	–3.3	3.9	4.0	2.0
Communication	7.6	5.1	6.2	9.0	2.1	6.8	5.9	4.9	6.0	6.9	12.3

(contd ...)

Table A1.6 (contd ...)

	1981–82	*1982–83*	*1983–84*	*1984–85*	*1985–86*	*1986–87*	*1987–88*	*1988–89*	*1989–90*	*1990–91*	*1992–93*
Finance, insurance, real estate services	8.3	10.4	10.0	8.5	10.2	11.3	8.4	11.4	12.6	7.7	5.9
Banking & insurance	7.3	15.1	9.4	10.2	14.1	15.0	8.7	14.7	20.8	6.0	4.1
Real estate, ownership of dwellings, business services	8.9	7.8	10.3	7.6	7.9	9.0	8.2	9.3	7.0	9.0	7.4
Community, social, personal services	2.6	8.0	3.9	6.8	6.5	7.0	7.2	6.4	8.3	4.2	4.6
Public administration, defence	2.3	9.6	3.4	9.1	7.1	8.9	9.4	6.1	7.8	1.3	4.9
Other services	2.9	6.7	4.4	4.9	6.1	5.4	5.2	6.7	8.8	6.8	4.3
	1993–94	*1994–95*	*1995–96*	*1996–97*	*1998–99*	*1999–2000*	*2001–02*	*2002–03*	*2003–04*	*2004–05*	*2005–06*
Agriculture, forestry, fishing	5.0	9.6	–2.4	6.2	0.3	–0.4	5.7	–7.2	10.0	0.0	6.0
Agriculture	5.1	10.1	–2.8	6.9	–0.1	–0.6	5.7	–8.1	10.9	–0.2	6.3
Forestry & logging	2.7	1.4	2.1	1.5	3.7	2.6	2.2	0.7	–1.1	1.6	1.6
Fishing	6.3	7.8	1.9	–3.9	7.0	2.2	8.1	4.1	3.6	1.5	4.1
Mining & quarrying	9.3	0.5	9.8	2.8	3.3	2.4	1.0	8.8	3.1	7.5	3.6
Manufacturing	12.0	9.7	1.5	2.7	4.0	7.3	3.4	6.8	6.6	8.7	9.1
Registered	14.4	10.8	–1.0	1.9	3.7	7.7	4.4	7.6	7.2	9.1	9.3
Unregistered	7.3	7.3	6.8	4.2	4.6	6.6	1.5	5.3	5.6	7.8	8.6
Electricity, gas, water supply	9.4	5.4	7.9	7.0	5.2	5.0	4.3	4.7	4.8	7.5	5.3

(contd ...)

Table A1.6 (contd ...)

	1993–94	*1994–95*	*1995–96*	*1996–97*	*1998–99*	*1999–2000*	*2001–02*	*2002–03*	*2003–04*	*2004–05*	*2005–06*
Construction	5.5	2.1	10.2	6.2	8.0	6.9	3.7	7.9	12.0	14.1	14.2
Trade, hotels, restaurants	10.7	7.7	7.6	7.6	7.2	4.1	8.8	6.9	10.3	8.4	8.2
Trade	10.9	7.7	7.6	7.2	6.9	3.9	8.7	7.0	10.5	8.3	8.1
Hotels & restaurants	7.4	6.6	8.2	13.0	11.2	6.9	11.2	5.7	8.5	8.7	9.4
Transport, storage, communication	9.8	8.2	8.2	8.1	11.1	12.2	8.5	13.6	15.1	15.2	13.9
Railways	2.1	4.8	1.8	1.8	9.0	4.3	6.0	5.6	6.5	5.7	7.7
Transport by other means	10.3	8.2	5.7	5.0	6.6	6.6	3.9	10.3	11.9	12.8	8.9
Storage	2.4	–3.0	–5.0	4.7	5.1	3.1	–0.8	–6.8	5.1	14.1	4.1
Communication	16.8	11.6	20.8	19.9	22.0	26.8	17.0	25.6	25.4	22.8	23.9
Finance, insurance, real estate services	5.6	7.0	11.6	7.4	10.6	3.5	4.5	8.0	5.6	8.7	10.9
Banking & insurance	8.5	9.7	17.9	8.8	13.4	–1.2	3.4	11.3	2.2	8.8	14.0
Real estate, ownership of dwellings, business services	3.0	4.3	5.4	5.8	7.4	9.2	5.7	5.4	8.3	8.6	8.6
Community, social & personal services	3.2	6.3	11.7	10.4	12.2	5.6	5.6	3.9	5.4	7.9	7.7
Public administration & defence	1.3	4.1	14.5	10.6	13.2	2.5	2.9	1.6	2.6	9.0	5.4
Other services	5.0	8.1	9.5	10.2	11.4	8.1	7.7	5.8	7.6	7.2	9.4

Source: Central Statistical Organisation—From INDIASTAT.

TABLE A1.7: Annual Growth Rate of Industrials Production for Two-Digit Industry Groups in India (1997–2006)

	1997–8	*1998–9*	*1999–2000*	*2000–1*	*2001–2*	*2002–3*	*2003–4*	*2004–5*	*2005–6*
Food products	–0.4	0.7	4.2	10.1	–1.6	11.0	–0.5	–0.4	2.0
Beverage, tobacco, & related products	19.4	12.9	7.6	4.3	12.2	27.9	8.5	10.8	15.7
Cotton textiles	2.4	–7.7	6.7	2.9	–2.2	–2.7	–3.1	7.6	8.5
Wool, silk and man-made fibre textiles	18.5	2.8	11.9	5.8	4.4	3.0	6.8	3.5	0.0
Jute and other vegetable fibre textiles	16.9	–7.3	–0.9	0.8	–5.9	8.3	–4.2	3.7	0.5
Textile products	8.5	–3.5	2	4.0	2.4	14.4	–3.2	19.2	16.3
Wood & wood products & furniture and fixtures	–2.6	–5.8	–16.2	2.9	–11.0	–17.6	6.8	–8.4	–5.7
Paper & paper products	6.9	16	–20.2	–9.1	3.0	6.8	15.6	10.5	–0.9
Leather & fur products	2.2	8.1	38.2	10.7	5.3	–3.2	–3.9	6.7	–4.8
Basic chemicals & chemical products (except petroleum products & coal)	14.4	6.6	10	7.3	4.8	3.7	8.7	14.5	8.3
Rubber, plastic, petroleum, and coal products	5.2	11.3	–1.1	11.8	11.1	5.5	4.5	2.4	4.3
Non-metallic minerals	13.4	8.3	24.4	–1.2	1.1	5.1	3.7	1.5	11.0
Basic metals & alloy industries	2.6	–2.5	5	1.8	4.3	9.2	9.2	5.4	15.8
Metal products & parts, except machinery & equipment	7.9	17	–1.2	15.0	–10.0	6.4	3.7	5.7	–1.1
Machinery & equipment, other than transport equipment	5.8	1.5	17.7	7.3	1.3	1.6	15.8	19.8	12.0

(contd ...)

Table A1.7 (contd ...)

	1997–8	*1998–9*	*1999–2000*	*2000–1*	*2001–2*	*2002–3*	*2003–4*	*2004–5*	*2005–6*
Transport equipment & parts	2.5	20.1	5.7	–2.0	6.8	14.6	17.0	4.1	12.7
Other manufacturing industries	–1.3	1	–16	11.6	8.9	0.1	7.7	18.5	25.2
Mining & quarrying	6.9	–0.8	1	2.8	1.2	5.8	5.2	4.4	1.0
Manufacturing	6.7	4.4	7.1	5.3	2.9	6.0	7.4	9.2	9.1
Electricity	6.6	6.5	7.3	4.0	3.1	3.2	5.1	5.2	5.2

Source: Ministry of Commerce and Industry, *Economic Survey*, various issues.

TABLE A1.8: Annual Growth Rates by Sector—the Maldives (1985–2005)

	1985	*1986*	*1987*	*1988*	*1989*	*1990*	*1991*	*1992*	*1993*	*1994*	*1995*
Primary sector	14.7	3.7	6.1	5.3	5.8	10.2	6.7	–1.9	–0.7	2.3	1.2
Agriculture	–3.9	9.4	2.5	2.6	2.9	6.0	3.8	3.8	3.9	3.8	3.3
Fisheries	25.8	1.1	7.8	6.5	6.9	11.2	7.8	–4.5	–3.0	1.5	0.0
Coral and sand mining	5.4	6.0	6.5	6.1	6.4	20.1	7.8	5.2	4.9	4.7	4.9
Secondary sector	7.6	7.8	10.0	9.9	10.5	16.2	10.1	9.0	9.2	7.3	8.0
Manufacturing (including electricity & water)	4.4	7.8	10.0	9.8	10.6	15.4	10.1	8.7	9.5	8.0	7.6
Construction	20.1	7.8	10.0	10.0	10.3	19.0	10.1	10.1	8.4	5.2	9.3
Tertiary sector	17.1	11.1	9.3	9.4	10.0	18.6	6.4	7.8	5.9	8.5	8.9
Distribution (trade)	10.8	6.6	11.5	11.5	11.9	15.8	10.0	10.5	11.8	7.0	8.0
Transport & communications	14.9	142.4	10.1	10.0	10.3	26.7	16.3	8.1	8.1	8.5	8.7
Tourism	35.3	2.8	9.4	9.4	10.0	20.7	3.2	8.0	3.0	10.5	10.6
Real estate	10.6	5.4	5.6	5.7	5.9	6.3	5.1	5.0	4.4	5.3	5.5
Business services	–10.2	–12.1	13.5	13.2	14.7	13.0	10.1	10.0	9.1	9.0	10.1
Government administration	7.0	21.4	8.8	9.1	9.4	24.8	4.4	6.1	9.5	5.0	5.6
Financial intermediation services indirectly measured	16.5	9.9	9.3	9.1	9.7	17.8	7.1	6.7	5.6	7.8	8.1

(contd ...)

Table A1.8 (contd ...)

	1996	*1997*	*1998*	*1999*	*2000*	*2001*	*2002*	*2003*	*2004*	*2005*
Primary sector	1.8	2.1	7.0	3.5	–0.7	5.1	15.9	1.9	3.0	11.3
Agriculture	3.3	1.8	1.8	2.0	3.5	3.8	4.0	4.1	4.3	–0.5
Fisheries	1.6	1.1	8.6	3.8	–1.8	5.6	22.9	0.7	2.0	16.8
Coral and sand mining	–3.4	15.2	14.9	7.0	–6.9	6.0	–0.3	6.1	9.2	3.8
Secondary sector	3.7	20.5	17.2	12.4	1.6	8.1	10.4	7.5	12.9	3.0
Manufacturing	–0.4	16.0	12.0	11.0	4.5	5.4	15.5	2.0	2.7	–9.9
Electricity and water supply	39.2	23.3	17.5	14.1	14.3	11.0	9.4	11.1	13.7	16.2
Construction	–6.9	30.3	29.7	14.0	–13.8	11.9	–0.6	18.3	36.7	15.2
Tertiary sector	11.0	10.0	8.9	6.8	6.0	2.4	4.7	9.6	9.7	–8.1
Wholesale and retail trade	4.0	7.3	3.6	3.2	3.2	0.4	2.3	4.3	5.8	3.0
Tourism (resorts. etc)	10.8	7.4	5.7	6.9	5.6	0.0	3.3	14.8	8.3	–33.1
Transport and communications	21.6	17.0	21.4	3.5	7.6	1.6	6.8	8.1	17.0	15.4
Financial services	8.4	8.8	9.2	7.3	3.1	2.5	6.7	6.9	7.3	–2.8
Real estate	5.4	5.7	6.0	5.1	2.6	2.1	4.6	3.7	3.9	0.6
Business services	8.4	8.8	9.2	7.3	3.1	2.5	6.7	5.1	5.4	–0.1
Government administration	13.5	18.5	9.9	14.8	10.7	11.0	6.1	6.7	12.6	15.0
Education, health and social services	2.2	2.1	2.1	2.0	2.0	1.7	1.7	1.6	1.5	1.5
Financial intermediation services indirectly measured	8.4	8.8	9.2	7.3	3.1	2.5	6.7	10.3	10.8	–7.4

Sources: 1984–2003 from *The 25 Years of Statistics—the Maldives*; 2004–5 from *Statistical Yearbook 2006*.

TABLE A1.9: Annual Growth Rates by Sector—Nepal (1989–2006)

	1989–90	*1990–91*	*1991–92*	*1992–93*	*1993–94*	*1994–95*	*1995–96*	*1996–97*	*1997–98*
Agriculture, fisheries, forestry	5.8	2.2	–1.1	–0.6	7.6	–0.3	3.8	4.4	0.9
Mining & quarrying	–5.4	8.9	8.1	2.2	6.1	3.5	13.0	6.8	1.3
Manufacturing	9.8	17.7	32.0	6.2	12.3	2.0	9.0	7.1	3.4
Electricity, gas and water	29.0	34.4	6.8	–9.2	6.2	12.0	19.3	1.8	–4.1
Construction	–2.0	8.1	7.8	4.8	6.6	5.2	7.1	6.6	2.2
Trade, restaurants, hotels	2.3	11.5	5.9	6.4	8.5	5.5	4.5	4.1	5.8
Transport, communication, storage	10.7	13.2	8.7	8.4	8.0	10.6	5.5	7.7	8.1
Finance & real estate	6.7	10.1	5.3	5.8	6.3	4.3	7.6	4.7	5.9
Community & social services	1.8	5.4	6.8	9.1	7.8	4.8	6.2	3.6	7.6

	1998–99	*1999–2000*	*2000–01*	*2001–02*	*2002–03*	*2003–04*	*2004–05*	*2005–06*
Agriculture, fisheries and forestry	2.8	4.9	5.5	2.2	2.5	3.9	3.0	1.7
Mining & quarrying	3.7	4.6	4.5	1.6	1.9	0.5	2.1	2.8
Manufacturing	5.3	7.2	3.8	–10.0	2.0	1.7	1.5	3.5
Electricity, gas, water	5.7	14.3	17.4	10.0	23.1	2.5	2.5	2.2
Construction	6.8	9.6	0.9	1.1	1.8	0.2	2.6	2.2
Trade, restaurants, hotels	3.9	6.8	1.5	–10.1	3.3	6.0	4.8	5.6

(contd ...)

Table A1.9 (contd ...)

	1998–99	*1999–2000*	*2000–01*	*2001–02*	*2002–03*	*2003–04*	*2004–05*	*2005–06*
Transport, communication, storage	6.8	7.0	6.2	1.6	4.3	5.3	–0.1	4.2
Finance & real estate	5.0	5.1	1.7	3.3	3.3	2.1	2.4	2.4
Community & social services	6.6	4.0	13.3	1.9	3.1	2.9	–2.1	3.9

Source: 1989–94 from *Statistical Yearbook of Nepal 1999*; 1995–2003 from *Statistical Yearbook of Nepal 2005*; 2004–5 and 2005–6 from Economic Report Nepal Rastra Bank 2005/2006.

Note: The *Statistical Yearbook of Nepal* does not provide growth figures or a series at constant prices before 1989. Note the data for 2005/6 is preliminary.

TABLE A1.10: Annual Growth Rates by Sector—Pakistan (1980–2006)

	1980	*1981*	*1982*	*1983*	*1984*	*1985*	*1986*	*1987*	*1988*
Industry	10.8	9.4	10.7	4.9	7.1	7.8	8.1	8.6	9.8
Mining & quarrying	13.1	13.2	10.8	–0.3	1.5	13.5	23.7	7.5	13.9
Manufacturing	10.3	10.6	13.8	7	7.9	8.1	7.5	7.5	10
Large-scale manufacturing	11	11.5	15.7	6.6	7.7	8	7.3	7.2	10.6
Small-scale manufacturing	8.4	8.4	8.4	8.4	8.4	8.4	8.4	8.4	8.4
Construction	11.5	4	5.7	–2.7	1	9.4	6.7	12.5	4.9
Electricity & gas distribution	12.1	10.9	1.6	6.7	13.5	2.6	11.7	10.1	16.3
Services	5.9	6.6	7.9	9.2	7.9	7.9	5.8	5.9	6.8

(contd ...)

Table A1.10 (contd ...)

	1980	1981	1982	1983	1984	1985	1986	1987	1988
Transport, storage, communication	6.7	8	8.3	8	8.3	7.9	4.9	7.2	6.8
Wholesale and retail trade	7.4	6.8	9.7	8.4	4.6	11.7	6.7	6	9
Finance and insurance	–1.9	–8.8	17	15.5	16.9	–0.2	3.5	0.6	3.7
Ownership of dwellings	3.6	3.6	9.8	14.5	14.7	10.2	5.3	5.3	5.3
Public administration & defence	6.2	10.6	1.4	10	7.9	3.1	5.3	5.5	4.2
Community and social & personnal services	5.7	5.7	6.5	6.5	6.5	6.5	6.5	6.5	6.5

	1989	*1990*	*1991*	*1992*	*1993*	*1994*	*1995*	*1996*	*1997*
Industry	4.7	6.4	6.9	7.7	5.5	4.5	0.7	4.7	–0.3
Mining & quarrying	2.1	9.6	10.4	2.4	3	4.7	–4.3	7.1	1.9
Manufacturing	4	5.7	6.2	8	5.4	5.5	–2.4	3.7	–0.1
Large-scale manufacturing	2.4	4.7	5.4	7.9	4.1	4.3	1.5	3.1	–2.1
Small-scale manufacturing	8.4	8.4	8.4	8.4	8.4	8.4	–11.5	5.3	5.3
Construction	2.3	3.1	5.7	6	5.8	1.6	1	3.3	1.1
Electricity & gas distribution	13.2	14.6	11	9.1	6.4	3.2	16.8	10.1	–2.9
Services	3.8	4.5	5.2	6.8	4.6	4.2	4.8	5	3.6
Transport, storage, communication	–4	6.5	6.3	10.5	6.7	3.7	4.1	0.8	3.8
Wholesale and retail trade	5.3	3.5	5.3	7.3	2.9	2.9	4.6	6.1	0.7
Finance and insurance	3.1	0.5	1.2	4.3	7	14.1	6.3	13.8	11.5

(contd ...)

Table A1.10 (contd ...)

	1989	*1990*	*1991*	*1992*	*1993*	*1994*	*1995*	*1996*	*1997*
Ownership of dwellings	5.3	5.3	5.3	5.3	5.3	5.3	5.3	5.3	5.3
Public administration & defence	7.9	2.7	3.3	2.6	2.5	1.4	3.1	3.2	2.2
Community and social & personnal services	6.5	6.5	6.5	6.5	6.5	6.5	6.5	6.5	6.5
	1998	*1999*	*2000*	*2001*	*2002*	*2003*	*2004*	*2005*	*2006*
Industry	6.1	4.9	1.3	3.6	2.6	4.7	12	11.4	5.9
Mining & quarrying	–4.9	3.2	6.2	–1.7	7.3	16.1	3.8	9.6	3.8
Manufacturing	6.9	4.1	1.5	9.3	4.5	6.9	14.1	12.6	8.6
Large-scale manufacturing	7.6	3.6	0	11	3.5	7.2	18.2	15.6	9
Small-scale manufacturing	5.3	5.3	5.3	6.2	6.3	6.3	6.2	6.2	7.6
Construction	1.3	–4.9	5.2	0.5	1.6	4	–6.9	18.6	9.2
Electricity & gas distribution	8.8	17.4	–3	–13.7	–7	–11.7	21.1	3.5	–8.4
Services	1.6	5	4.2	3.1	4.8	5.2	6	8	8.8
Transport, storage, communication	7.2	5.1	3.6	5.3	1.2	4.3	5.5	3.6	7.2
Wholesale and retail trade	–1.1	3	1.9	4.5	2.8	6	8.1	11.1	6.8
Finance and insurance	–24	18.9	–4.1	–15.1	17.2	–1.3	4.5	29.7	23
Ownership of dwellings	5.3	5.3	5.3	3.8	3.5	3.3	3.5	3.5	3.5
Public administration & defence	2	2.5	9.4	2.2	6.9	7.7	4.2	0.6	2.8
Community and S & P services	6.5	6.5	6.5	5.6	7.9	6.2	5.2	5.9	6.5

Sources: 1975–2004: *Handbook of Statistics on Pakistan Economy 2005*, Table 1.3; 2005–6: *Annual Report* (2005–6), State Bank of Pakistan, Table 2.1; Real GDP growth at constant 1999–2000 prices.

TABLE A1.11: Annual Growth Rates by Sector—Sri Lanka (1988–2006)

	1988	*1989*	*1990*	*1991*	*1992*	*1993*	*1994*	*1995*	*1997*
Mining & quarrying	9.0	5.4	9.1	–10.0	–6.0	11.9	6.0	3.4	7.7
Manufacturing	4.7	4.4	9.5	6.8	8.8	10.5	9.1	9.2	3.8
Processing of tea, rubber, & coconut kernel products	–2.0	–0.5	8.4	–5.6	–12.6	8.4	13.0	4.4	9.1
Factory industry	7.0	10.5	10.2	9.5	13.0	11.3	8.8	10.0	3.5
Small industry	1.1	–25.4	4.7	5.4	5.1	5.6	6.2	7.1	10.3
Electricity and water	3.5	1.8	10.2	7.1	5.4	12.0	10.8	9.3	7.0
Electricity									8.2
Water									8.5
Construction	1.5	0.6	2.9	3.1	8.1	6.5	6.0	4.9	6.1
Wholesale and retail trade, hotels, and restaurants	2.7	1.7	3.6	7.8	5.3	8.4	6.4	3.6	7.1
Import trade	1.9	–2.0	–2.0	14.9	8.2	14.7	9.4	2.1	6.5
Export trade	3.6	6.7	11.2	4.9	15.1	13.4	12.8	12.6	9.6
Domestic trade	3.2	3.5	6.0	3.6	1.0	2.0	1.9	2.2	12.0
Hotels and restaurants									2.2
Transport, storage, communication	0.6	1.9	3.8	7.8	6.9	4.1	3.1	5.5	13.1
Transport									8.8
Cargo handling, storage, warehousing									5.7
Post and telecommunications									15.5
Financial services, real estate, business services	6.0	6.0	6.3	4.2	6.0	10.8	9.5	10.5	29.7
Financial services									8.3

(contd ...)

Table A1.11 (contd ...)

	1988	*1989*	*1990*	*1991*	*1992*	*1993*	*1994*	*1995*	*1997*
Real estate, renting, business services									10.3
Public administration, other government services, S & P services, defence, other community, social, and personal services									2.9
Public administration, other govt services, & defence	0.5	12.4	3.5	–0.8	2.3	3.0	3.1	5.4	4.7
Other community, social, and personal services	1.5	2.4	9.1	8.4	6.7	2.0	2.5	4.5	5.2

	1998	*1999*	*2000*	*2001*	*2002*	*2003*	*2004*	*2005*	*2006*
Mining & quarrying	–5.4	4.1	4.8	0.7	–1.1	5.7	7.9	14.1	8.0
Manufacturing	6.3	4.4	9.2	–4.2	2.1	4.2	5.1	6.0	5.3
Processing of tea, rubber, & coconut kernel products	–1.2	3.8	4.2	–6.7	–0.9	–0.1	1.3	2.7	1.1
Factory industry	7.6	4.5	10.4	–3.9	2.5	4.6	6.1	6.1	5.9
Small industry	6.6	4.8	5.5	–3.5	2.1	6.1	0.0	9.8	5.3
Electricity and water	10.1	9.5	4.5	–2.9	–0.7	21.6	–2.5	24.5	20.2
Electricity	9.8	8.9	4.5	–3.7	–1.5	25.2	–3.6	27.7	22.2
Water	12.1	13.7	4.5	2.1	3.8	1.4	5.3	3.8	4.2
Construction	7.1	4.8	4.8	2.5	–0.8	5.5	6.6	8.9	8.0
Wholesale and retail trade, hotels, and restaurants	4.4	1.3	8.5	–6.9	5.4	7.8	6.1	2.8	5.9

(contd ...)

Table A1.11 (contd ...)

	1998	1999	2000	2001	2002	2003	2004	2005	2006
Import trade	8.2	–1.4	12.9	–10.7	8.4	11.2	9.0	2.3	7.5
Export trade	0.1	6.1	18.3	–8.0	2.0	3.5	7.7	6.9	4.4
Domestic trade	2.1	2.1	2.4	–2.0	3.9	4.5	2.0	4.6	4.5
Hotels and restaurants	2.2	12.8	1.5	–15.3	–2.1	26.4	13.1	–27.5	6.3
Transport, storage, and communication	7.6	8.1	7.8	3.8	7.6	10.6	13.7	11.7	13.1
Transport	3.2	2.9	3.9	–1.6	3.7	4.6	4.2	3.3	5.1
Cargo handling, storage, warehousing	2.6	2.1	2.6	–1.9	2.1	9.9	12.8	8.4	13.2
Post and telecommunications	42.1	37.1	24.5	22.3	18.9	23.9	31.4	24.7	22.7
Financial services, real estate, business services	5.4	4.3	5.6	6.6	9.1	8.8	5.6	6.5	9.7
Financial services	6.4	4.6	6.4	7.9	11.1	10.6	6.6	7.5	10.5
Real estate, renting, business services	2.7	3.2	3.1	2.6	2.9	2.4	1.7	2.8	6.2
Public administration, other government services, and S & P services, defence, other community, social, and personal services	3.1	6.0	3.1	2.7	1.3	2.1	3.9	5.4	2.8
Public administration, other govt services, and defence	3.0	4.2	4.2	1.0	0.0	0.6	2.1	5.1	1.5
Other community, social, & personal services	3.3	9.5	1.0	6.0	3.6	4.7	7.1	6.0	4.8

Sources: 1987–95: Authors' calculation using Economic and Social Statistics of Sri Lanka, 1997 GNP at 1982 factor cost, Central Bank of Sri Lanka; 1997–2006: Authors' calculation using Economic and Social Statistics of Sri Lanka, GDP constant 1996 factor costs prices, online from Central Bank of Sri Lanka.

Note: Before 1987 data are available from the older books, but not in such a disaggregated fashion.

Table A1.12: Growth in Employment, Regional Comparisons (in percentage)

	Total Growth in Employment														
	1992	*1993*	*1994*	*1995*	*1996*	*1997*	*1998*	*1999*	*2000*	*2001*	*2002*	*2003*	*2004*	*2005*	*2006*
World	2.17	1.42	1.78	1.34	1.57	1.63	1.53	1.56	1.68	1.44	1.51	1.64	1.76	1.72	1.67
Developed Economies & EU	–0.11	–0.22	0.74	1.18	0.83	1.23	1.11	0.95	1.10	0.44	–0.21	0.49	1.30	0.97	1.12
Central & SE Europe (non-EU) & CIS	2.07	–1.42	–0.53	–1.17	–0.27	–0.82	–0.51	–1.88	2.65	1.83	1.19	0.36	1.82	1.02	0.99
East Asia	2.48	1.32	1.20	0.84	0.99	1.00	0.53	1.02	1.28	0.93	1.13	1.03	1.23	1.00	0.94
South East Asia & the Pacific	2.67	1.58	1.85	2.77	3.13	1.85	1.59	2.57	2.07	1.80	1.70	1.72	2.03	2.53	1.93
South Asia	1.82	2.50	2.89	1.06	2.42	2.04	2.80	2.24	1.52	1.82	2.46	2.55	1.32	2.31	2.36
Latin America & the Caribbean	5.74	3.04	2.55	2.17	1.14	3.63	2.32	2.37	2.21	1.93	2.05	2.53	2.10	1.87	1.75
Middle East	3.08	3.57	3.84	3.71	3.46	4.53	4.91	4.74	3.85	2.85	4.44	4.88	4.81	3.36	3.80
Sub-Saharan Africa	3.12	3.10	3.76	3.24	2.43	2.52	2.49	2.49	2.48	2.51	2.45	2.51	3.30	2.61	2.66
North Africa	2.48	1.74	3.95	1.37	4.00	2.98	3.23	3.03	1.54	2.56	3.16	3.55	4.41	3.94	2.80

(contd ...)

Table A1.12 (contd ...)

	Growth in Employment in Agriculture														
	1992	*1993*	*1994*	*1995*	*1996*	*1997*	*1998*	*1999*	*2000*	*2001*	*2002*	*2003*	*2004*	*2005*	*2006*
World	1.58	–0.33	0.14	–0.90	–0.11	0.37	1.44	1.68	0.76	–0.34	0.34	0,.06	–1.40	–0.73	–1.11
Developed Economies & EU	–3.88	–4.02	0.42	–1.39	–3.25	–1.59	–2.04	–2.80	–0.90	–3.58	–5.41	–7.51	–4.99	–0.91	–0.62
Central & SE Europe (non-EU) & CIS	0.13	–2.20	2.23	0.39	0.23	–1.09	0.25	4.15	–1.72	–11.93	–3.61	–2.18	–0.55	–2.34	–2.42
East Asia	0.45	–2.31	–2.59	–3.12	–2.33	–0.25	0.49	1.62	0.95	0.80	1.07	–0.77	–3.31	–3.52	–3.79
South East Asia & the Pacific	2.64	–3.06	–2.65	–1.59	0.13	–2.63	4.66	0.24	2.89	–0.70	0.76	1.69	–2.18	1.99	1.43
South Asia	1.79	2.08	3.11	0.28	2.18	1.52	3.13	2.01	0.19	–0.58	–1.08	–0.16	–1.35	–0.57	–0.70
Latin America & the Caribbean	3.07	0.41	0.09	–1.75	–3.76	3.20	–5.88	3.51	–3.08	–3.37	1.75	2.42	2.31	2.77	2.88
Middle East	1.27	1.95	2.22	1.83	6.30	5.07	5.52	4.13	3.03	1.73	3.12	1.41	1.50	0.02	0.74
Sub-Saharan Africa	3.79	4.00	2.94	2.55	1.80	1.36	1.11	1.80	1.64	1.79	1.99	1.32	1.21	1.46	0.04
North Africa	8.78	–2.11	3.00	–0.44	0.65	1.45	0.33	0.85	1.17	0.19	0.82	5.01	6.93	4.63	3.78

(contd ...)

Table A1.12 (contd ...)

	Growth in Employment in Industry														
	1992	*1993*	*1994*	*1995*	*1996*	*1997*	*1998*	*1999*	*2000*	*2001*	*2002*	*2003*	*2004*	*2005*	*2006*
World	1.49	1.72	1.54	1.51	2.08	1.64	0.23	0.43	1.69	1.39	1.06	2.00	3.64	3.98	4.02
Developed Economies & EU	–2.21	–2.09	–1.09	0.05	–0.27	0.46	0.00	–0.89	–0.01	–1.18	–2.14	–1.72	0.12	–0.40	–0.24
Central & SE Europe (non-EU) & CIS	0.62	–3.12	–3.30	–3.97	–2.68	–2.51	–3.41	–5.43	2.53	–2.29	1.37	1.63	0.85	1.79	1.78
East Asia	3.50	3.94	2.32	2.04	2.78	1.12	–0.28	–0.78	–0.68	0.06	–2.72	1.87	4.89	6.22	5.97
South East Asia & the Pacific	3.55	10.11	12.62	5.54	6.69	6.04	–8.31	6.15	5.35	4.24	6.26	1.66	5.18	3.50	3.08
South Asia	1.84	2.91	2.82	2.80	3.08	3.22	2.58	3.17	6.08	6.35	8.19	7.04	5.48	6.48	6.61
Latin America & the Caribbean	7.00	2.90	–1.04	1.39	3.52	3.41	6.44	1.70	2.87	2.50	2.70	0.15	1.34	1.23	0.73
Middle East	2.72	4.69	4.99	5.33	3.56	4.67	5.15	5.05	3.74	4.02	5.37	4.84	4.51	2.98	3.62
Sub-Saharan Africa	–0.45	2.15	7.05	7.19	4.58	4.33	5.35	3.90	4.33	4.93	2.95	4.40	9.53	7.19	8.67
North Africa	–2.52	2.21	4.04	2.54	7.63	0.96	4.51	4.43	–0.11	2.94	2.51	2.58	4.87	5.34	4.35

(contd ...)

Table A1.12 (contd ...)

	Growth in Employment in Services														
	1992	*1993*	*1994*	*1995*	*1996*	*1997*	*1998*	*1999*	*2000*	*2001*	*2002*	*2003*	*2004*	*2005*	*2006*
World	3.39	3.55	4.02	4.00	3.25	3.05	2.36	2.03	2.66	3.36	2.97	3.05	3.89	2.85	2.96
Developed Economies & EU	1.38	1.10	1.62	1.96	1.73	1.83	1.87	2.06	1.71	1.42	0.95	1.91	2.15	1.58	1.70
Central & SE Europe (non-EU) & CIS	4.44	0.35	–0.19	–0.15	1.04	0.44	0.86	–3.36	5.56	12.52	3,.37	0.85	3.31	2.04	1.95
East Asia	7.10	8.17	9.16	8.17	5.75	3.09	1.33	1.56	3.50	1.85	4.29	3.30	5.53	3.58	3.41
South East Asia & the Pacific	2.32	7.84	5.62	9.38	6.34	6.77	2.19	4.36	–0.59	4.25	0.79	1.80	6.25	2.71	1.98
South Asia	1.90	3.28	2.41	1.89	2.58	2.58	2.17	2.25	1.85	4.49	6.57	5.14	3.72	4.79	4.78
Latin America & the Caribbean	6.64	4.44	5.19	4.28	2.42	3.88	4.16	2.20	3.94	3.57	1.91	3.45	2.30	1.82	1.74
Middle East	3.98	3.71	3.96	3.71	2.33	4.26	4.55	4.83	4.22	2.73	4.50	6.23	6.16	4.72	4.91
Sub-Saharan Africa	1.74	–0.37	6.08	4.60	4.14	6.51	6.75	4.49	4.76	4.09	3.81	5.74	7.57	4.28	7.93
North Africa	–0.85	5.33	4.77	2.49	5.33	5.17	5.01	4.10	2.54	4.15	5.08	2.95	2.47	2.85	1.42

Source: Estimates ILO.

Note: From personal communication dated 13 September 2007.

Table A1.13: Selected Growth Rates, Regional Comparisons (in percentage)

	1991	1992	1993	1994	1995	1996	1997	1998	1999	2000	2001	2002	2003	2004	2005	2006
	GDP Growth															
EAP	8.31	11.13	11.35	11.08	9.92	9.04	7.30	2.25	6.32	7.62	6.62	7.87	8.82	9.04	8.96	9.43
ECA	–6.30	–8.24	–3.58	–6.66	0.96	1.78	3.91	0.75	2.05	6.71	1.78	4.95	6.03	7.38	6.02	6.77
LAC	4.65	3.84	3.68	4.74	0.56	3.55	5.49	2.40	0.20	3.93	0.27	–0.53	2.07	6.21	4.60	5.52
MNA	6.18	4.18	0.90	2.94	3.10	5.98	3.35	5.66	4.00	3.22	3.37	3.65	2.22	6.01	4.40	5.37
SAS	1.83	5.56	4.44	6.62	6.96	6.72	4.16	5.43	6.42	4.28	4.64	3.69	7.62	7.95	8.61	8.58
SSA	0.69	–1.18	0.55	1.88	3.76	5.06	3.54	2.40	2.59	3.46	3.69	3.43	4.13	5.52	5.67	5.59
	GDP/Capita Growth															
EAP	6.68	9.58	9.87	9.64	8.55	7.73	6.05	1.12	5.16	6.69	5.64	6.92	7.89	8.14	8.03	8.60
ECA	–8.30	–6.97	–3.87	–6.81	0.84	1.72	3.78	–1.00	1.96	6.60	1.80	4.97	5.99	7.46	5.98	6.76
LAC	2.80	2.05	1.93	3.00	–1.10	1.90	3.85	0.84	–1.30	2.39	–1.12	–1.87	0.72	4.82	3.25	4.20
MNA	3.66	1.80	–1.36	0.68	0.92	3.81	1.28	3.60	2.07	1.30	1.49	1.74	0.43	4.14	2.59	3.57
SAS	–0.31	3.43	2.32	4.50	4.89	4.71	2.24	3.52	4.50	2.41	2.86	1.90	5.81	6.18	6.90	6.93
SSA	–2.06	–3.84	–1.54	–0.77	1.07	2.34	0.89	–0.20	0.01	0.89	1.19	1.02	1.70	3.10	3.26	3.19

(contd ...)

Table A1.13 (contd ...)

	Population Growth															
	1991	*1992*	*1993*	*1994*	*1995*	*1996*	*1997*	*1998*	*1999*	*2000*	*2001*	*2002*	*2003*	*2004*	*2005*	*2006*
EAP	1.53	1.42	1.35	1.31	1.26	1.22	1.18	1.12	1.10	0.87	0.93	0.89	0.87	0.84	0.86	0.76
ECA	2.17	–1.36	0.30	0.16	0.12	0.06	0.12	1.77	0.08	0.11	–0.02	–0.02	0.04	–0.08	0.05	0.01
LAC	1.80	1.76	1.72	1.69	1.67	1.61	1.58	1.55	1.52	1.50	1.40	1.37	1.35	1.33	1.31	1.27
MNA	2.44	2.34	2.30	2.24	2.16	2.09	2.05	1.98	1.90	1.90	1.86	1.88	1.79	1.80	1.77	1.74
SAS	2.15	2.07	2.07	2.02	1.97	1.92	1.88	1.84	1.83	1.83	1.73	1.76	1.72	1.66	1.60	1.55
SSA	2.81	2.77	2.12	2.67	2.66	2.66	2.62	2.60	2.58	2.55	2.47	2.39	2.39	2.35	2.33	2.33
	Labour Force Growth															
EAP	1.86	1.70	1.58	1.56	1.60	1.61	1.38	1.33	1.48	1.21	1.45	1.10	1.18	1.39	1.34	1.14
ECA	–1.02	–0.98	–0.98	–0.09	–0.59	–0.41	0.09	0.36	–1.37	0.61	1.13	0.37	–0.09	1.15	0.46	0.25
LAC	4.04	4.16	2.74	2.72	2.75	1.47	3.40	2.66	2.84	2.16	2.04	2.51	2.42	1.81	2.02	1.95
MNA	1.96	3.07	3.47	4.05	2.81	3.33	3.62	3.64	4.79	3.22	3.21	3.81	3.80	3.90	3.45	3.23
SAS	1.68	1.66	1.58	1.62	1.87	2.01	2.00	2.07	2.14	2.05	2.26	2.30	2.36	1.71	2.16	2.11
SSA	2.95	3.01	2.11	2.92	2.52	2.66	2.58	2.57	2.52	2.41	2.49	2.29	2.20	2.66	2.39	3.72

Source: *World Development Indicators 2007.*

Notes: EAP: East Asia and Pacific; ECA: Europe and Central Asia; LAC: Latin America and the Caribbean; MNA: Middle East and North Africa; SAS: South Asia; SSA: Sub-Saharan Africa.

Table A1.14: Doing Business Indicators, South Asia, 2006

	Afghanistan	*Bangladesh*	*Bhutan*	*India*	*Maldives*	*Nepal*	*Pakistan*	*Sri Lanka*
Total Rank	162	88	138	134	53	100	74	89
Starting a Business								
Rank	17	68	79	88	31	49	54	44
Procedures (number)	3	8	10	11	5	7	11	8
Time (days)	8	37	62	35	13	31	24	50
Cost (% of income per capita)	67.4	87.6	16.6	73.7	18.1	78.5	21.3	9.2
Min. capital (% of income per capita)	0	0	0	0	6.6	0	0	0
Dealing with Licenses								
Rank	..	67	145	155	9	127	89	71
Procedures (number)	..	13	26	20	10	15	12	17
Time (days)	..	185	204	270	118	424	218	167
Cost (% of income per capita)	..	272.3	263.5	606	40.2	324	972.9	151
Employing Workers								
Rank	74	75	116	112	5	150	126	98
Difficulty of Hiring Index	67	11	78	33	0	67	78	0
Rigidity of Hours Index	40	40	40	20	0	20	20	20
Difficulty of Firing Index	30	40	0	70	0	70	30	60
Rigidity of Employment Index	46	30	39	41	0	52	43	27

(contd ...)

Table A1.14 (contd ...)

	Afghanistan	*Bangladesh*	*Bhutan*	*India*	*Maldives*	*Nepal*	*Pakistan*	*Sri Lanka*
Nonwage labour cost (% of salary)	0	0	1	16.8	0	10	12	15
Firing costs (weeks of wages)	4.3	51	94.7	55.9	8.7	90	90	177.7
Registering Property								
Rank	169	167	41	110	172	25	68	125
Procedures (number)	11	8	5	6	No practice	3	6	8
Time (days)	252	425	93	62	No practice	5	50	63
Cost (% of property value)	9.5	10.5	0	7.8	No practice	6.4	4.4	5.1
Getting Credit								
Rank	174	48	159	65	143	101	65	101
Legal Rights Index	0	7	3	5	4	4	4	3
Credit Information Index	0	2	0	3	0	2	4	3
Public registry coverage (% adults)	0	0.6	0	0	0	0	0.3	0
Private bureau coverage (% adults)	0	0	0	6.1	0	0.1	1.1	3.1
Protecting Investors								
Rank	173	15	118	33	60	60	19	60
Disclosure Index	0	6	6	7	0	6	6	4
Director Liability Index	0	7	3	4	8	1	6	5
Shareholder Suits Index	2	7	4	7	8	9	7	7
Investor Protection Index	0.7	6.7	4.3	6	5.3	5.3	6.3	5.3

(contd ...)

Table A1.14 (contd ...)

	Afghanistan	*Bangladesh*	*Bhutan*	*India*	*Maldives*	*Nepal*	*Pakistan*	*Sri Lanka*
Paying Taxes								
Rank	30	72	68	158	1	88	140	157
Payments (number)	2	17	19	59	1	35	47	61
Time (hours)	275	400	274	264	0	408	560	256
Profit tax (%)	0	29.2	35.5	14.3	0	19.7	27	36.8
Labour tax and contributions (%)	0	0	1.3	19.4	0	11.6	14.6	17.4
Other taxes (%)	36.3	11.1	6.3	47.4	9.3	1.5	1.8	20.8
Total tax rate (% profit)	36.3	40.3	43	81.1	9.3	32.8	43.4	74.9
Trading across Borders								
Rank	152	134	150	139	91	136	98	99
Documents for export (number)	7	7	10	10	8	7	8	8
Time for export (days)	66	35	39	27	15	44	24	25
Cost to export (US$ per container)	2,500	902	1,230	864	1,000	1,599	996	797
Documents for import (number)	11	16	14	15	9	10	12	13
Time for import (days)	88	57	42	41	21	37	19	27
Cost to import (US$ per container)	2,100	1,287	1,950	1,244	1,784	1,800	1,005	789
Enforcing Contracts								
Rank	165	174.0	56.0	173.0	83.0	105.0	163.0	90.0

(contd ...)

Table A1.14 (contd ...)

	Afghanistan	*Bangladesh*	*Bhutan*	*India*	*Maldives*	*Nepal*	*Pakistan*	*Sri Lanka*
Procedures (number)	..	50.0	34.0	56.0	28.0	28.0	55.0	20.0
Time (days)	1,642	1,442.0	275.0	1,420.0	665.0	590.0	880.0	837.0
Cost (% of debt)	25	45.7	20.2	35.7	16.2	24.4	22.6	21.3
Closing a Business								
Rank	151	93.0	151.0	133.0	114.0	95.0	46.0	59.0
Time (years)	No practice	4.0	No practice	10.0	6.7	5.0	2.8	2.2
Cost (% of estate)	No practice	8.0	No practice	9.0	4.0	9.0	4.0	18.0
Recovery rate (cents on the dollar)	0	24.9	0.0	13.0	18.2	24.5	39.9	35.6

Source: *Doing Business 2006.*

Note: Available from www.worldbank.org

CONTRIBUTORS

SADIQ AHMED is Senior Manager of Regional Programs, South Asia Region of the World Bank.

KAUSHIK BASU is C. Marks Professor of Economics and Director at the Centre for Analytic Economics, Columbia University, USA.

ANA M. FERNANDES is an Economist in the Development Economics Research Group of the World Bank.

EJAZ GHANI is Economic Adviser, Poverty Reduction and Economic Management Department, South Asia Region of the World Bank.

VENKATARAMAN KRISHNASWAMY is a Consultant with the World Bank.

ANNEMIE MAERTENS is a PhD Candidate at Applied Economics and Management, Cornell University, and a Consultant, World Bank.

AADITYA MATTOO is a Lead Economist in the Development Economics Research Group of the World Bank.

HOWARD PACK is Professor at the Wharton School, University of Pennsylvania, USA.

ARIEL PAKES is a Steven McArthur Heller Professor of Economics, Department of Economics, Harvard University, USA.

MICHELLE RIBOUD is Former Education Sector Manager, Human Development, South Asia Region of the World Bank.

JEFFREY D. SACHS is Professor at The Earth Institute, Columbia University, USA.

HONG TAN is a Consultant, South Asia Region, World Bank.

Late SIMON THOMAS was Lead Transport Economist in the Sustainable Development Transport Unit of the South Asia Region of the World Bank.

PAUL A. VOLCKER is Former Chairman of the Federal Reserve System, USA.

VLADISLAV VUCETIC is a Lead Energy Specialist in the Middle East & North Africa Sustainable Development Unit of the World Bank.

L. ALAN WINTERS is Professor of Economics, University of Sussex, UK.